PETER CORBIN *An Artist's Creel*

PETER CORBIN

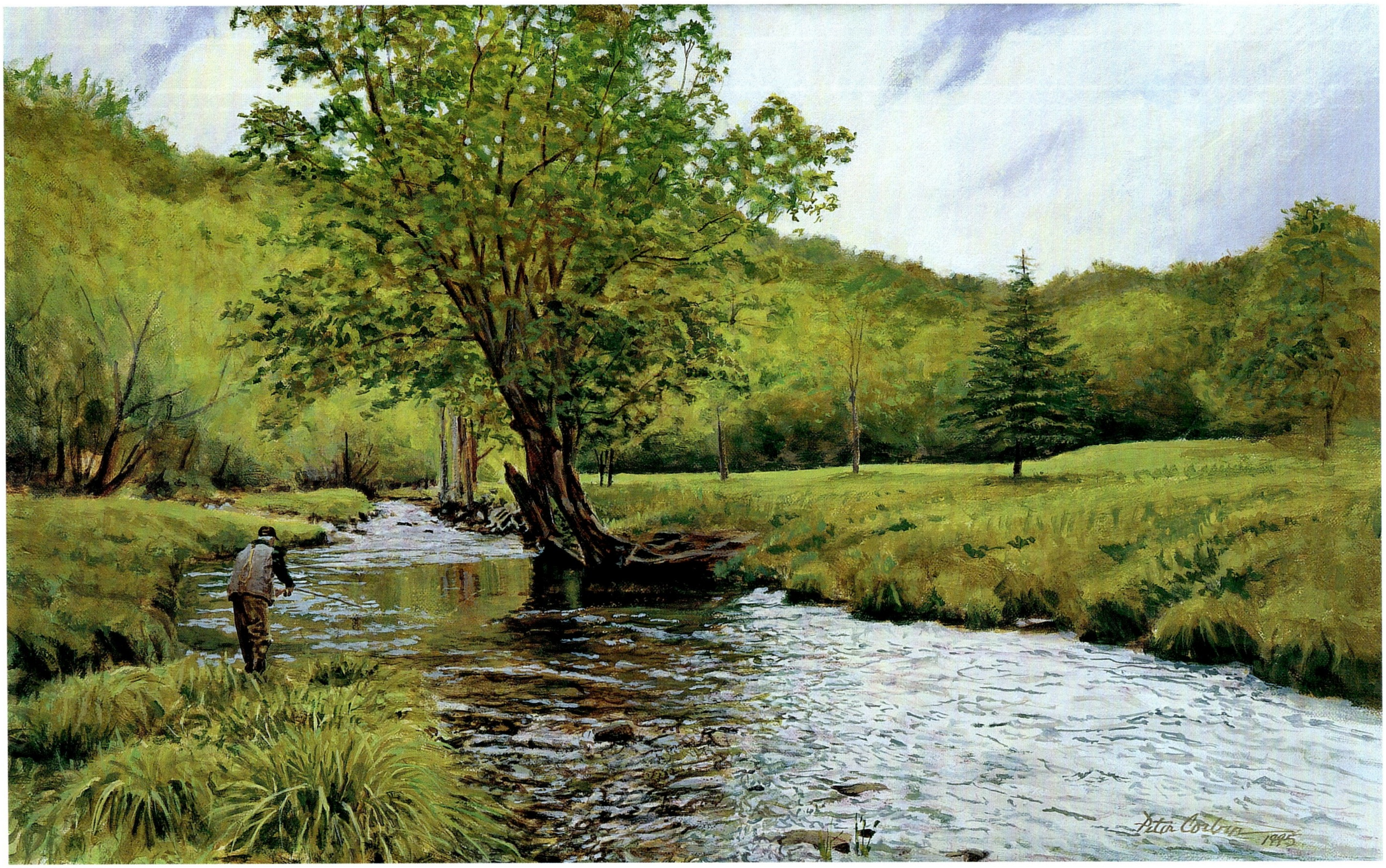

An Artist's Creel

FOREWORD BY John Merwin

ESSAY BY Tom Davis

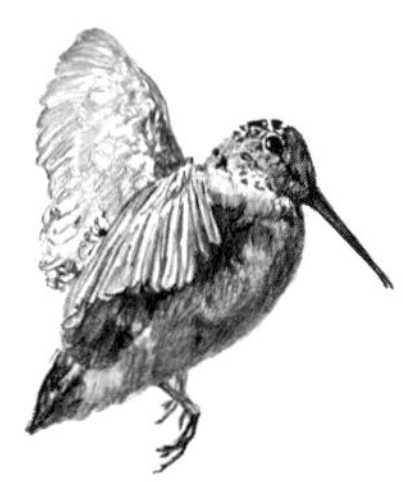

HUDSON HILLS PRESS

New York and Manchester

Published in the United States by Hudson Hills Press LLC,
74-2 Union Street, Manchester, Vermont 05254.

Distributed in the United States, its territories and possessions, and Canada by National Book Network, Inc. Distributed in the United Kingdom, Eire, and Europe by Windsor Books International.

Co-Directors: Randall Perkins and Leslie van Breen
Founding Publisher: Paul Anbinder

Designer: Christopher Kuntze
Editor: Margot Page
Production Manager: David Skolkin
Proofreader: Laura Addison
Indexer: Karla Knight
Printed and bound by CS Graphics, Singapore
Color Separation by Pre Tech Color, Wilder, Vermont

LIBRARY OF CONGRESS CATALOGING-IN-PUBLICATION DATA

Davis, Tom.
Peter Corbin : an artist's creel / by Tom Davis ; introduction by John Merwin.
p. cm.
ISBN 1-55595-256-9 (alk. paper)
1. Corbin, Peter, 1945– —Criticism and interpretation.
2. Wildlife art—United States. I. Corbin, Peter, 1945– II. Title.
N6537.C6593D38 2005
760'.092—dc22 2005019696

FRONTISPIECE: *The Pool in the Meadow,* 1995. Acrylic on canvas, 12 × 20 inches, signed and dated lower right.

Contents

Acknowledgments / 9

Foreword / 11
by John Merwin

Introduction / 15
by Tom Davis

An Artist's Creel / 27
by Tom Davis

COLOR PLATES / 39
Fly Fishing / 41
Shotgunning / 93
Equine & Portraits / 137
Sculpture / 163
Limited-Edition Prints / 171

Chronology / 185

Exhibitions / 189

Bibliography / 191

Index / 193

Dedication

To my dear wife, Lillian, and my two wonderful children, Parker and Lindsey, who have long tolerated my disappearances to places far and near to research paintings. To Korky Podmaniczky, who has helped record and market my paintings for many years. To Donald Christ and the many other wonderful people who have invited me to record their love of the outdoors and the places and sports they cherish. And to my fellow artists and teachers who have shared their wisdom and encouragement through my career. And, finally, to my late father, who demanded that I make my own choices in life.

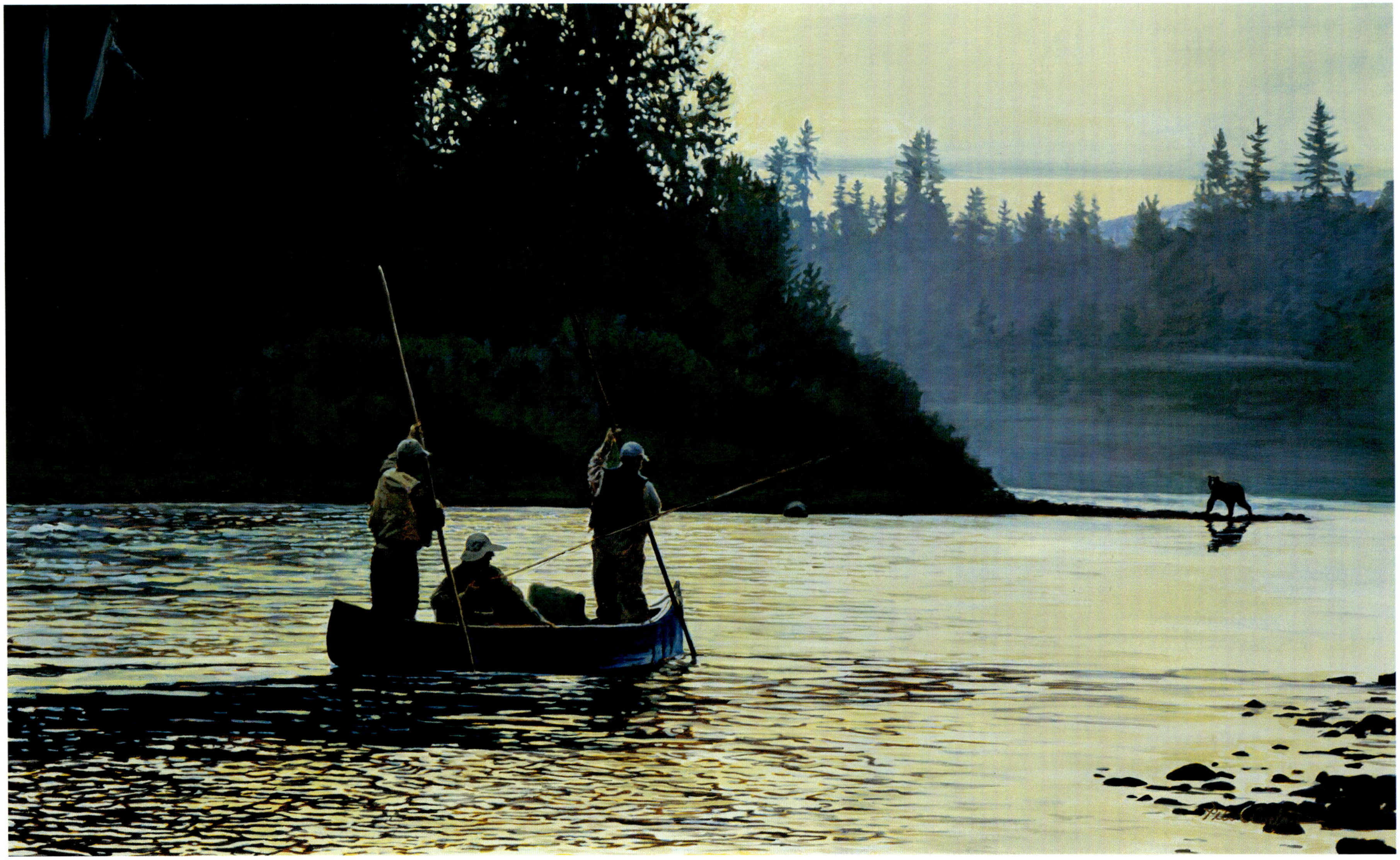

Evening Encounter, 2003
oil on canvas
24 × 40 inches

Acknowledgments

THERE ARE MANY PEOPLE to acknowledge and thank for making possible not only this book but also my career. They have supported and encouraged me artistically, financially, and emotionally through the years, and I am deeply indebted to all of them.

My first thanks go to my father and mother, Robert and Elizabeth Corbin, and my father-in-law, Eben Pyne.

To my close friends Lee Mortimer and Jim Kline, who have shown me the compass reading in both the deep wood and in life—they taught me to read the water in life's stream and to see not only where the fish lie but where life values are revealed.

To my teachers and fellow artists, Charles Cole, Alice Dunbar, John Risley, Harry Nadler, Bob Blazek, Allen Blagden, C. D. Clark, Walter Matia, Bob Kuhn, and Bob Abbett, who have taught me not only technical skills but also, more importantly, how to express my individuality.

To Donald Christ and many other wonderful clients, who have shared their love of sport and far-off places.

I would also like to thank the people who made the production of this book possible: Leslie van Breen, Margot Page, and, especially, Randall Perkins, who have encouraged and cajoled a relatively disorganized mind to order. Thanks also to Tom Davis, who has written on my work for more than twenty years, and to John Merwin for both his fine contribution to this book and his support at the start of my painting career.

Finally, my deepest appreciation to my wife, Lillian, and, my children, Parker and Lindsey, who have supported me in every possible way in my life.

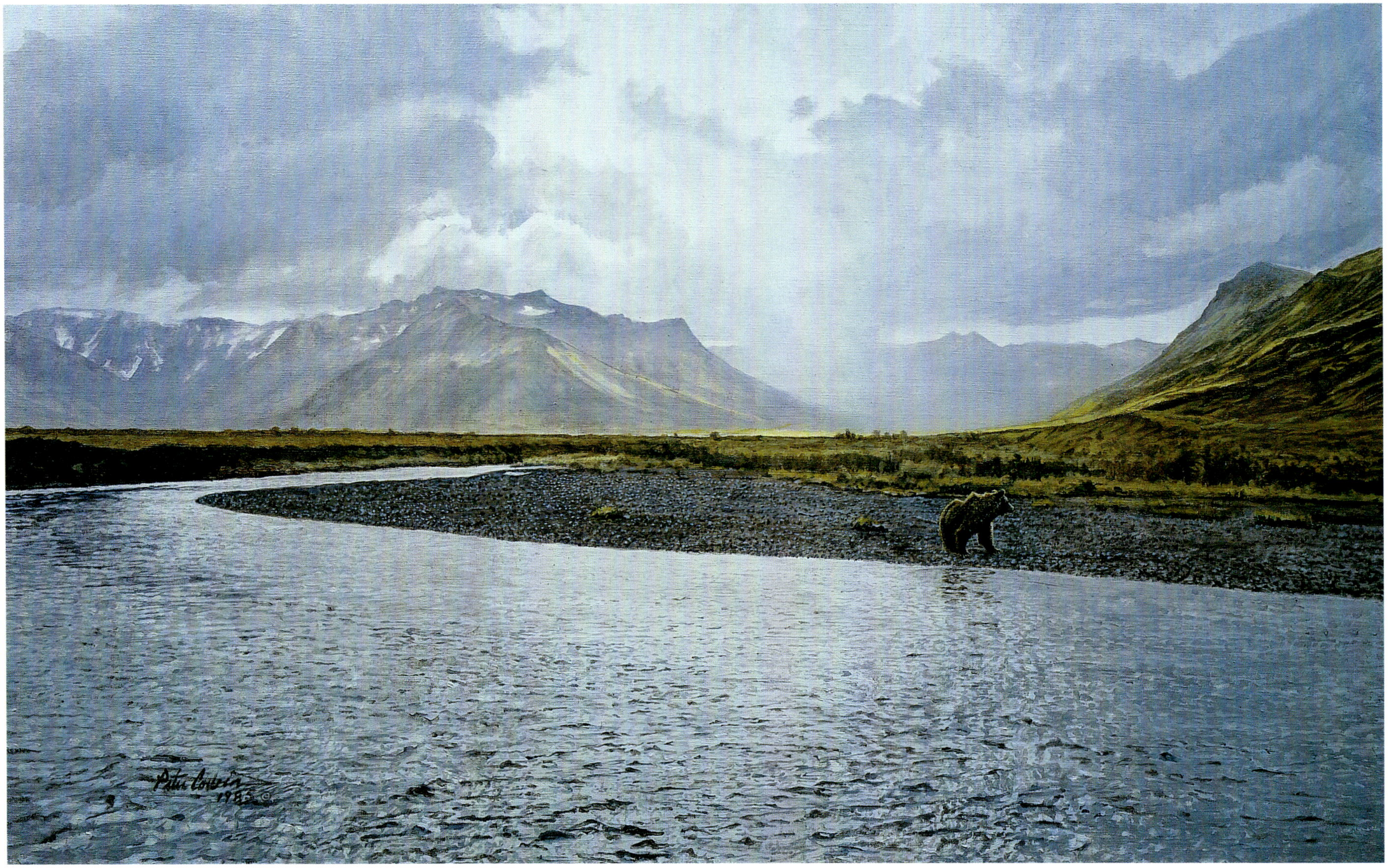

Alaskan Solitude, 1985
acrylic on canvas
24 × 40 inches

Foreword

It was almost thirty years ago that a brash young artist named Peter Corbin stopped in Vermont to meet with an equally brash young editor (me) about having his work appear in *Fly Fisherman* magazine, where I was then working. What we needed at the time was some illustration work, which didn't interest Peter. He told me he wanted to paint instead, and this led to a conversation that continued over a long dinner that night about the differences between sporting illustration and sporting art. This evening was the beginning of a shared feast of ideas between us; future discussions were conducted over other dinners and even a trout stream or two.

I had at least a passing acquaintance with the work of the artists Thomas Eakins, Ogden Pleissner (who was then still living and painting in Manchester, Vermont, only a few miles from my office), A. B. Frost, and Winslow Homer—familiarity enough to at least be able to talk with Peter about them late into that night. He explained that Frost had been rigidly classified as "just an illustrator," albeit a great one, yet Homer also began his career as "just an illustrator" with his first work for the old *Harper's Weekly* magazine. Illustration can be a kind of artistic quicksand from which fine art never emerges, but Winslow Homer eventually, and most certainly, transcended the trap.

Corbin admired A. B. Frost, especially his shooting scenes, and told me that Frost once complained of a "tight fist," the illustrator's compulsive attention to detail that had hampered his transition from illustration to art. The potential for such a "tight-fist" handicap was clearly a frustrating prospect for Corbin as well.

That first evening ended with my expressed hope that I would be around in twenty years or so to see what had happened with Peter's career. Then I went back to my writing and he went back to his painting.

This book, *An Artist's Creel*, reflects what happened to Peter Corbin over the ensuing thirty years, and it is simply an extraordinary journey. Because Corbin possesses that sort of restless intellect that never stops evolving, he has become an artistic success, both critically and commercially, without having become "just an illustrator" in the process.

In these pages is evident the artist's nearly superhuman dedication to developing his own work over decades. Choosing a life of creative endeavor over a business career is a common dream that has, in Corbin's case, been uncommonly realized. That his family was of some means is almost immaterial. What he has accomplished cannot be bought, only earned over time. It is the evolving sense of self, the nurturing of a fragile spark of self-confidence, which enables the progression of paintings over such a long time period. Maintaining determination, dedication, and discipline in the midst of the tumult of everyday life is obviously no small matter. Many try; few succeed.

Then there is the business of art. Corbin has long been adamant that his paintings should sell well, viewing the marketplace itself as a critic of sorts. He is a businessman of necessity, having founded Shooter's Hill Press as the fine-art publisher of his own work, and what I find most interesting is that Corbin has been able to handle the business skillfully while at the same time continuing to develop as an artist—a remarkably successful balancing act.

The paintings themselves are "right." Corbin is a traditional sportsman in the best possible sense, and, be it a painting of a salmon river, bonefish flat, or grouse cover, the fishing and shooting sports he portrays are invariably accurate. Much of his equestrian work is, on one level, the meticulous study of horse anatomy (harkening back to the painter Thomas Eakins). However well executed, this correctness of his paintings has its basis in the realm of illustration.

But what makes Corbin's paintings so successful is what each carries beyond simple illustration. The "tight fist" he experienced at the beginning of his career has indeed loosened. He is not merely painting a photographic slice of time—the illustrator's exhaustive detail of a perfect moment afield. He is painting the sum of all such moments and is doing so by suggestion rather than by overworked detail. It is the artist as magician; the painting is utterly real and an illusion at the same time.

As a result, his paintings don't just look right; they feel right. I don't merely see them; I can smell the spruces, I can feel the water. This sense of the surrounding land- and waterscapes is a very primal response that somehow extends three-dimensionally from a two-dimensional canvas.

In one example, the water in many of his angling scenes often has a remarkable transparency, not fully clear as a window but as a window partly fogged. As a result, we may see only flashes of bonefish as they move slowly along a wind-rippled flat. In the real world, bonefish never swim fully revealed: One struggles to see a fin, part of a shadow amid the waves and reflections of the sea. So Corbin gives us only suggestions of fish. It is a deft touch.

Consider the light, as well. Natural light models objects, giving them dimension. In changing conditions of weather or time of day, it also alters colors or at least the way we see them. Light plays a primary role in much of Corbin's work, so much so that when I wrote a commentary on his work for a 1981 copy of *Atlantic Salmon Journal* I entitled the piece "A Fascination of Light," reflecting the painter's fascination with light and the viewer's opportunity to watch the interplay between subject and atmosphere.

The flat, gray light of a cloudy day on Idaho's Henry's Fork (*Harriman's Ranch*) first avoids the bright sun and blue sky cliché of most sporting art. The reflected sky plays hard with the water, nibbling at it with color here and there that becomes neither flat nor gray. The action of light here is extraordinarily intense, and the combination of flat water and flat landscape in flat light becomes immensely powerful.

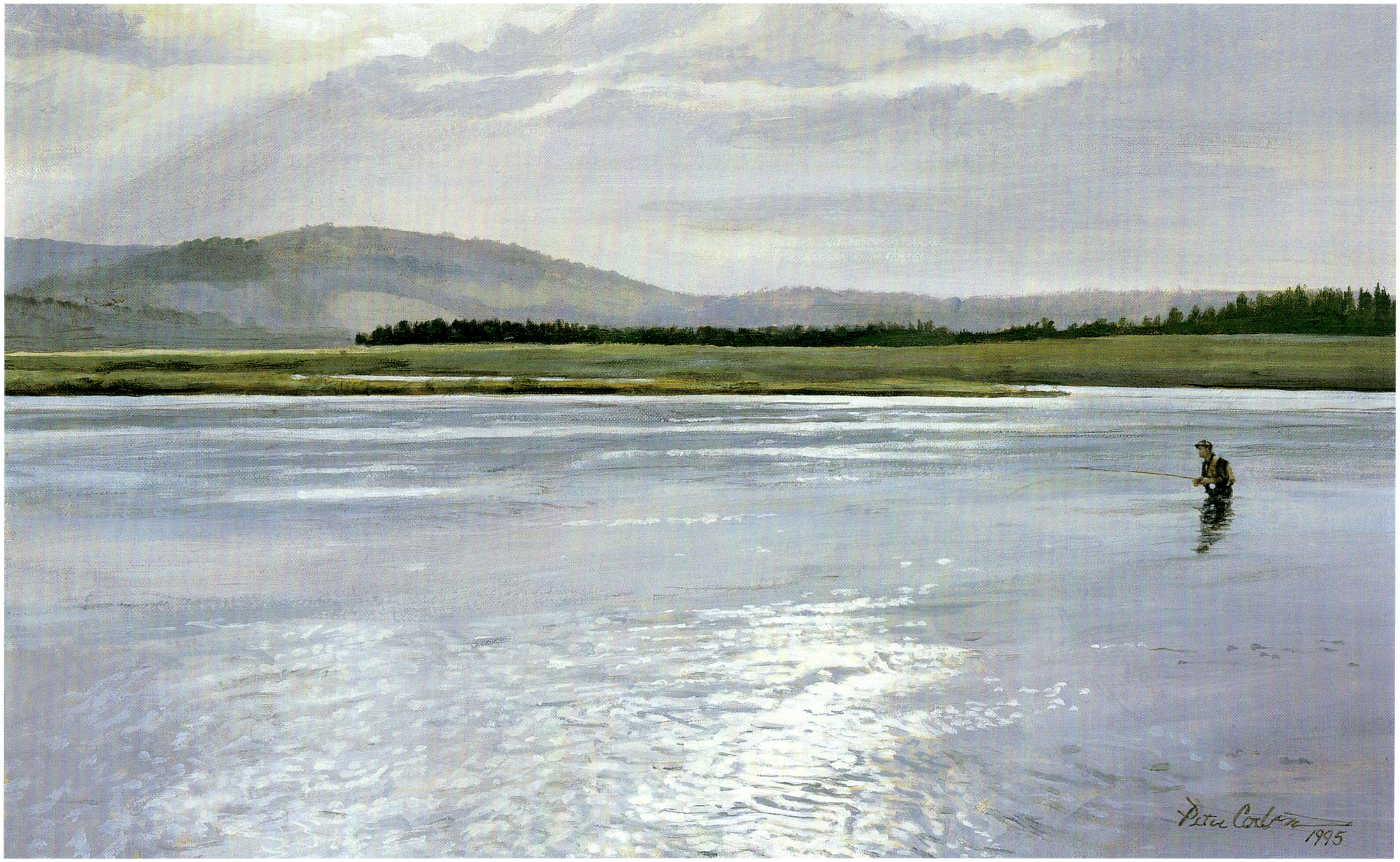

Harrimans Ranch, 1995
acrylic on canvas
12 × 20 inches

I find the same idea, executed differently, in the painting *Alaskan Solitude* with the strongly painted surface of its river. It is the broken, rippled surface of the water that gives such strong texture to this canvas, a texture that then becomes a vehicle for both light and color. It looks like Alaska, but, more importantly, it *feels* like the Alaskan waters that have rippled around my own waders.

As you read this book, you might find yourself wondering, how did he do that? But mostly what you will find in these pages is a gift. A sporting life offers the gift of collective memory, in which the overall impression of a day spent in the water or woodlands remains long after its details are forgotten. It is that lingering, powerful sense that we share deeply as sportsmen, and it is that essence, that gift, that graces a Peter Corbin canvas.

—John Merwin

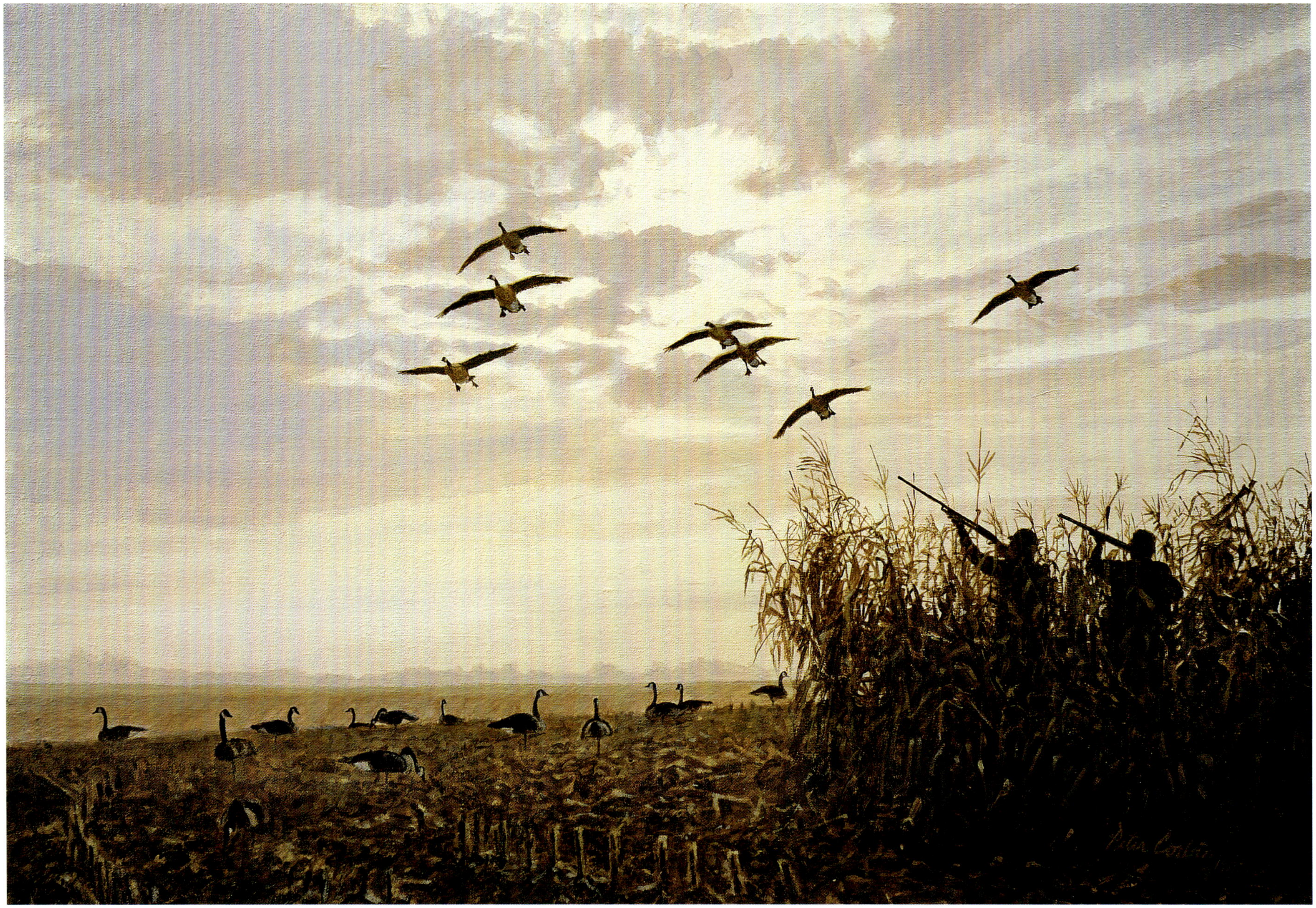

Standing Corn, 1981
acrylic on canvas
20 × 30 inches

Introduction

On a chilly December morning, the leaden skies are threatening snow. In a cut cornfield on one of the few working dairy farms left in the neighborhood of his home in Millbrook, New York, Peter Corbin is lying on his back in full camouflage with a shotgun across his chest. He is surrounded by Canada goose decoys; a few yards away, the great animal painter Bob Kuhn and I are crouching in a blind of standing cornstalks. A flock of about twenty-five geese is on final approach and Corbin is multitasking: "flagging" with charcoal-gray paddles (to create an impression of moving wings that geese find irresistible) while, at the same time, making sweet, brassy music on a mouth call. The big birds are utterly fooled, and when Corbin shouts, they seem to stop in mid-air, suspended by the filaments of their amazement.

One would expect an artist who is renowned for his scenes of wingshooting, fly fishing, and the sporting life to know this world intimately, to be comfortable and confident in its environments and skilled with the tools that connect us to it. Peter Corbin is as competent an outdoorsman, in the old-fashioned, broadly inclusive sense of the word, as one will ever meet.

Yet Corbin spends as much, if not more, time in the outdoors with a camera in his hands than a fly rod or shotgun. It is his sketchpad and his recording secretary. He photographs everything, from panoramic landscapes to autumn leaves etched with frost, from the glare on a sun-hammered bonefish flat to the arch of a dressage horse's neck, from trout to tarpon, teal to turkeys, Texas quail hunters to British Columbia steelhead fishermen, looking for any and all information that might conceivably contribute toward the making of a painting.

Reflecting on the process, he muses, "My paintings are done on four or five levels. They tell a story; and I'm always trying to work the light to the dark, the dark to the light, trying to draw the viewer into the painting. I try for an asymmetrical balance, so there isn't something sitting in the center of the canvas. The landscape is important to me: Having that perspective, being able to paint the whole landscape and then put a figure into it, I am able to set up some tensions, some dynamics, by the placement of the figure. When I do a hunting or fishing painting, my goal is always to capture the essence of the experience. It may not be exactly as it happened, but it is faithful to the way it is *remembered*."

Corbin's studio is a loft on his property in Millbrook, New York, located in the hayloft over the horse barn. Sometimes, wanting to see how a painting "reads" at a distance, he will open the door and step out into the space where the hay is actually kept, a fluctuating number of half-wild cats eyeing him suspiciously from their perches atop the stacked bales.

The studio itself is humble and decidedly low-tech. Corbin's lighting system consists of a skylight with a retractable shade, a large square of cardboard balanced on the rafters, and a length of broomstick-diameter dowel with a screw-hook in one end with which Corbin can adjust the quantity of natural light entering the studio and, to a limited extent, the area it illuminates. A curtained-off area, where Corbin photographs all his finished canvases with a large-format view camera, allows him to maintain a comprehensive pictorial record of his output with four-by-five-inch transparencies. Apart from a smattering of hung objects—mounted birds (Canada goose, ruffed grouse, woodcock), animal skulls (white-tailed deer, grizzly bear, wolf), a map of the salmon pools of Quebec's fabled Moisie River, a few other odds and ends—the walls of Corbin's studio are dominated by his slide collection.

An arm's length to the right of his easel, surrounded by a garrison of brushes, is the work surface on which he mixes his paint. After working exclusively in acrylics for more than a quarter century, Corbin switched to oil paint about five years ago; one of the few state-of-the-art items in his studio is the ventilation system he installed to mitigate the health concerns associated with breathing paint fumes over a long period of time.

"That is one of the big reasons I resisted switching to oils," he explains. "I've known a number of oil painters who developed cancer relatively early in life, and I didn't want to become a statistic. Acrylics offer a lot of practical advantages—they are easy to handle, they dry quickly, and they're excellent for capturing fine detail—but oils have so much more *punch*. With oils, you can do things with glazes to achieve a saturation of color that you just can't duplicate in acrylics."

Sharp Tail Country, 1994
acrylic on canvas
12 × 20 inches

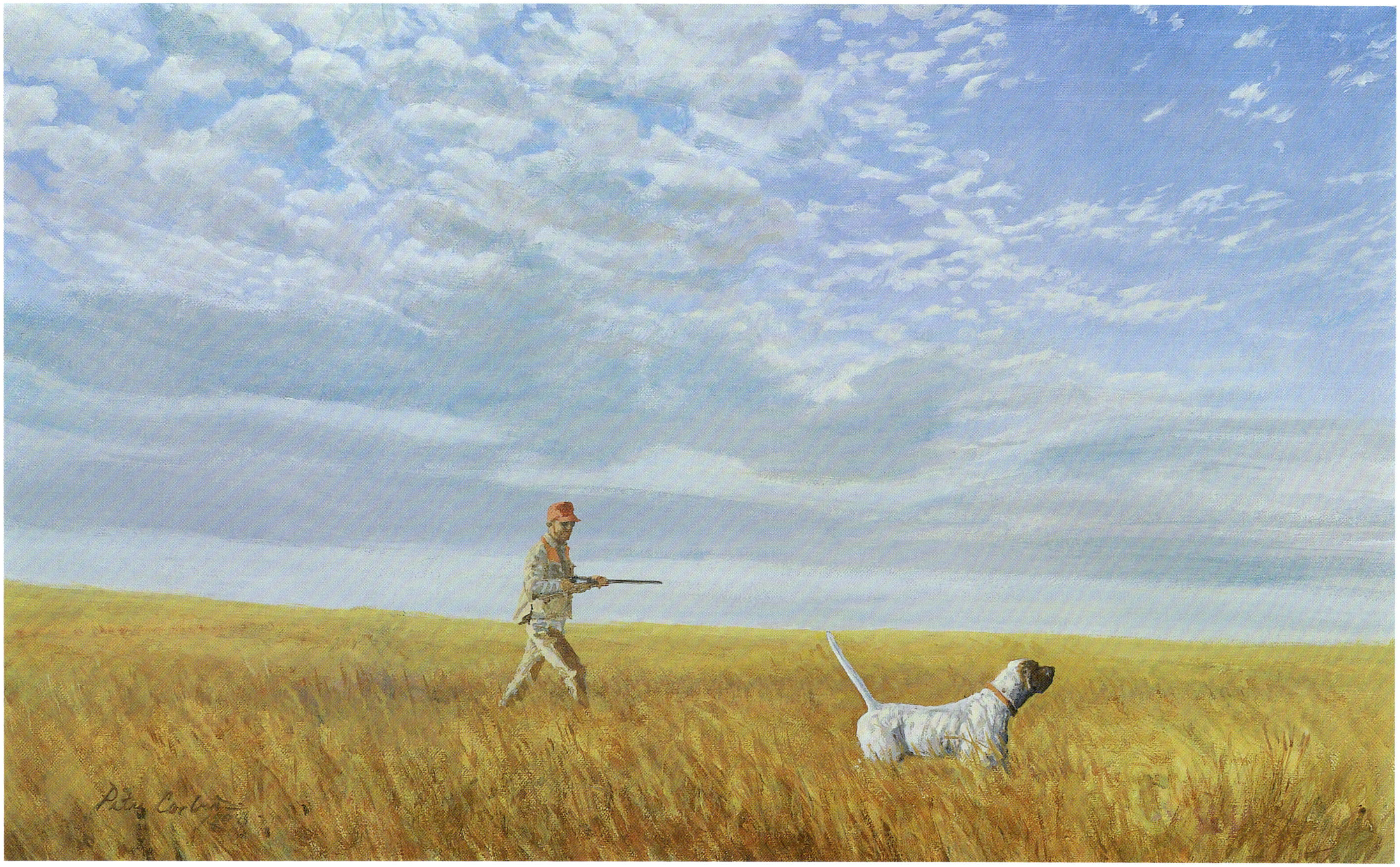

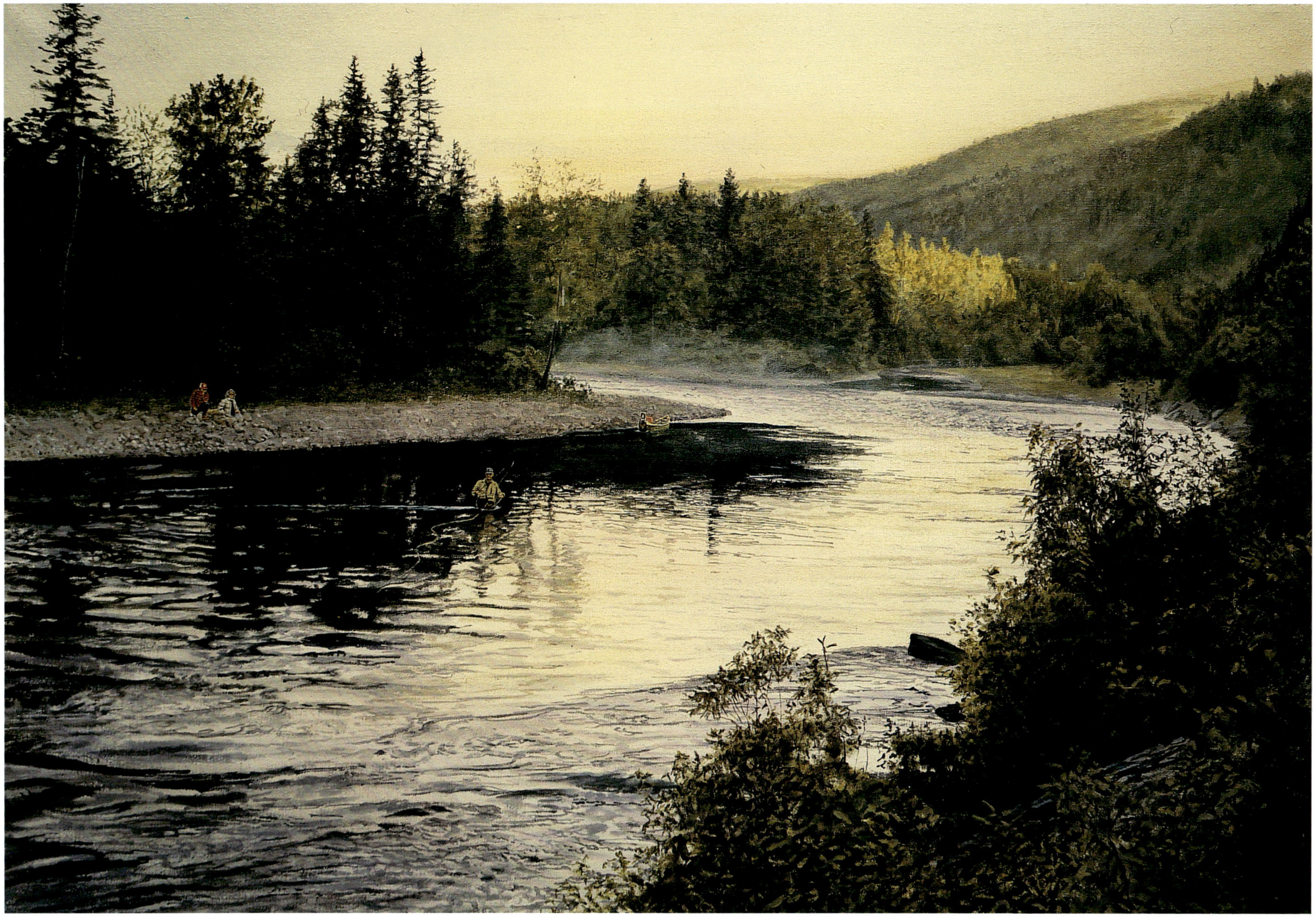

Shadow Water, 1987
acrylic on canvas
24 × 36 inches

Above his paints and brushes, sharing space on a shelf with a small collection of carefully chosen art books, is the studio's other concession to the 21st century, Corbin's satellite radio, usually tuned to a station that specializes in radio dramas from the 1940s and 1950s like *The Shadow* and *The Lone Ranger* that Corbin remembers listening to as a child, although an eclectic variety of music channels receives its share of air time as well.

Taped to the studio's back wall, behind and to the right of the easel so that Corbin can lean over on his stool to study it, is a reproduction of Ogden Pleissner's masterpiece

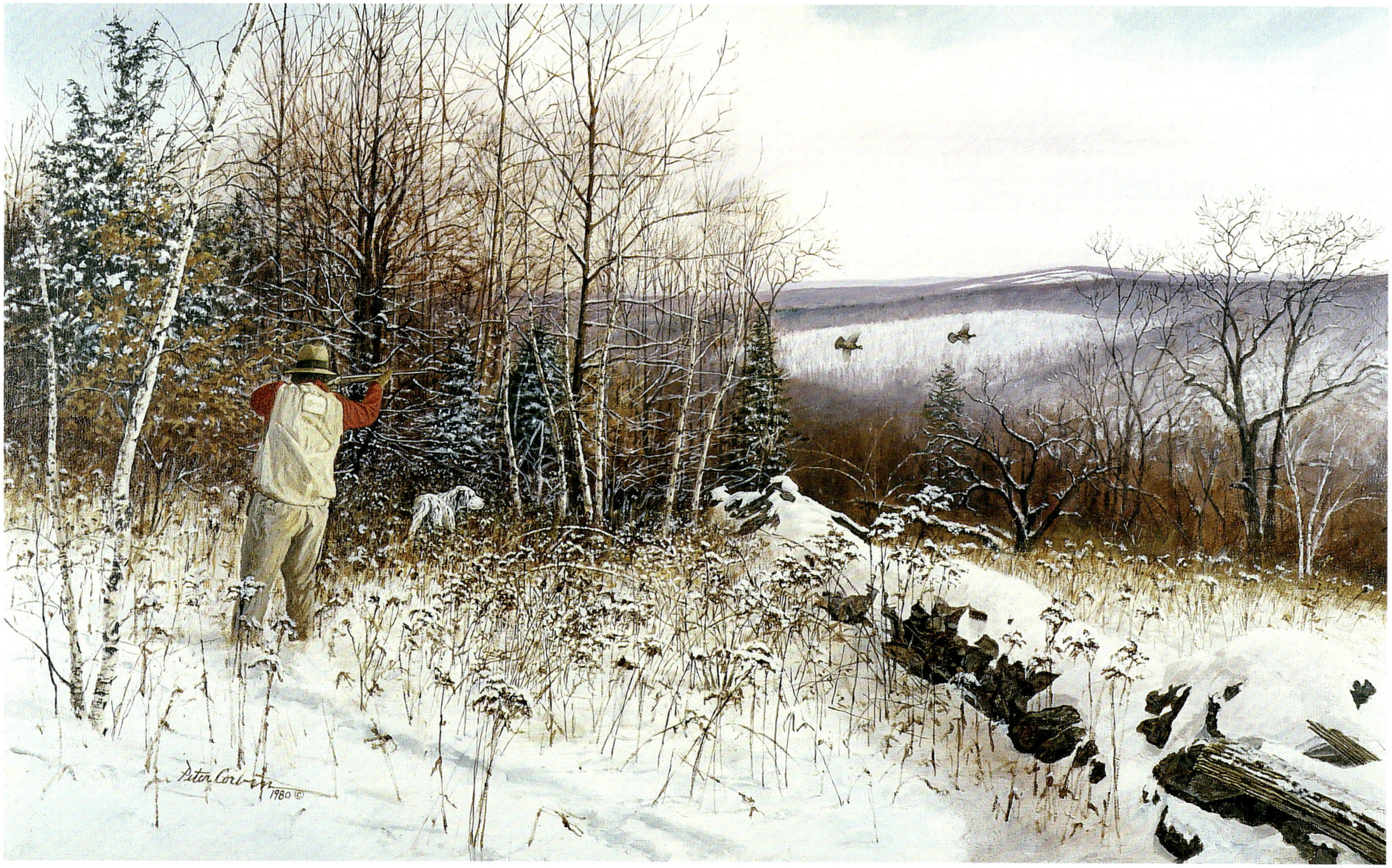

A Chance to Double, 1980
acrylic on canvas
24 × 40 inches

Blue Boat on the Saint Anne. Corbin cites Pleissner, who died in 1983, as one of the two artists (A. B. Frost being the other) who have most influenced him, arguing that Pleissner deserves to be ranked alongside Winslow Homer in the pantheon of American realist painters.

When Peter was ten, his father took him to New Brunswick's famed Miramichi River to fish for Atlantic salmon. The lodge where the Corbins stayed featured a Pleissner print on the wall, and the image made a deep impression on the newly minted salmon angler. A. B. Frost's *Shooting Pictures*, which hung in Corbin's childhood home, had already fired his imagination; so, too, had the masterful paintings of North American game birds by Lynn Bogue Hunt, Francis Lee Jaques' graphically dramatic

Ogden Pleissner
Blue Boat on the Ste. Anne, 1958
watercolor on paper, 17¼ × 27 inches

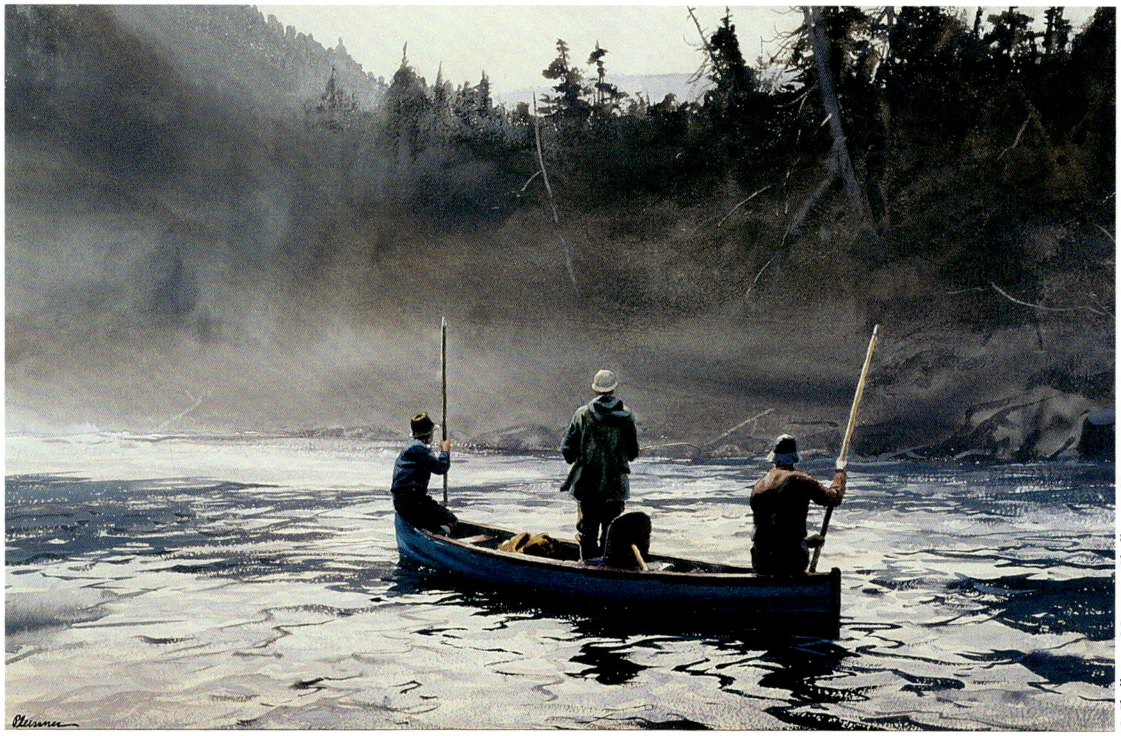

images of prairie birds and wildlife, and Carl Rungius' iconic depictions of big-game animals, all of which he knew from books.

Corbin divides his paintings of hunting and fishing into three major classifications. The first are scenes of *anticipation*: casting to a tailing permit or rising trout, calling the flock of Canadas that has yet to commit.

The second are scenes of *the moment*: the tarpon's gill-rattling leap, the thunderous flush of a ruffed grouse in front of a setter's point. These are the hardest to get "right," in Corbin's opinion, not only because of the specific artistic demands created by the action, but also because it is so easy for them to look trite and formulaic instead of fresh and exciting.

The third and final category comprises scenes of *reflection*, the mellow, contemplative afterglow when images, sensations, and emotions coalesce into living memories. It is probably no coincidence that as Corbin himself has mellowed, he finds himself more and more attracted to this aspect of the sporting experience.

"I have always felt I was a landscape painter," Corbin says, "with the added element that something 'happens' in my landscapes. And because of what I know, and what I love, that 'something' is usually fishing or hunting. I am happiest when the figures are one-third, or less, the height of the canvas. Fairly early on, I did some catalog covers for L. L. Bean. They were good for me at that point in my career, but after I painted them it took me a year to get my figures back down to the size I really wanted them."

The Permit Fisherman, 1991
acrylic on canvas
8 × 12 inches

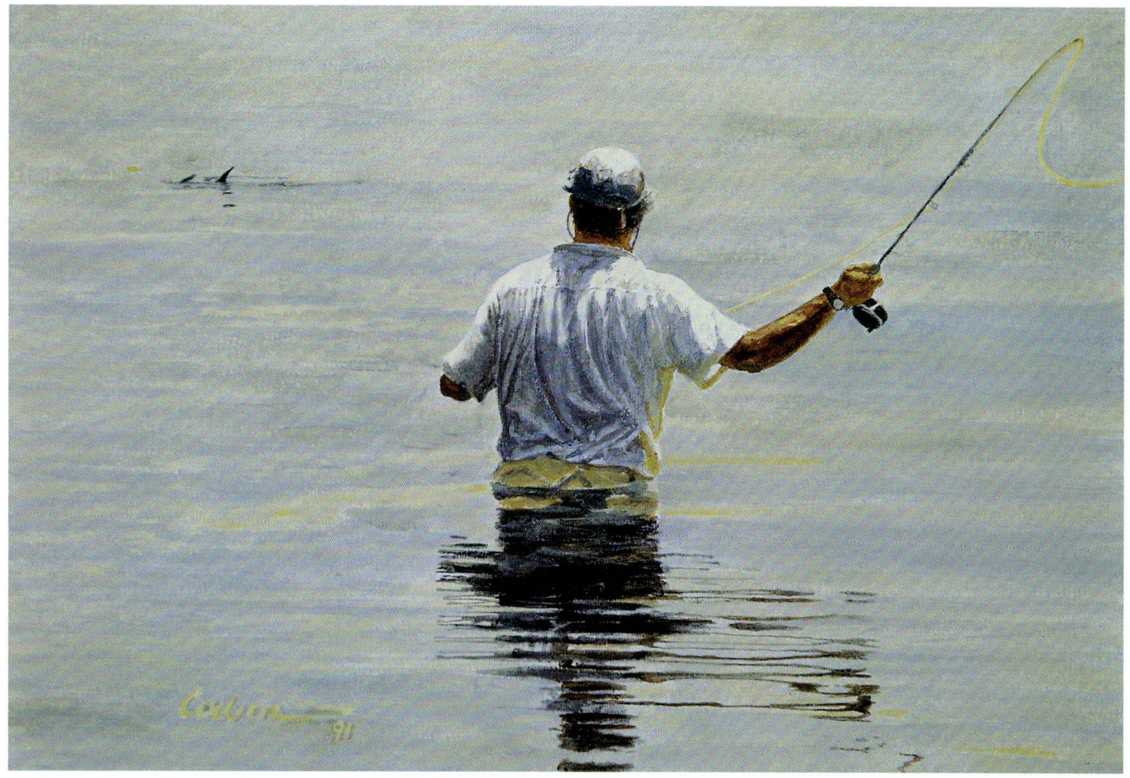

Evening Stripers, 2001
oil on canvas
20 × 30 inches

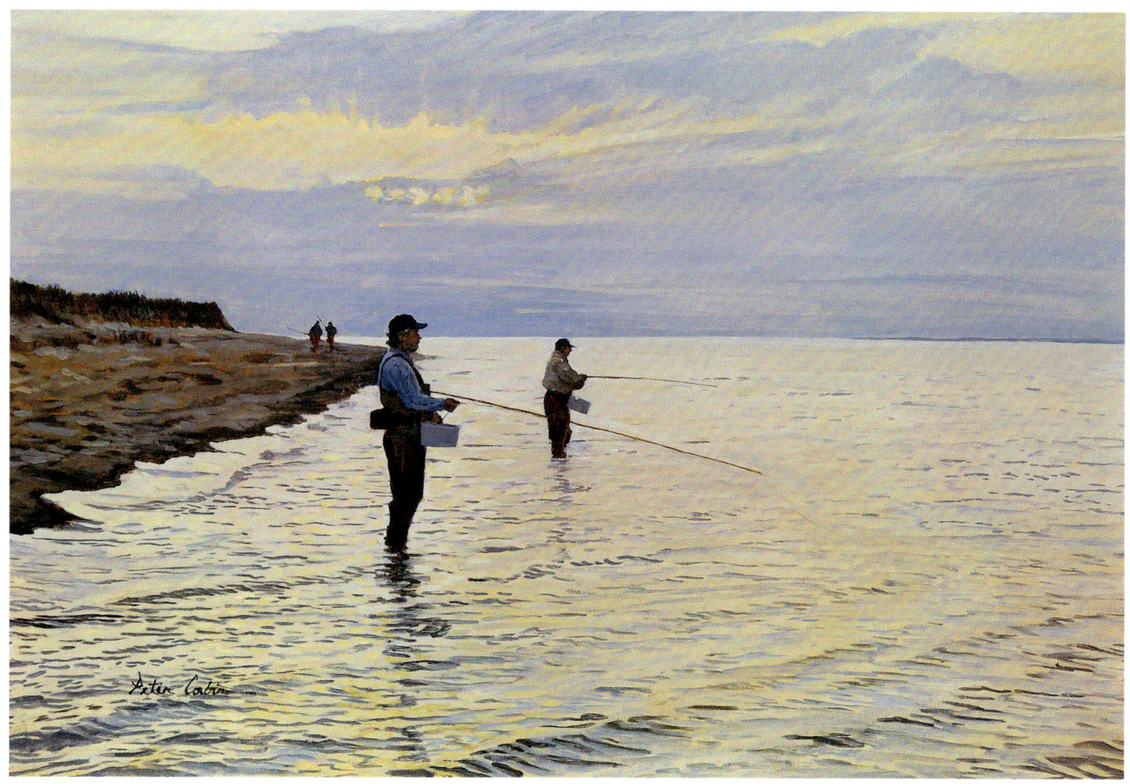

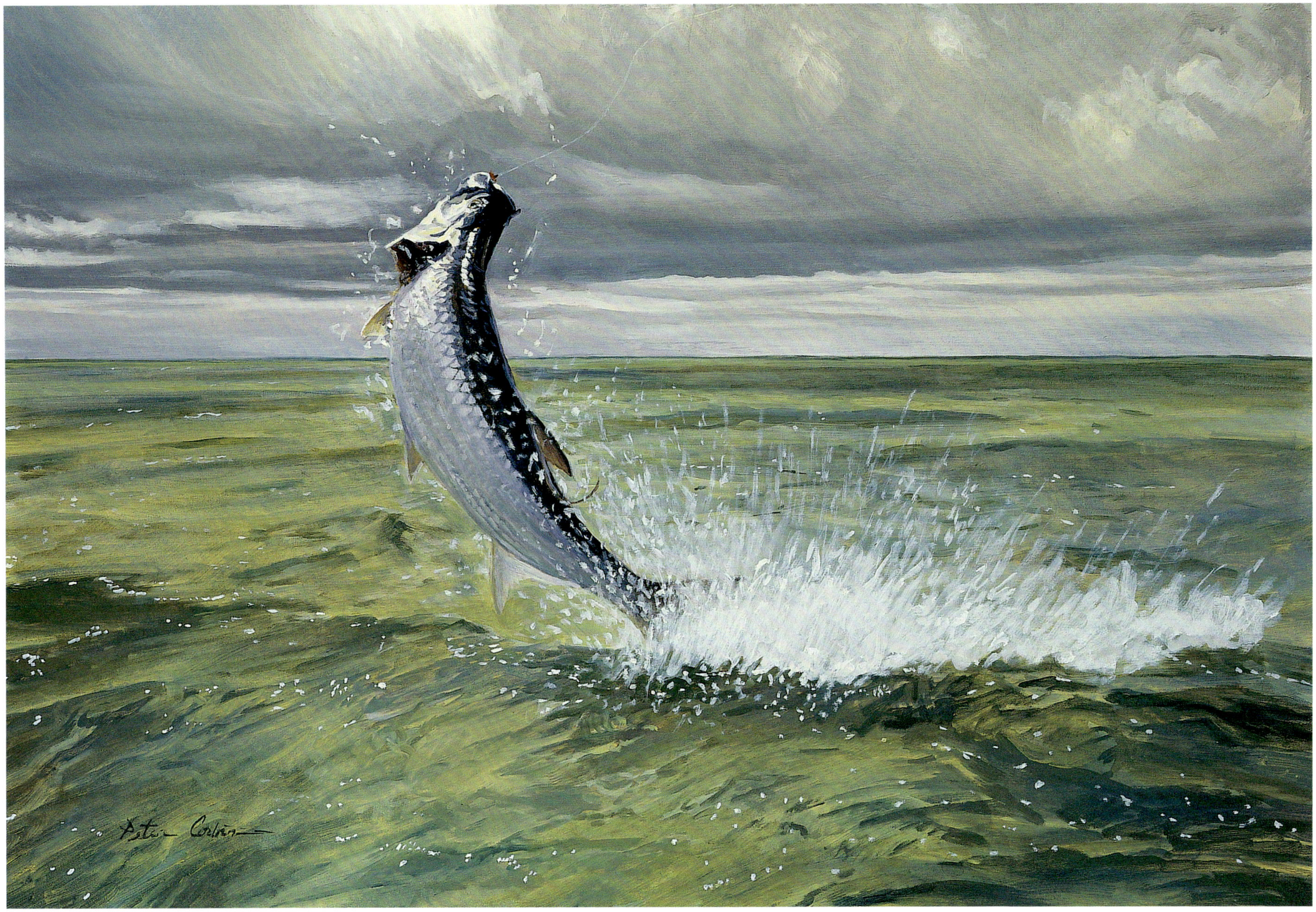

Power and Grace, 2001
oil on canvas
24 × 36 inches

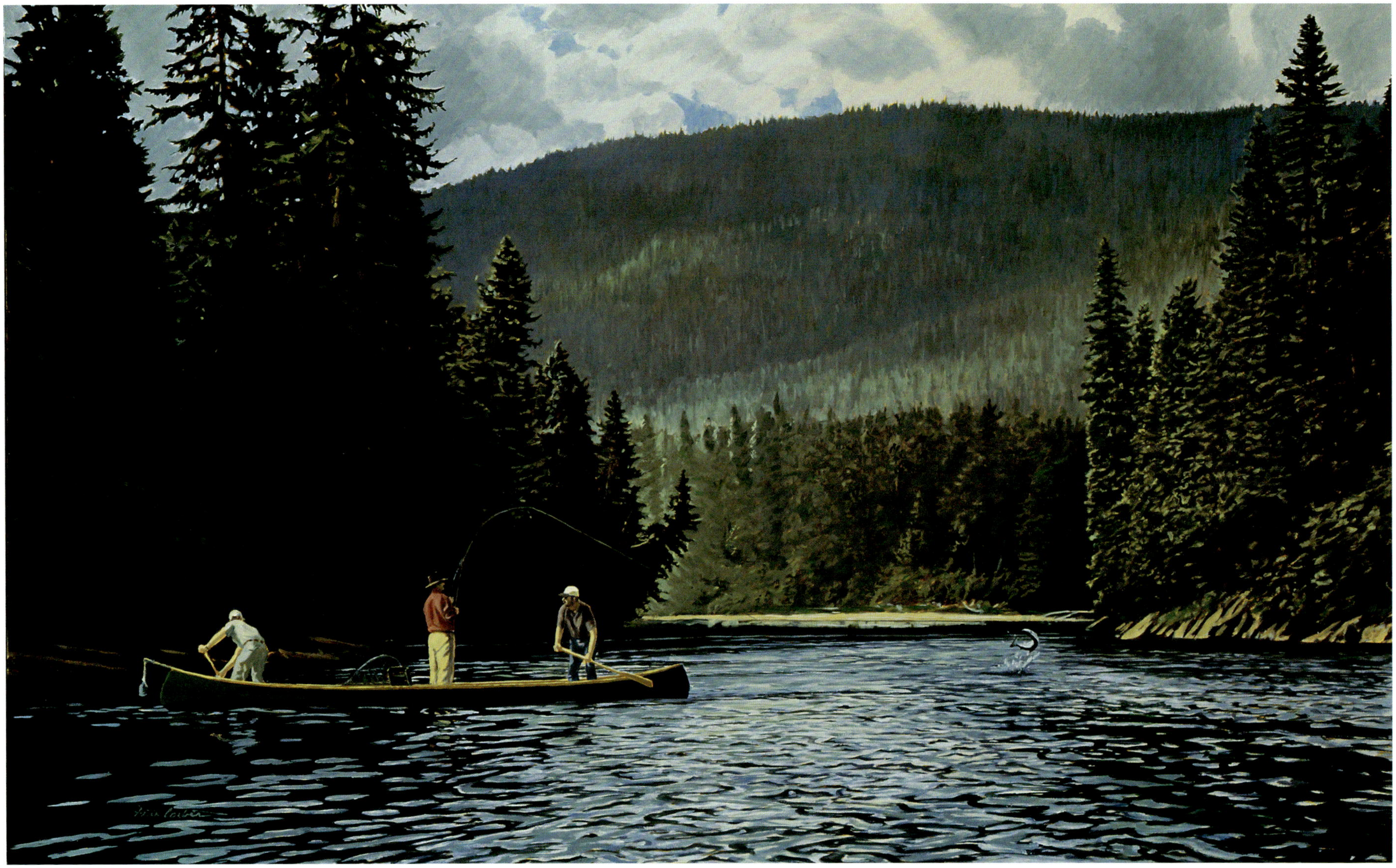

Headed for Quiet Water, 2004
oil on canvas
24 × 40 inches

The current work-in-progress on his easel is a scene of Atlantic salmon fishing on Quebec's fabled Grande Cascapédia River. The pair of guides in a canoe, who flank an angler who is attached by monofilament to an impressively airborne salmon, hews to Corbin's "one-third" rule. The emphasis is on the landscape and its interplay of light and shadow; the action, while not "secondary," is downplayed, even subdued. Earmarked for the annual Coeur d'Alene Art Auction, the piece, called *Headed for Quiet Water*, is nearly finished.

While Corbin speaks often of the abstract qualities that underpin his paintings and of the need to "move beyond" the subject matter in discussing and appraising them, Atlantic salmon fishing on the Cascapédia represents the heart of his body of work. In

Edge of the Orchard, 1982
acrylic on canvas
24 × 20 inches

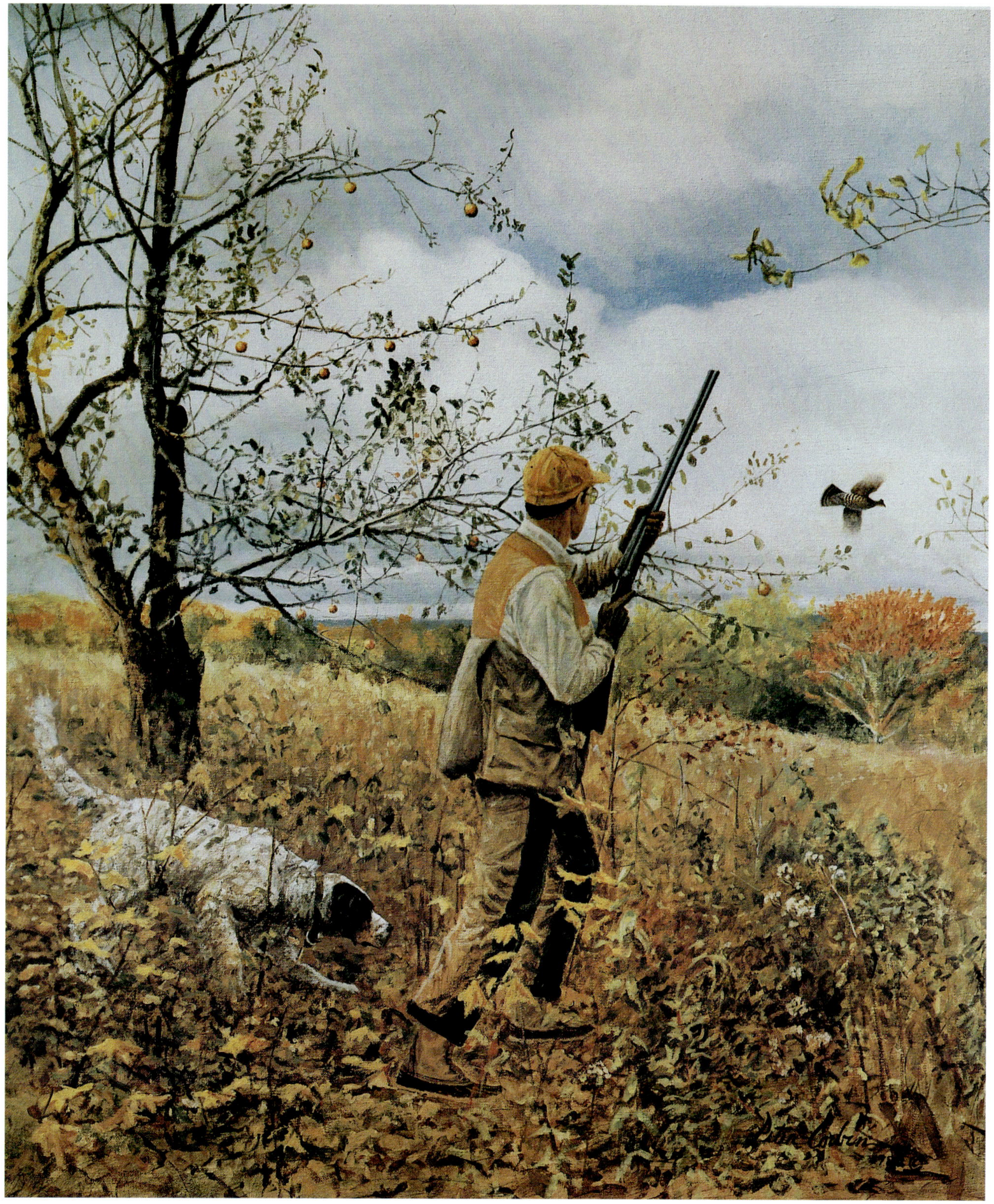

general, and despite the extraordinary breadth of his pursuits as both sportsman and artist, Corbin is identified more prominently with depictions of Atlantic salmon fishing than with any other subject.

He has a history with the Grande Cascapédia River, and, as every sportsman knows, the places with personal history are the ones that pull most tenaciously and most joyfully on the soul. For one thing, the Cascapédia's long-established camps, evocatively named pools, and formal style of fishing, with two guides for each wood-and-canvas

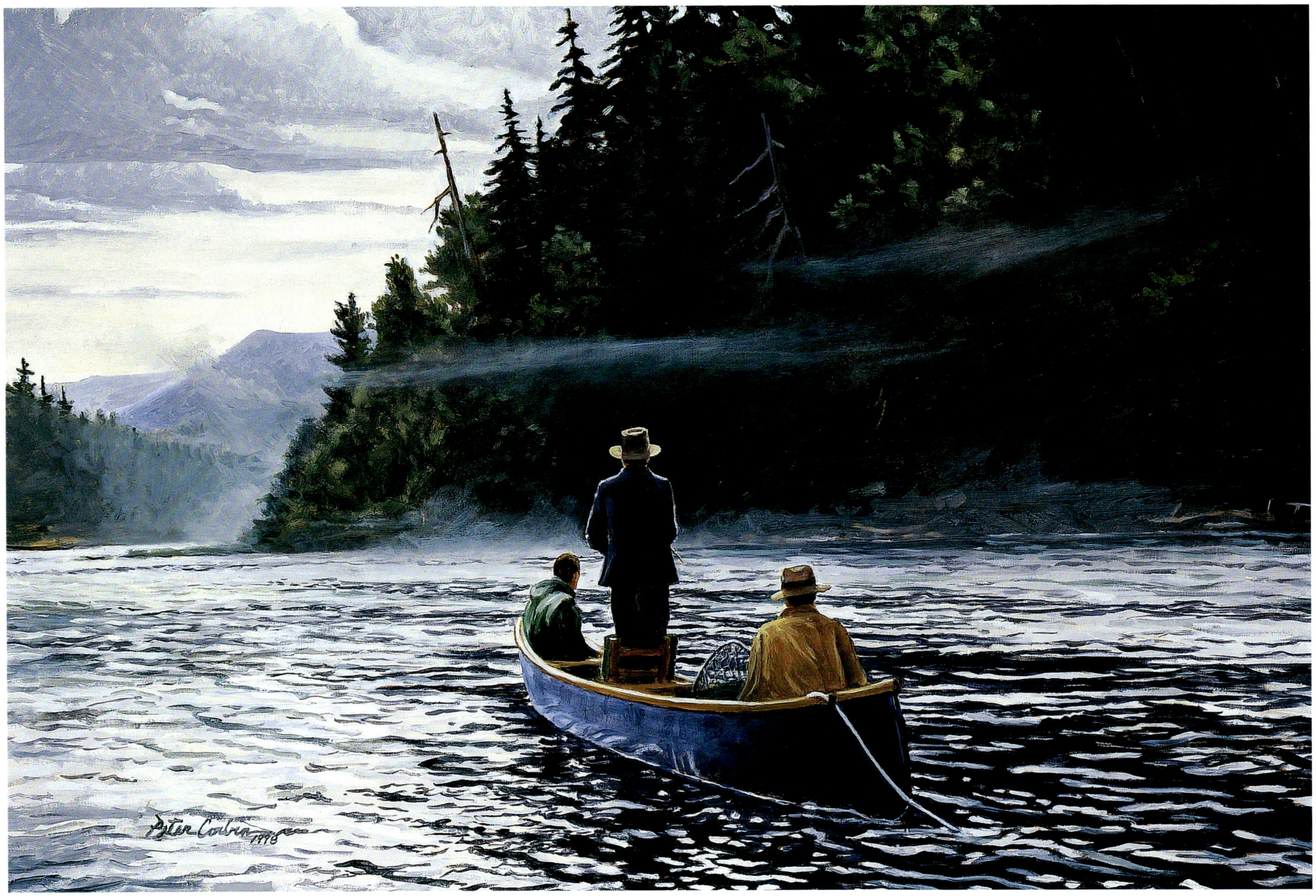

The Blue Canoe, 1998
oil on canvas
20 × 30 inches

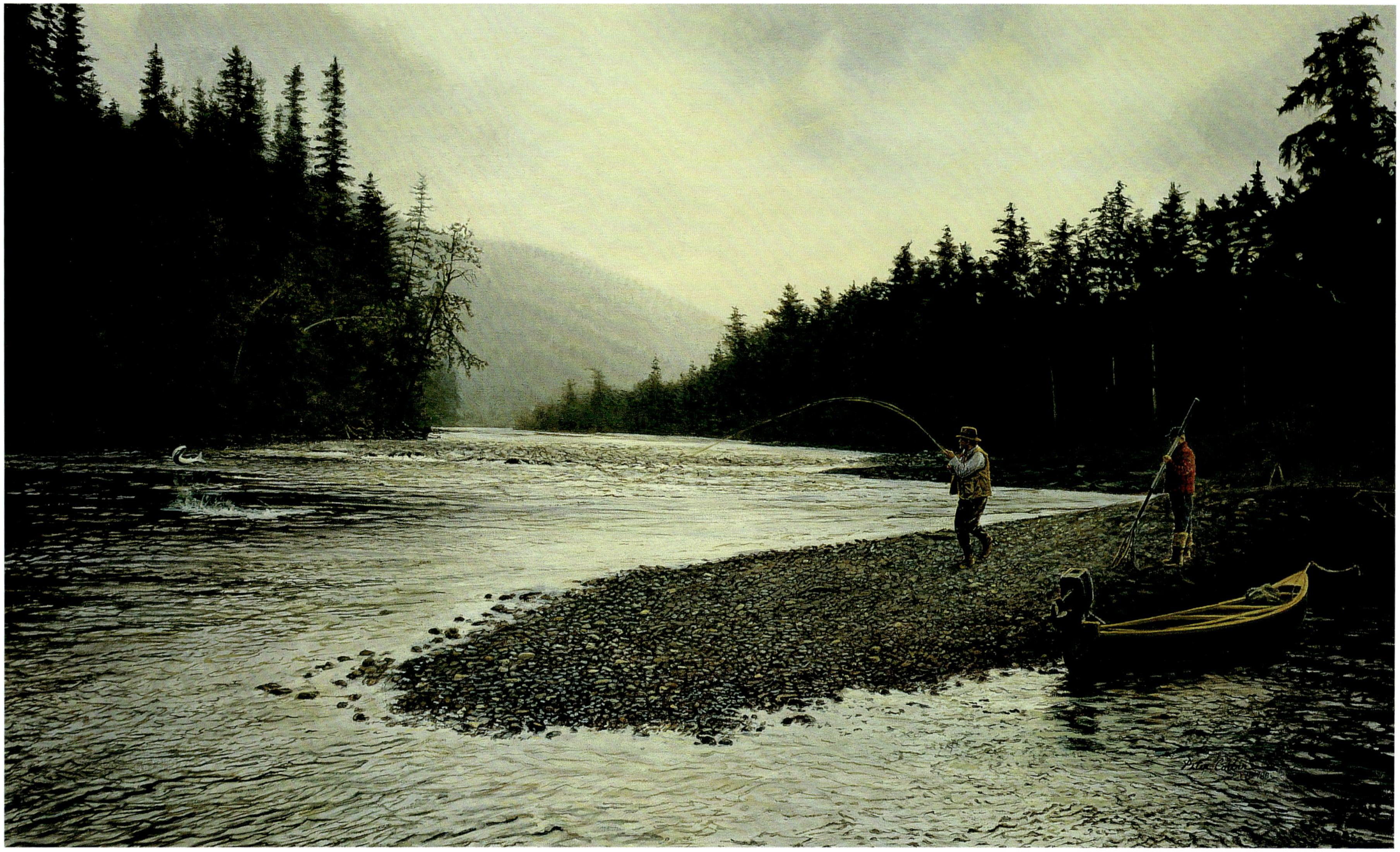

A Cascapédia Morning, 1988
acrylic on canvas
24 × 40 inches

canoe, are steeped in tradition, and Corbin is nothing if not a traditionalist. Ironically, this poses something of a dilemma for him: As a sporting artist, he has made a conscious and deliberate choice to depict his subjects in what he calls "my time" rather than in the classic, romanticized outdoors style—and in Corbin's time, salmon guides are today more likely to wear ball caps, T-shirts, and blue jeans than the felt hats, button-down poplin shirts, and pressed khaki pants that were *de rigueur* in Pleissner's time.

Of ultimate importance, however, is the majesty of the river itself, and the sweep, scale, and drama of the landscape through which it flows on its surging way to the sea. The allure of the Grande Cascapédia for Peter Corbin is an alloy compounded of brilliant sport and overwhelming visual grandeur.

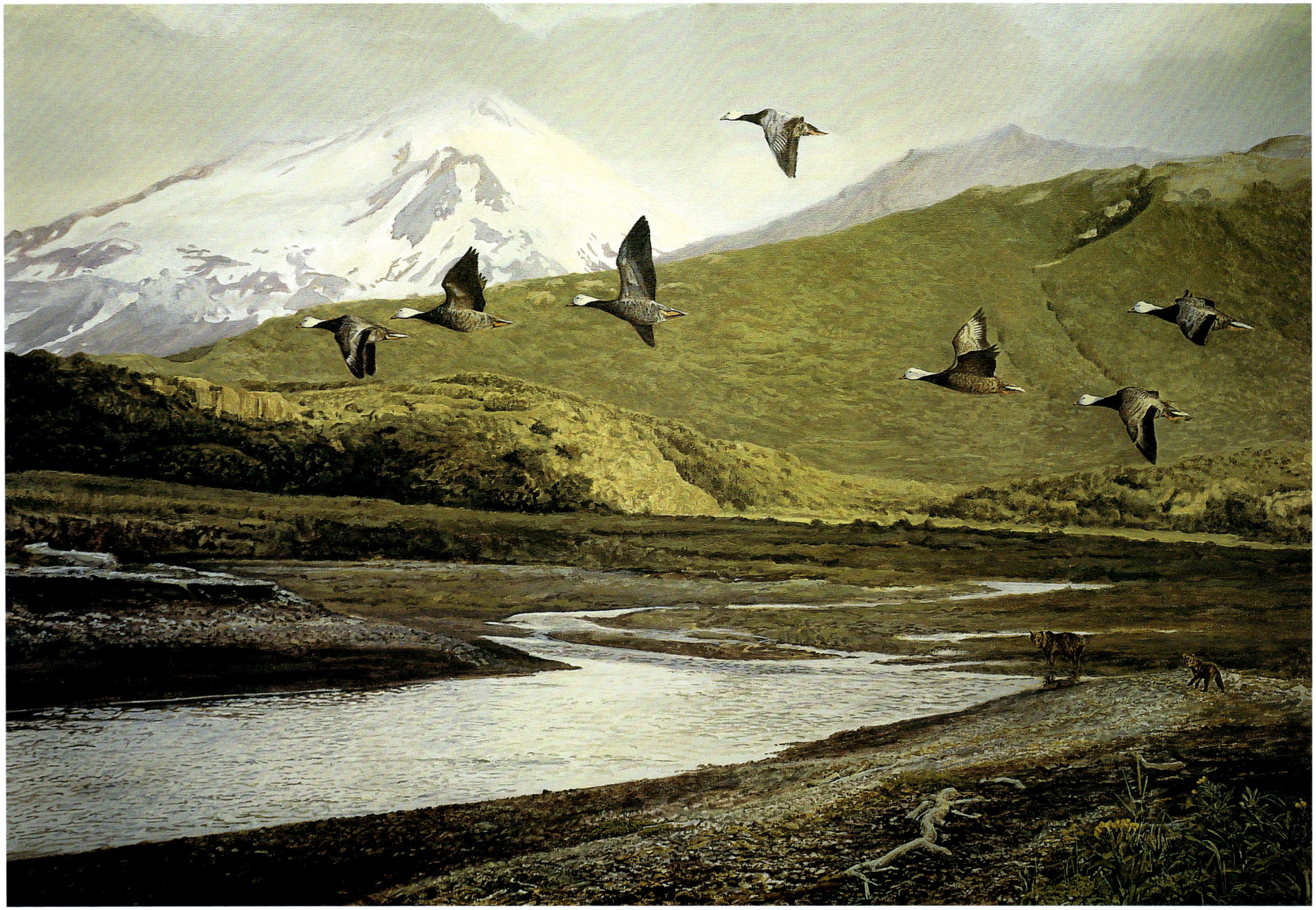

Crossing the Estuary, 1987
acrylic on canvas
40 × 60 inches

PETER CORBIN
An Artist's Creel

by Tom Davis

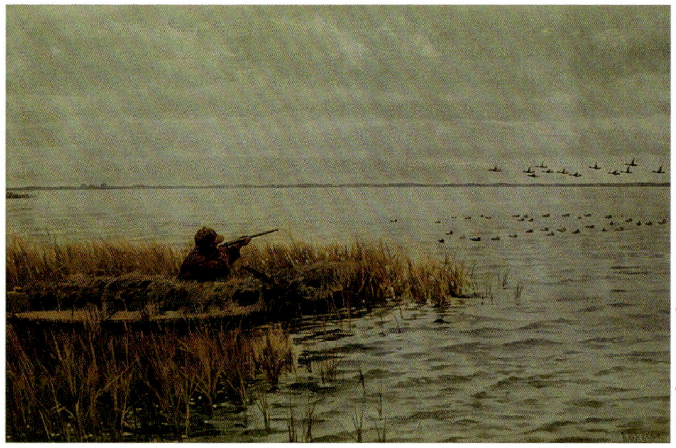

© Frederic Hamilton

A. B. Frost, *Duck Shooting from a Blind*, watercolor and gouache on paper, 13½ × 21½ inches

PETER STOCKTON CORBIN was born on October 18, 1945, in West Orange, New Jersey. The younger of two sons born to parents Robert and Elizabeth, he grew up in a home full of art, books, Labrador retrievers, and the tools and trappings of sport.

Over the years, Peter developed an abiding attachment to the rituals, protocols, and traditions, as codified and handed down by his father, of hunting and fishing. Or, more specifically, of wingshooting and fly fishing. "I love fly casting," he notes. "It's like ballet with an aesthetic elegance that I find very appealing. The other thing I really enjoy about fly fishing is that when you hook up you feel a direct connection to the fish. When I use other kinds of tackle, I feel *dis*connected. Fly fishing has just been a passion of mine forever."

Corbin's serious study of art began during his years at Pomfret, the rigorous college preparatory school in Pomfret, Connecticut. He credits his sculpture teacher there, Alice Dunbar, with instilling an awareness of the possibilities for artistic expression; prefiguring things to come, one of the projects he tackled in her classes was sculpting a goose, although he chose to interpret it abstractly. His painting instructor at Pomfret, Chick Cole, also helped expand his horizons.

When Corbin entered Wesleyan University in the fall of 1964, his plan was to major in math, star in football, hockey, and track, and, upon graduation, work at a prep school as a teacher and coach. But between flunking calculus and barely scraping by in everything else, he ended up flirting with academic probation and jeopardizing a promising athletic career.

While Corbin was eventually forced to retire as an athlete, due to a series of concussions (in an unhappy family tradition, his son Parker would suffer a horrific head injury playing football in prep school that took him four years to fully recover from), he found his niche in Wesleyan's art department. He literally exhausted the studio art curriculum, and when there were no more courses to take, he cajoled his professors into sponsoring various independent study projects. Sculpture was his primary focus; under the direction of Professor John Risley, for his senior honors thesis Corbin created a group of three monumental outdoor sculptures, jarringly abstract welded steel-and-fiberglass pieces through which he explored and articulated his growing preoccupation with light.

Corbin also continued to add to his fund of outdoor experiences. For two consecutive summers, he and his close friend Gus Blagden, an All-American lacrosse player at the University of Virginia and five years Peter's senior, trekked to the Cassiar Mountains of British Columbia. He found work at a hunting camp there and also the time to do a little hunting of his own for Stone sheep and mountain goats. Blagden's sudden death at the age of twenty-four—a bout of rheumatic fever in childhood left him with a weakened heart—was a devastating blow to Corbin, then a sophomore at Wesleyan.

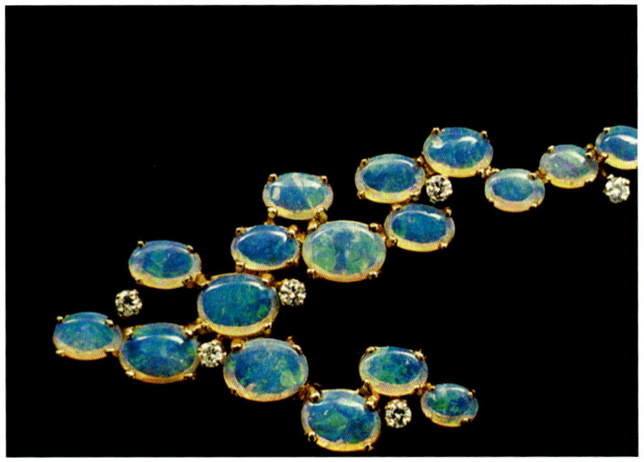

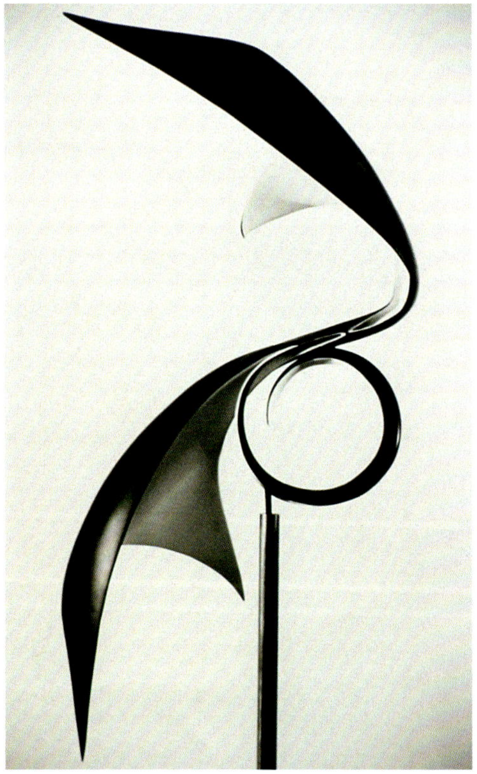

Pin, 1973
opal and diamond

Reflected Light Sculpture #1, 1969
mild steel and epoxy

He suffered another shock that same year when his parents divorced. "It was tough," he concedes. "I never saw it coming. So I kind of withdrew for a while and just immersed myself in art and sports."

After graduating with high honors in 1968, Corbin traveled with his mother for an extended tour of two of the world's great art capitals, Florence and Madrid. It amounted to a pilgrimage for him, and he seized every opportunity to visit the museums, study their masterworks, and simply open himself up to the genius of Titian, Velázquez, Raphael, and others. The experience inspired Corbin, upon his return stateside, to begin a new series of sculptures. Blending his fascination with light, in this case light as reflected from highly polished, curvilinear metal surfaces, with the challenge of conveying motion in a static medium, these pieces occupied his artistic attentions for the next several years.

He also continued his formal study of art, heading west to the California College of Arts and Crafts in Oakland. He didn't stay long, though. While Corbin was accepting of all the modern art "isms" (his love of traditional artists such as Frost and Pleissner notwithstanding) and at the time considered himself an abstract expressionist, he found the Bay Area "funk art" scene "wacky." After a year, he returned to New Jersey in 1970 to a management job with a jewelry manufacturer, Robert S. Fisher & Co., in Newark, where he had the opportunity to design a few jewelry pieces.

On a ski trip to Colorado in 1971, Corbin met Lillian Pyne. The two hit it off immediately and they eventually married in October 1973. Peter was by then an ardent Atlantic salmon angler, taking at least one trip every summer to fish the Grande Cascapédia (or another of Quebec's salmon rivers) with a group of like-minded friends. He had even begun drawing some salmon-fishing scenes with the combination of landscape, water, and canoes proving irresistible to the artist in him. Impressed by what they saw, his friends urged him to spread his wings even wider.

In fairly short order the newlyweds had quit their jobs (Lillian was working at a bank in New York City) and moved to a rented cottage in the southern Catskills so Corbin could focus all his energies on sporting art before they had children or owned property.

Slowly but steadily, Corbin established himself in the outdoor world. Early on, the beloved outdoor writer Gene Hill, a former Madison Avenue advertising executive, advised him to illustrate a few books. "It doesn't pay much," Hill cautioned, "but it helps put your name out there. It's advertising." So he drew forty drawings in a month's time—for $500. But when you are starting out, you have to do those kinds of things.

Another crucial step in the blueprint of his career was developing relationships with various conservation and non-profit organizations, such as Ducks Unlimited, the Ruffed Grouse Society, the Coastal Conservation Association, and the GameCoin. The two

The Georgia-Florida Field Trials, 1983
acrylic on canvas
30 × 48 inches

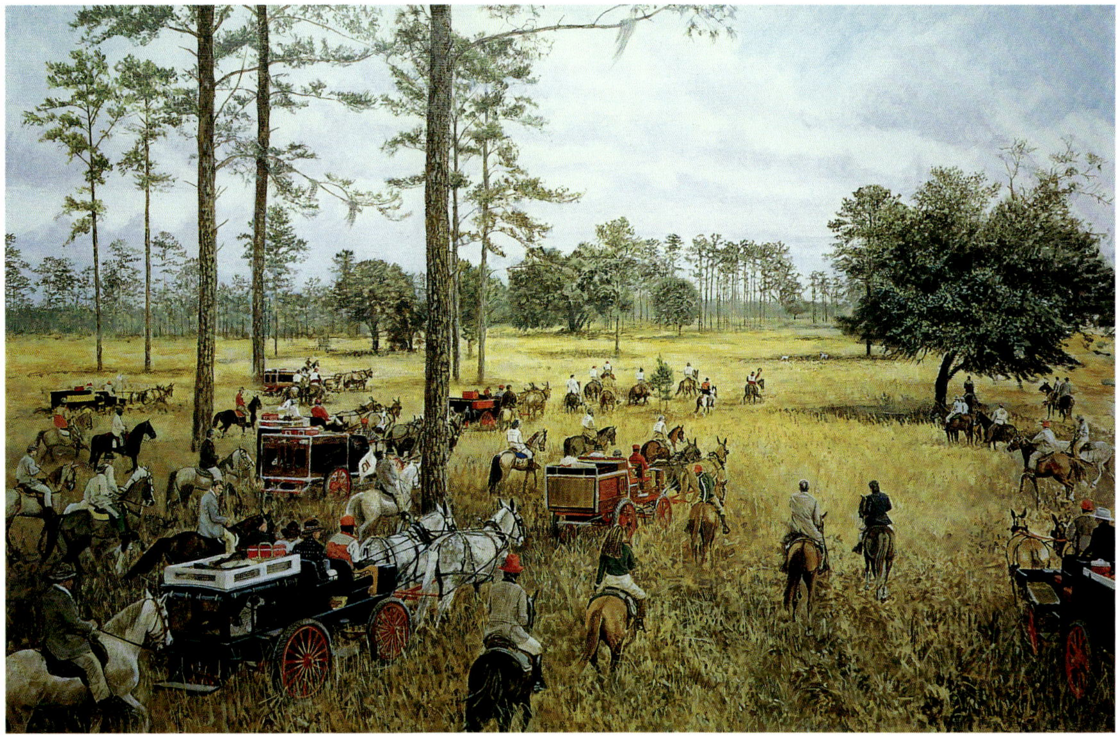

groups he is most prominently identified with, though, are the Atlantic Salmon Federation and the American Museum of Fly Fishing.

Then there were the catalog covers for L. L. Bean; other shows and exhibits, including the internationally prestigious *Birds in Art* show at the Leigh Yawkey Woodson Art Museum in Wausau, Wisconsin (where Corbin's monumental painting of emperor geese, *Crossing the Estuary*, hangs in the permanent collection); limited-edition prints published by Orvis, Petersen Prints, and Mill Pond Press; and laudatory articles in magazines such as *Sports Afield*, *Wildlife Art*, and *Sporting Classics*.

Peter Corbin will tell you that he's a "very slow" painter. "I probably do as many paintings in a year as some of my contemporaries do in a month," he admits. "It goes back to the way I constructed sculpture. It is a long, thoughtful process, although I like to think that it is still somewhat organic. The most paintings I have ever done in a year is twenty-nine. Lately I've been doing fifteen to seventeen a year, but they have been bigger canvases, a number of them twenty-by-thirty inches and some even larger than that."

It is more instructive to characterize Corbin not as a slow painter, but as a deliberate and meticulous one; the Dutch master Vermeer, for instance, was a painter of transcendent genius who agonized at incredible length over the most minute details of his work. The questions are timeless: When is a painting finished? When does a painting arrive at the place where nothing more can be done to improve it? "It is really important to know when to stop," Corbin observes, "or at least when to stop for a while. You get to a point where you're not adding anything. Bob Abbett calls it the point where you are just 're-arranging paint.' For me, it's an inner feeling that there is nothing I can do to make the painting better, and that if I *do* try to do anything I'm likely to make it worse. Maybe it is not as successful as I had hoped it would be—I always come back to Ogden's remark that every painting is perfect until you start it—but I learn something from each painting that I can apply to the next one."

While sporting art depicts specific individuals in specific locations, the best sporting art conveys the universality of the experience, engages the viewers' own memories, dreams, and imagination, and irresistibly draws them into the scene. Having taken his cues from Frost and Pleissner, Corbin cultivates this sense of universality by intentionally keeping his figures small in relation to the overall size of the painting and by typically depicting them from the back or side rather than head-on, obscuring their identities and shifting the emphasis to the landscape, the light, and that ineffable quality known as mood.

"My interest in getting past the subject is why I don't do formal head-and-shoulder portraits," Corbin says. "I call my portraits 'informal formal portraits'; there is a foreground and a background, but not much middle ground. Like my sporting paintings,

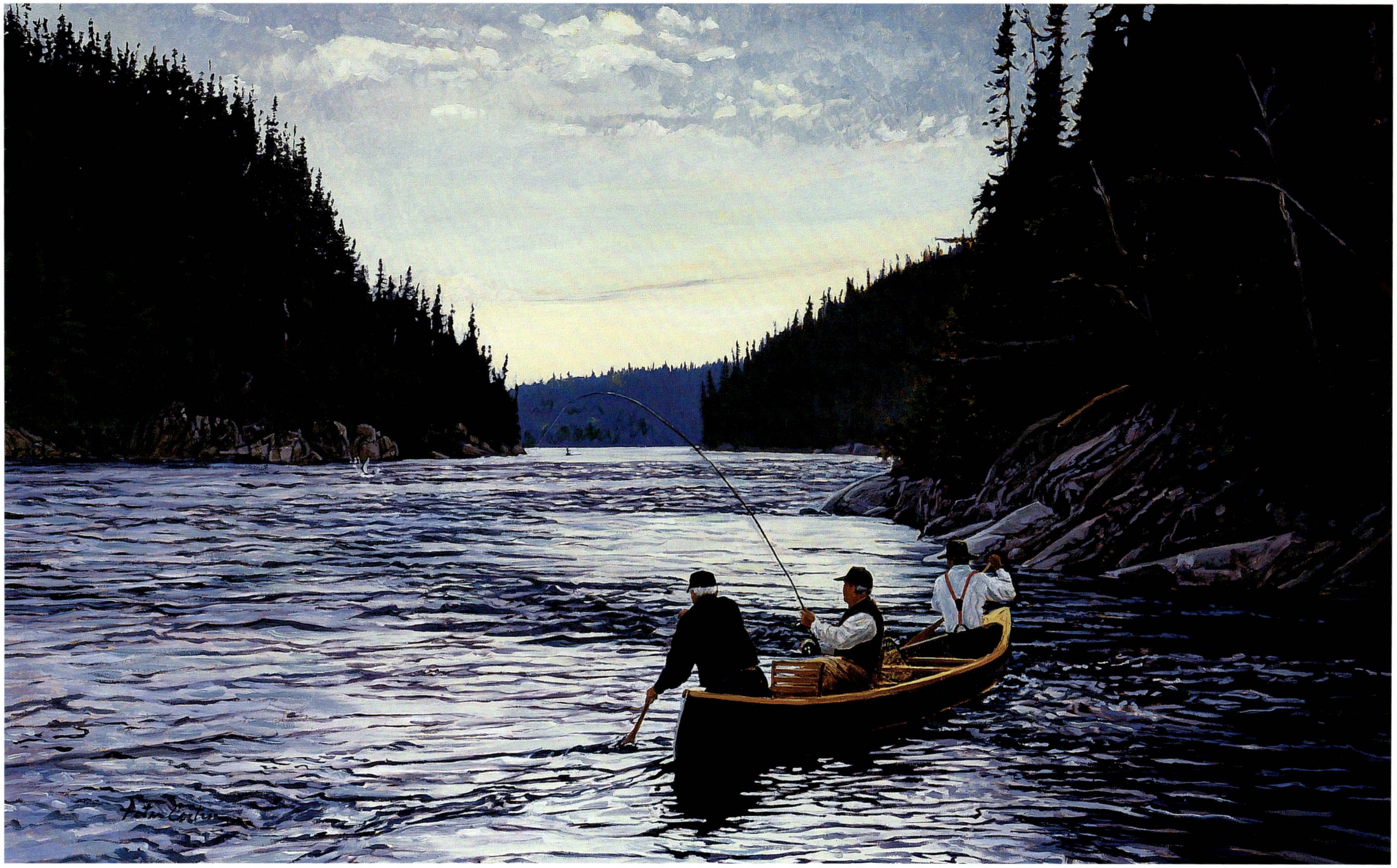

Down River, 2000
oil on canvas
24 × 40 inches

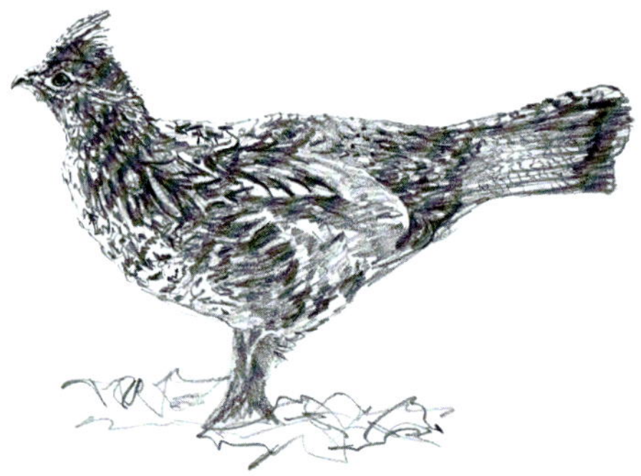

Ruffed Grouse, 2005
original pencil drawing
4 × 5 inches

they are basically landscapes with people in them, and I approach them the same way: I spend time with the person I'm depicting in a place they are comfortable and relaxed in, take tons of photos, and try to be as unobtrusive as possible, like the proverbial 'fly on the wall.' The more I bother them, the stiffer and more self-conscious they get."

Although Corbin has tried his hand over the years at *plein air* painting, and admires the spontaneity and freshness of expression that on-location painting can bring to the canvas, he has never felt as comfortable, or as pleased with the results, as he does when he paints in his studio, where the air is redolent of hay and horses, the filtered light is gauzy, and a fifty-year-old drama plays on the satellite radio.

In addition to his paintings, Corbin always has a number of drawings in inventory. Some of these drawings served as preliminary sketches for paintings; others are "free-standing" images that Corbin simply felt inspired to do.

"I've always loved pencil," he says. "My drawings used to be fairly 'tight,' but over the years they've loosened up and become softer and more impressionistic. I call them 'inexpensive originals,' and while they're not the priority that my paintings are, I still take a great deal of pride in them."

First Retrieve
original pencil drawing
4 × 7 inches

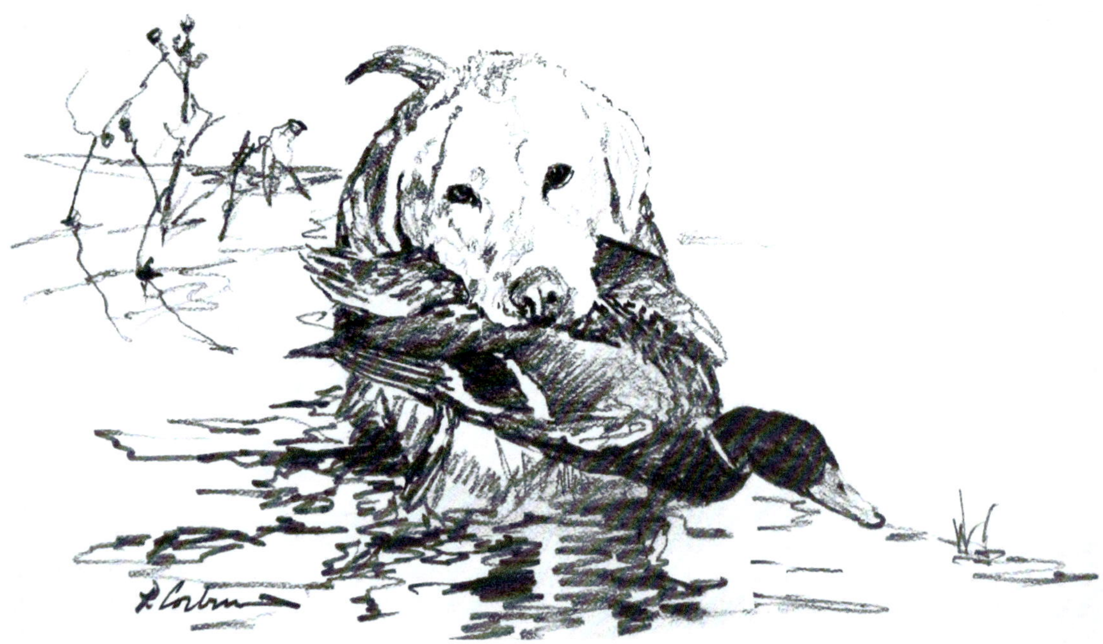

Changing the Fly
original pencil drawing
4 × 7 inches

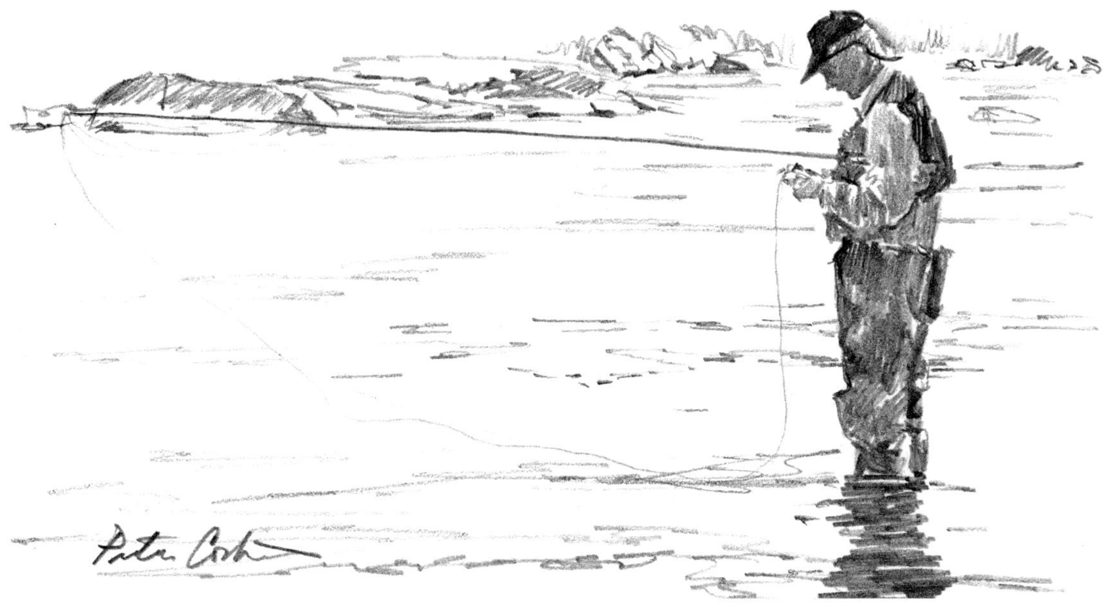

It is natural to wonder if, after so many paintings of Atlantic salmon fishing and ruffed grouse hunting, Corbin ever runs out of inspiration. The short answer is no; the longer, more complex answer cuts to the heart of his entire philosophy of art, a philosophy that has certainly evolved over the course of his career but remains rooted in the same soil that nurtured the budding abstract-expressionist sculptor at Wesleyan University. In Peter Corbin's view, there is no fundamental difference between the expansive welded steel-and-fiberglass sculptures he created in college, the smaller, more decorative polished steel sculptures that came a little later, and the painting that sits on his easel at this very moment. It comes back, once again, to getting beyond the nominal subject—"the tyranny of the thing seen," as Picasso supposedly put it—and exploring the qualities that underpin all enduring visual art, whether two- or three-dimensional, abstract or representational.

For Corbin, while it would be wrong to say that it is all about light, in both its transmitted and reflected forms, that is what it is *mostly* about. "What you did as a sculptor in the 1960s and 1970s," he explains, "was define a theme, which was usually couched as a 'problem,' then you worked through that theme or problem via a series of sculptures until you had taken it as far as it could go. The three outdoor sculptures I made at Wesleyan dealt primarily with transmitted light; the series that followed, eight pieces, all told, were examples of reflected light, although they were responses to my fascination with linear movement as well.

Reflected Light Sculpture #3, 1969
nickel silver and mild steel

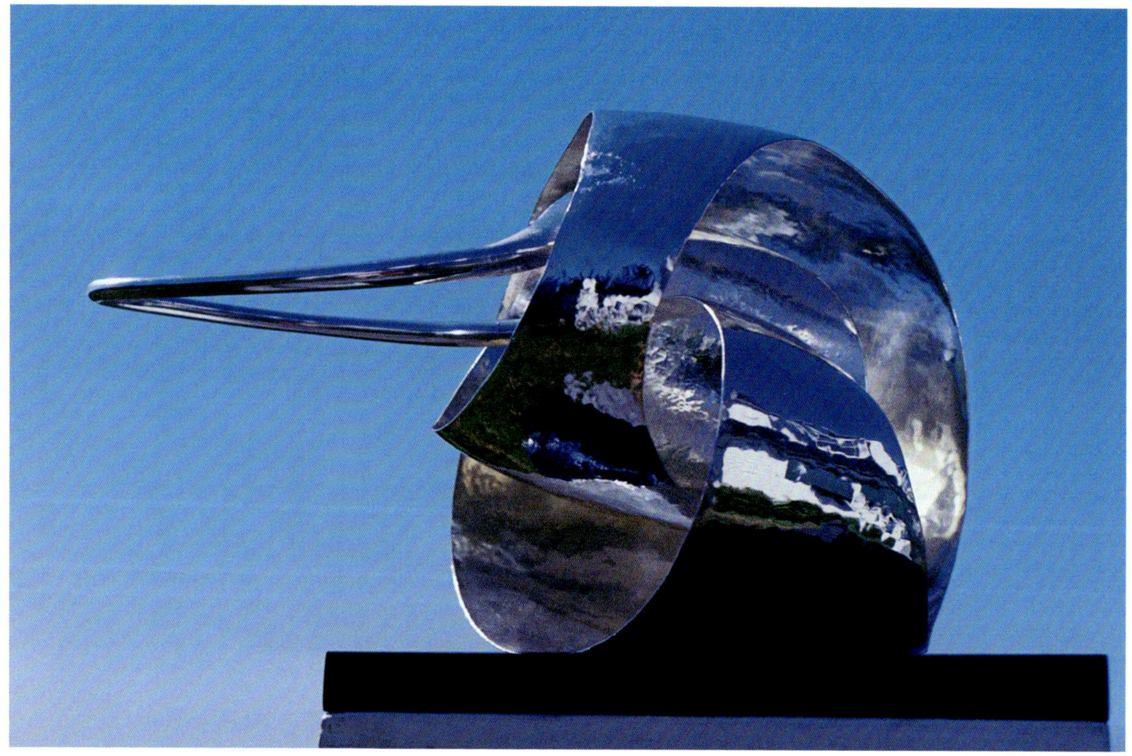

"In those days I was influenced by modern abstract sculptors like Steve Smith, Alexander Calder, and José de Rivera. But when I turned to sporting art and began to revisit Frost, Pleissner, and also Thomas Eakins, whom I had come to admire somewhat later, I saw that their compositions were based on very much the same principles. When you depict water in a duck-hunting or salmon-fishing scene, you are dealing with reflected light; when you paint autumn foliage in a grouse-hunting scene, you are dealing with transmitted light.

"Everyone talks about how beautifully these artists depicted their subject matter and conveyed a sense of place and mood, and that is absolutely true. But it is the way they designed their paintings, and especially the way they handled light, that gave their work its underlying strength, and it is why their example continues to challenge and inspire me.

"So I don't find myself getting burned out at all. I'm still working through those same basic problems that I posed for myself when I was doing sculpture. If anything, by becoming a sporting artist and having to pay attention to the painting's 'story line' as well as to the abstract qualities of the composition, I have added a few more challenges."

Nor is it a coincidence that as he has grown older his work has become looser and more impressionistic, or that he is increasingly preoccupied with mood, atmosphere,

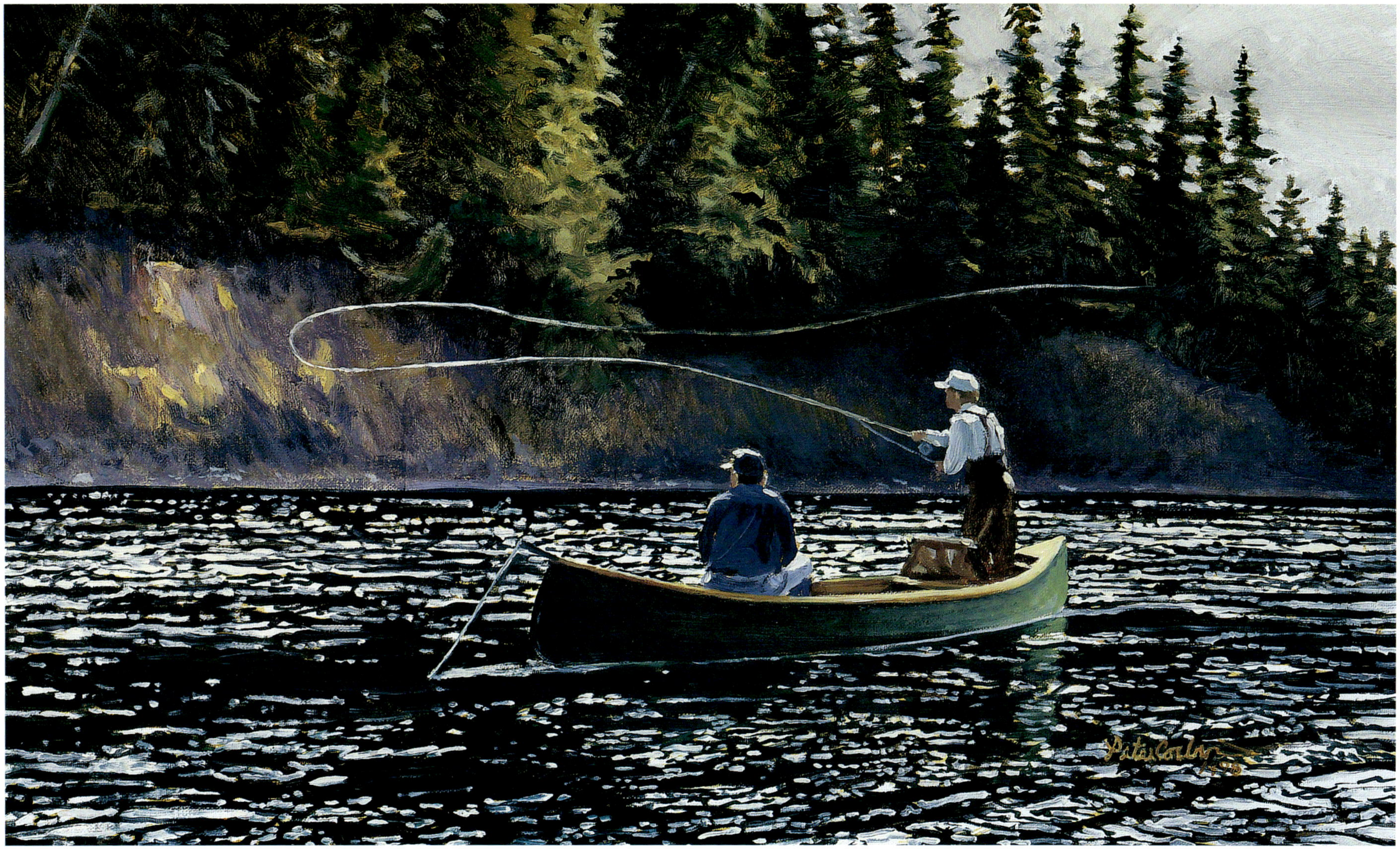

The Run on the Bank, 1998
oil on canvas
12 × 20 inches

and other "intangibles." There was a time when it would have been fair to categorize Corbin as a "detail" painter (early in his career, he even did a few photographically realistic waterfowl paintings for various duck stamp competitions); now, as his friend Bob Kuhn would put it, his paintings "convey the illusion of detail by dint of intelligent editing."

"You need to keep the eye moving," Corbin notes, "and the hard edges that appear in highly detailed paintings tend to stop the eye. That is why I'm always working the light to the dark, the warm to the cool, pushing and pulling the different elements of the painting to create some tension, some visual interest. There are no lines in nature, just surfaces meeting.

"That's why color is so important, too. My painting teacher at Wesleyan, Harry Nadler, introduced me to Josef Albers' theory of color perception, the gist of which is that colors, as the human eye perceives them, change hue in response to the colors around them. The change can be very subtle, but it is always something I'm aware of, something I try to use to contribute to the dynamics of the composition.

"I have to admit, though, that evolution and artistic growth aren't the only reasons that I have become more interested in color, value, and mass, and less interested in line. The other reason is that, like a lot of us, I don't see as well as I used to!"

Corbin has lately become enamored of the artistic possibilities of dressage; while equestrian paintings have long been a staple of his repertoire—some years ago he took sculptor Jon Zahourek's intensive course in equine anatomy—he finds the combination of grace, power, and precision inherent in dressage irresistible.

"Dressage is the ballet of equestrian sport," he enthuses. "I see these magnificent horses and the exquisite choreography of their movements, and I am reminded of Degas' ballerinas."

Corbin's son Parker likes to say that what he is looking for when he casts his fly is "a tug on the line." In his search for scenes to paint, Peter Corbin will tell you he is looking for the same thing. "I've been collecting images that tug on my line my whole life," he muses. "Hunting, fishing, horses, landscapes, whatever. The thing that really separates artists from the people who are sane on this planet is that you don't consciously pick out this or that career. Art picks you. When people tell me they have a son or daughter who is interested in art and ask if I'll talk to them, I say that I will be happy to critique their work but I won't encourage them to become an artist. You don't pick art as a career; it picks you. You are compelled to do what you do by what you see."

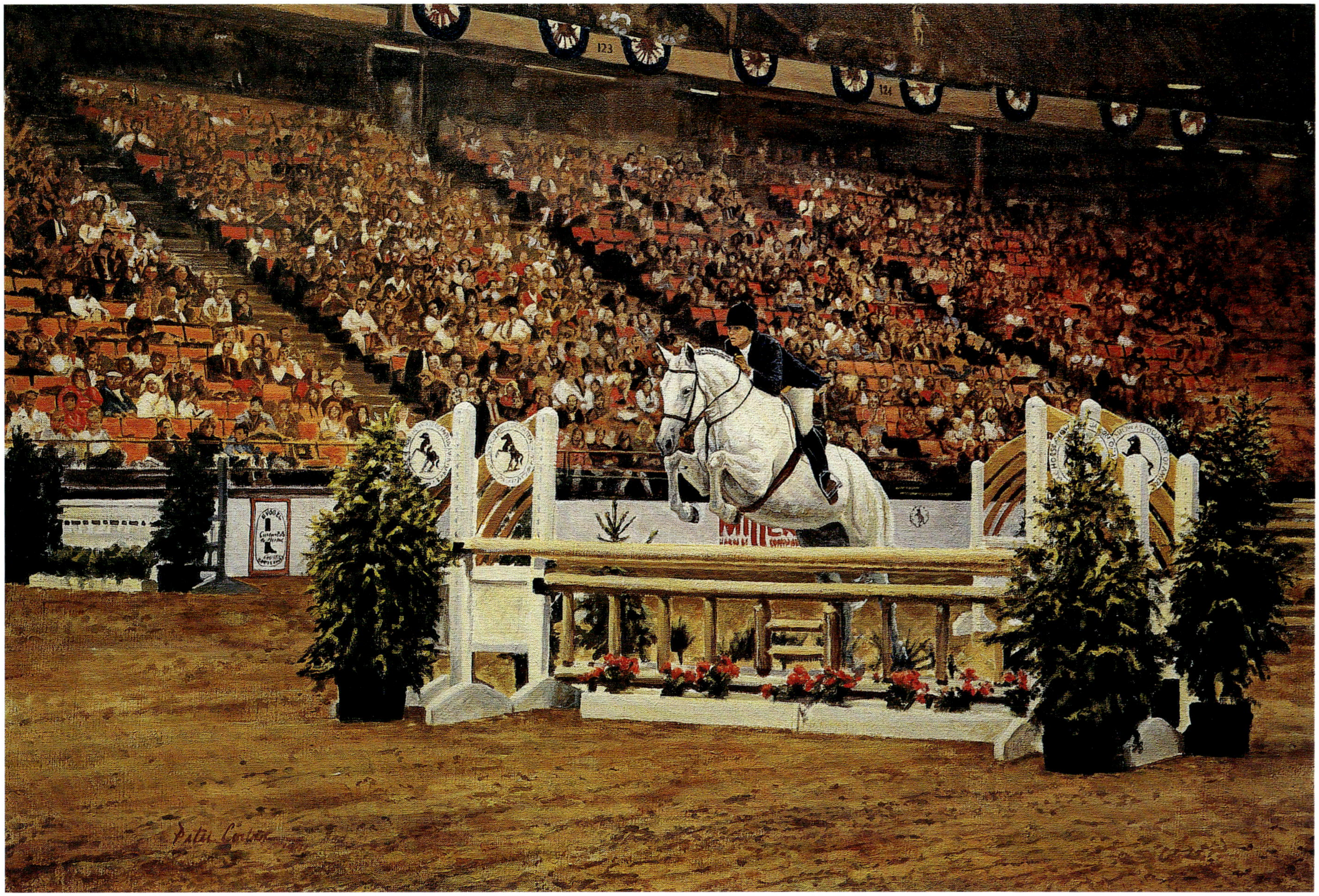

At the National, 1991
acrylic on canvas
24 × 36 inches

COLOR PLATES

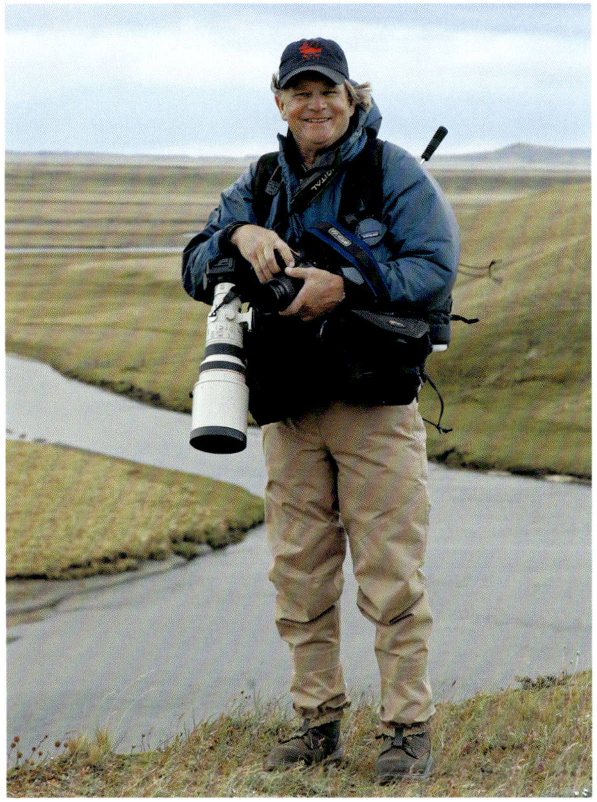

On a commission in Patagonia, January 2005.
Photo by Craig Derby, Derby Digital Images.

Although I now release nearly every fish I catch and don't even carry a fishing creel, I have preserved the images from a lifetime in the natural world with both my mind and my camera. They are not complete "finished" images, but, rather, the essence of my experiences that I want to relate or share with people. Most often, the essence is a certain light as transmitted either through clouds or trees or as reflected off water. Or it may be the focused attitudes of a shotgunner or angler or the expression of their appreciation of a day afield. I put these thoughts and images in my creel to take home, sort through, and piece together, selecting parts with which to construct the paintings. Like the sculpture I created early in my career, these paintings are woven together to combine abstract elements with realism and to convey the essences of the natural world and my experiences in it.

Fly Fishing

My fascination with both reflected and transmitted light, and the elements of asymmetrical balance and linear motion, all come together in the realism of the sport of fly fishing, which, for me, is the most direct form of fishing that exists. Stripping a fly back and feeling the take of a large striped bass is a very primary and intimate experience, and the delivery of the fly with the fly rod to the water is as close as fishing and ballet can get.

An old mentor of mine said, "It's not so much that I like to catch fish as I like the places where they live." This is also true of painting. From the intimacy of small streams to the ballet of saltwater flats and all the river scenes in between—the sport of fly fishing has comprised the bulk of my work.

Eastern Trout

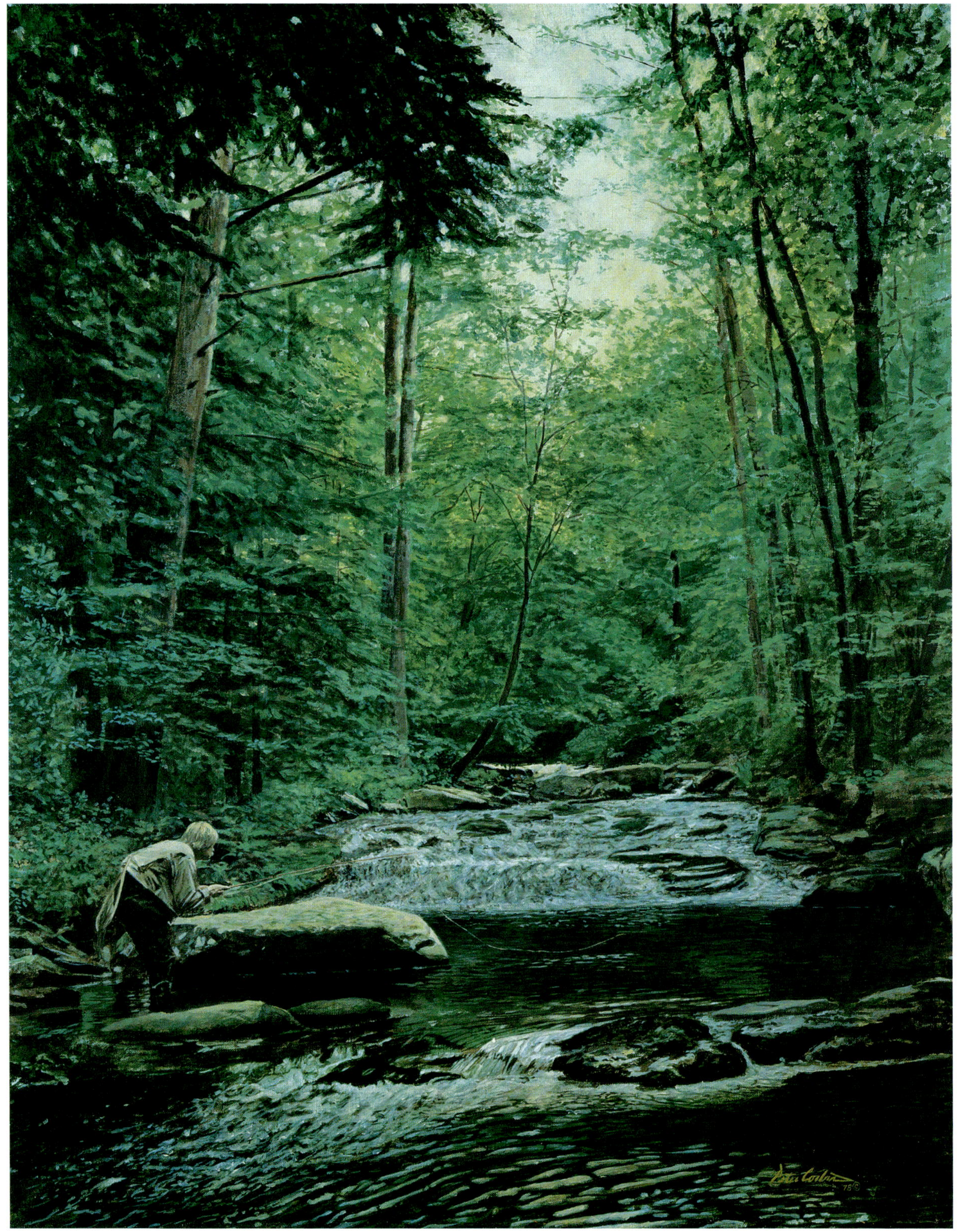

Stalking, 1978
acrylic on canvas
30 × 24 inches
signed and dated lower right

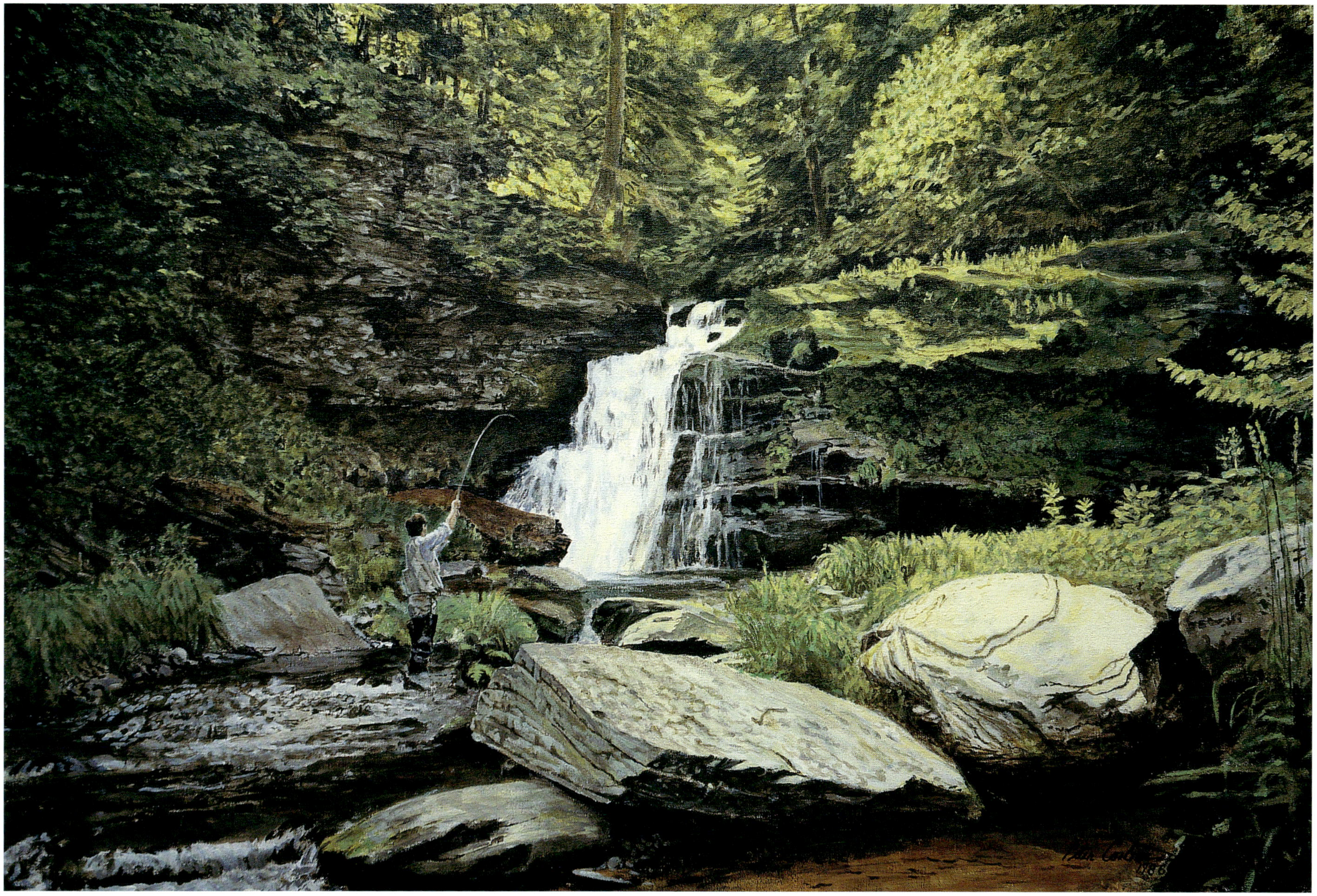

Upper Falls, 1986
acrylic on canvas
24 × 36 inches
signed and dated lower right

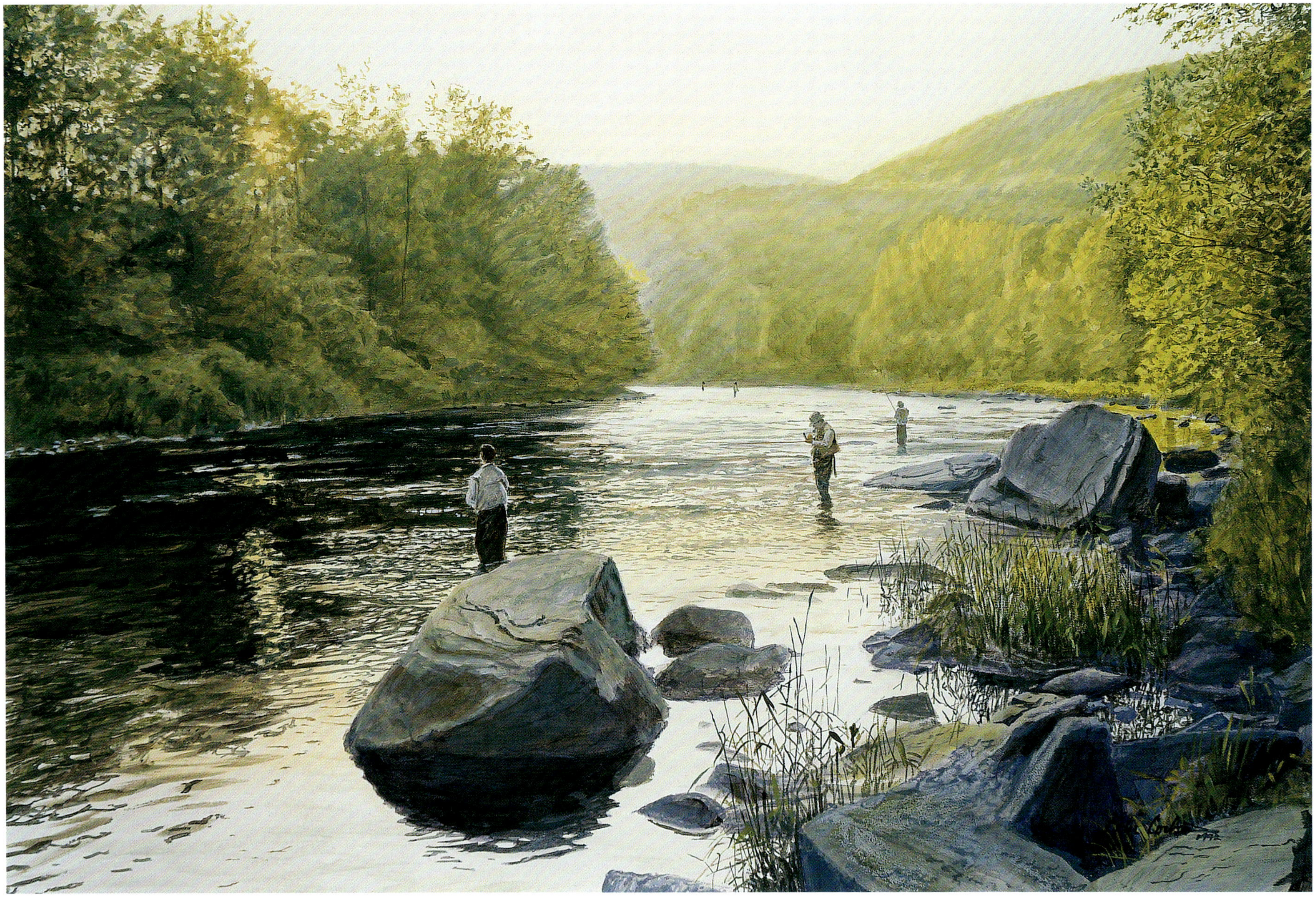

Beaverkill Afternoon, 1992
acrylic on canvas
20 × 30 inches
signed and dated lower right

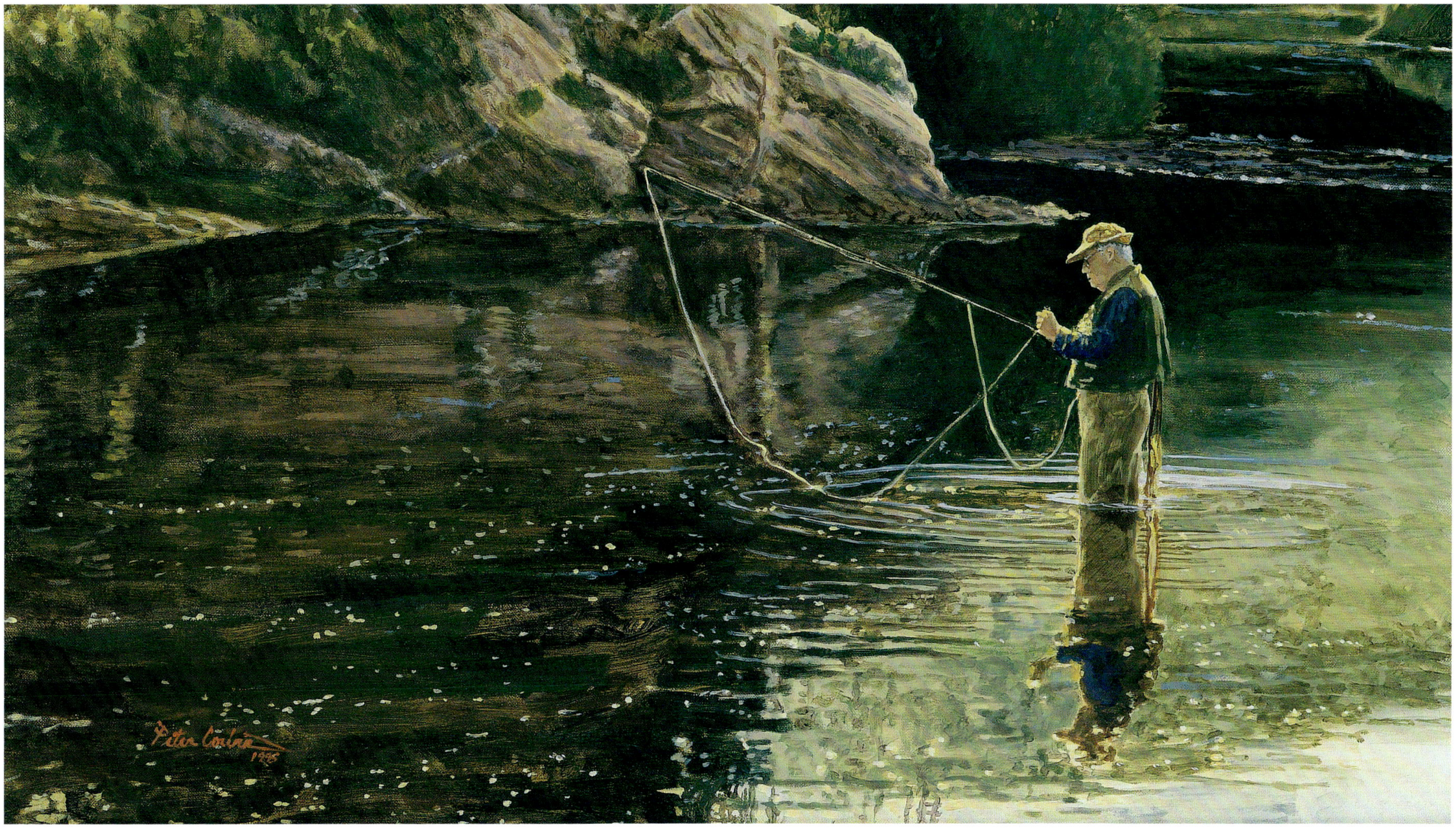

Adirondack Reflection, 1995
acrylic on canvas
15 × 28 inches
signed and dated lower left

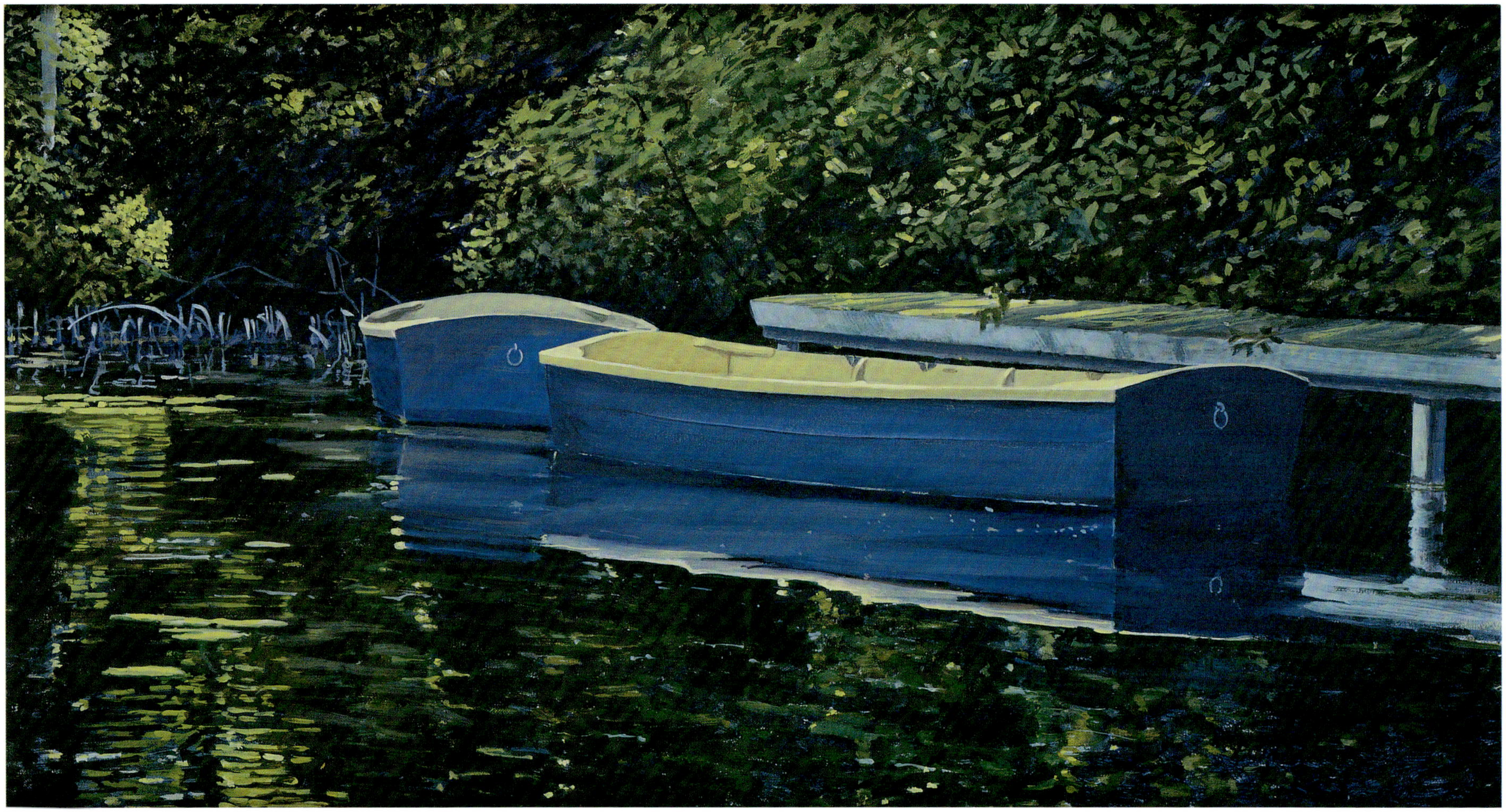

Blue Boats, 1993
acrylic on canvas
16 × 30 inches
signed and dated lower right

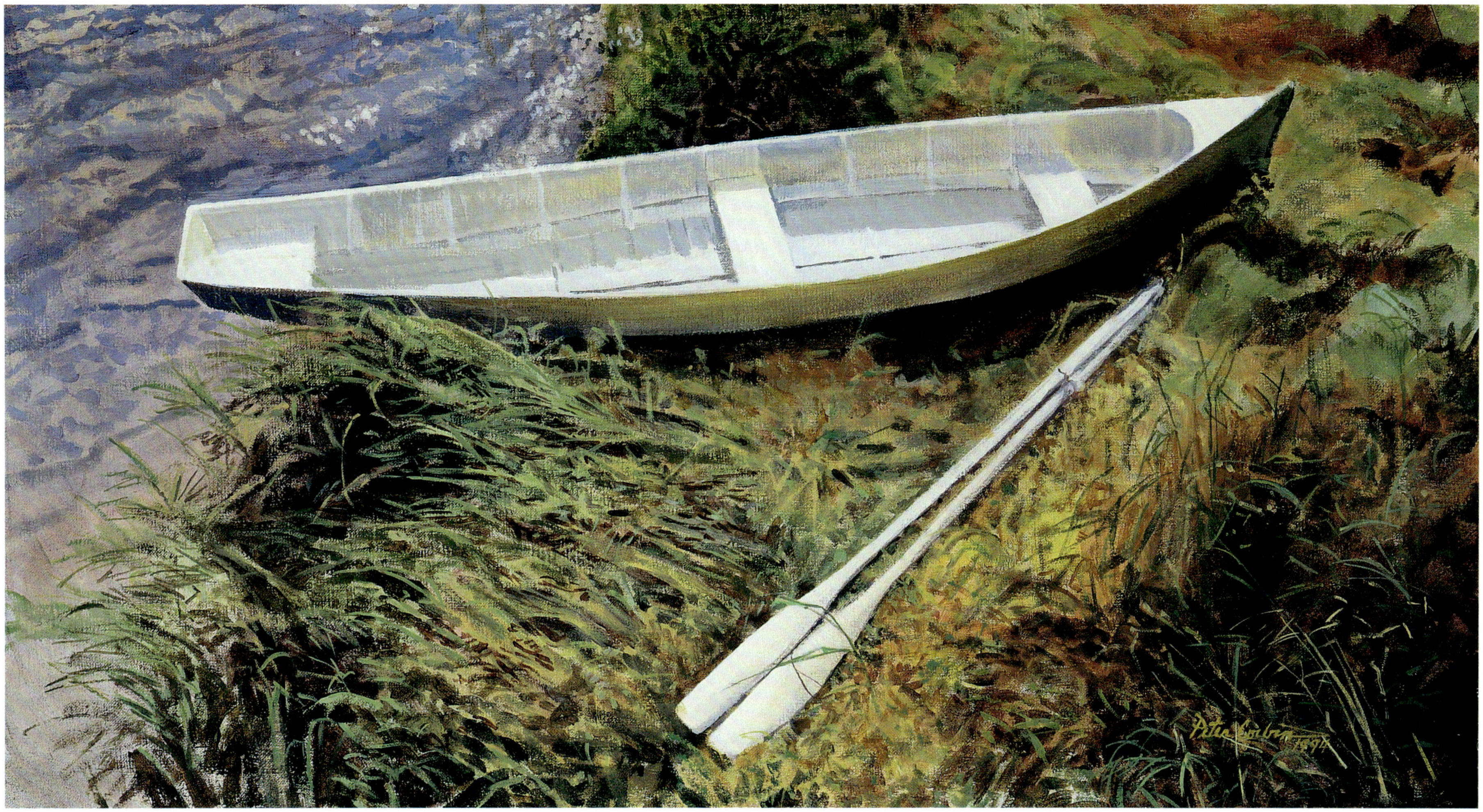

The White Skow, 1994
acrylic on canvas
16 × 30 inches
signed and dated lower right

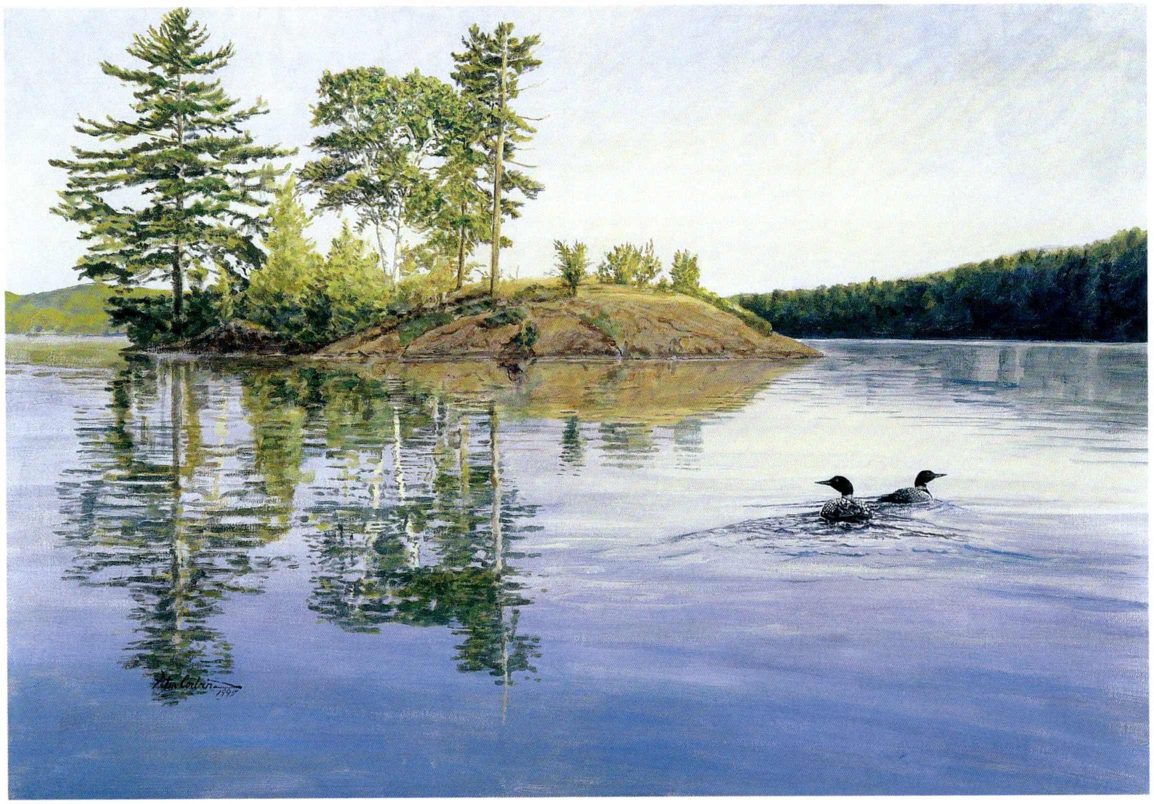

Two Loons, 1995
acrylic on canvas
20 × 30 inches
signed and dated lower left

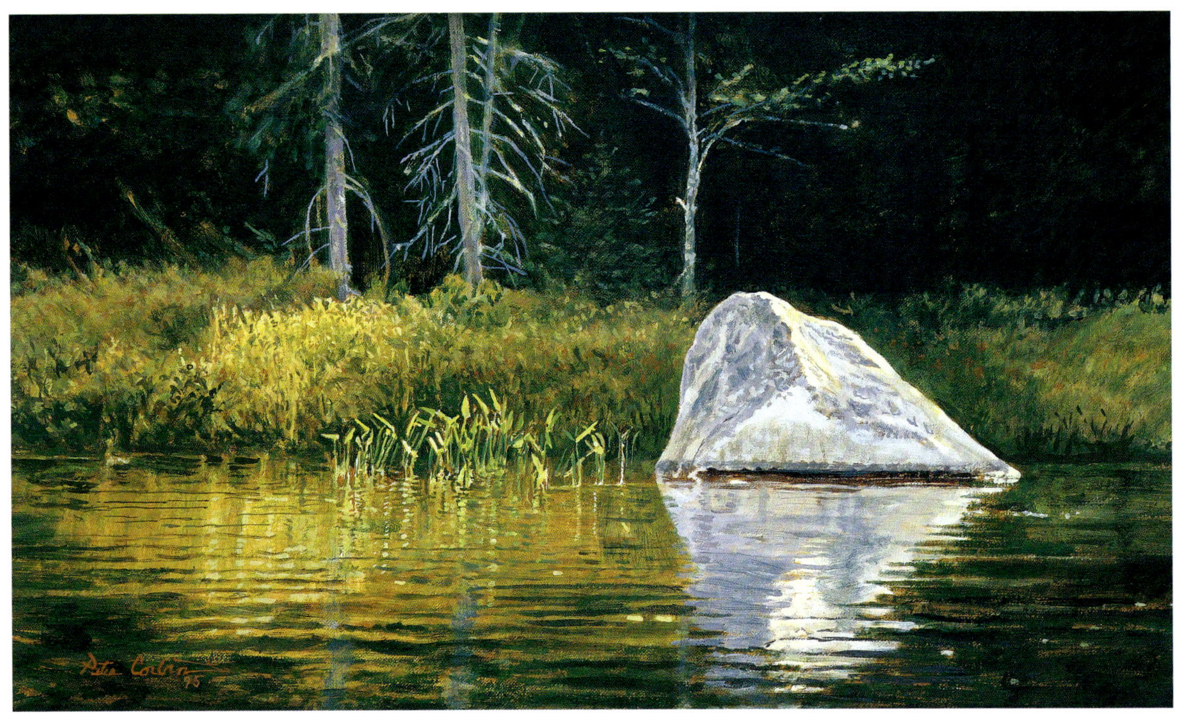

Arrowhead Weed, 1995
acrylic on canvas
12 × 20 inches
signed and dated lower left

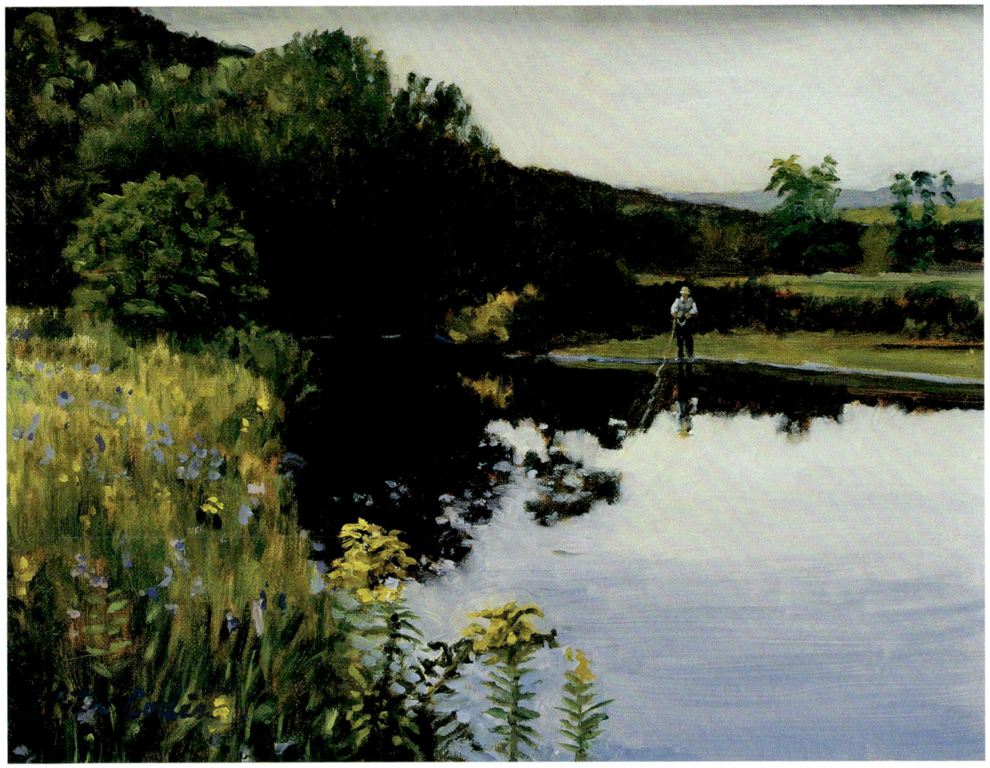

Summer Evening, 1997
oil on canvas
9 × 12 inches
signed lower left

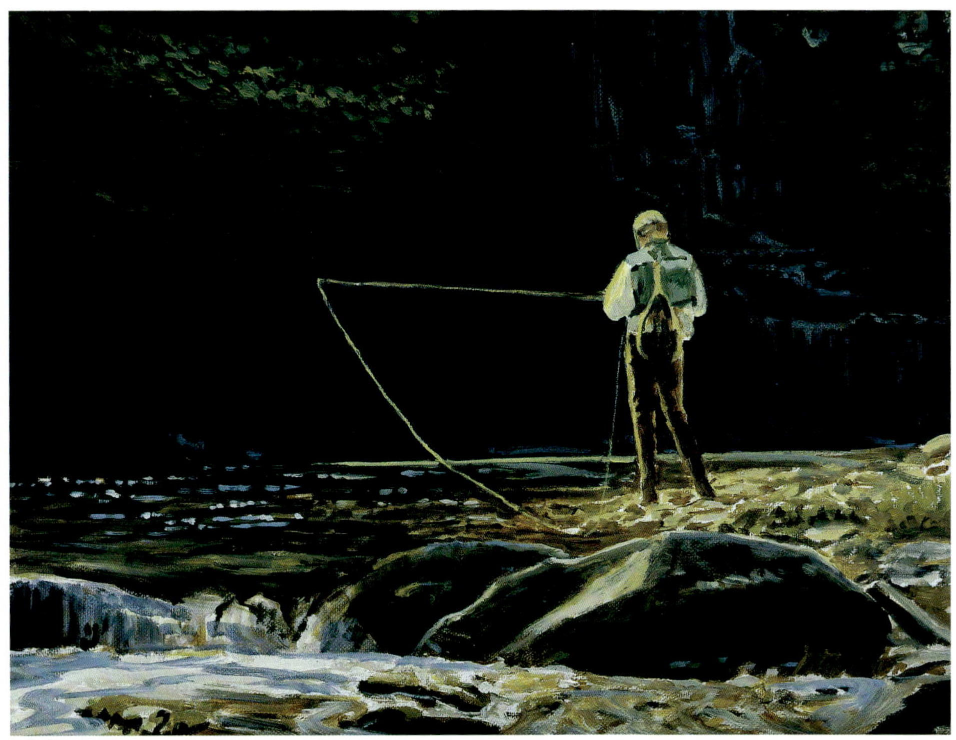

Summer Hatch, 1997
oil on canvas
9 × 12 inches
signed lower right

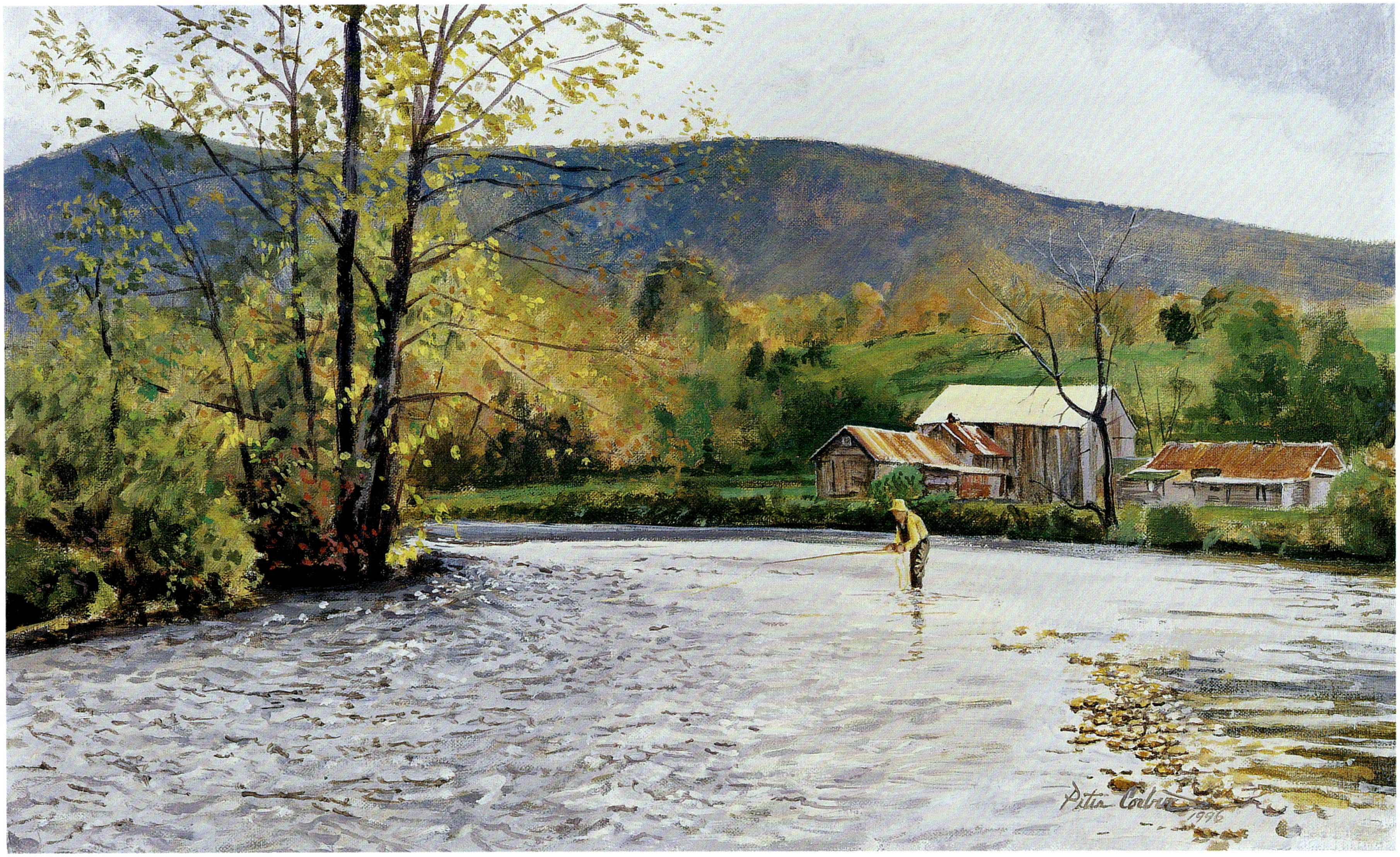

Battenkill, 1996
acrylic on canvas
12 × 20 inches
signed and dated lower right

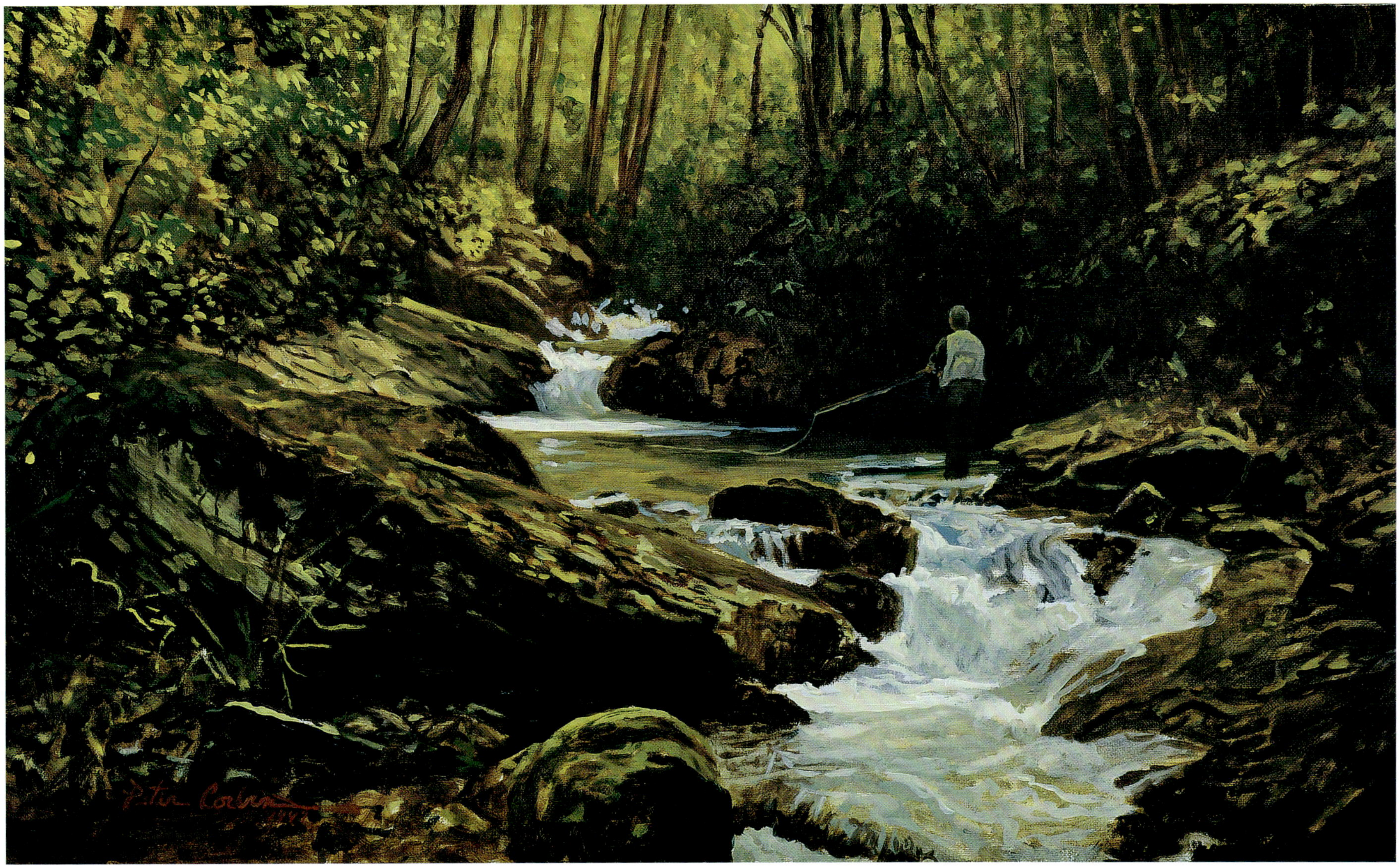

Mountain Pool, 1997
oil on canvas
12 × 20 inches
signed and dated lower left

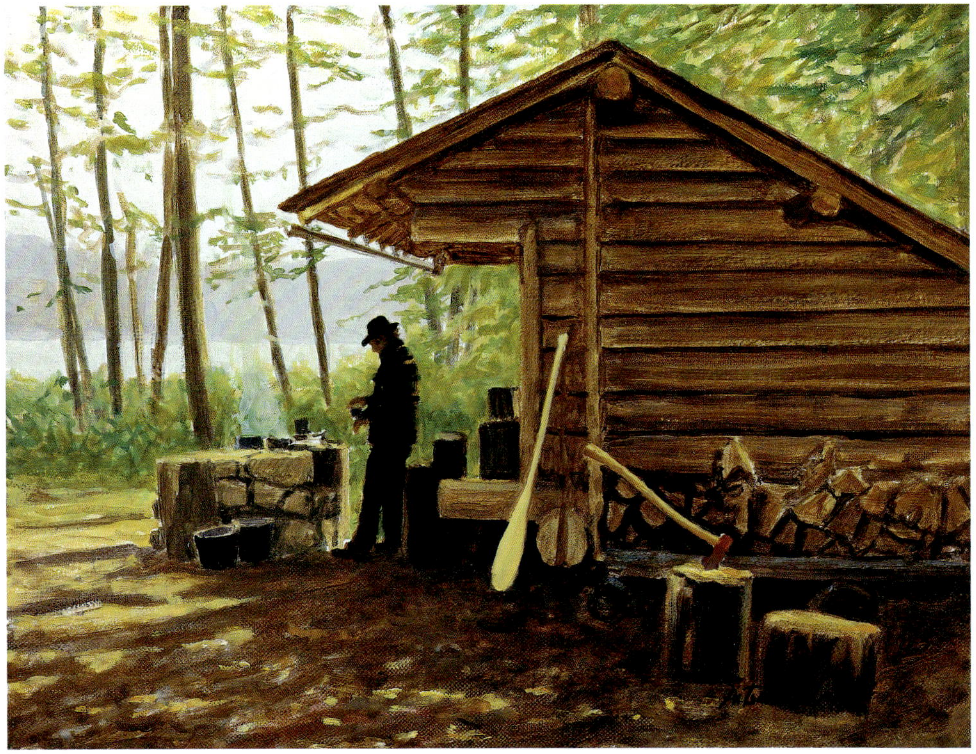

Morning Coffee, 1998
oil on canvas
9 × 12 inches
signed lower right

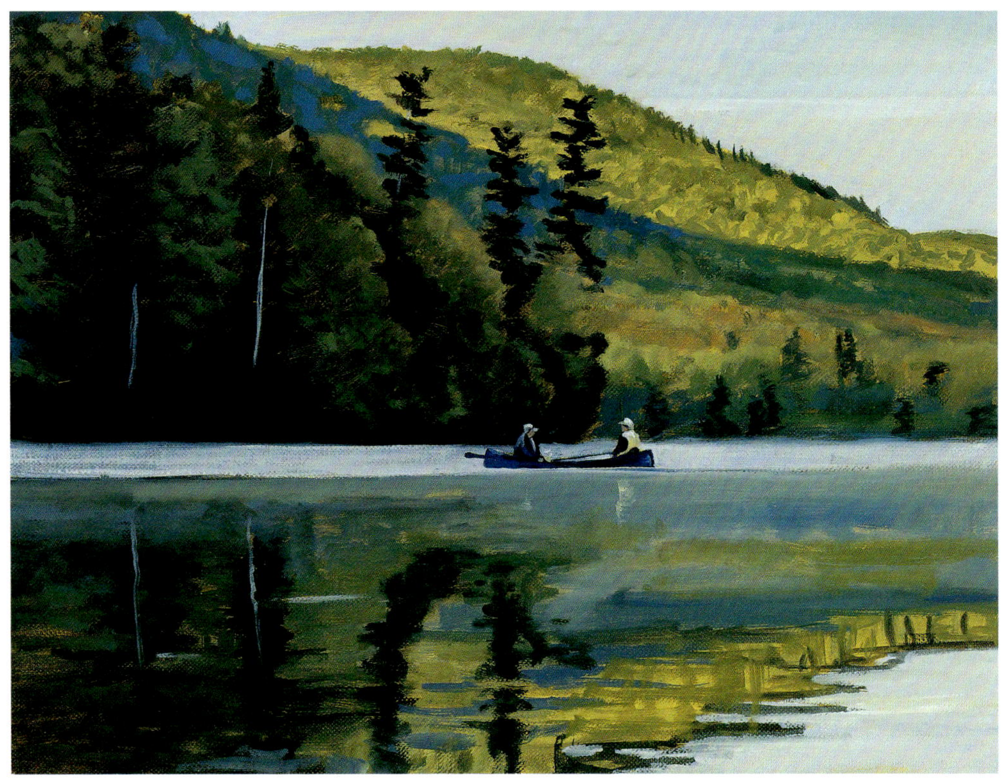

Upper Lake, 1999
oil on canvas
9 × 15 inches
signed lower left

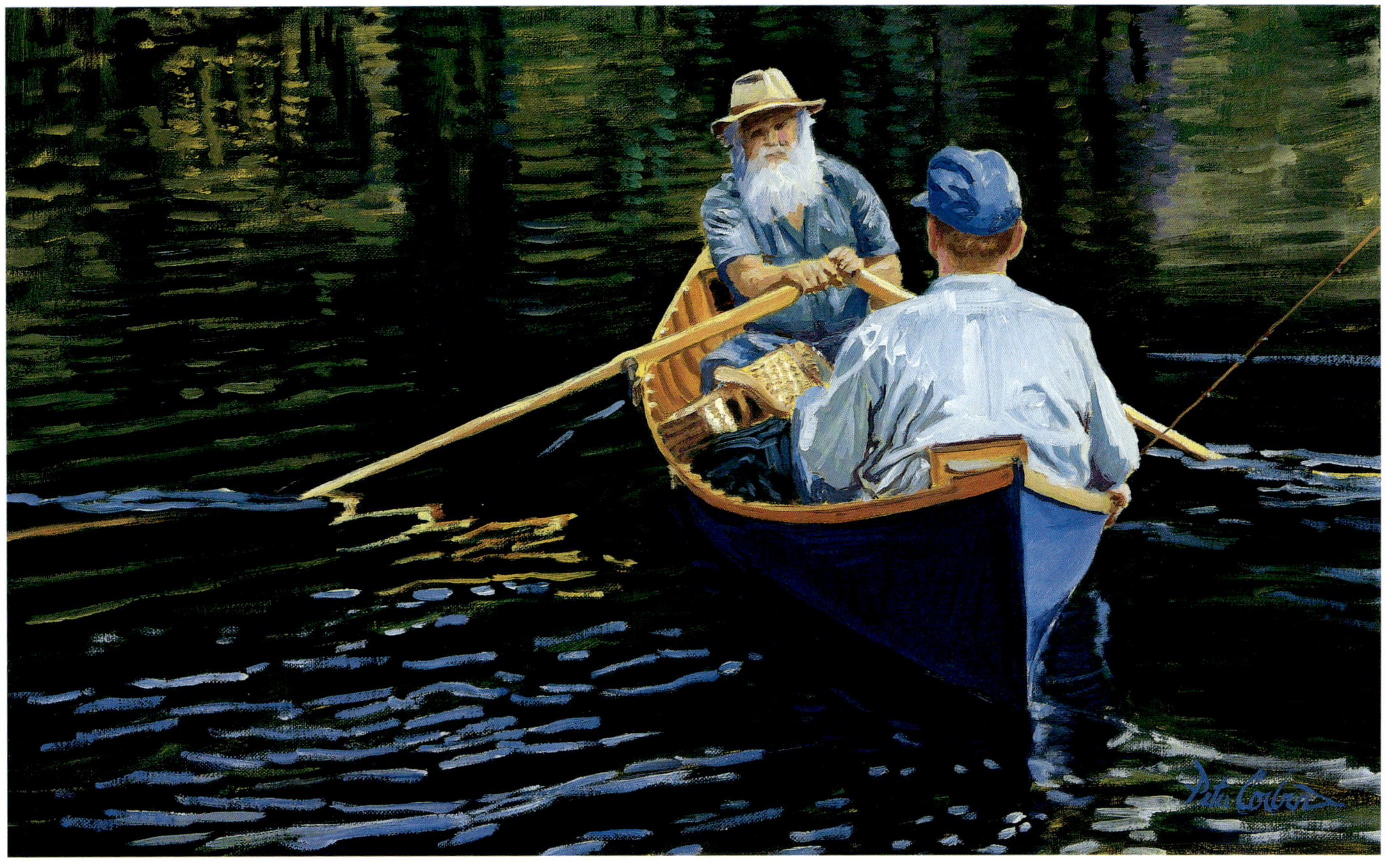

Adirondack Guide, 1999
oil on canvas
12 × 20 inches
signed lower right

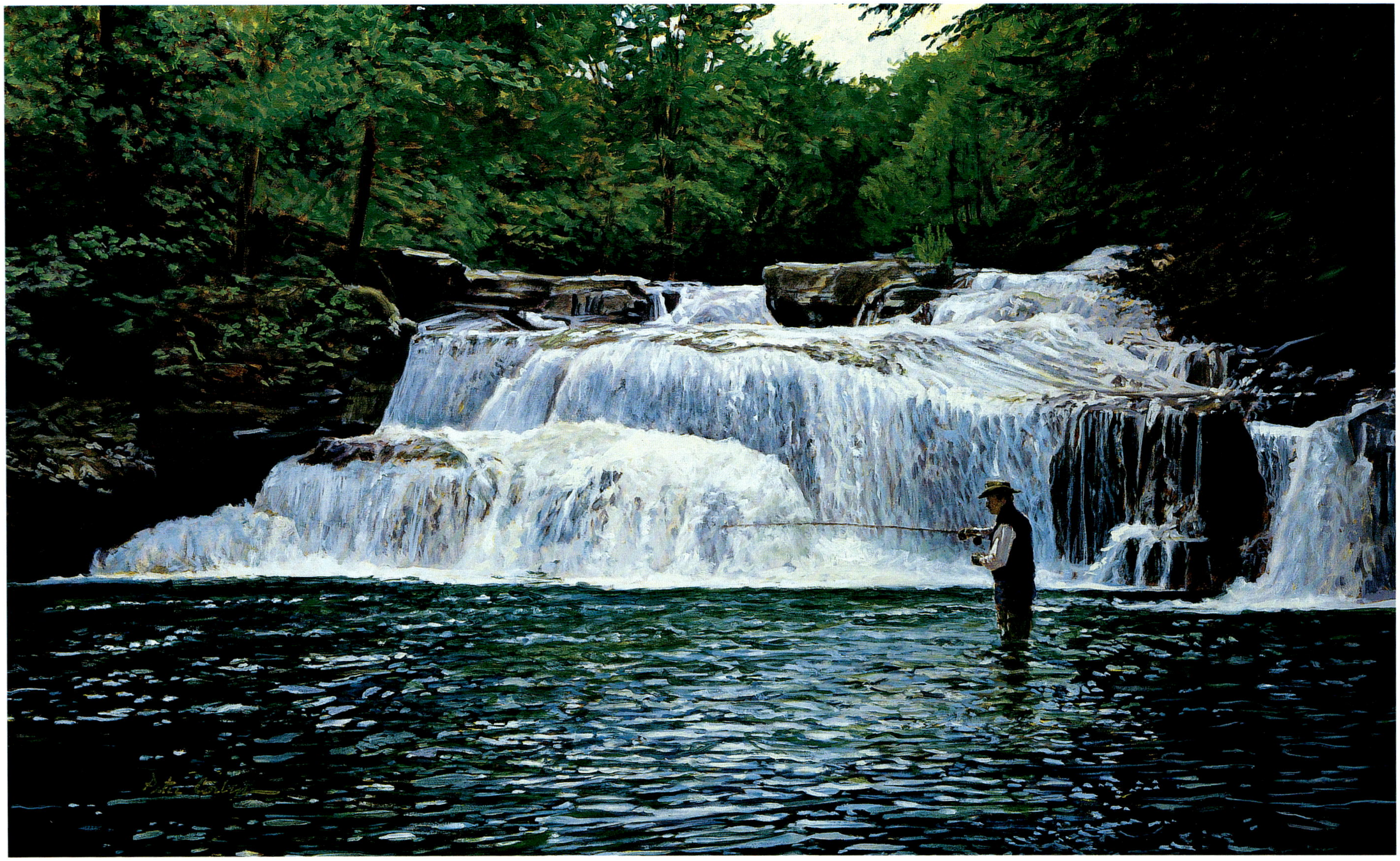

The Sound of the Falls, 2002
oil on canvas
24 × 40 inches
signed lower left

Atlantic Salmon

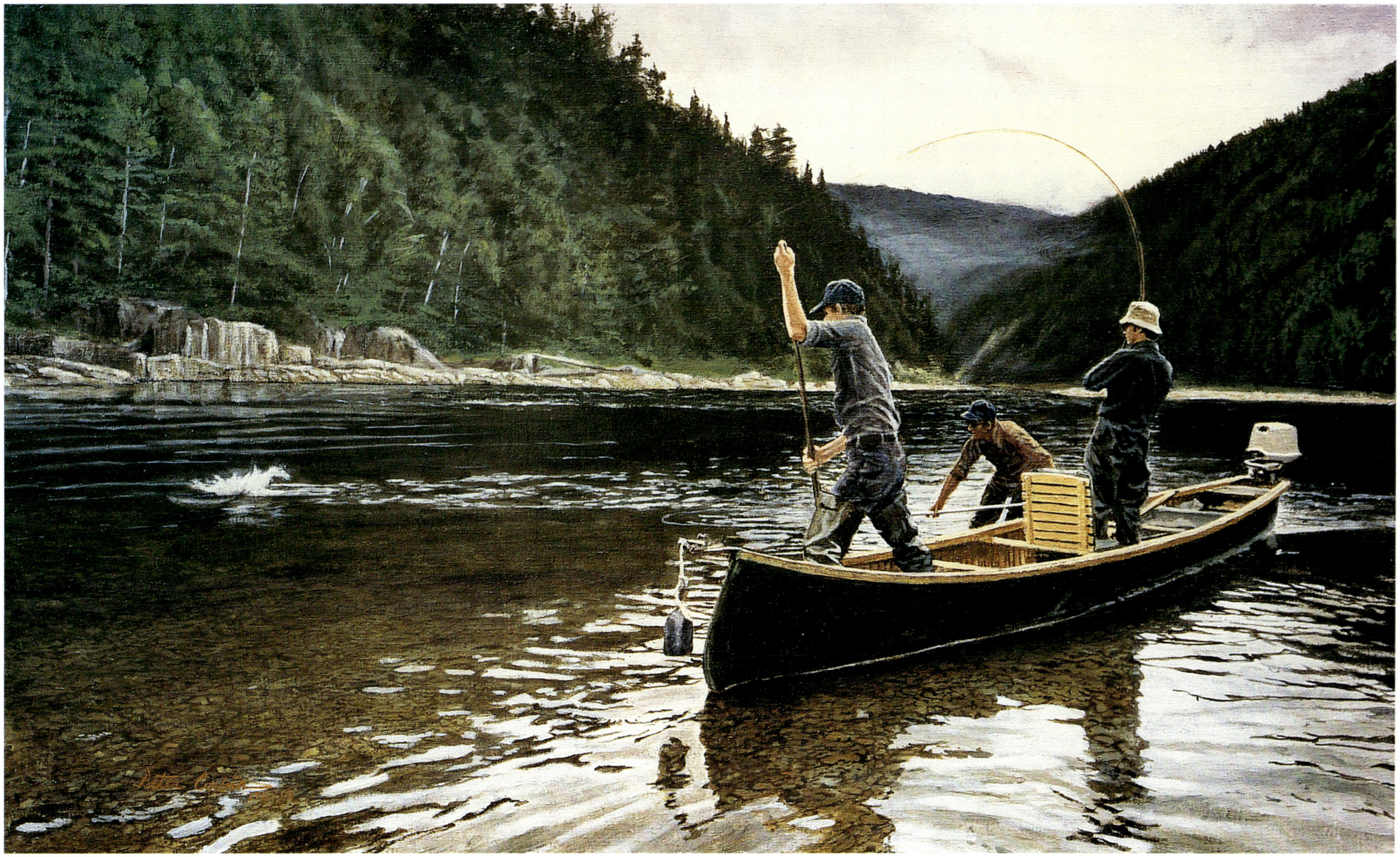

Near the Net, 1980
acrylic on canvas
20 × 30 inches
signed and dated lower left

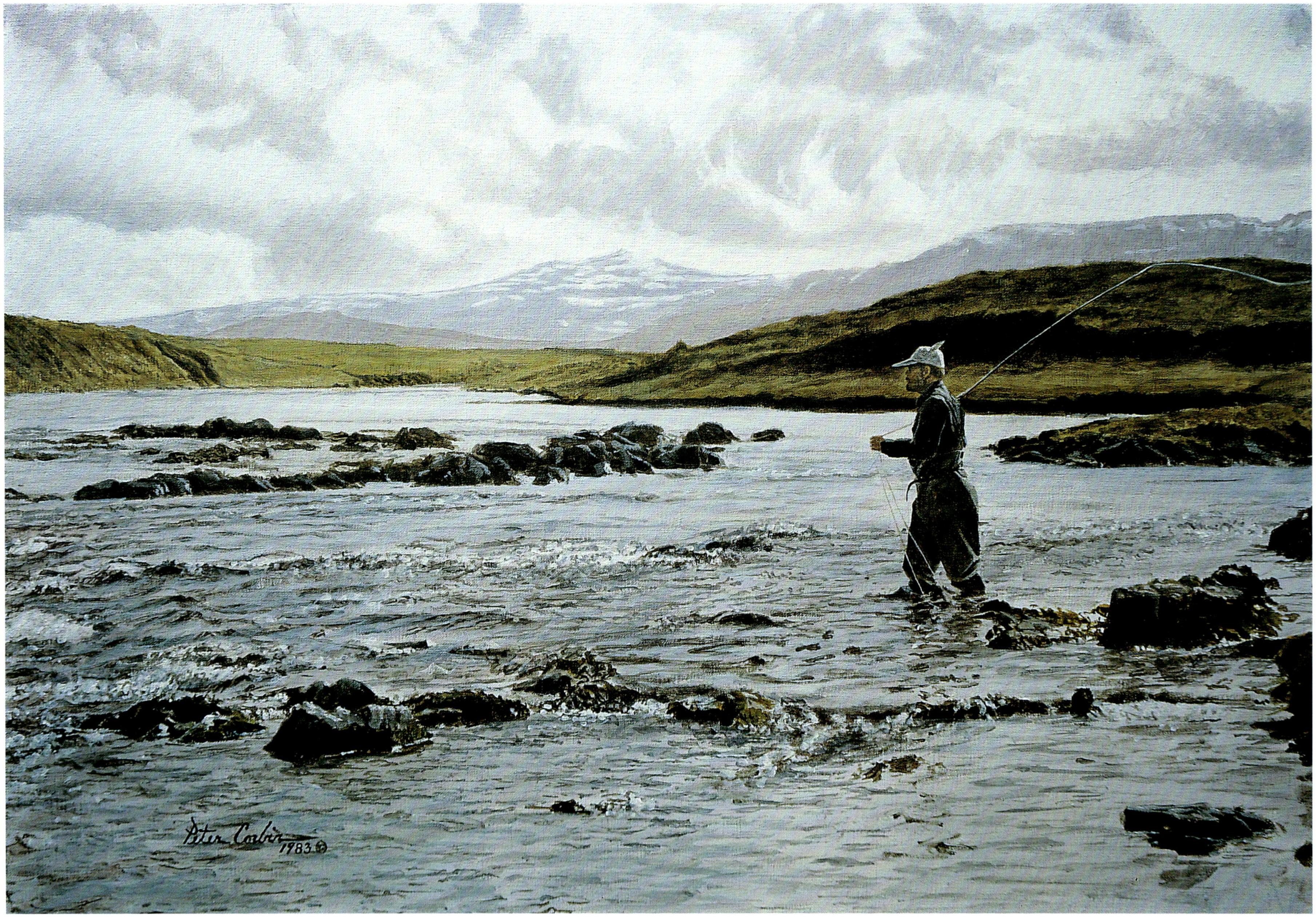

Wading for Salmon—Iceland, 1983
acrylic on canvas
20 × 30 inches
signed and dated lower left

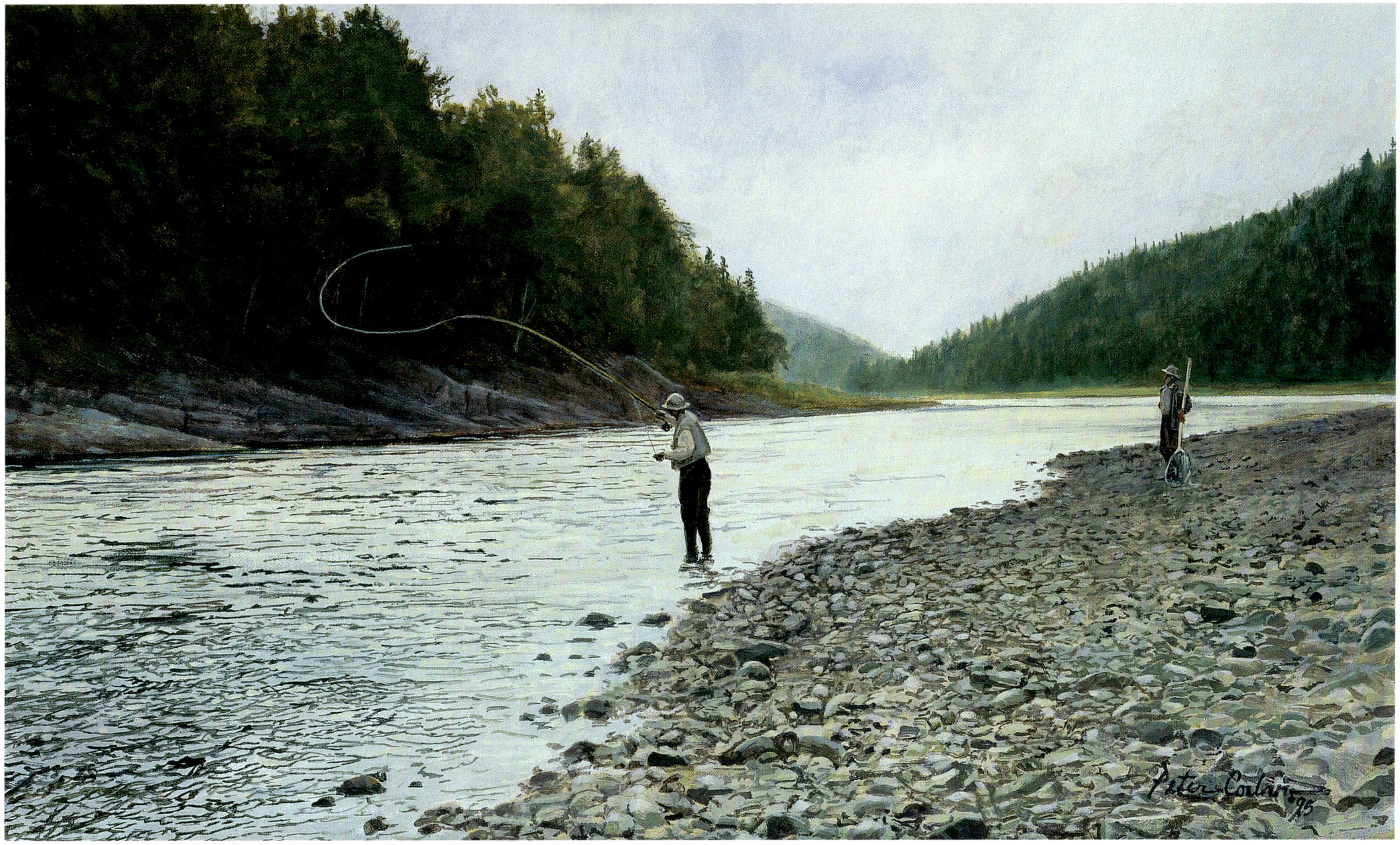

Great Expectations, 1995
acrylic on canvas
12 × 20 inches
signed and dated lower right

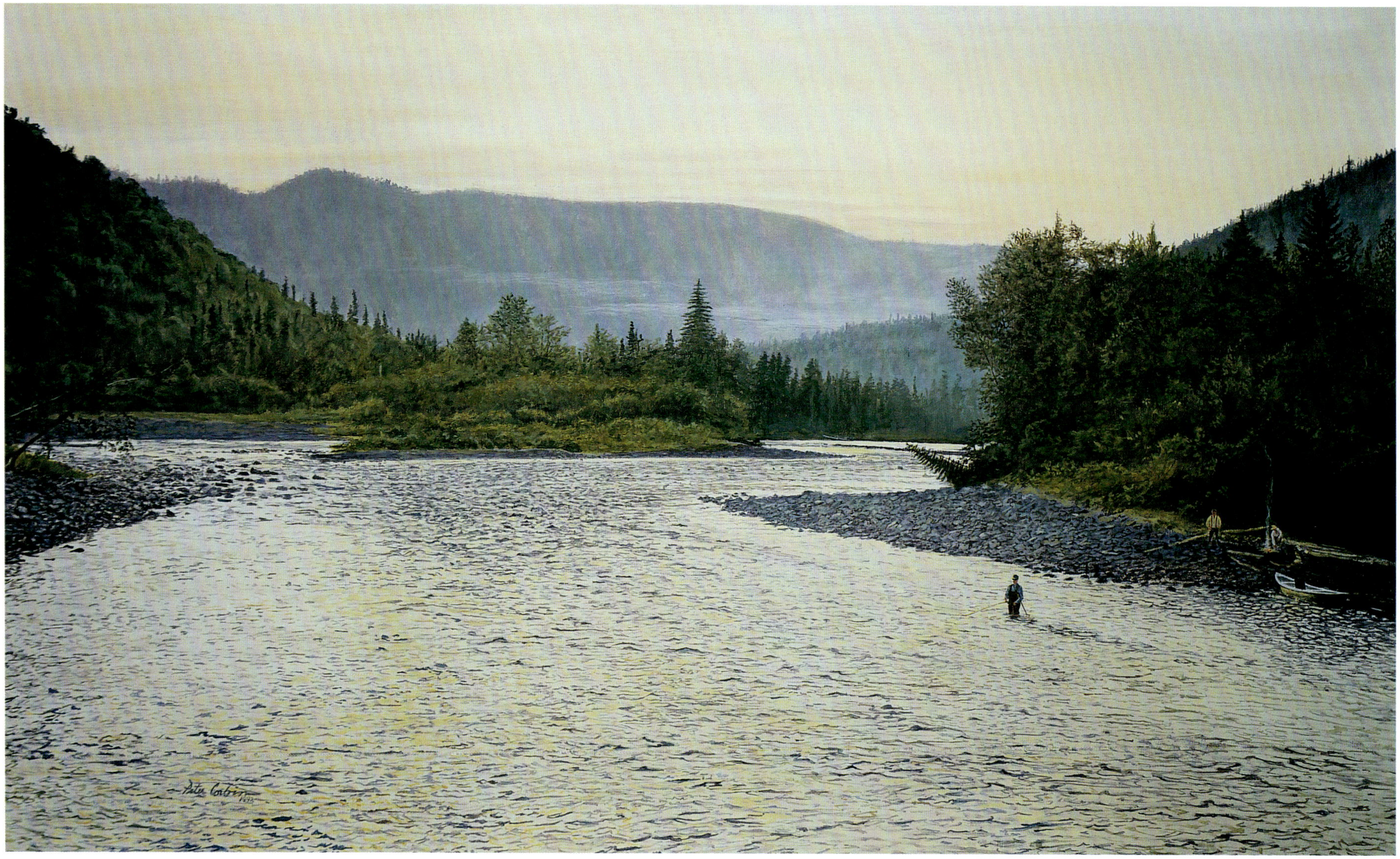

A Cascapédia Evening, 1992
acrylic on canvas
24 × 40 inches
signed and dated lower left

Low Water at the Point, 1998
oil on canvas
9 × 12 inches
signed and dated lower left

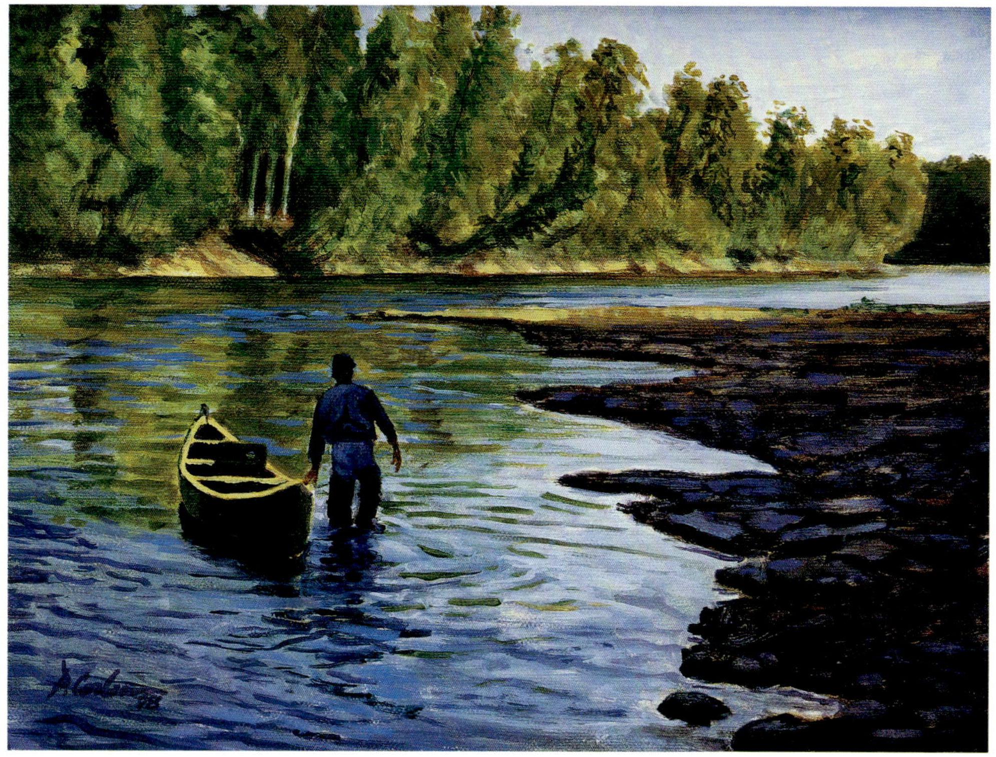

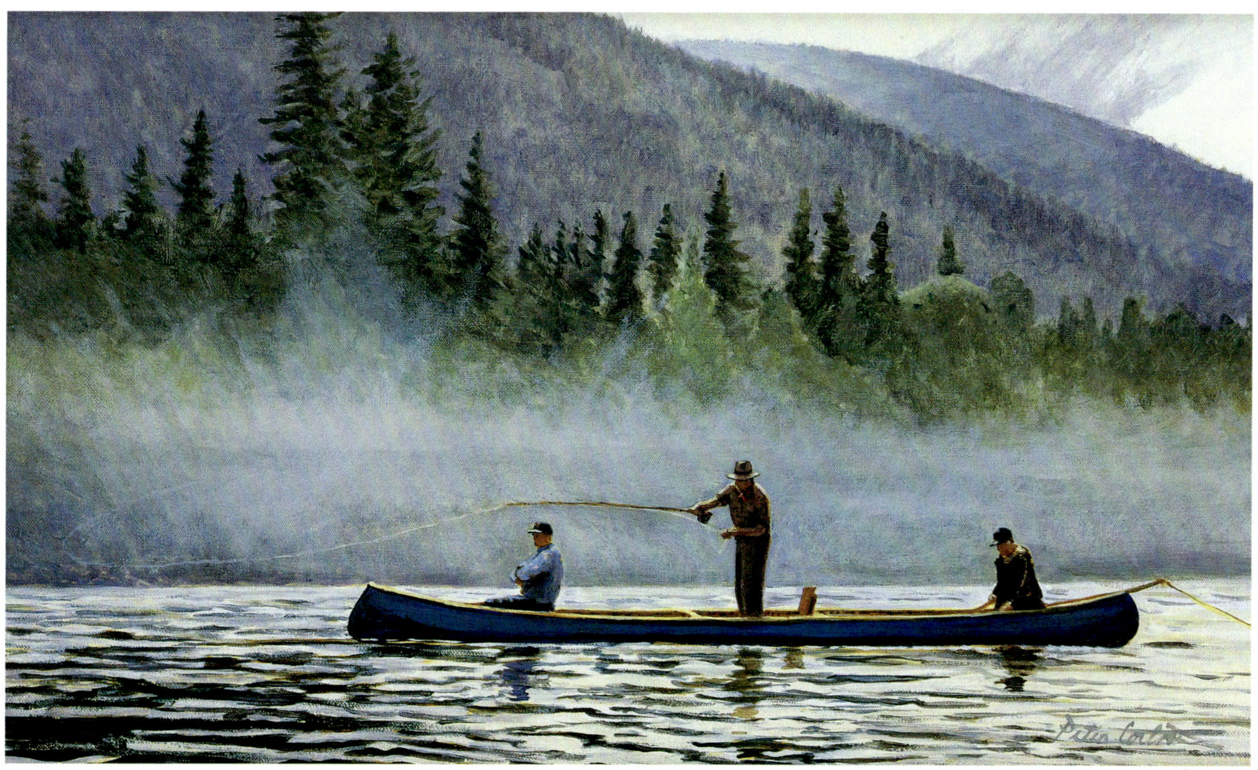

Morning on the Grand, 1998
oil on canvas
12 × 20 inches
signed lower right

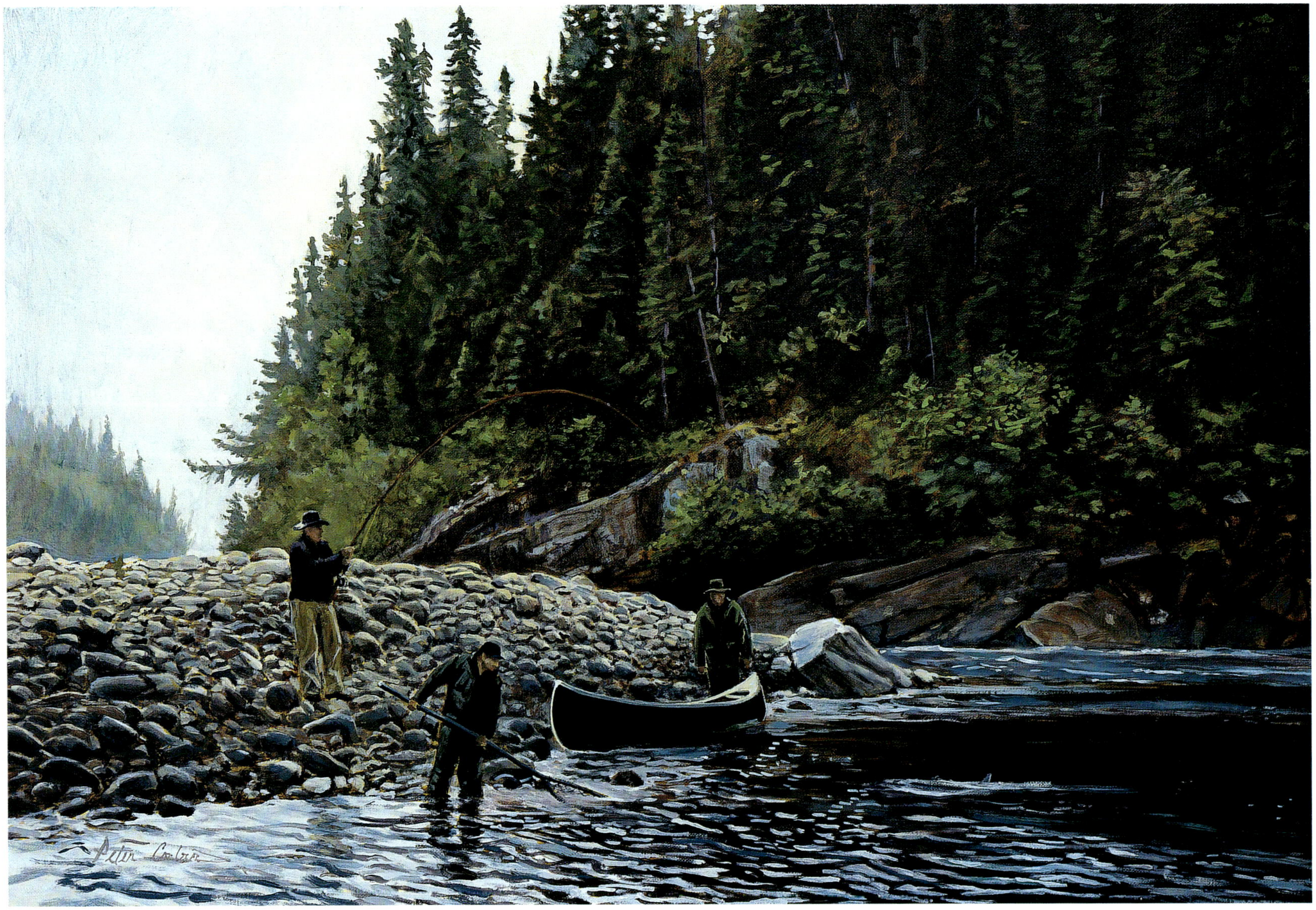

The Landing, 1999
oil on canvas
16 × 24 inches
signed lower left

Lower Beat, 2000
oil on canvas
8 × 12 inches
signed lower left

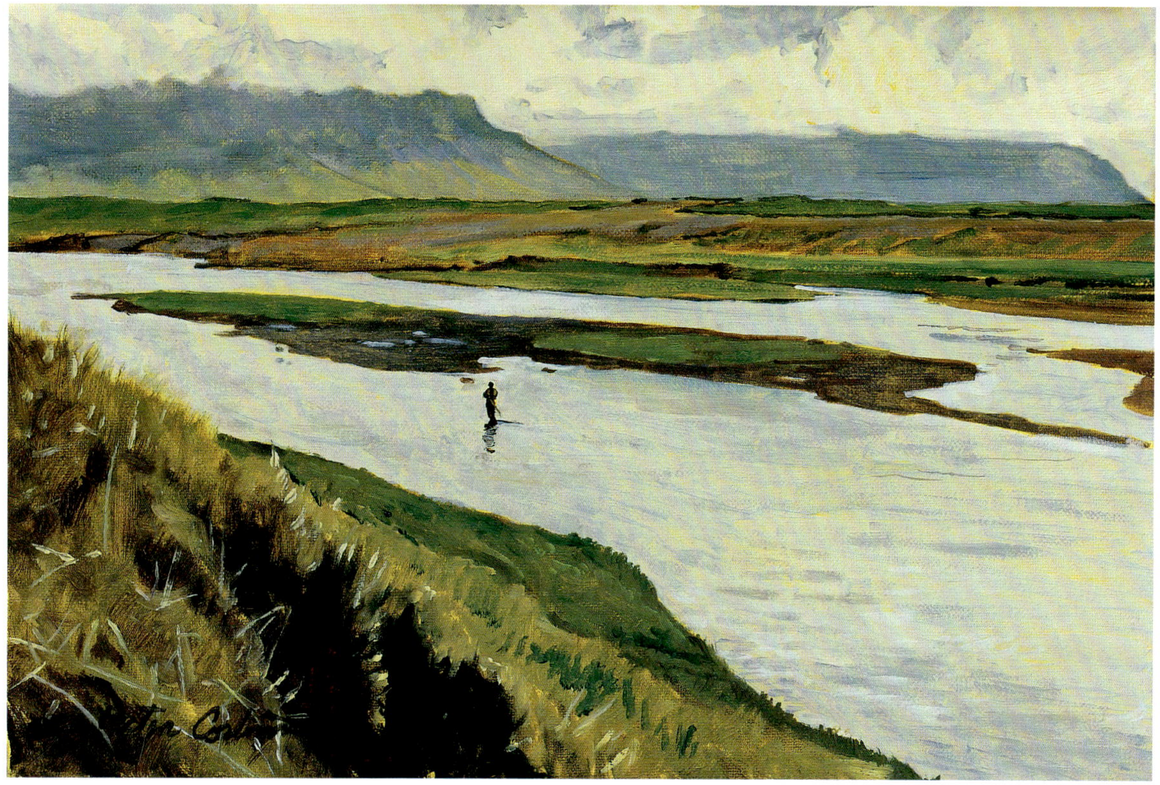

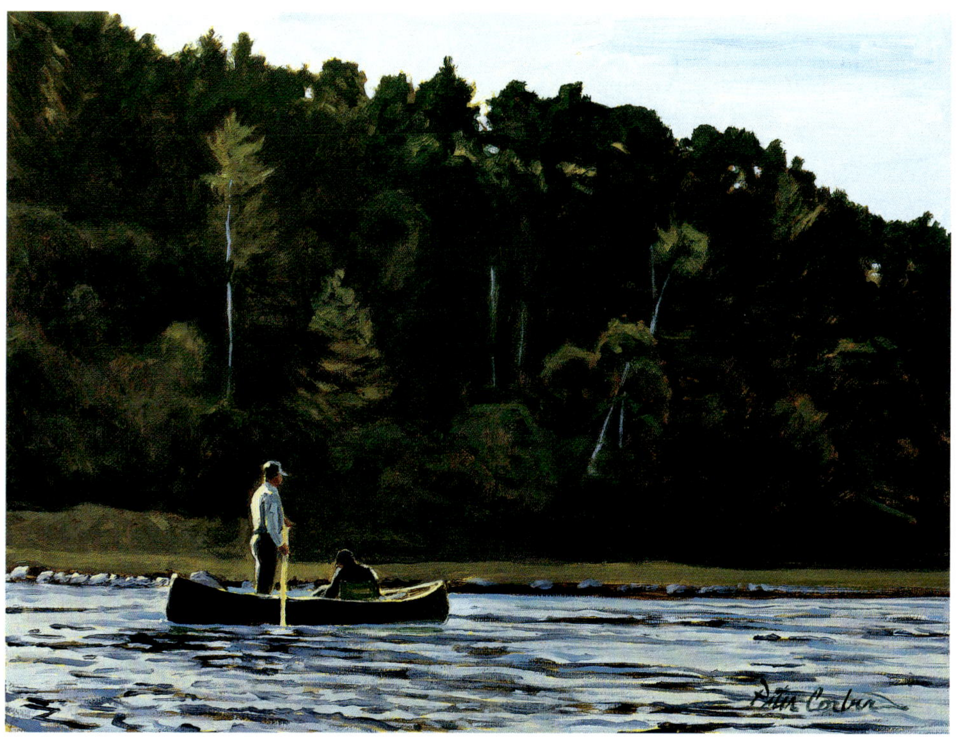

Miramichi Morning, 2000
oil on canvas
9 × 12 inches
signed lower right

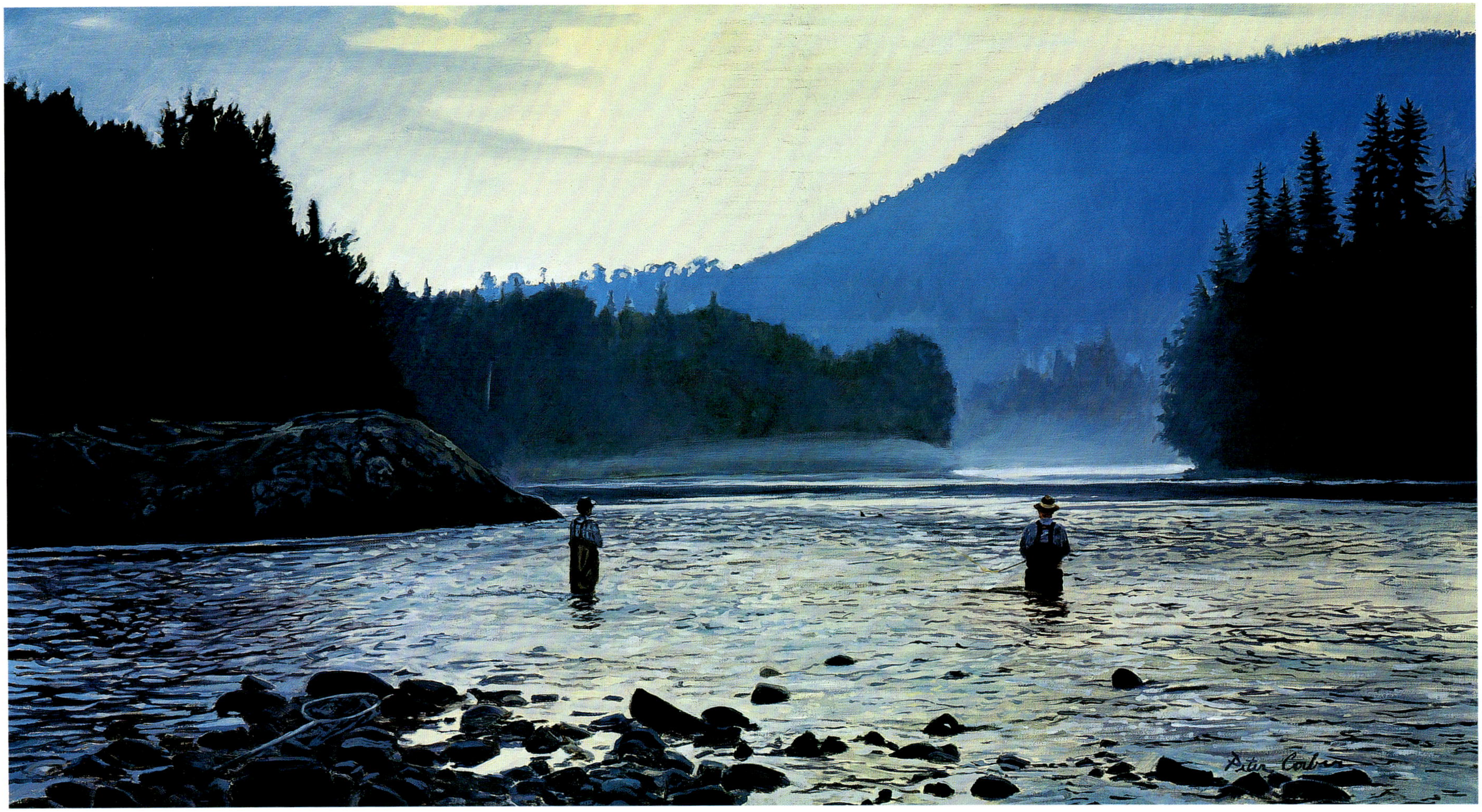

Charlie Valley Rock, 2000
oil on canvas
16 × 30 inches
signed lower right

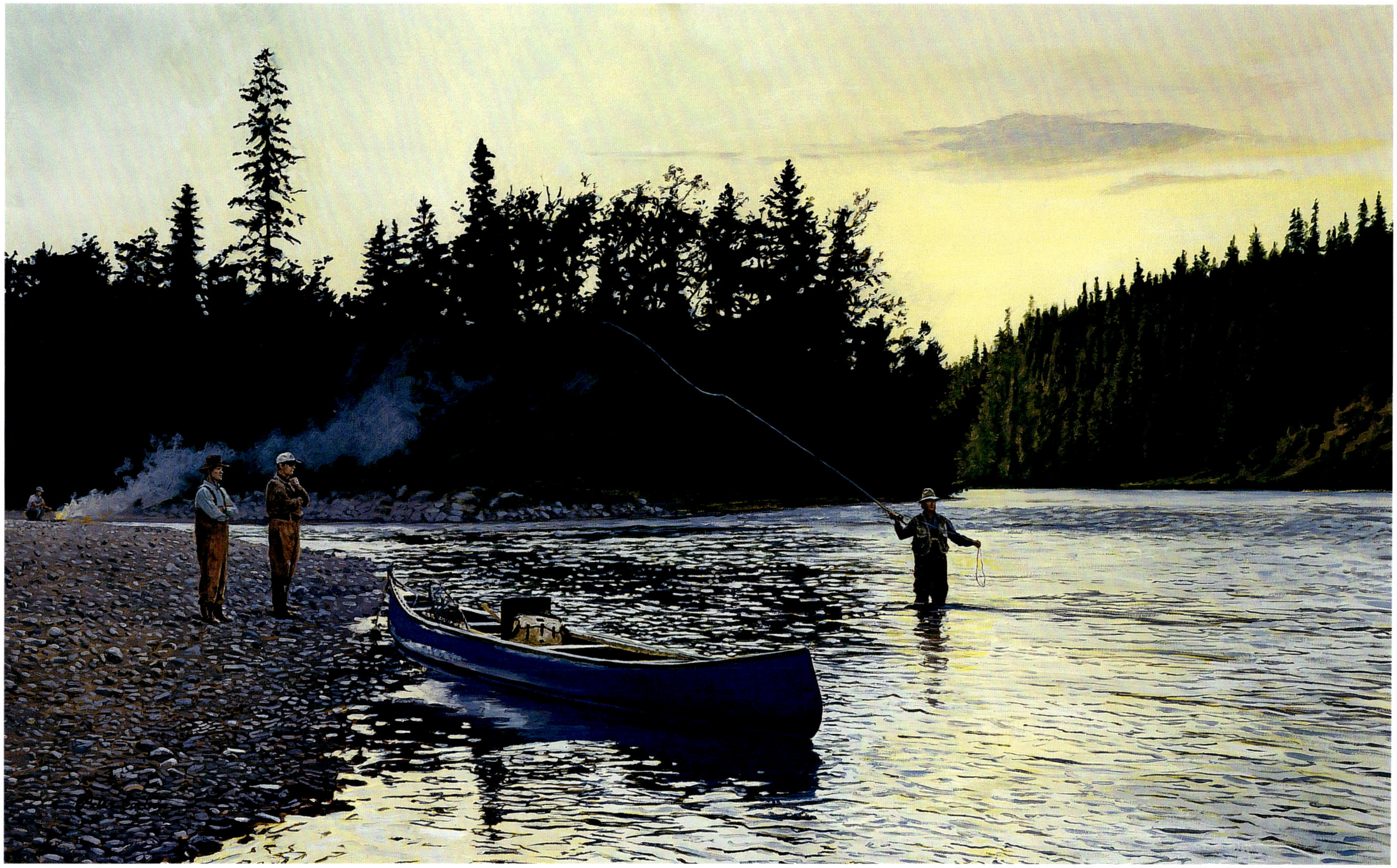

Evening at the Forks, 2000
oil on canvas
24 × 40 inches
signed lower left

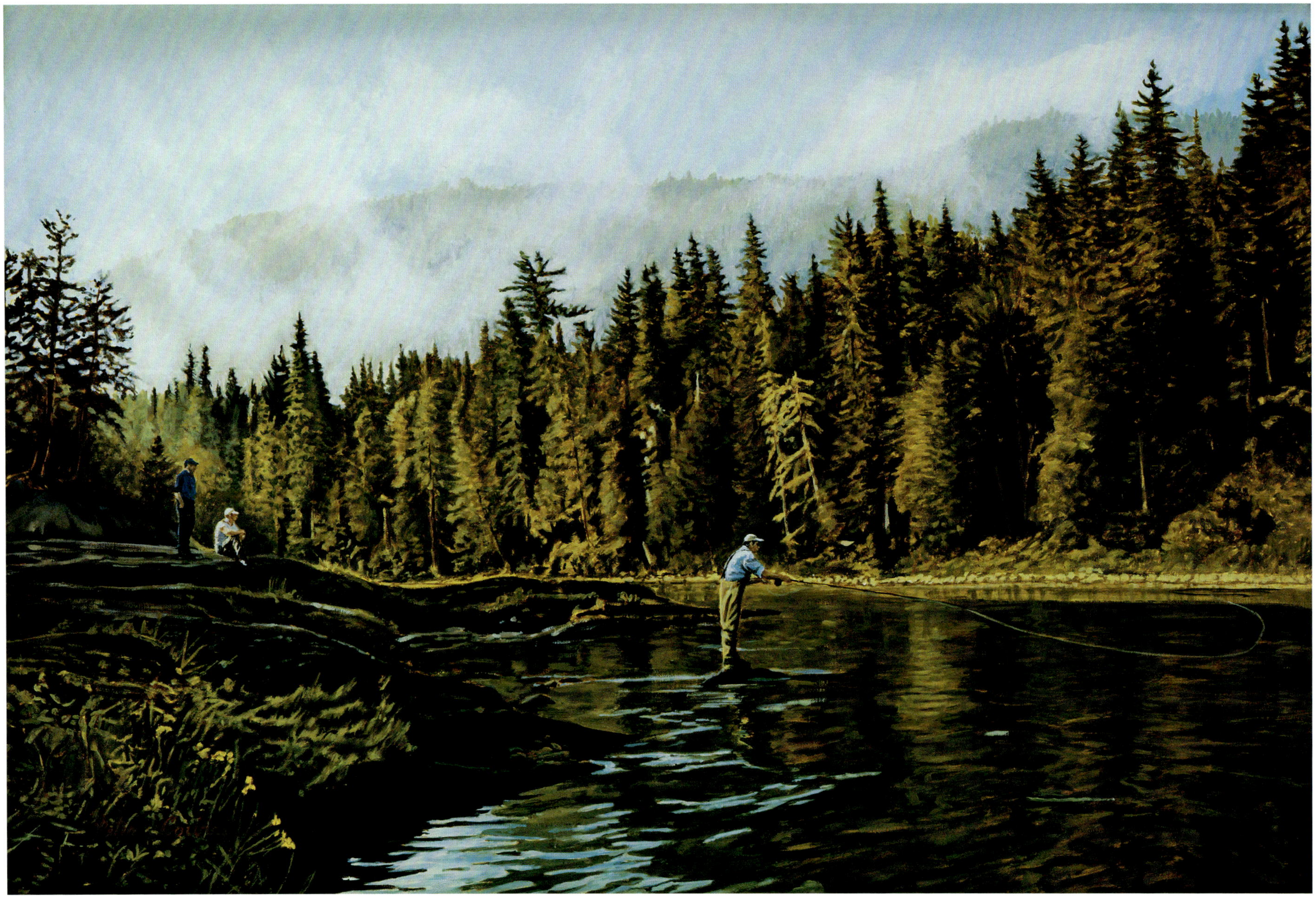

The Long Cast, 2003
oil on canvas
20 × 30 inches
signed lower left

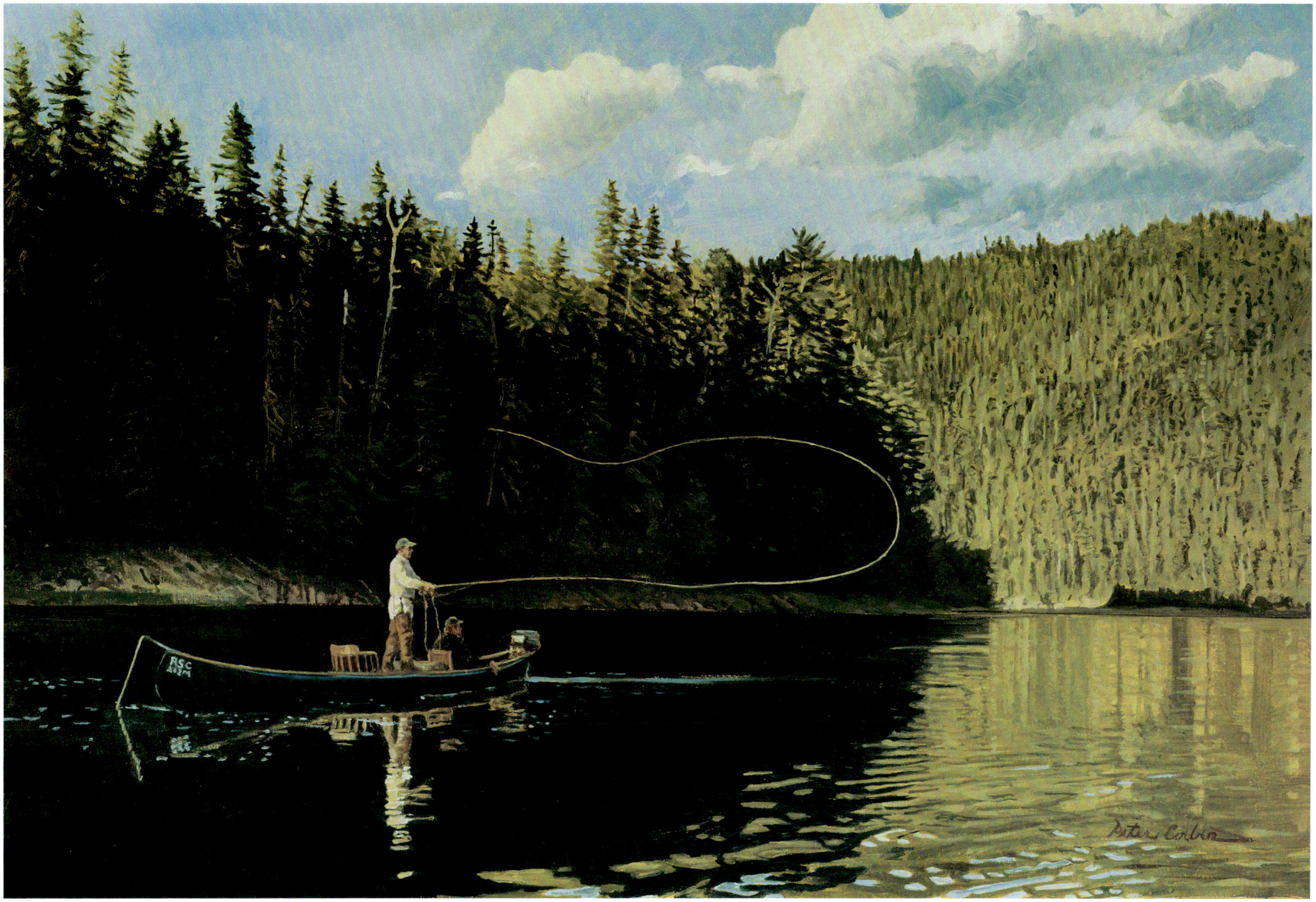

Evening on Ladies Pool, 2003
oil on canvas
20 × 30 inches
signed lower right

Western Trout

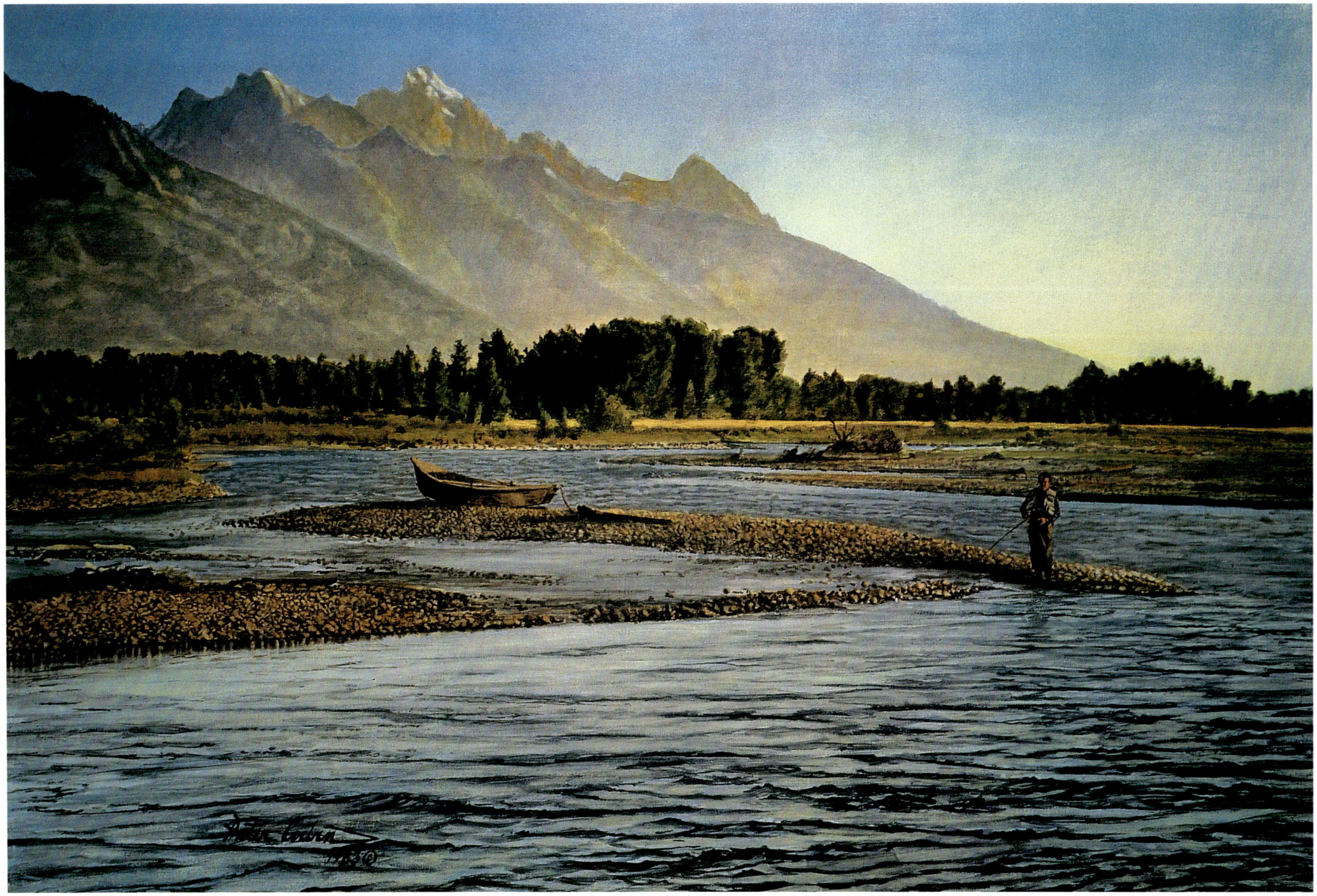

The Gravel Bar, 1983
acrylic on canvas
20 × 30 inches
signed and dated lower left

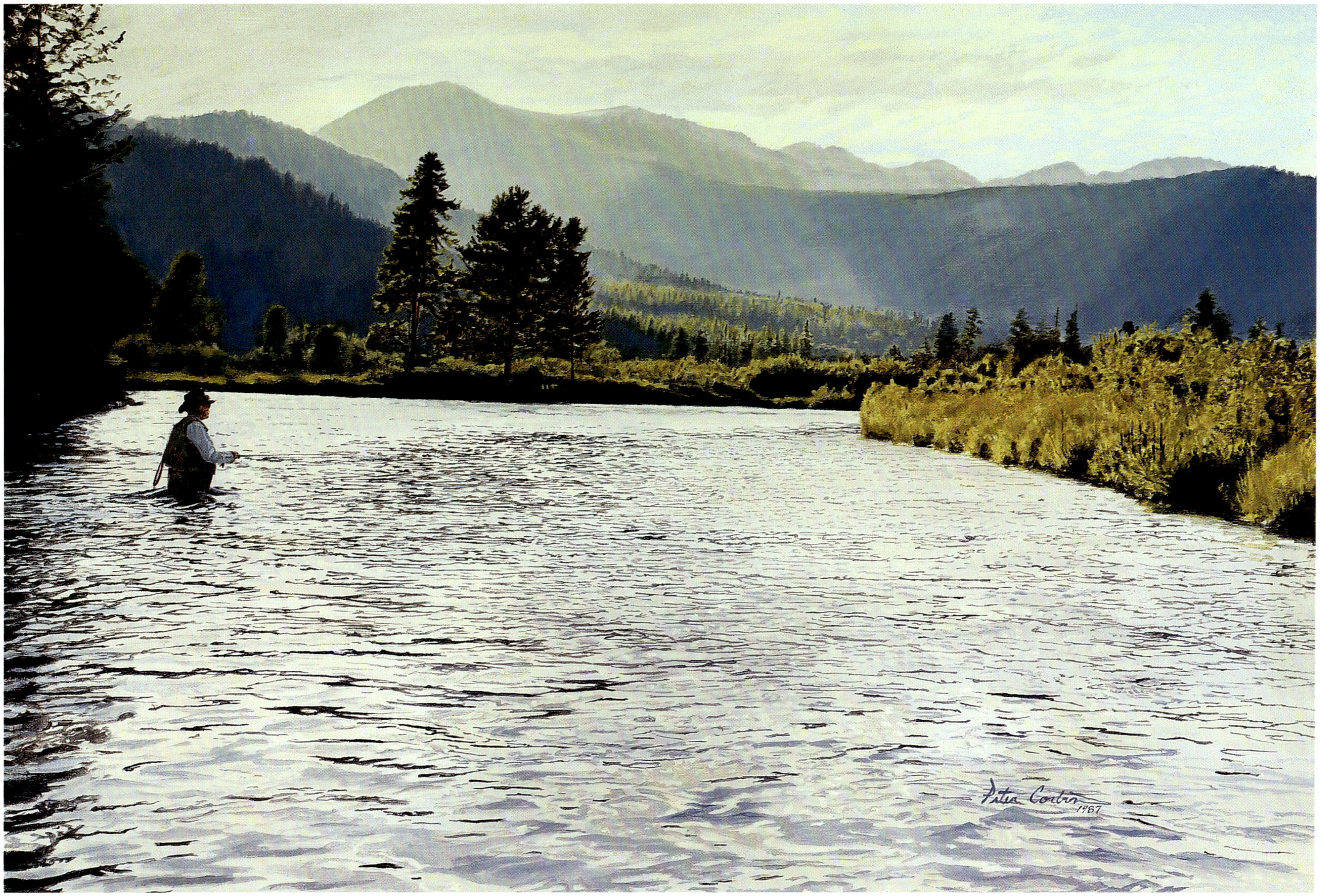

A Fishcreek Evening, 1987
acrylic on canvas
20 × 30 inches
signed and dated lower right

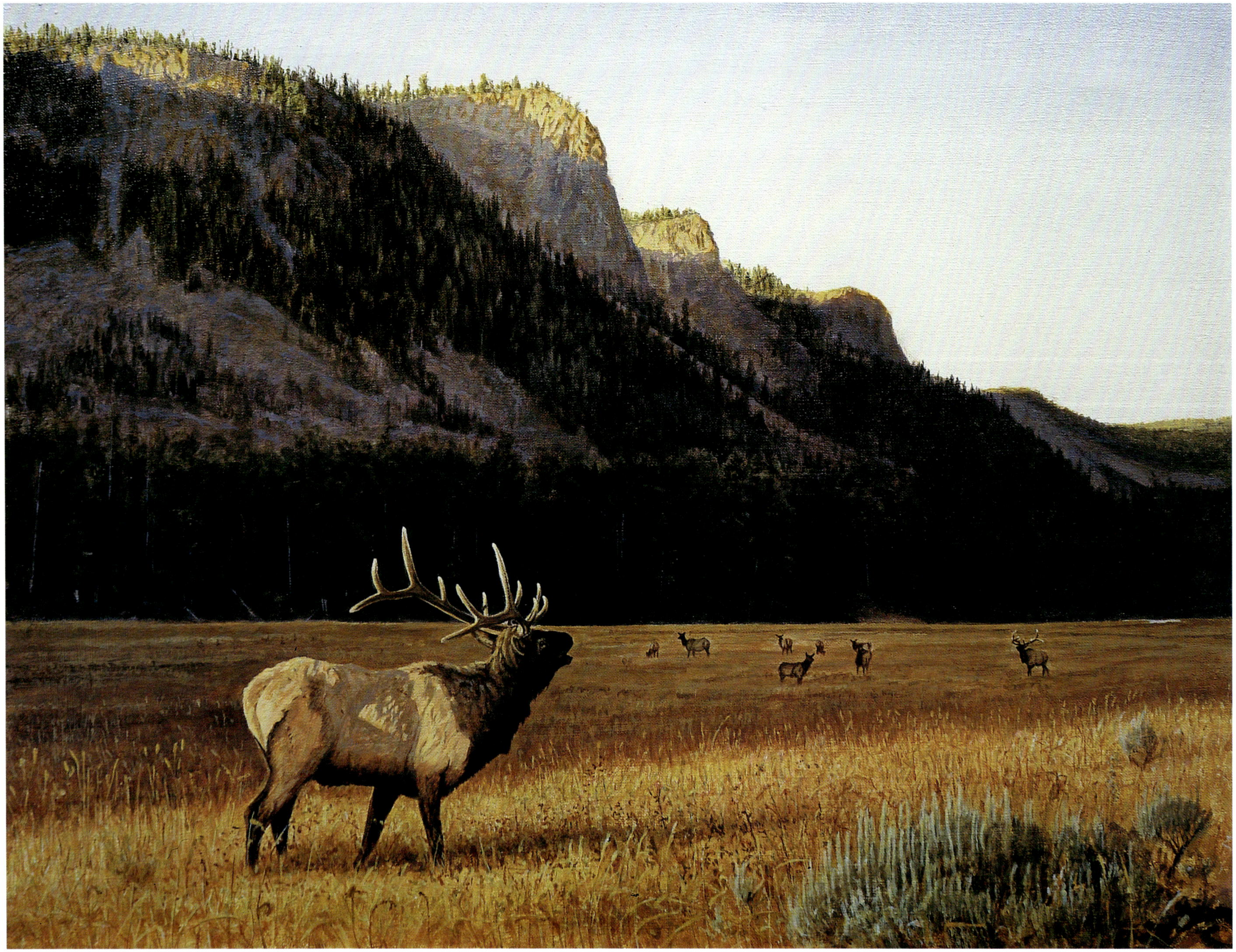

September's Song, 1988
acrylic on canvas
18 × 24 inches
signed and dated lower right

Sleeping Indian—Rising Trout, 1989
acrylic on canvas
8 × 12 inches
signed and dated lower left

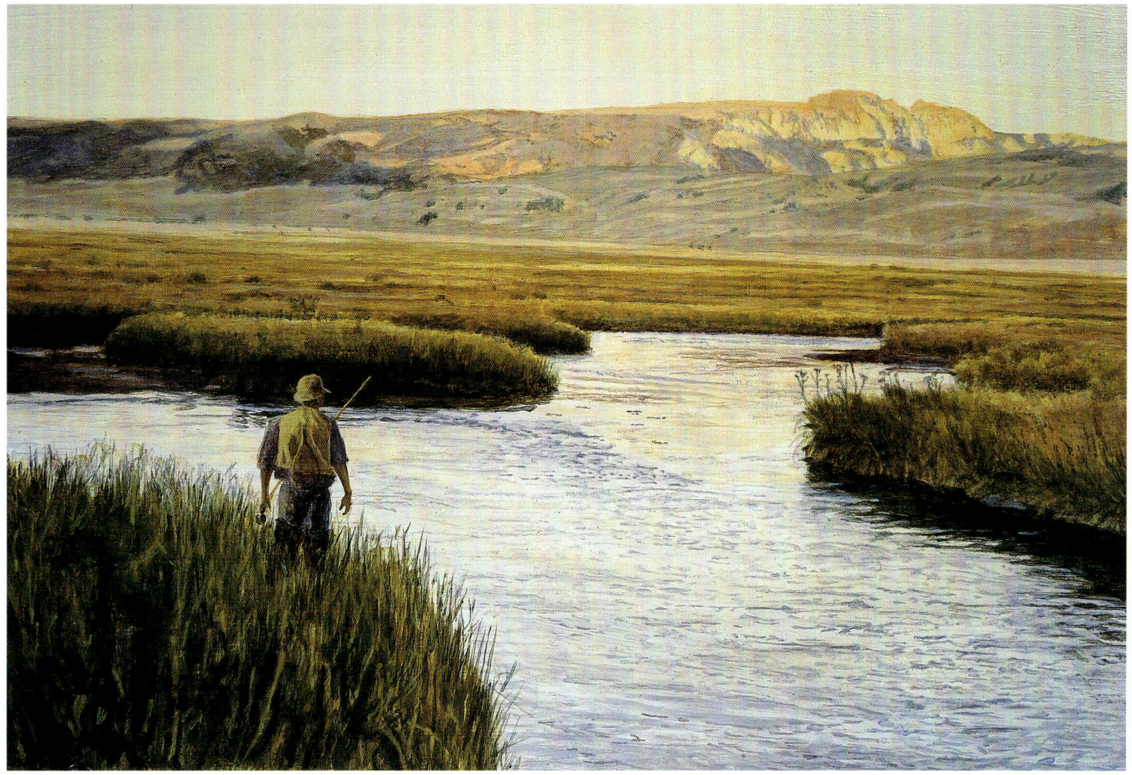

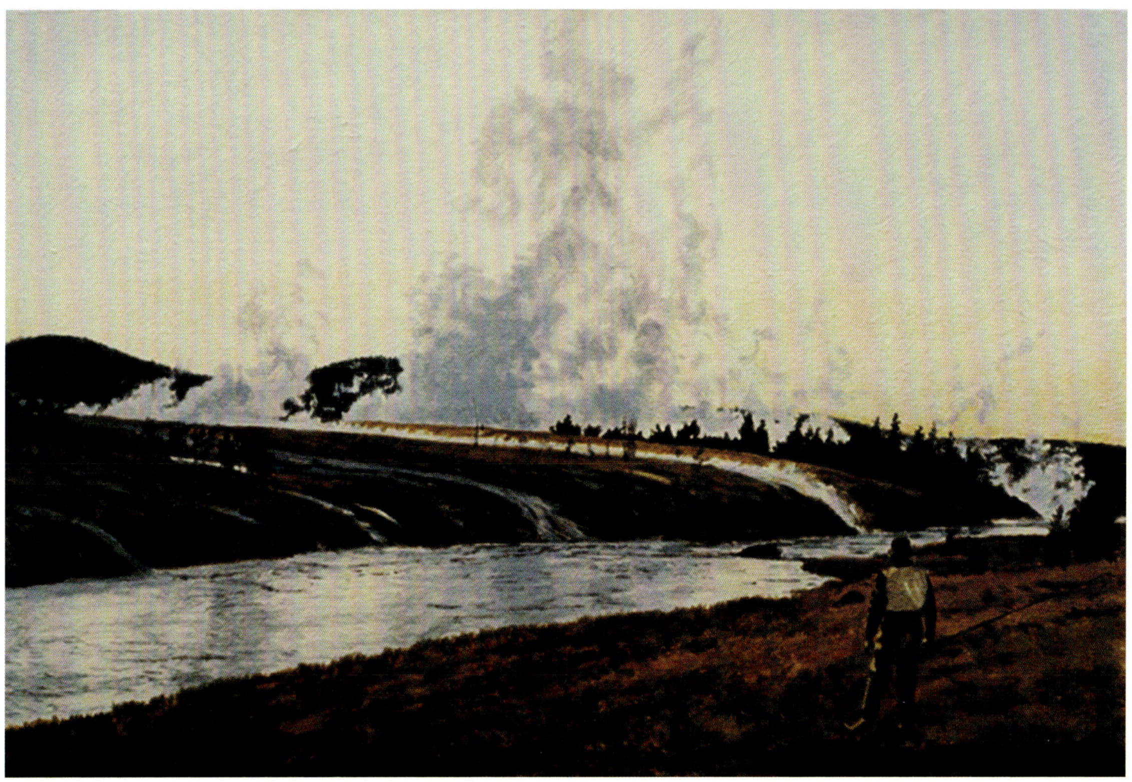

Firehole Evening, 1990
acrylic on canvas
8 × 12 inches
signed lower left

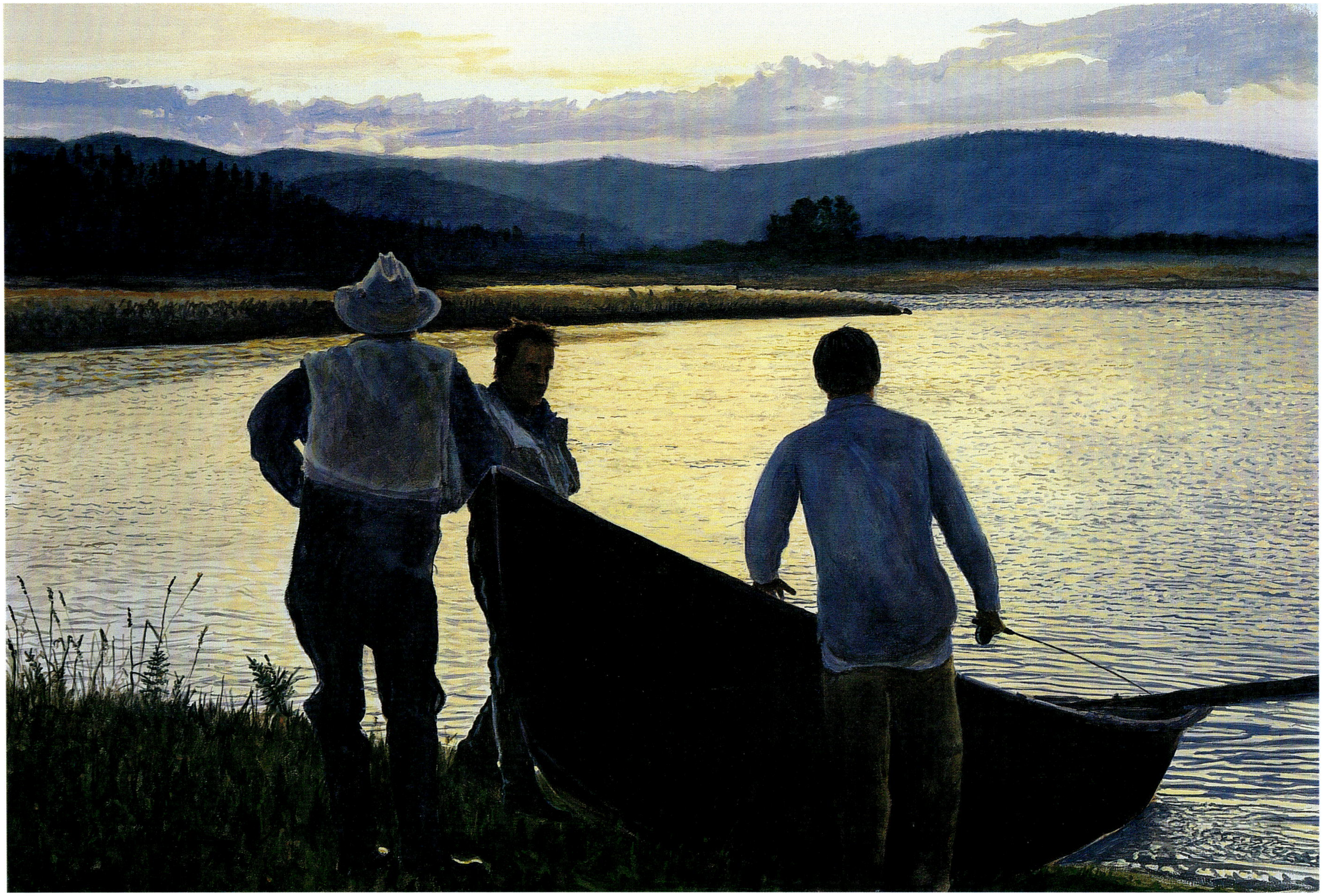

Evening on the River, 1992
acrylic on canvas
20 × 30 inches
signed and dated lower left

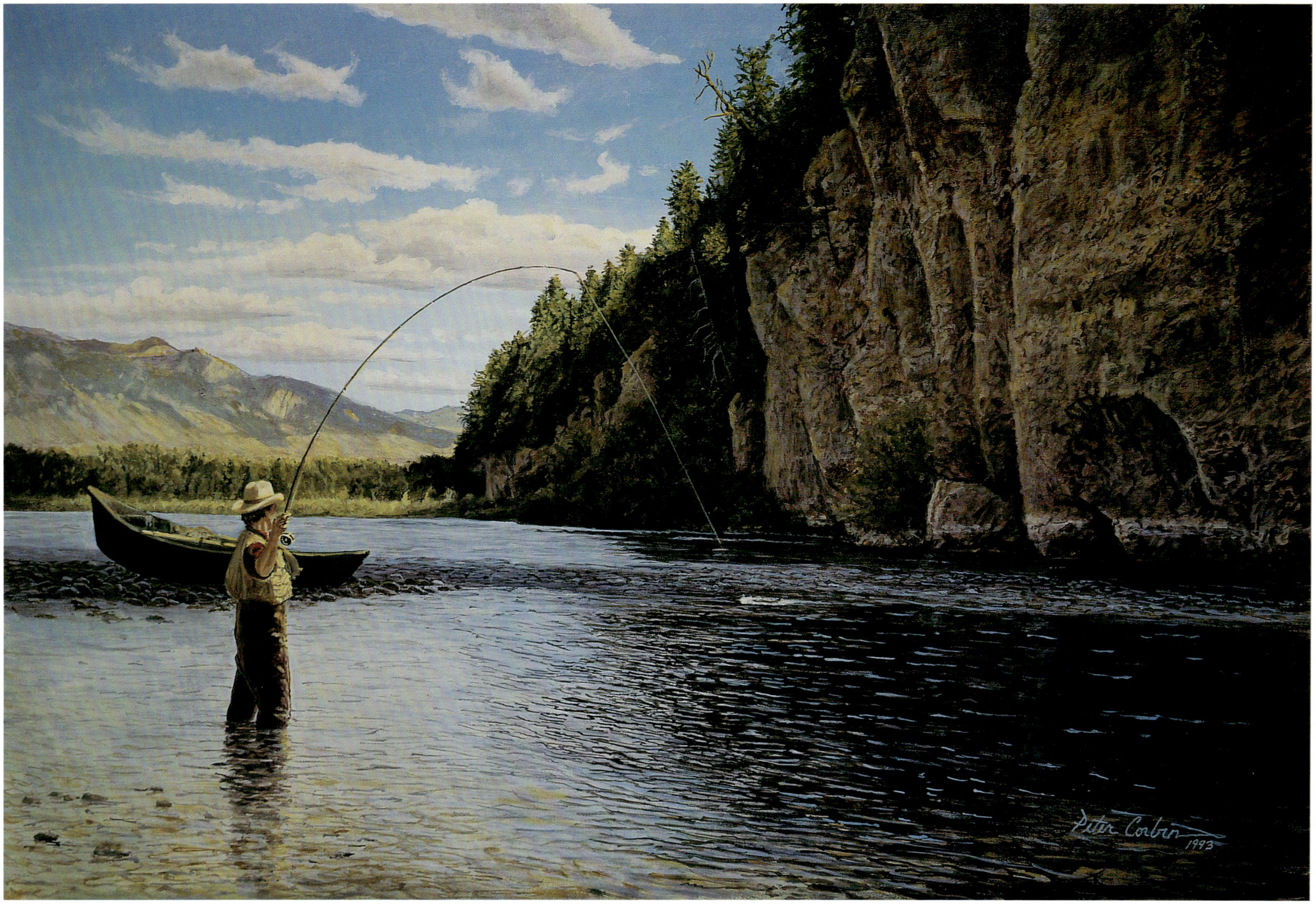

Head of the Canyon, 1993
acrylic on canvas
20 × 30 inches
signed and dated lower right

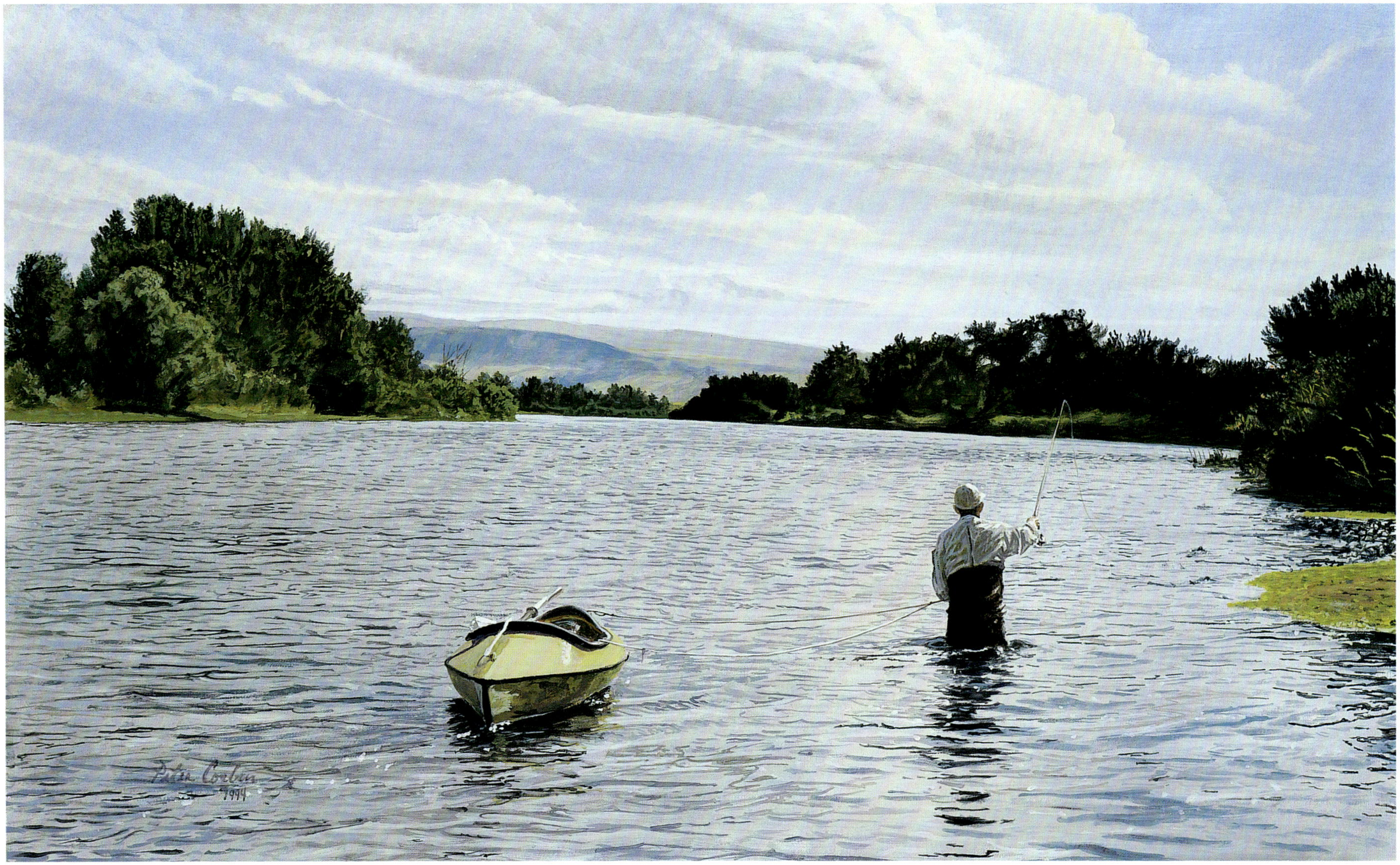

Fishing the Edges, 1994
acrylic on canvas
18 × 30 inches
signed and dated lower left

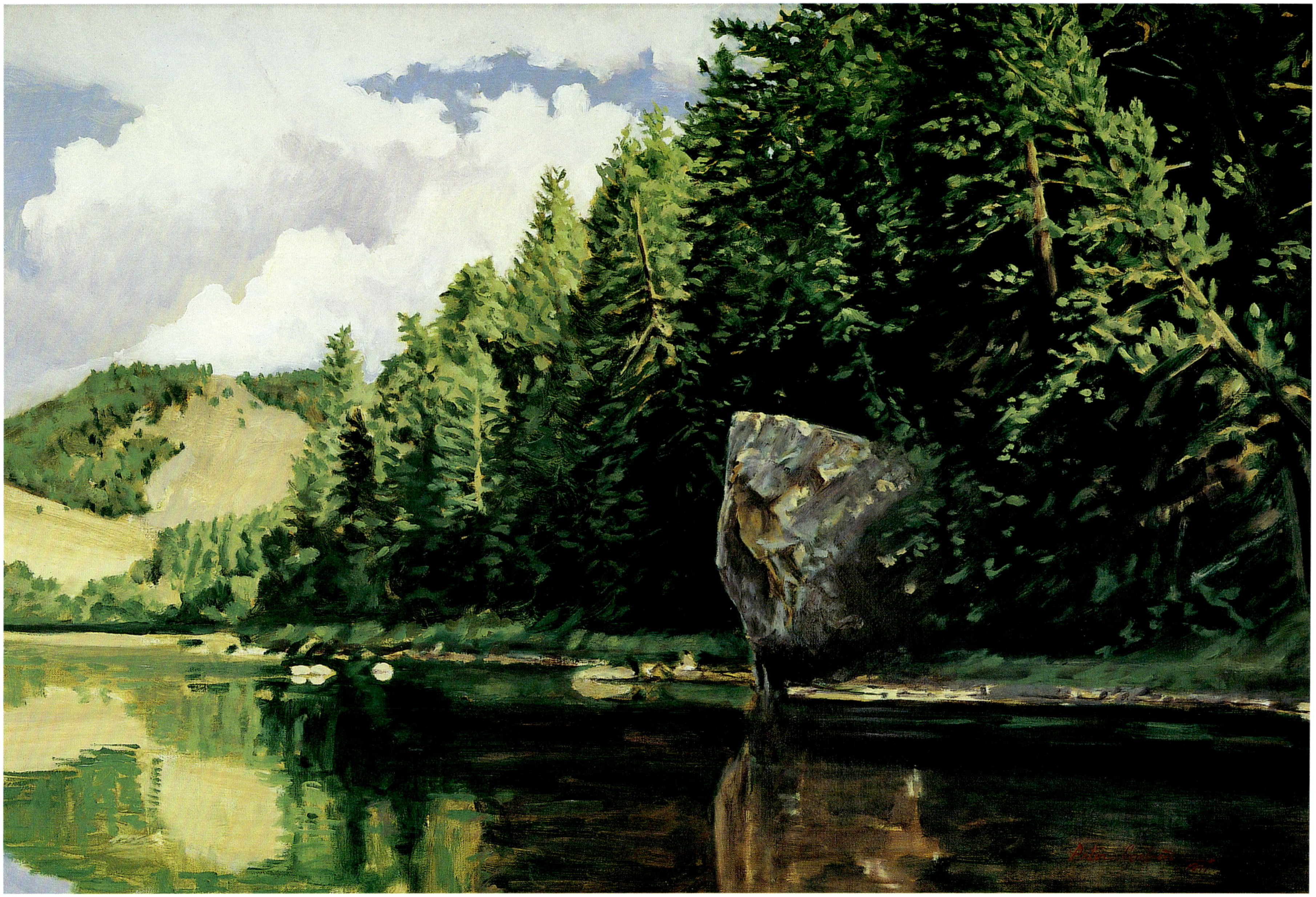

John's Rock, 1997
oil on canvas
20 × 30 inches
signed and dated lower right

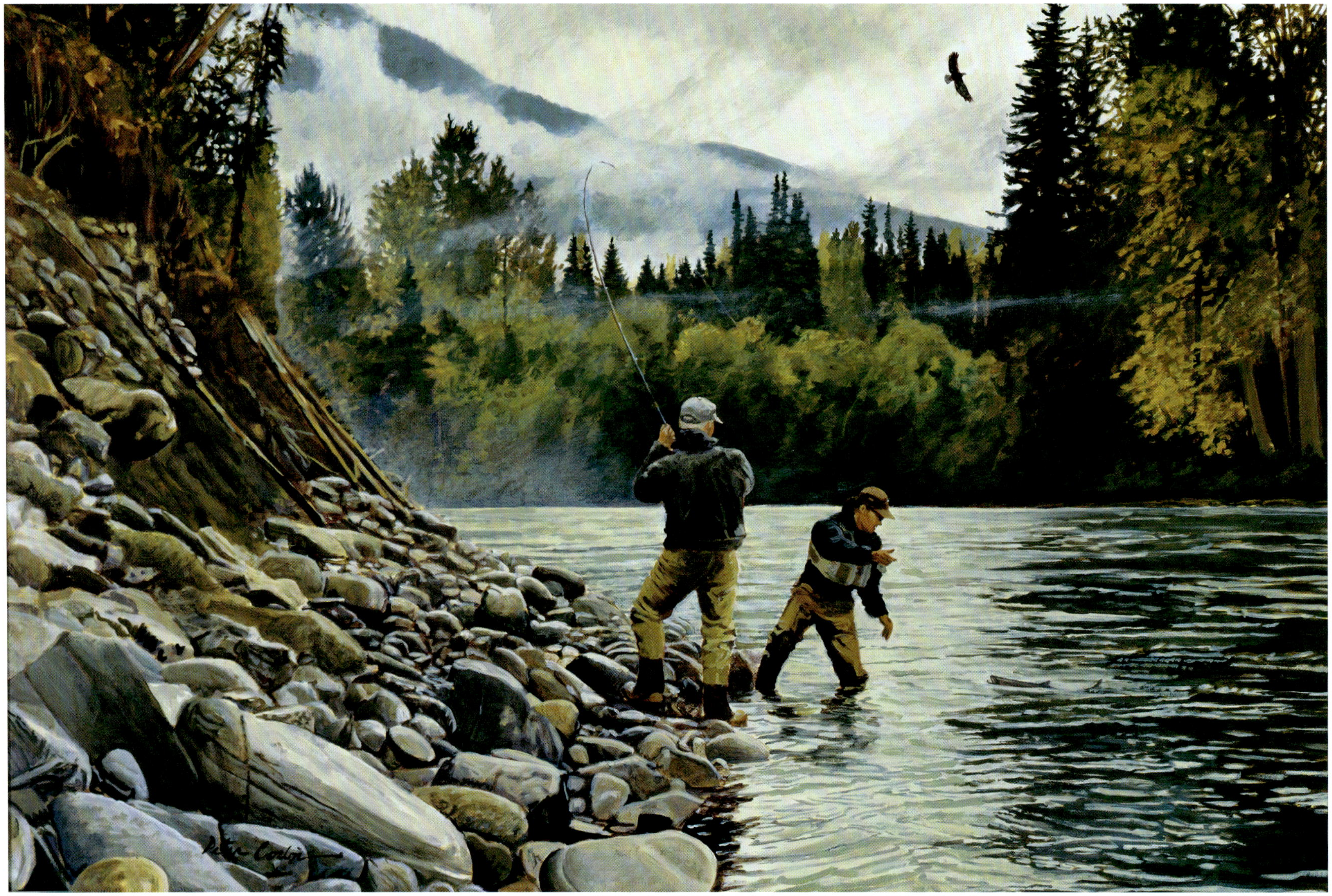

Close at Hand, 2002
oil on canvas
24 × 36 inches
signed lower left

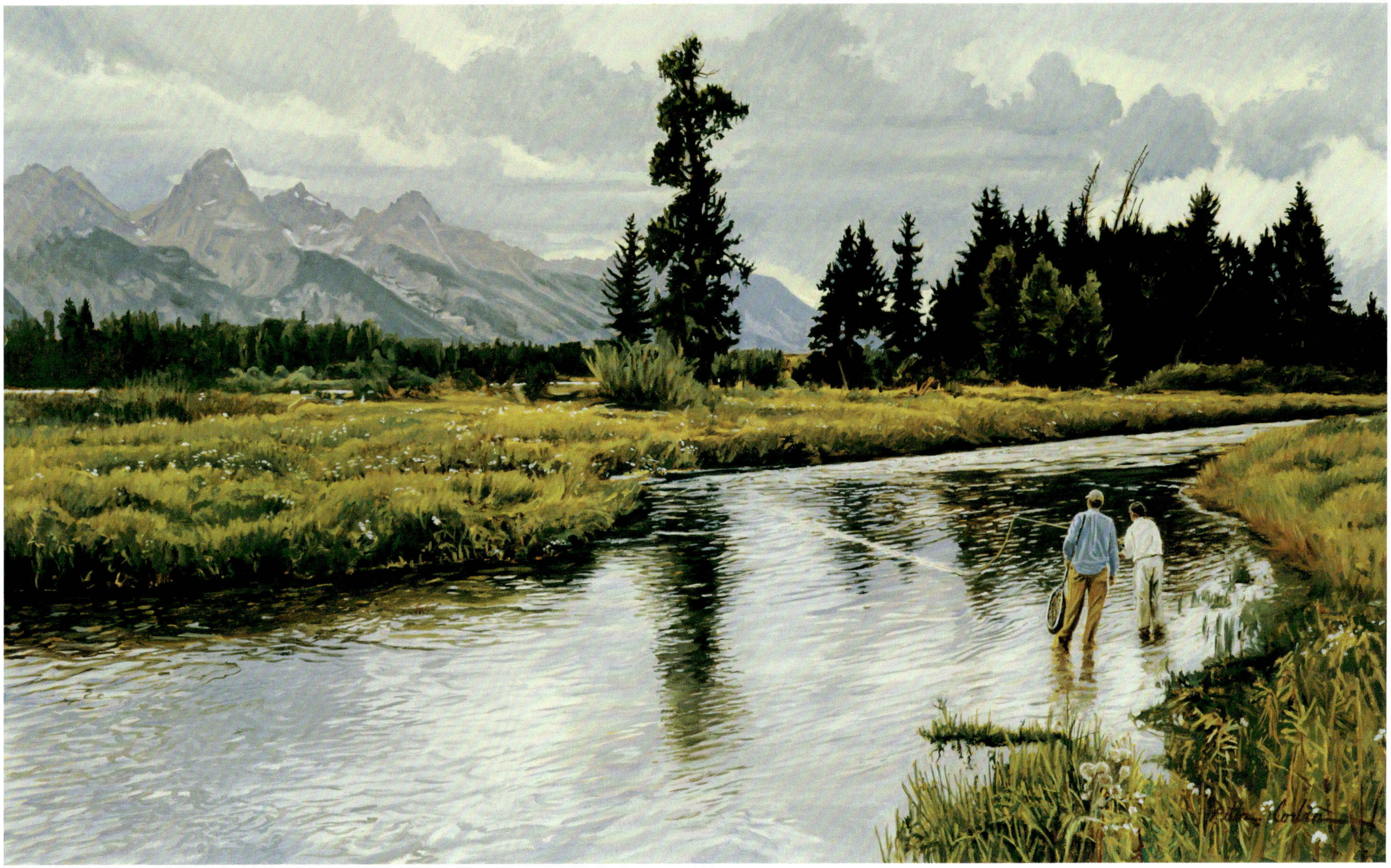

Partners, 2004
oil on canvas
24 × 40 inches
signed lower right

Salt Water

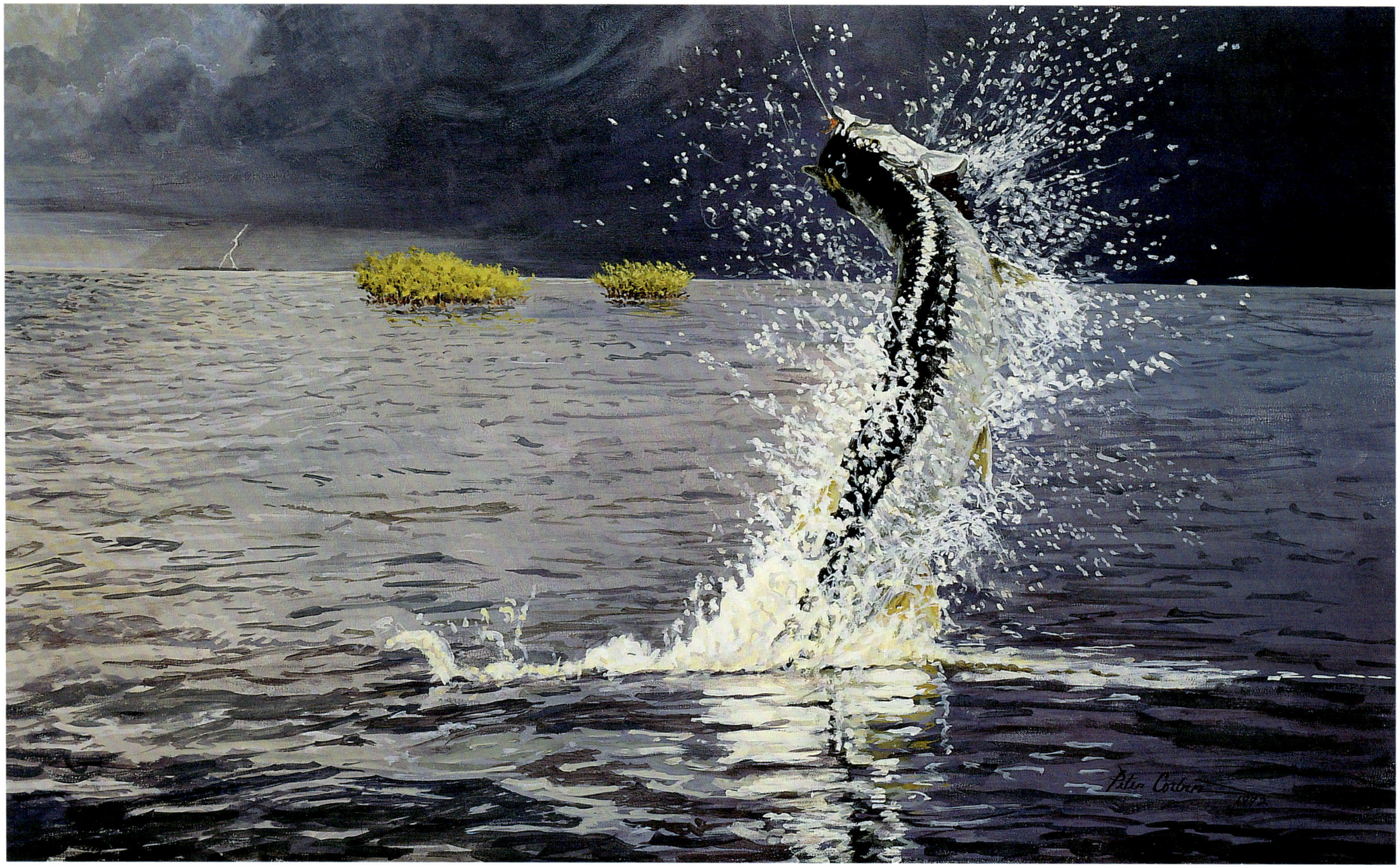

Thunder & Lightning, 1995
acrylic on canvas
$16\frac{5}{8} \times 24\frac{7}{8}$ inches
signed and dated lower right

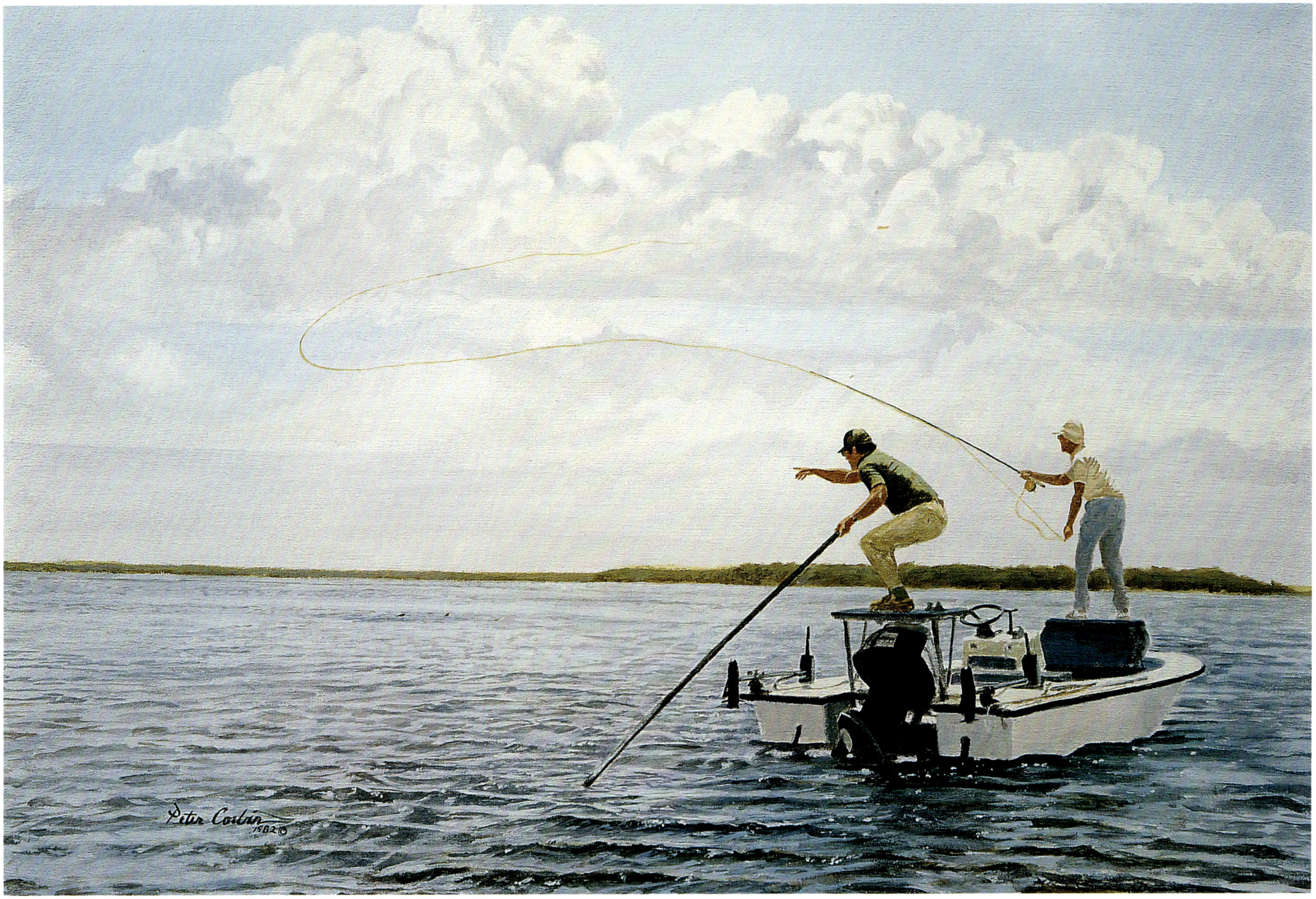

One Chance, 1982
acrylic on canvas
22 × 30 inches
signed and dated lower left

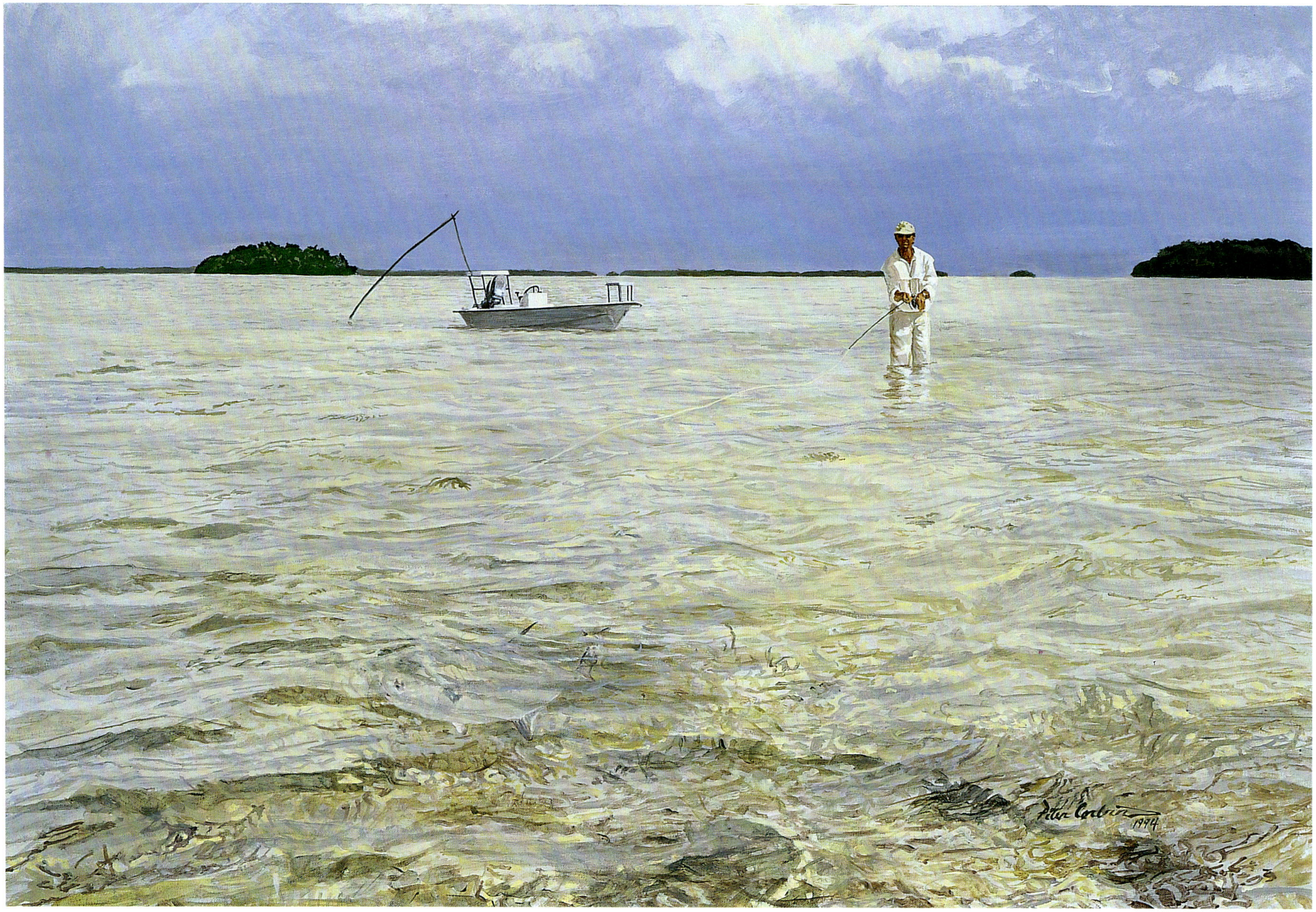

Permit Flats, 1994
acrylic on canvas
20 × 30 inches
signed and dated lower right

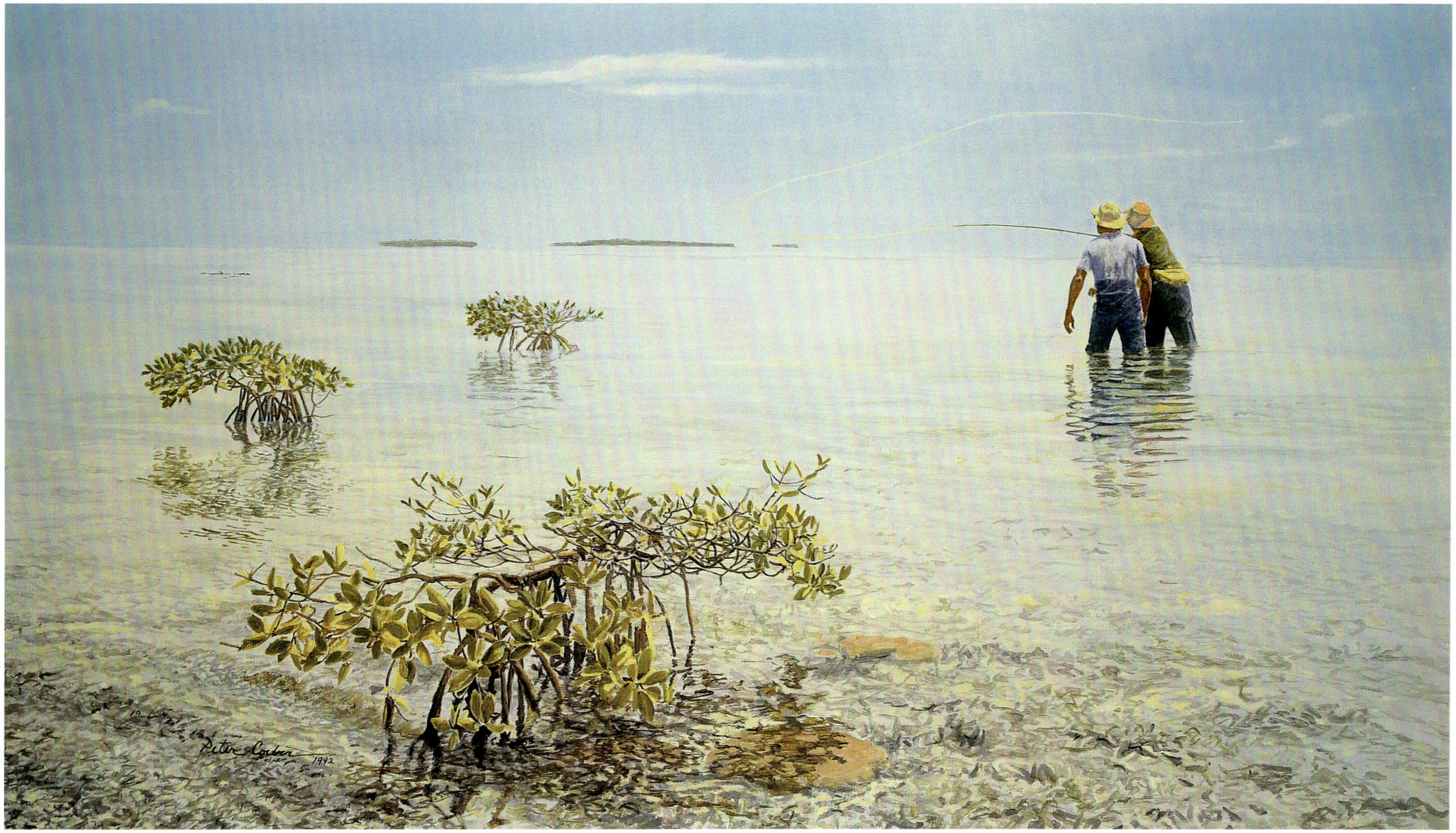

The Flats Fisherman, 1992
acrylic on canvas
20 × 36 inches
signed and dated lower left

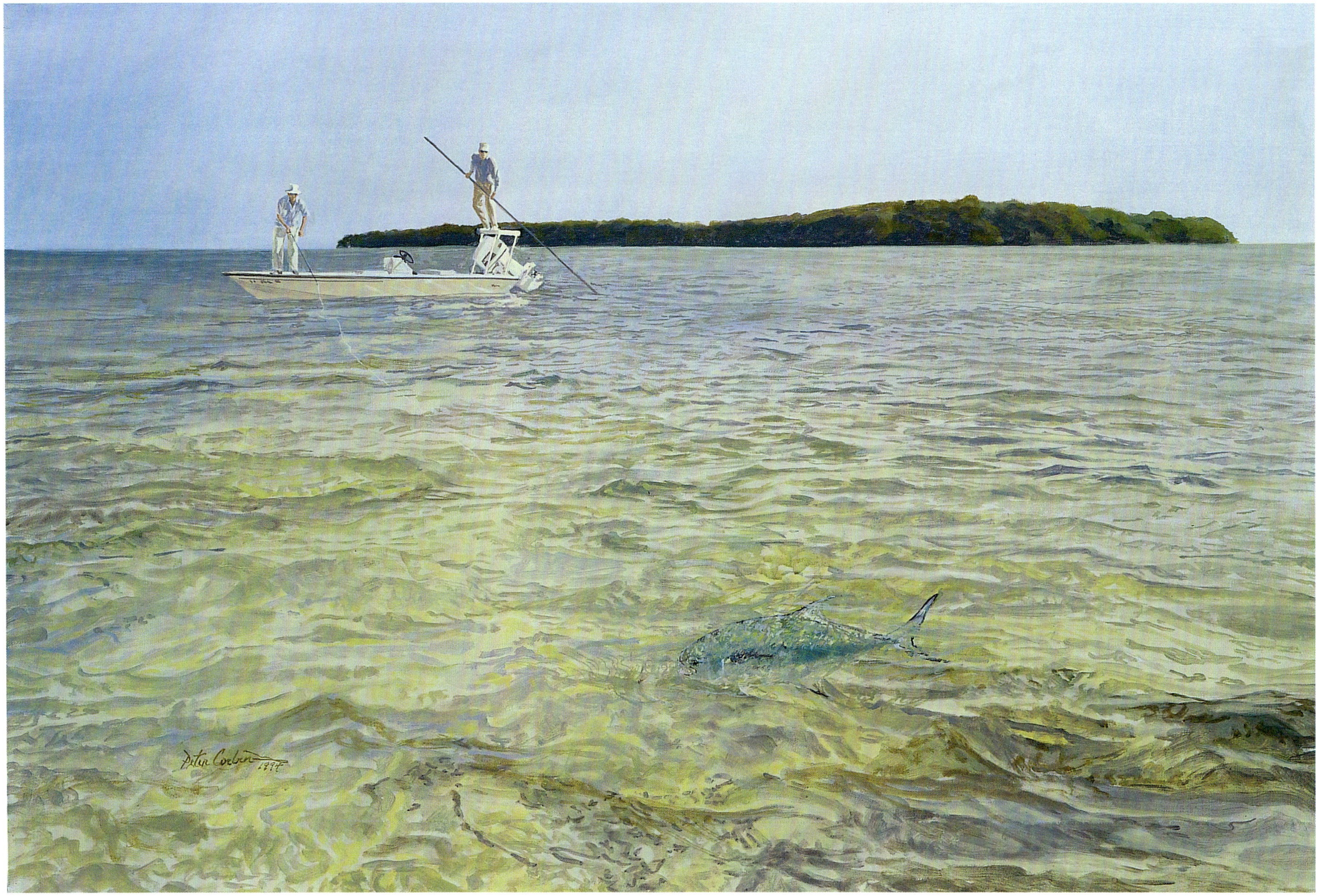

Portrait of John Hettinger, 1994
acrylic on canvas
20 × 30 inches
signed and dated lower left

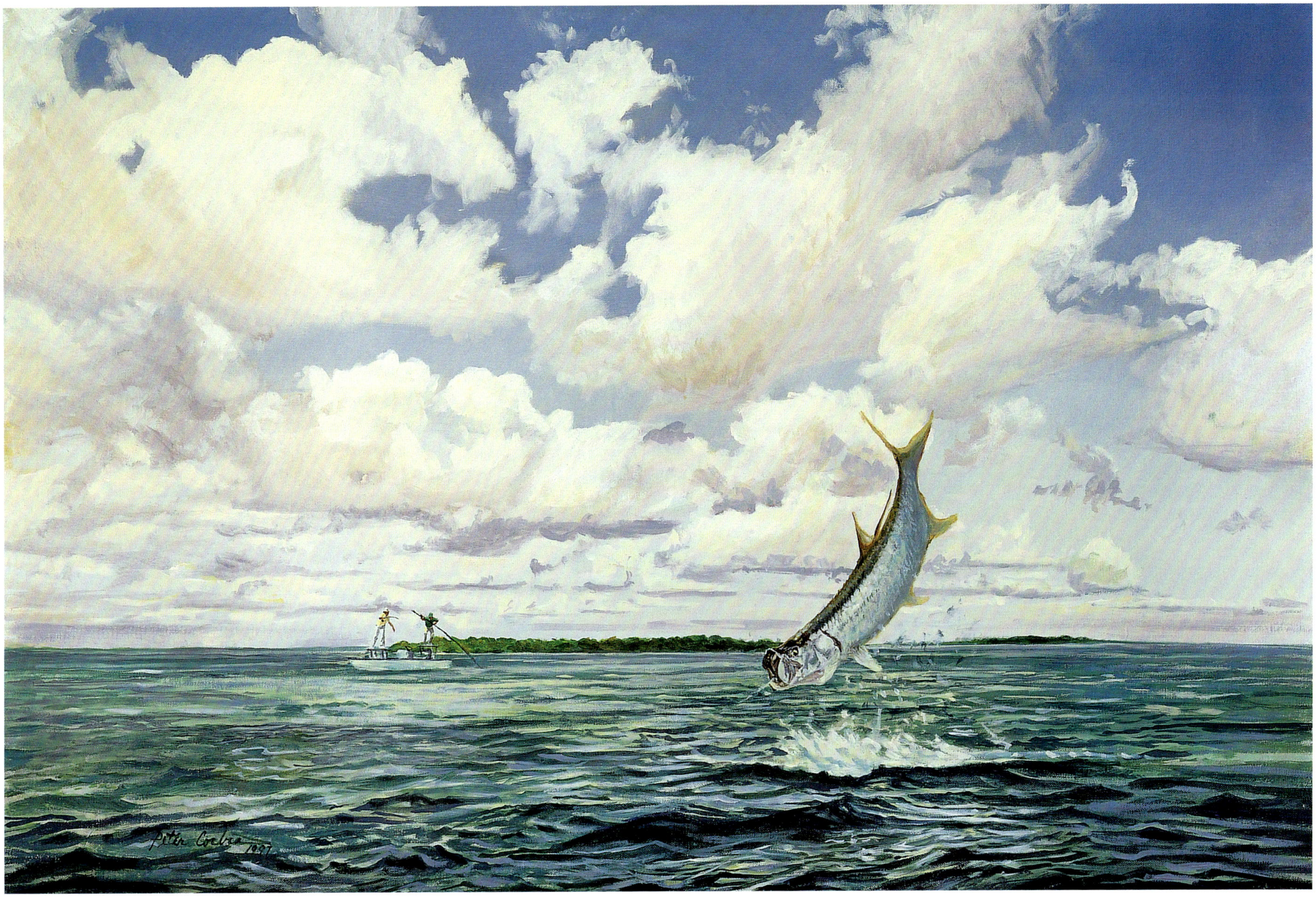

Broken Sky/Broken Water, 1997
oil on canvas
20 × 30 inches
signed and dated lower left

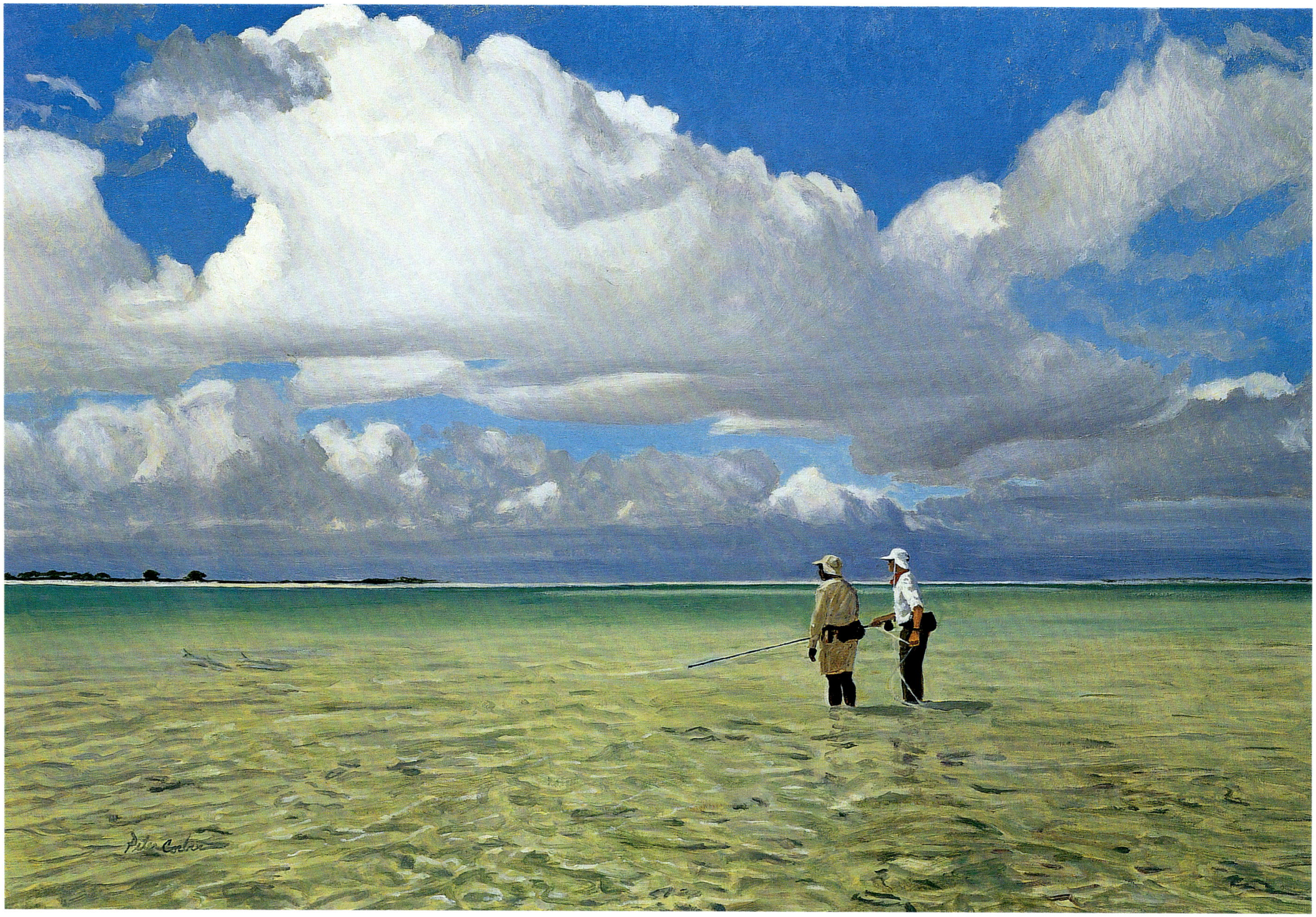

On the Edge—Bonefish, 2001
oil on canvas
20 × 30 inches
signed lower left

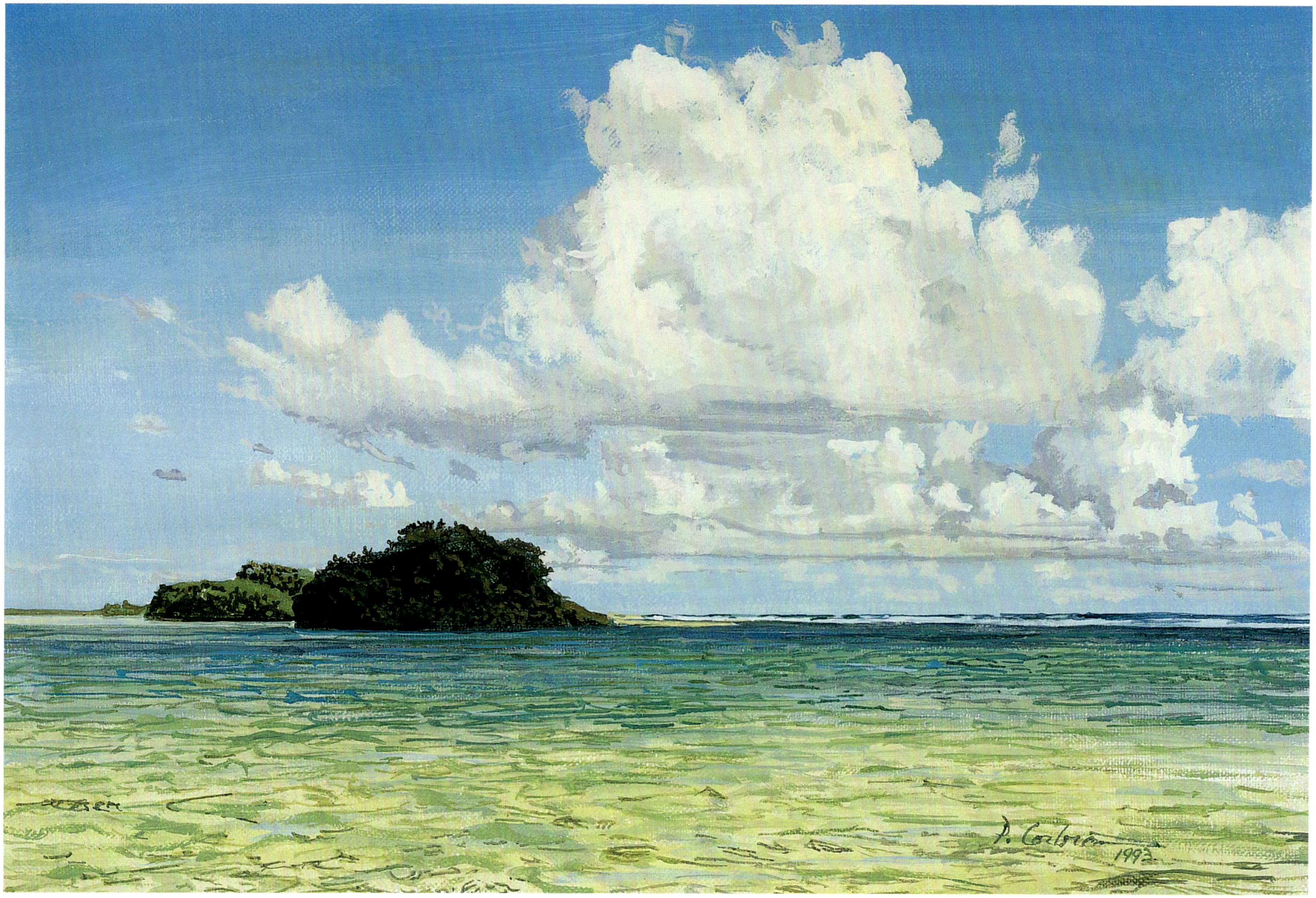

Bonefish Flats, 1993
acrylic on canvas
9 × 12 inches
signed and dated lower right

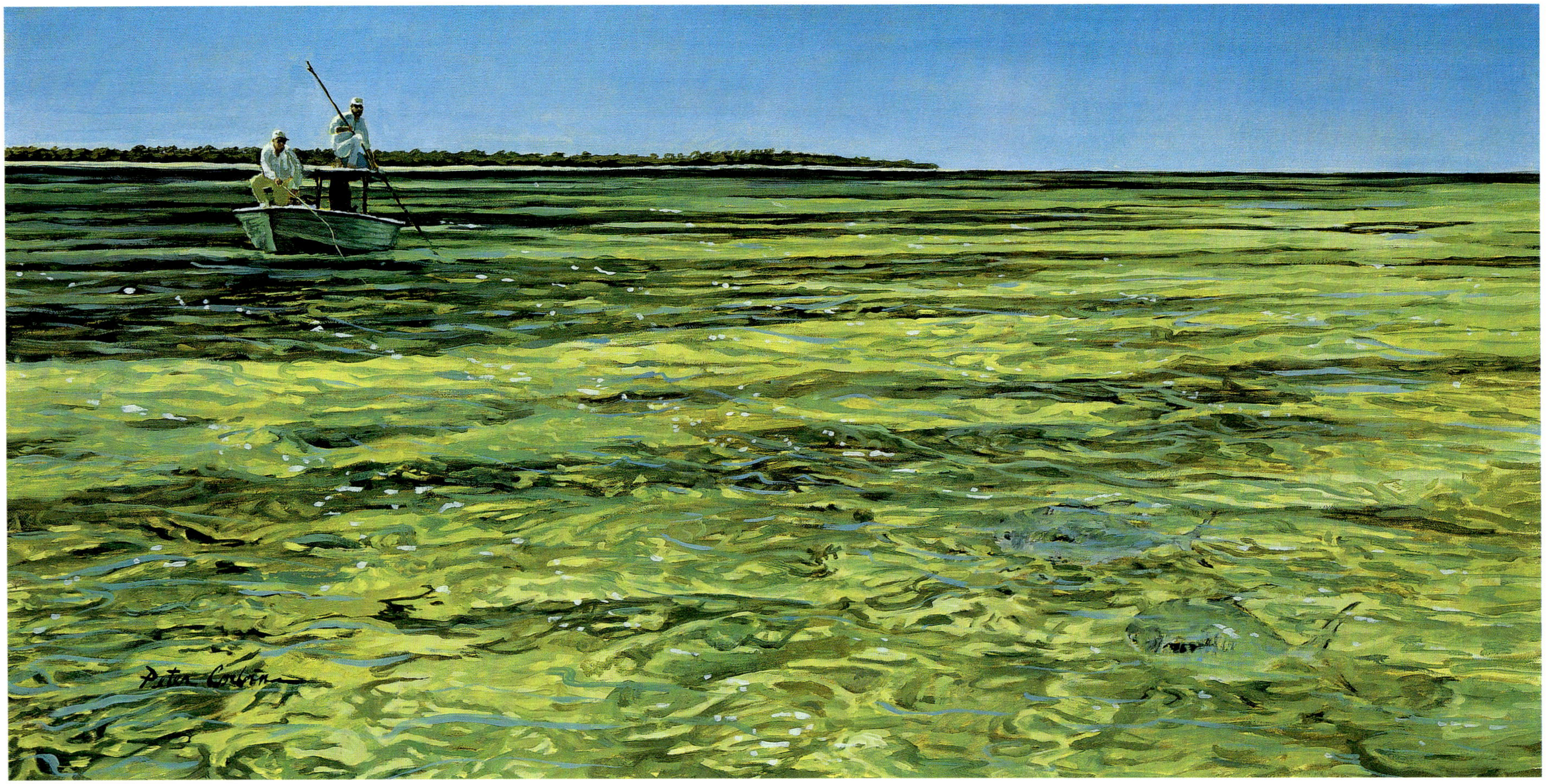

Poling the Permit Flats, 2000
oil on canvas
15 × 30 inches
signed lower left

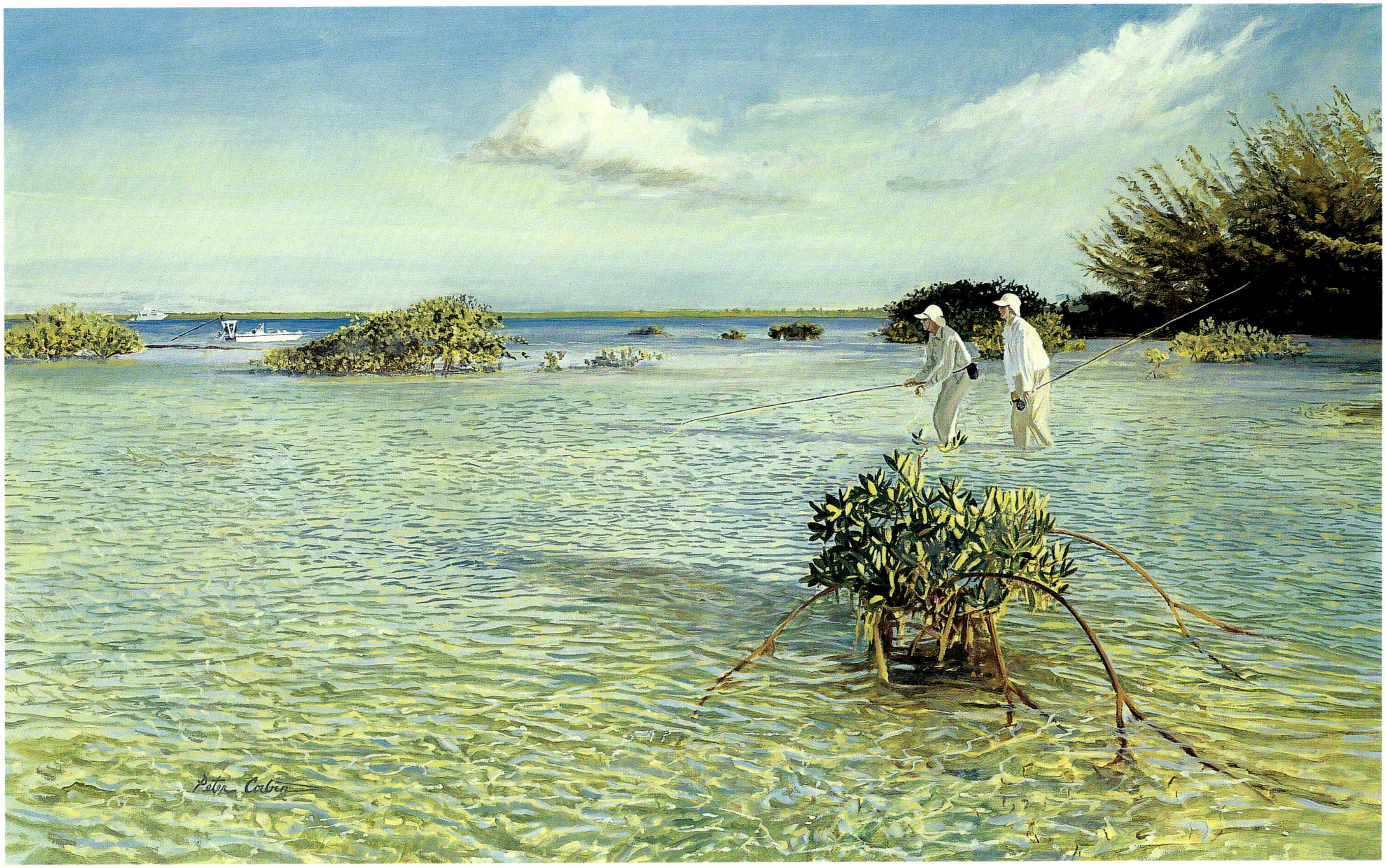

South Bite—Andros, 2002
oil on canvas
24 × 40 inches
signed lower left

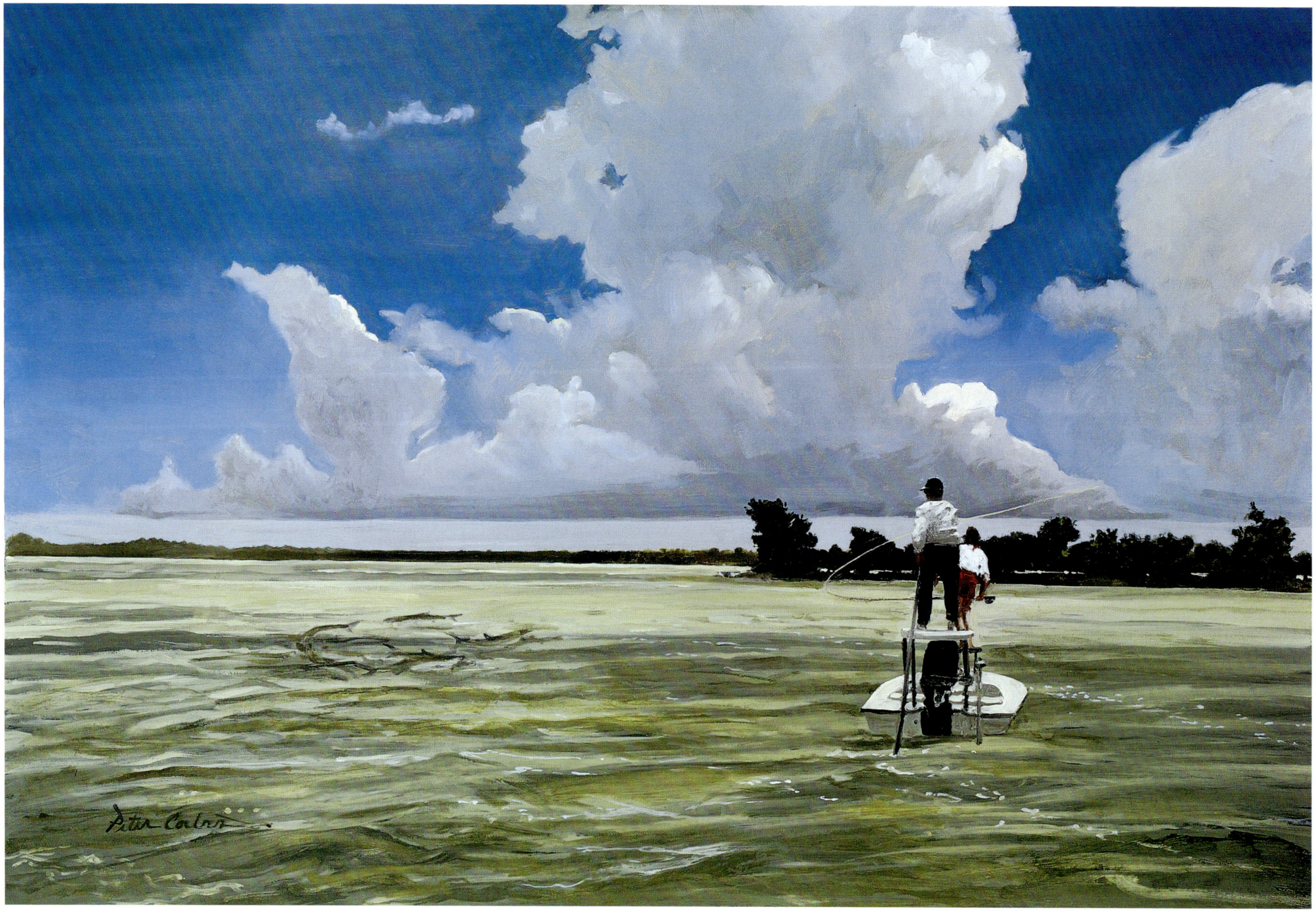

The Daisy Chain, 2004
oil on canvas
20 × 30 inches
signed lower left

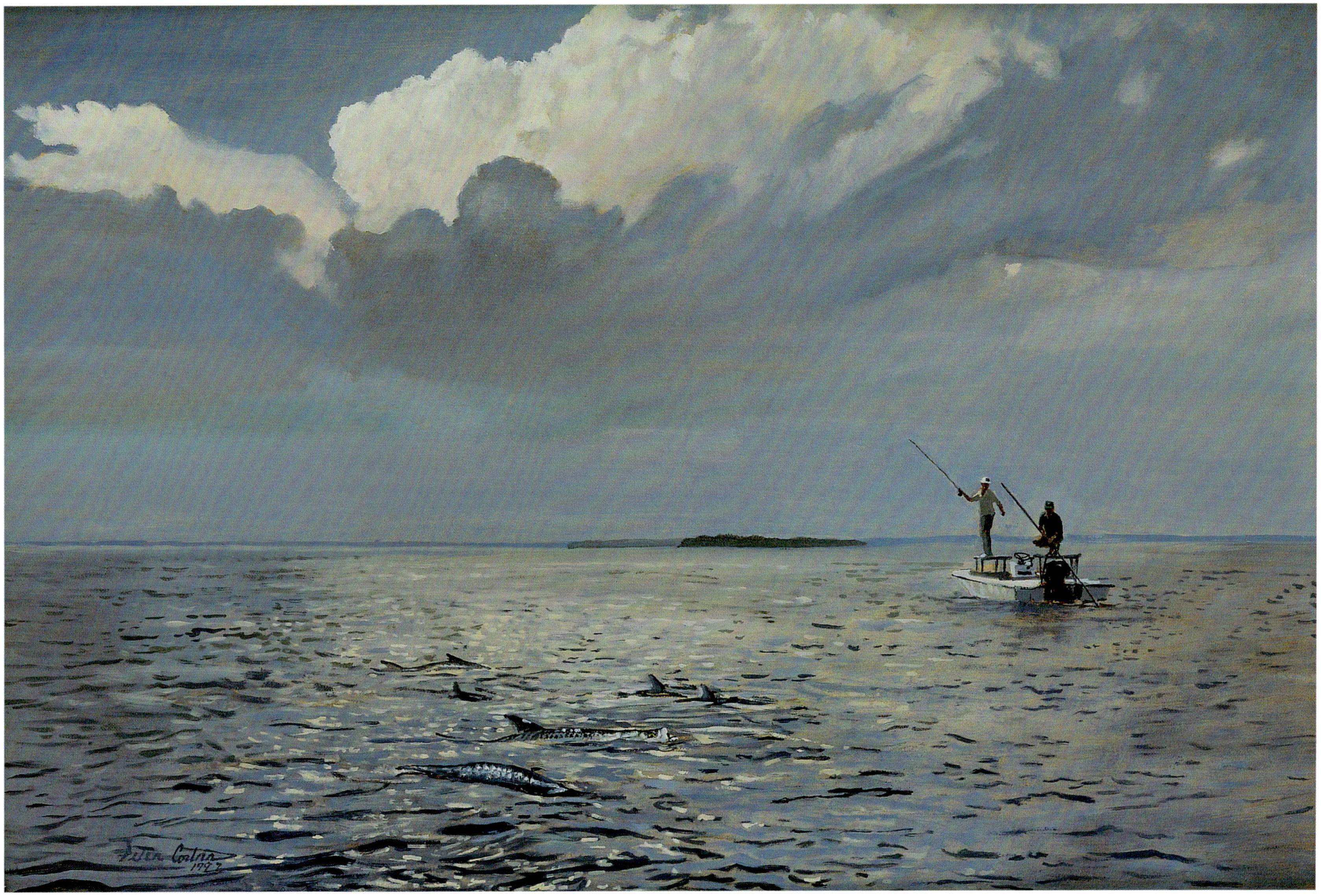

Rolling Tarpon, 1997
oil on canvas
16 × 24 inches
signed and dated lower left

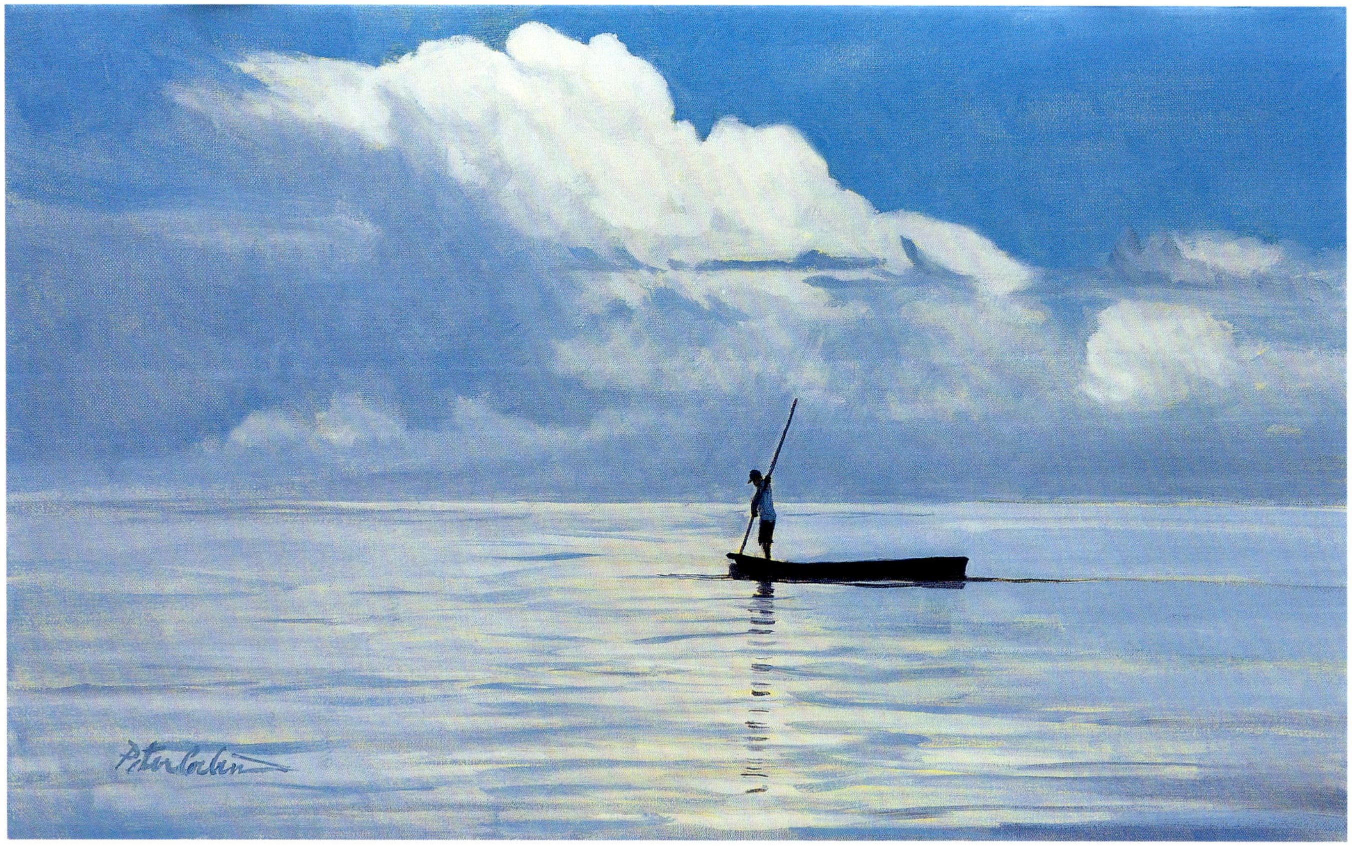

Key West Sponger, 1998
oil on canvas
12 × 20 inches
signed lower left

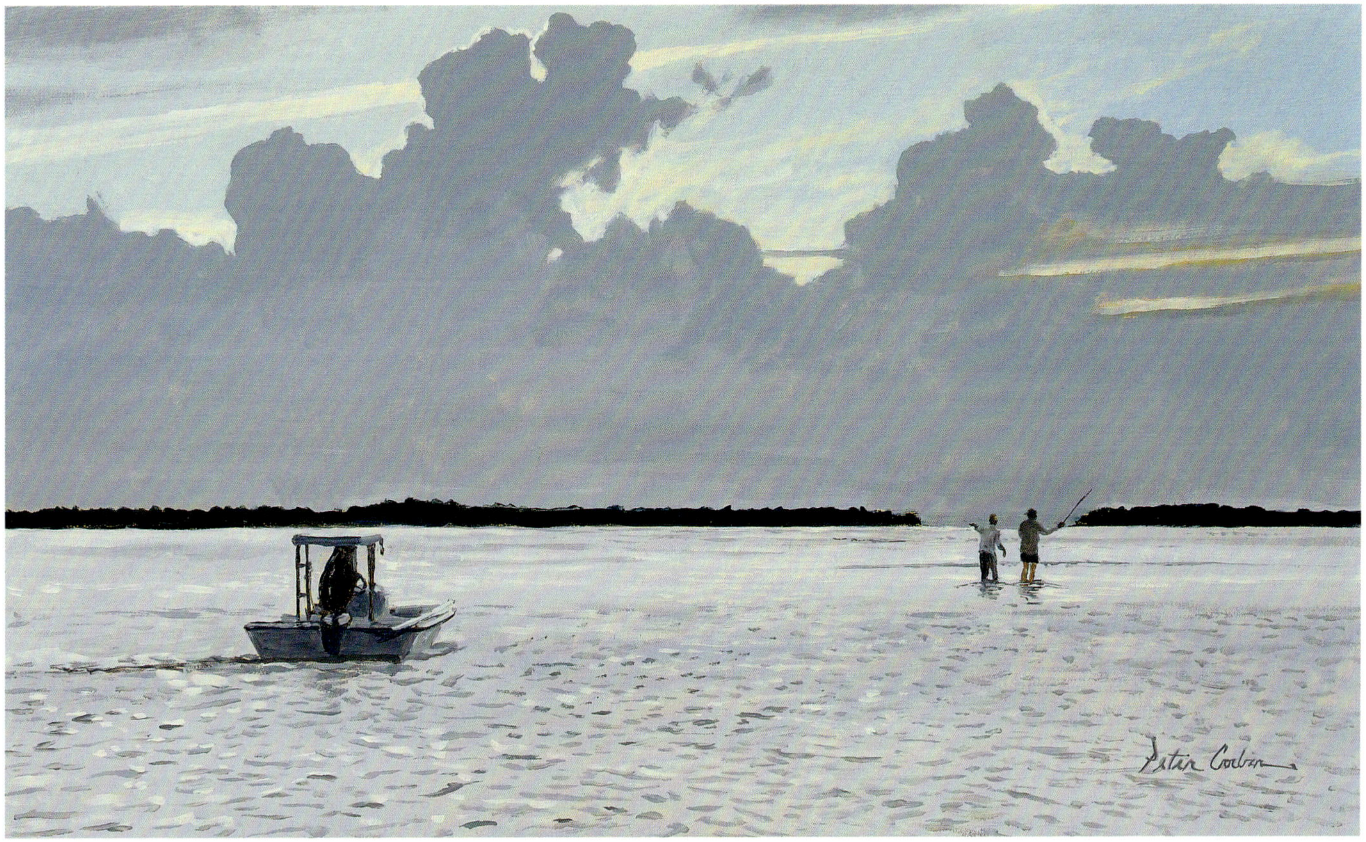

Wading for Bones, 2000
oil on canvas
12 × 20 inches
signed lower right

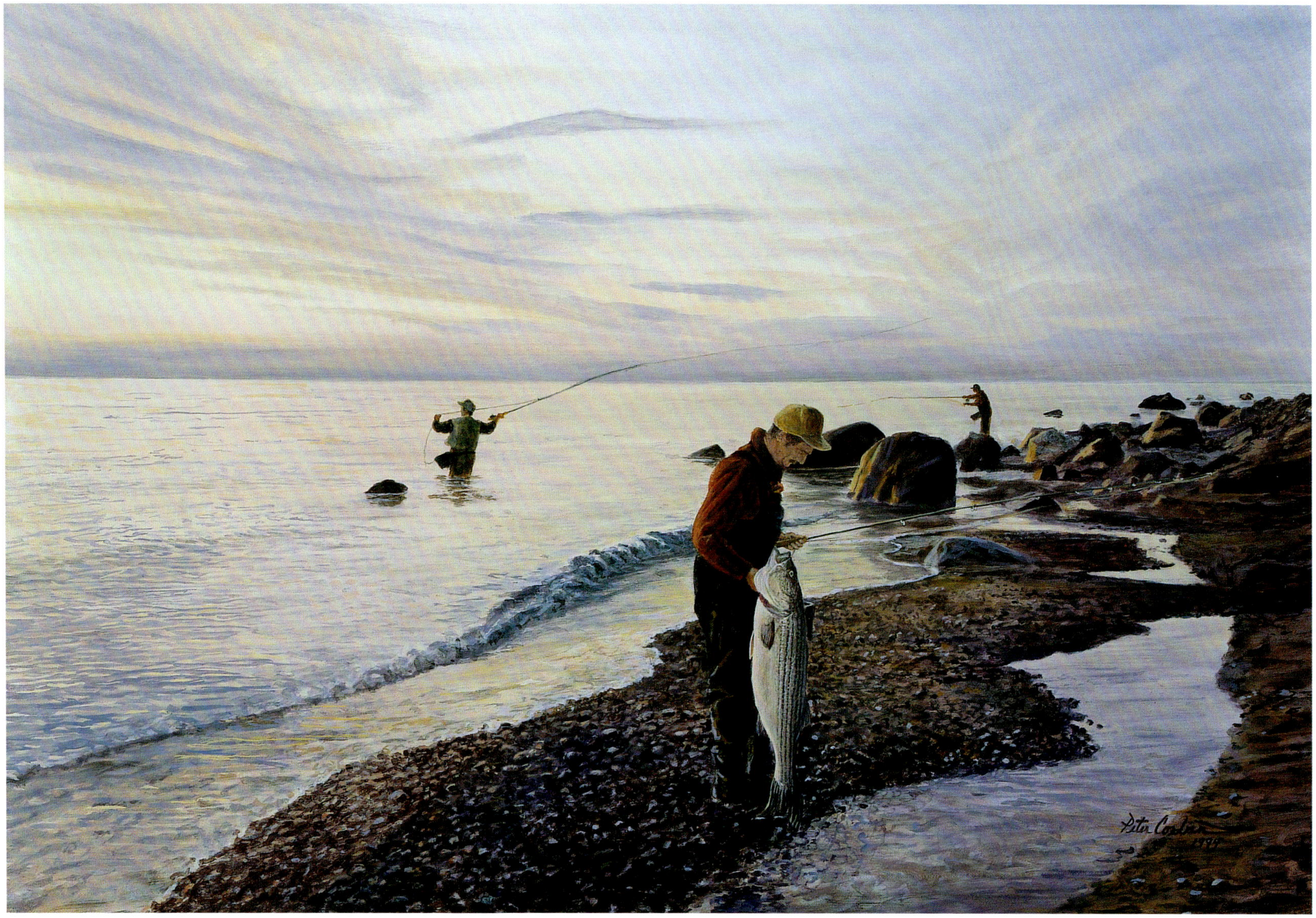

Trophy Fish, 1994
acrylic on canvas
24 × 36 inches
signed and dated lower right

Working for a Living, 1994
acrylic on canvas
9 × 16 inches
signed and dated lower left

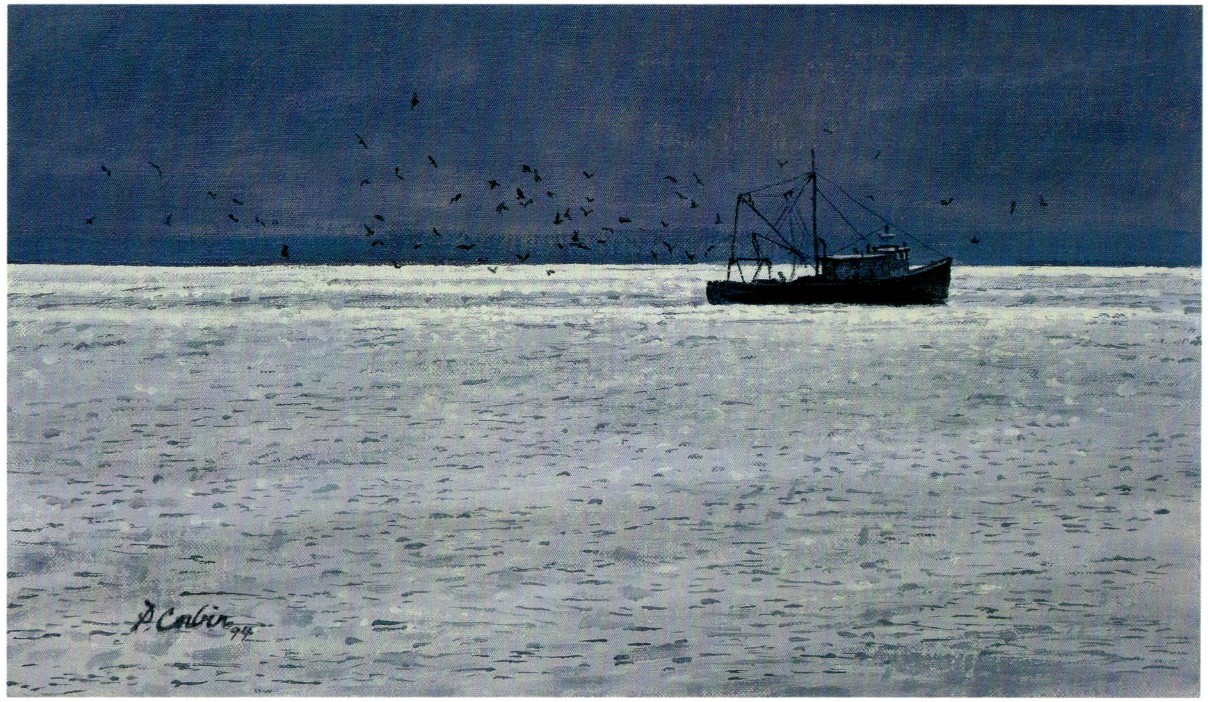

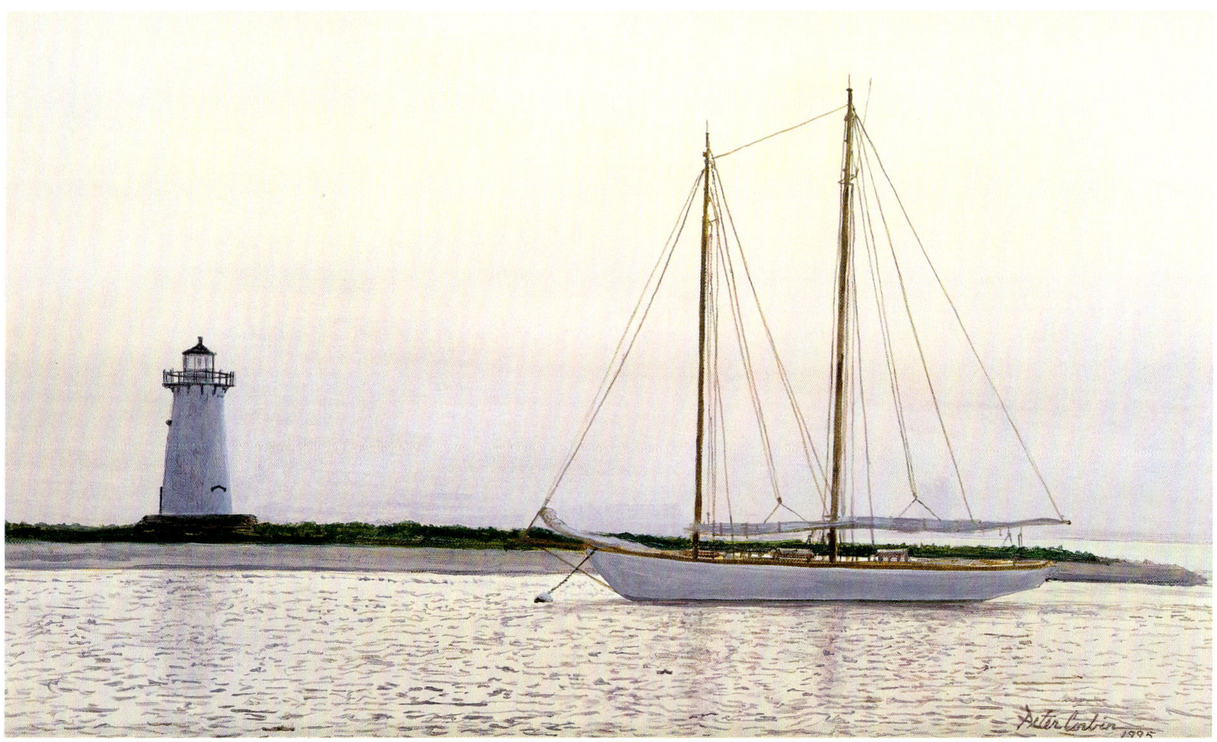

Evening Tide, 1995
acrylic on canvas
12 × 20 inches
signed and dated lower right

Shotgunning

I have always been fascinated by the flight of birds, whether the wild flush of a single grouse or the ordered chaos of several hundred Canada geese gliding into a field. The patterns of flight and the scope of bird hunting have always quickened my pulse and stirred my imagination.

And the elements and perspective of a bird-hunting scene create a wonderful painting. Because of the limited range of the shotgun and the size of the quarry, I am allowed to compose a believable scene that includes the hunter, the dogs, and the birds presented in the variously colored landscape where they meet. Duck marshes, goose fields, grouse and woodcock covers, and quail plantations all feature gentle landscapes that provide a perfect background to the drama of the hunt. When it is really successful, a landscape can even capture the earth's moisture and smells. It also allows me to record real scenes of my time, though many of these scenes are timeless.

Upland

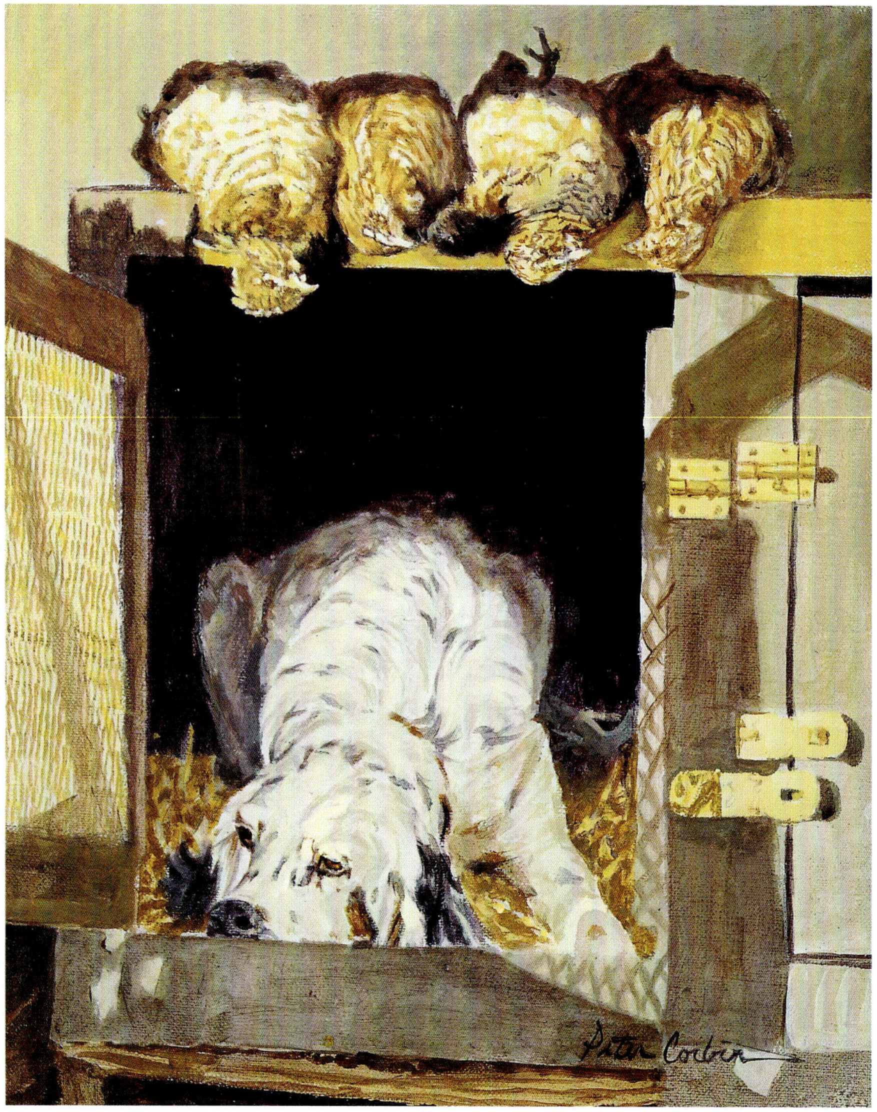

A Hard Day's Work, 1992
acrylic on canvas
12 × 10 inches
signed lower right

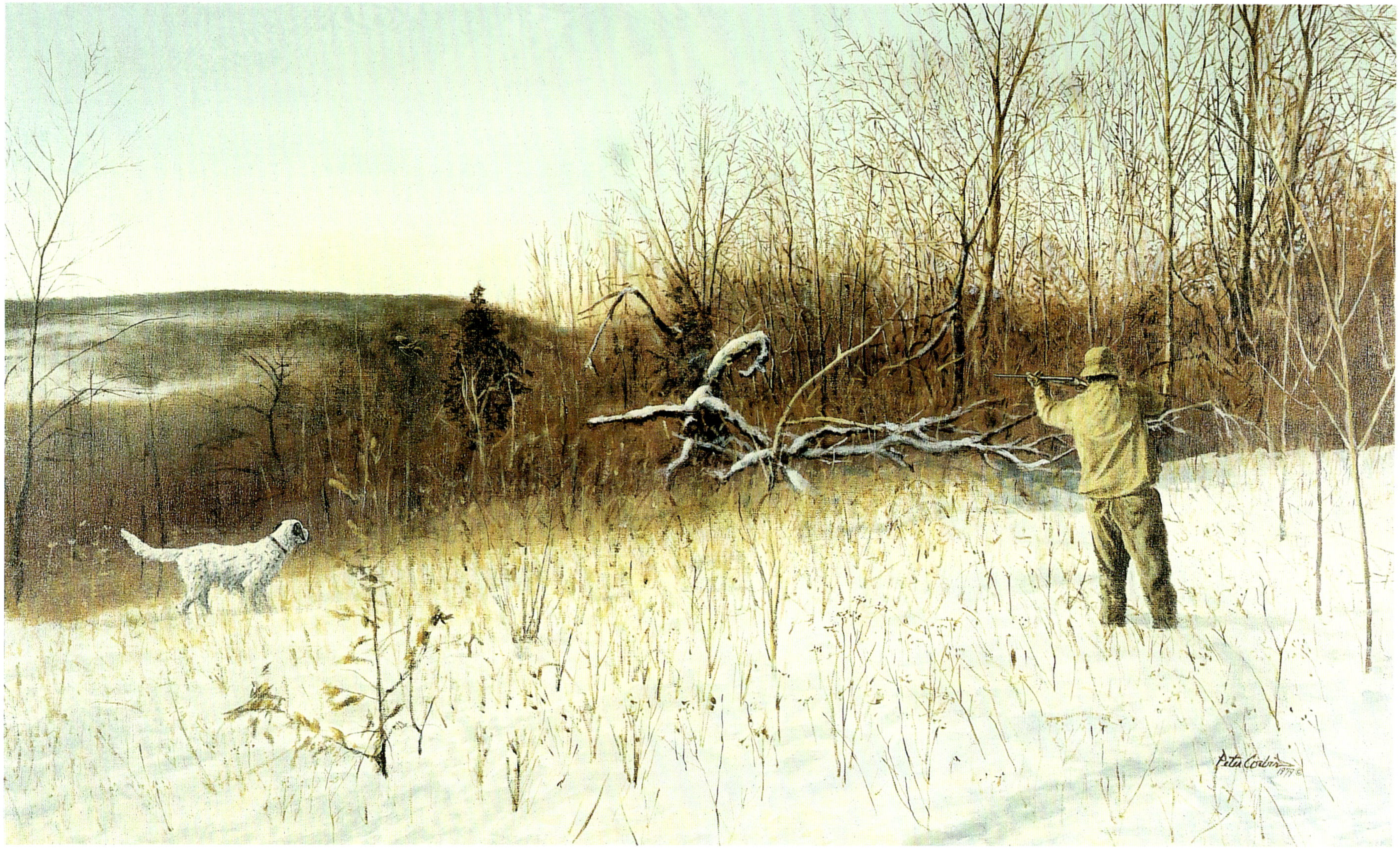

Deadfall Flush, 1979
acrylic on canvas
24 × 40 inches
signed and dated lower right

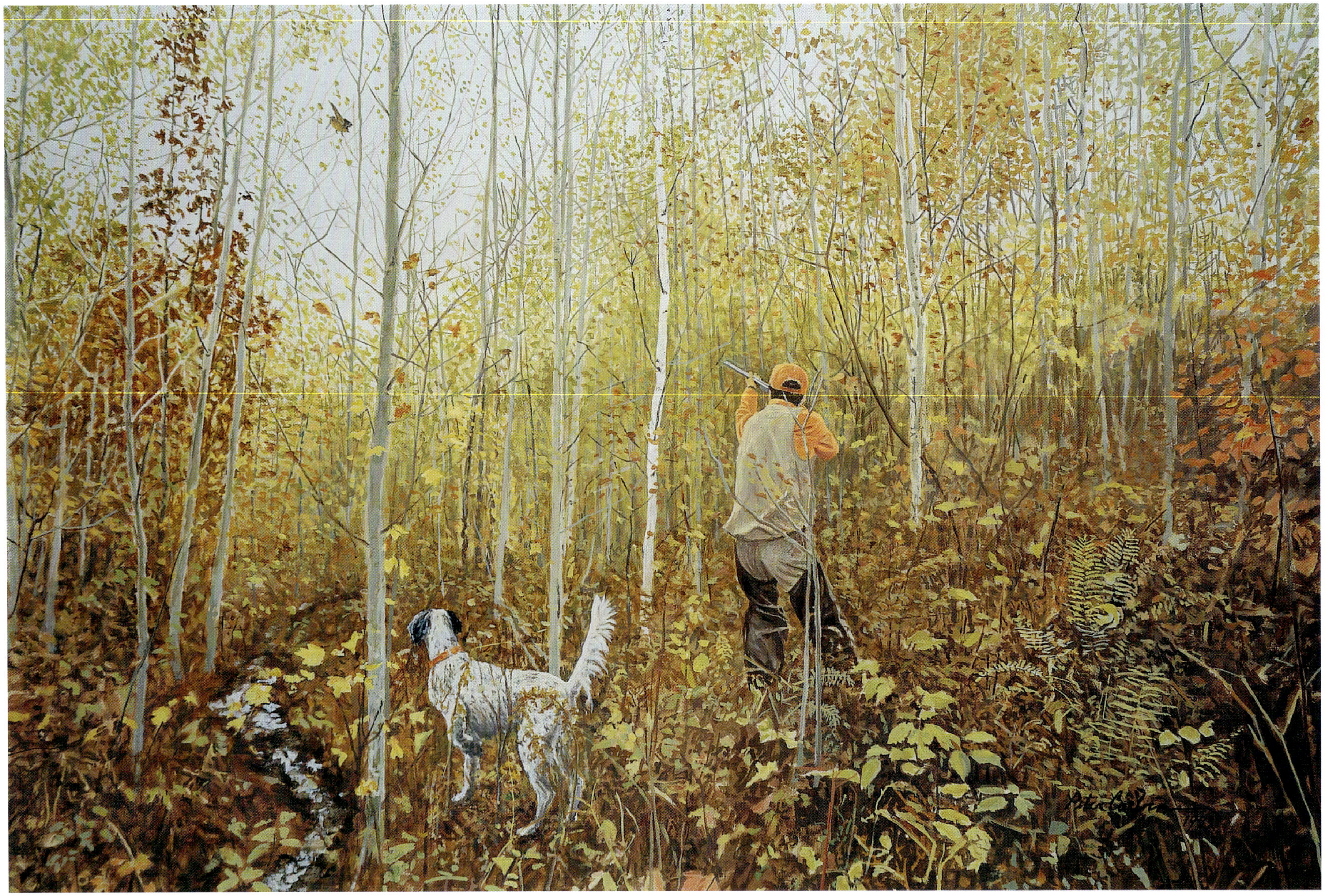

October Afternoon, 1992
acrylic on canvas
20 × 30 inches
signed and dated lower right

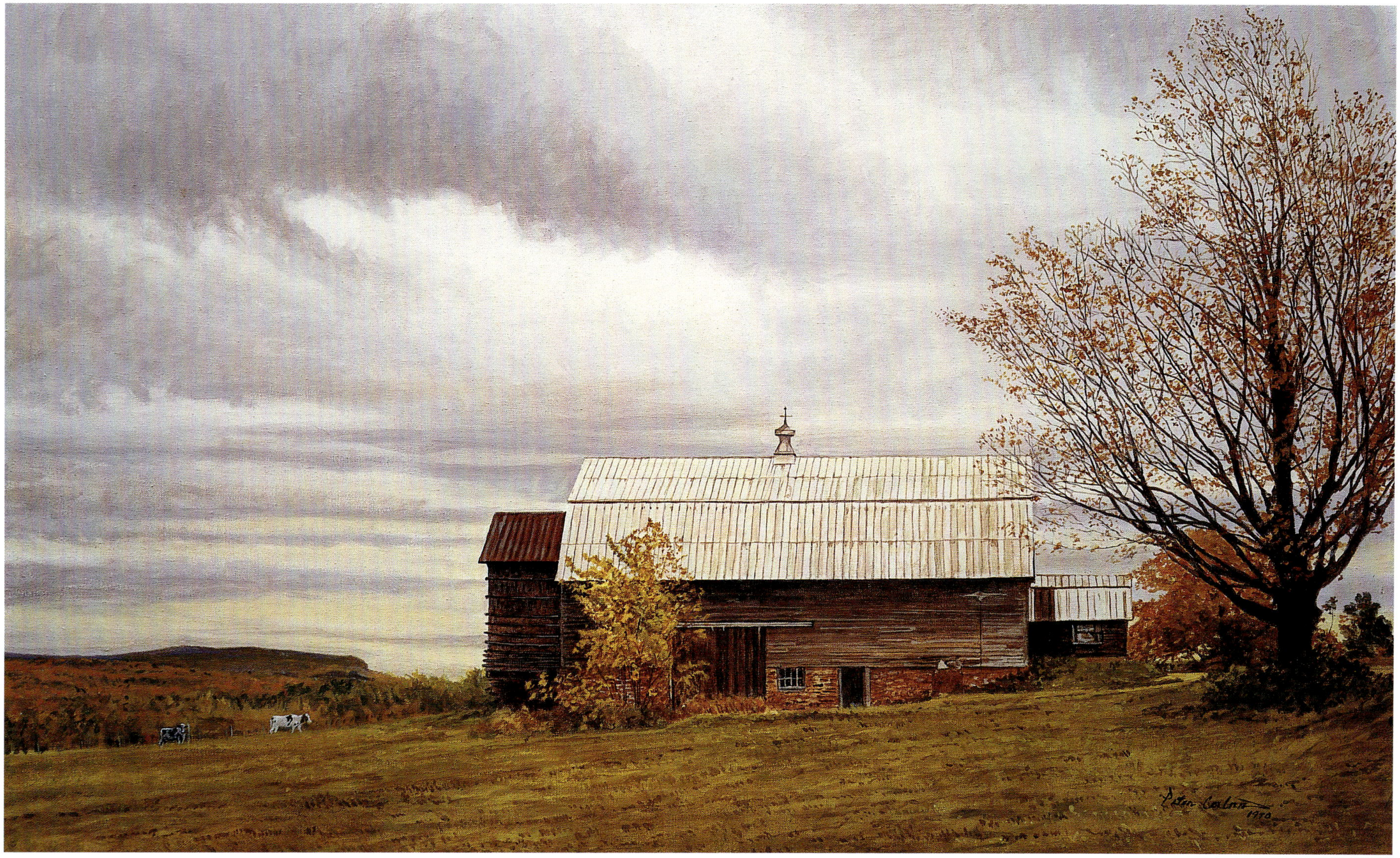

September Thunder, 1991
acrylic on canvas
24 × 40 inches
signed and dated lower right

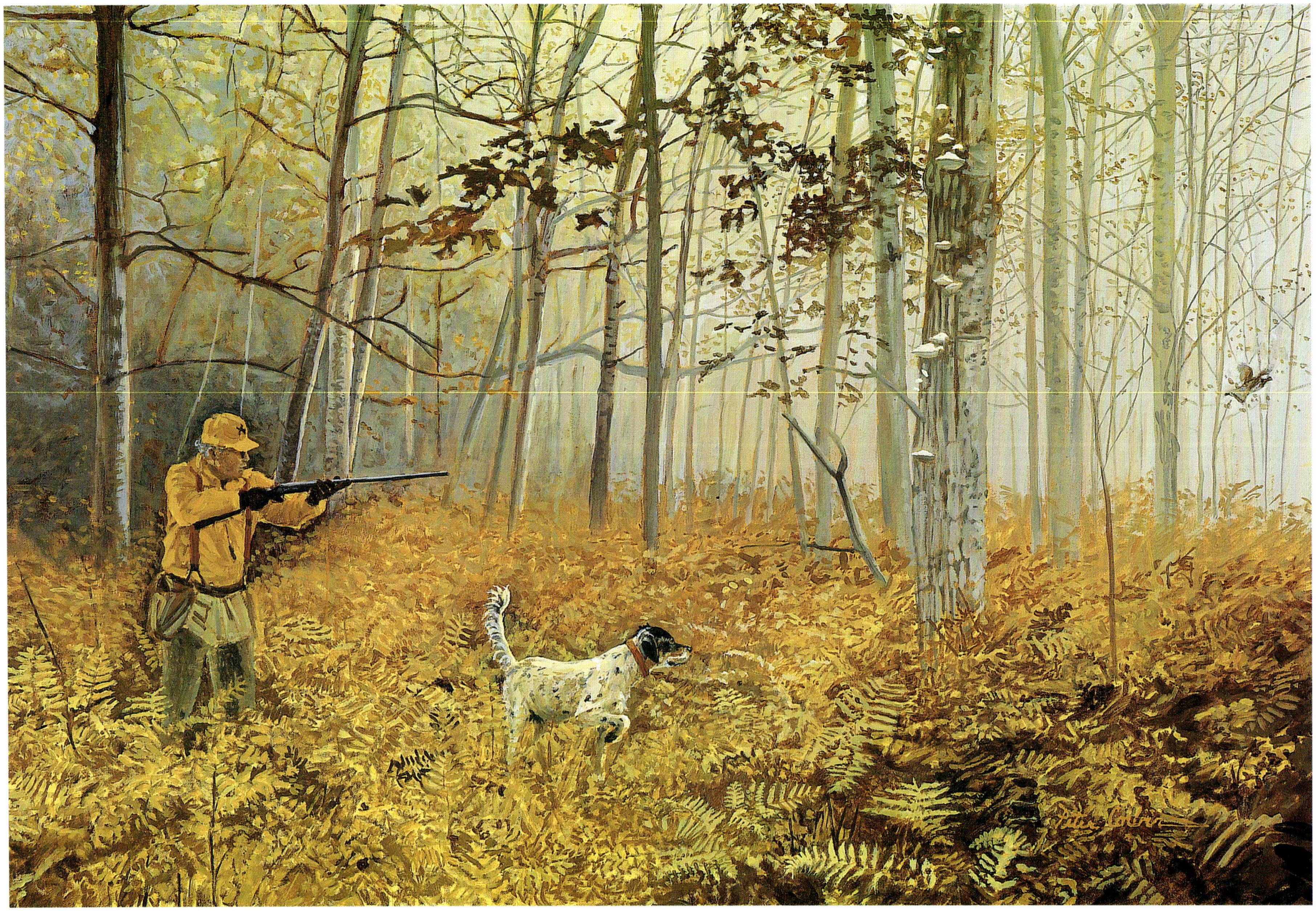

Michigan Morning, 2001
oil on canvas
20 × 30 inches
signed lower right

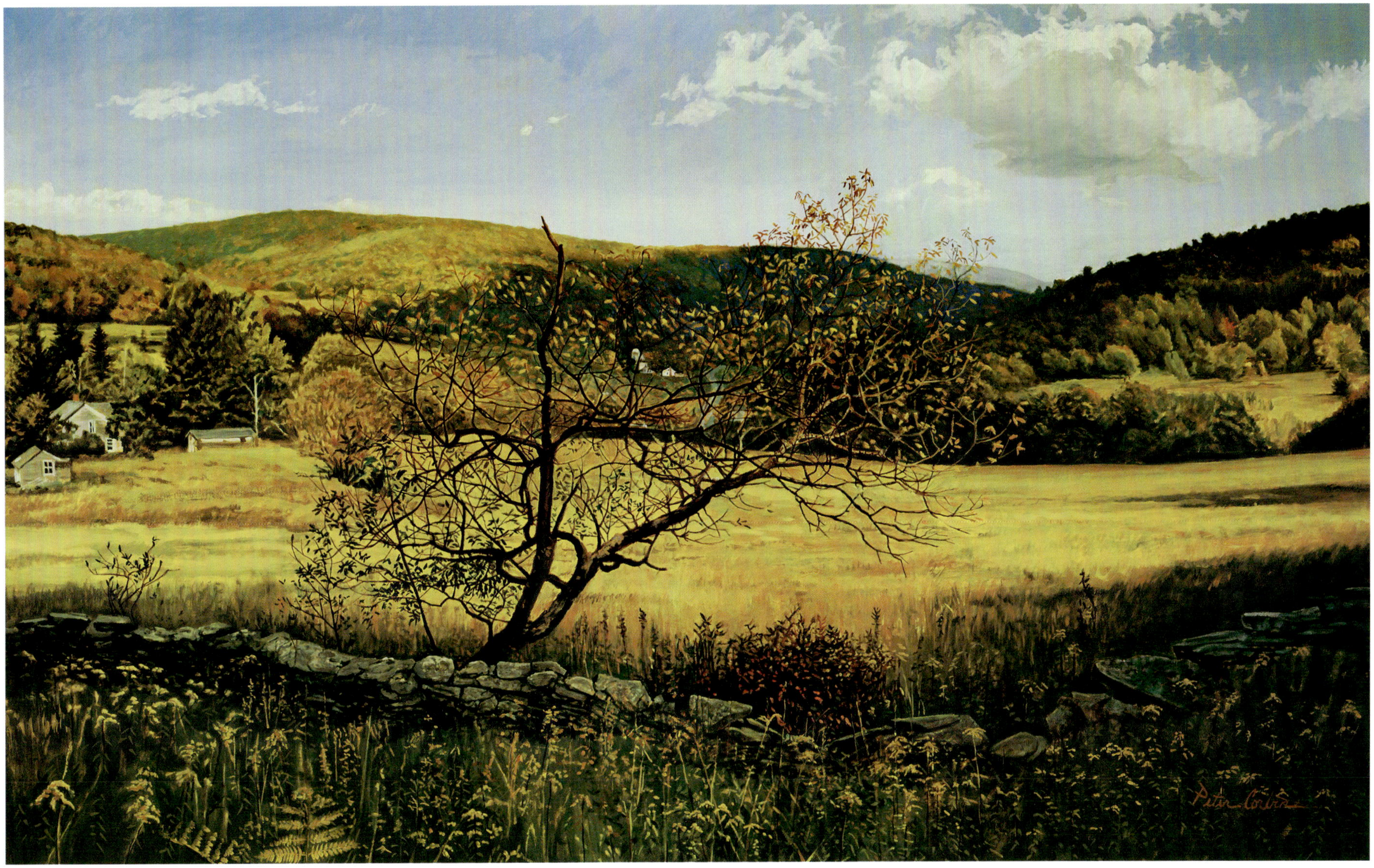

A Catskill Valley, 2004
oil on canvas
34 × 56 inches
signed lower right

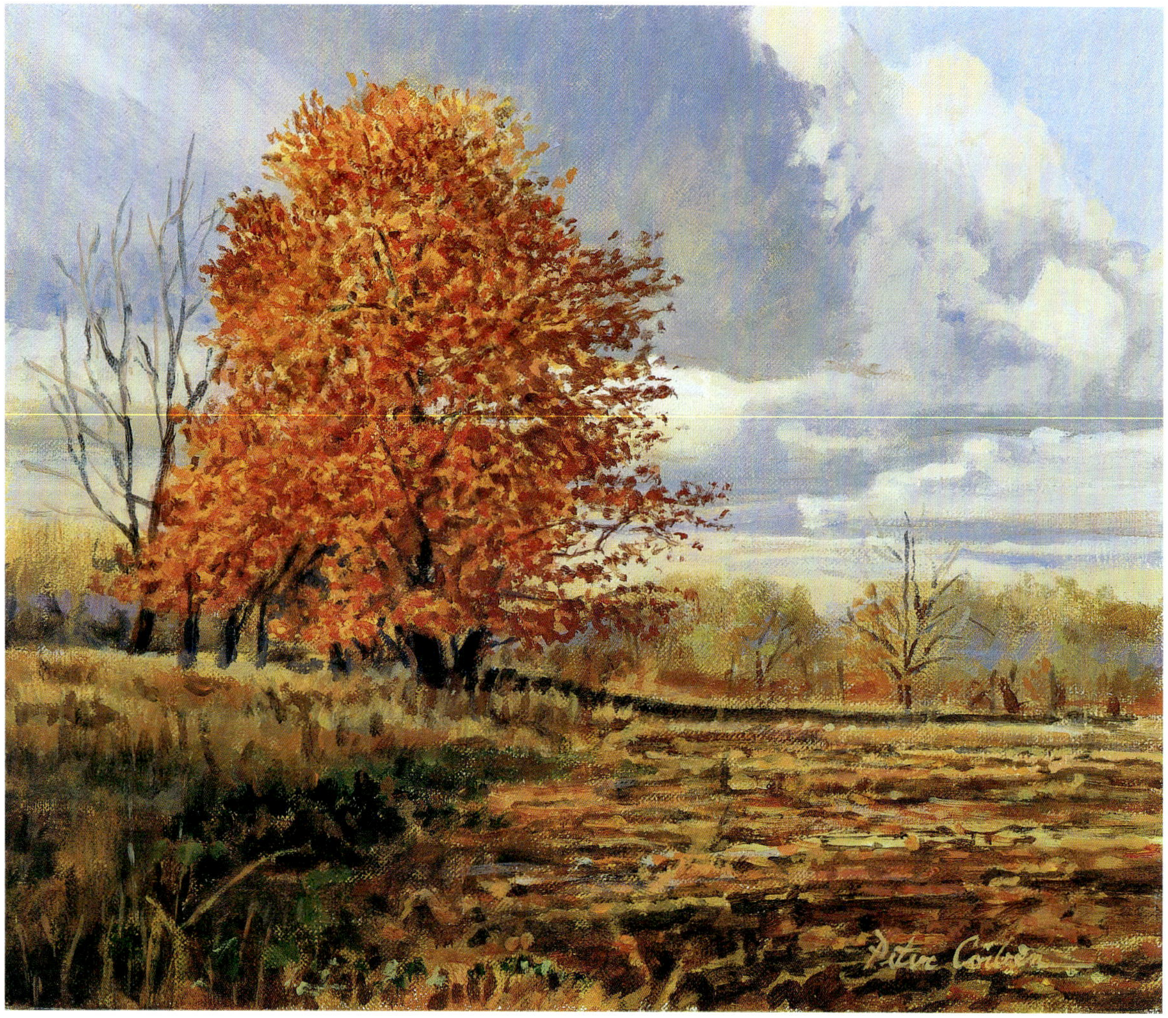

Shade Tree—Fall, 1994
acrylic on canvas
10 × 12 inches
signed lower right

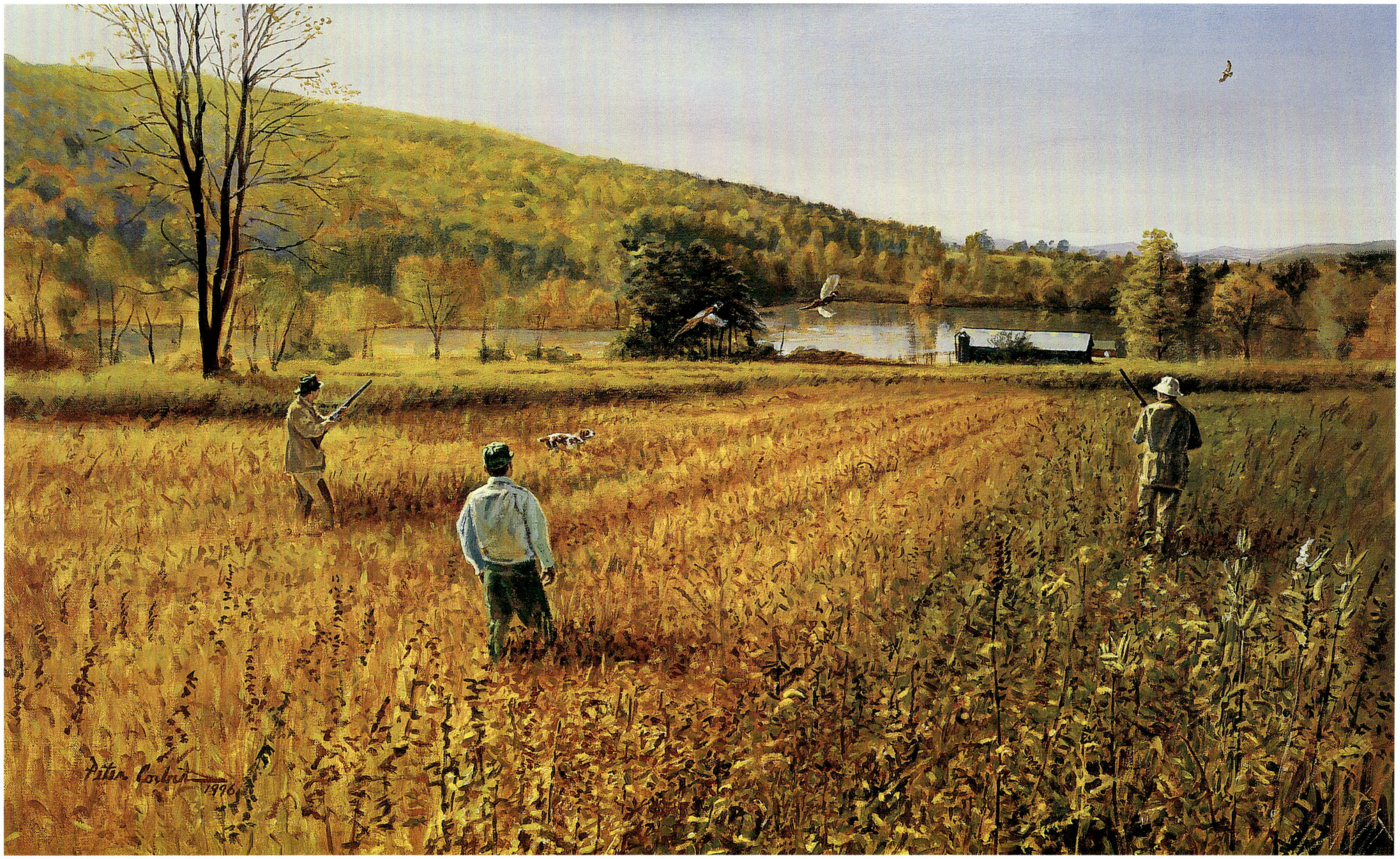

The Valley, 1996
acrylic on canvas
18 × 30 inches
signed and dated lower left

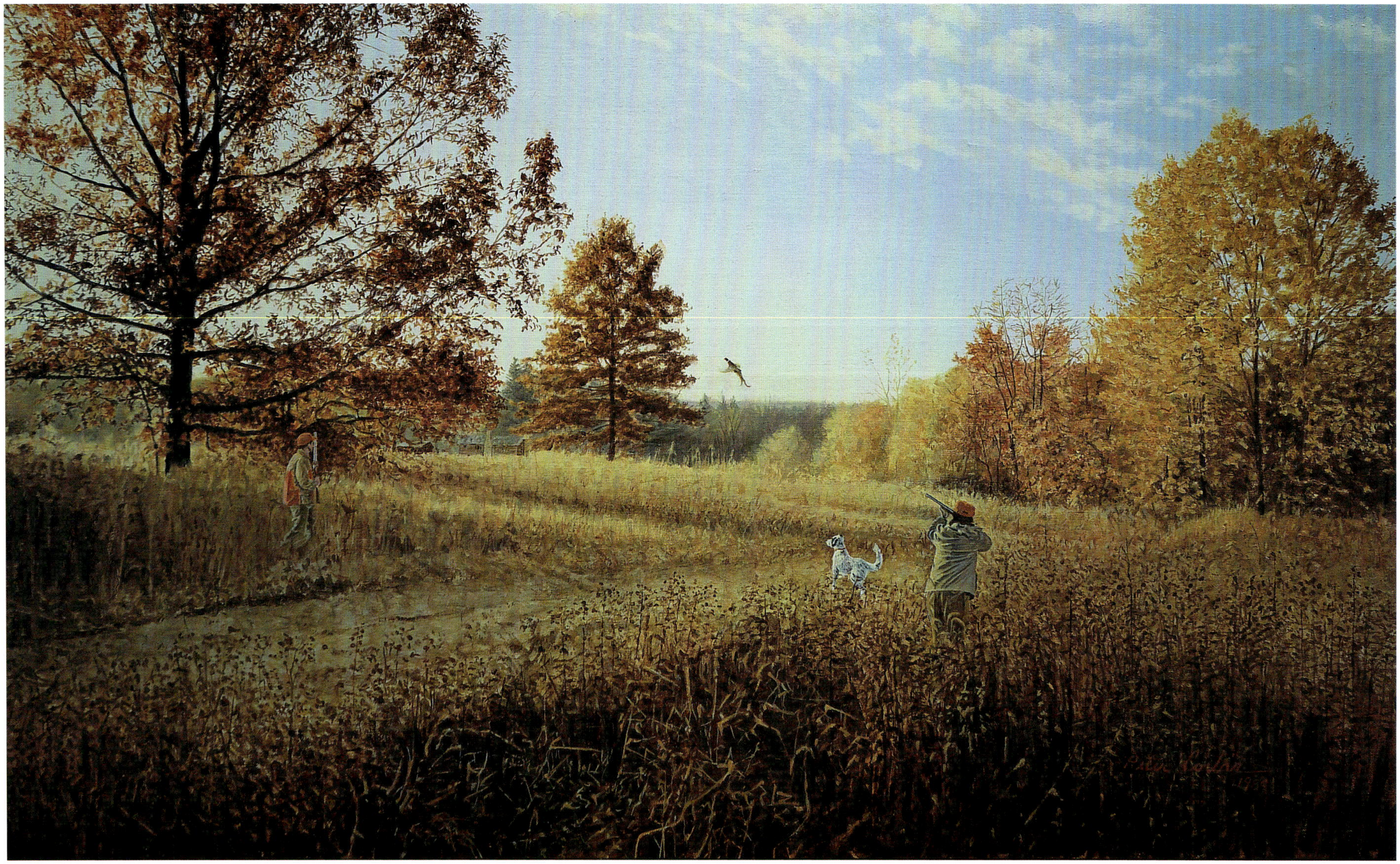

Amwell Autumn, 1989
acrylic on canvas
24 × 40 inches
signed and dated lower right

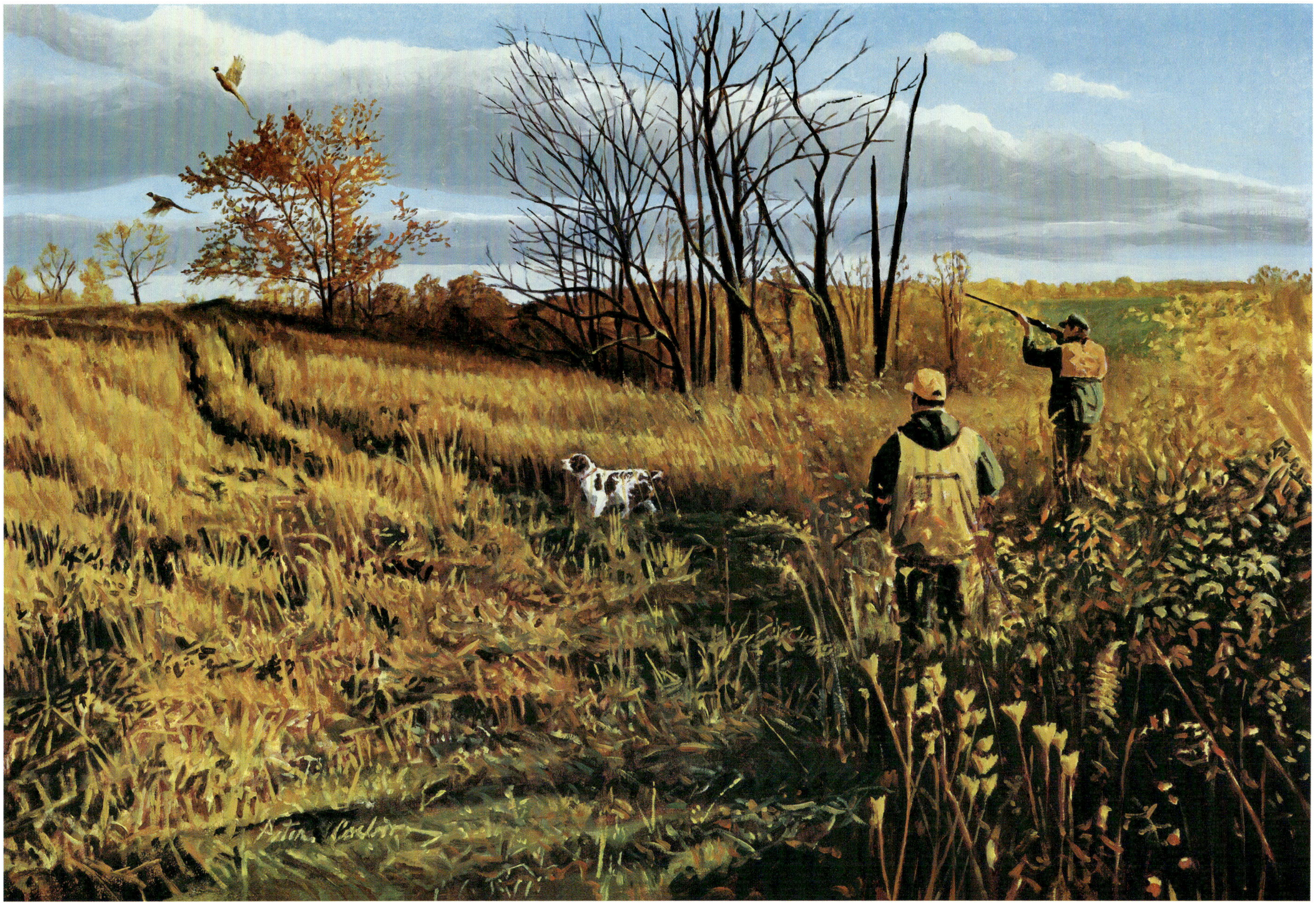

Tamarack Double, 2002
oil on canvas
20 × 30 inches
signed lower left

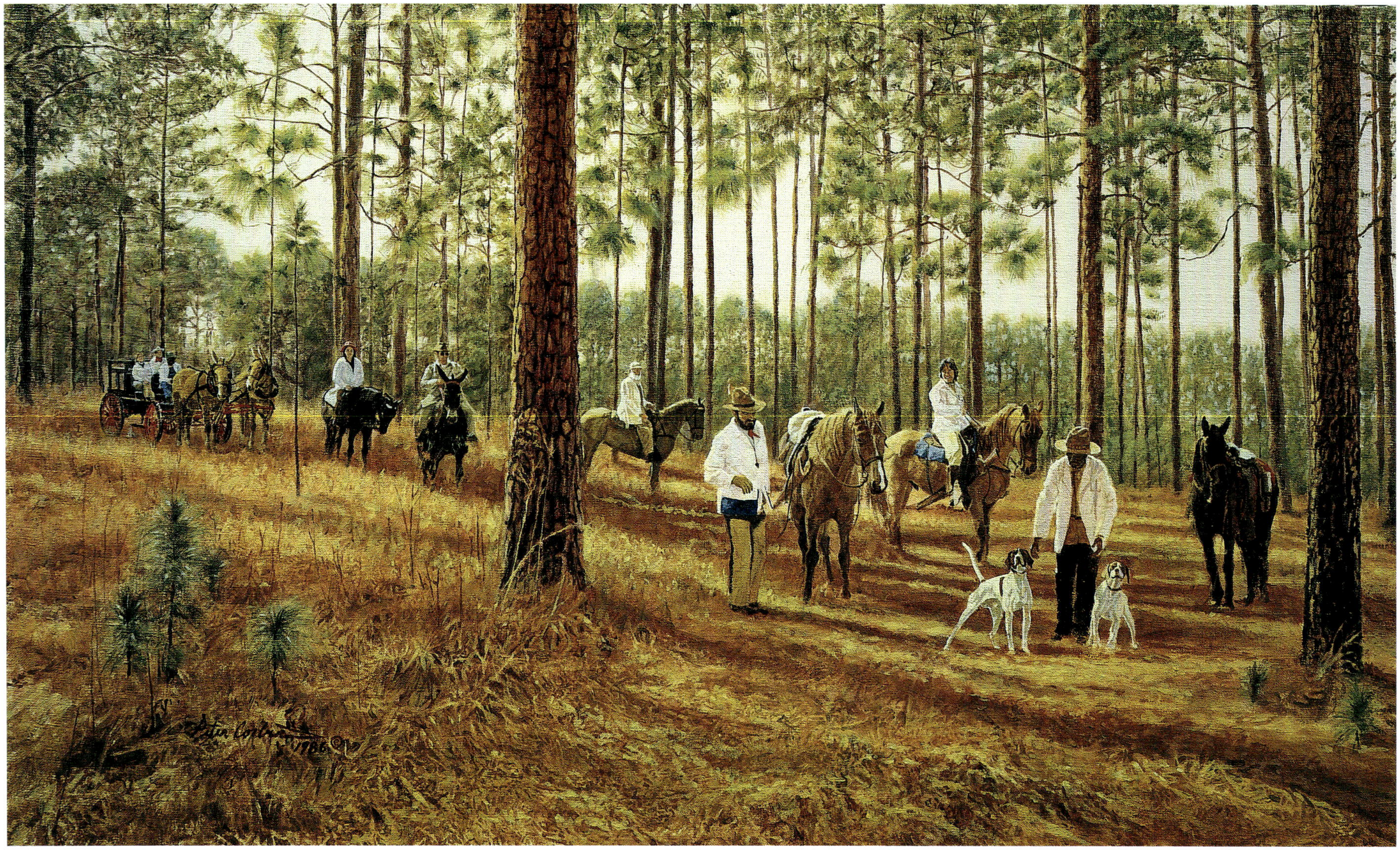

Putting Down a New Pair, 1986
acrylic on canvas
20 × 34 inches
signed and dated lower left

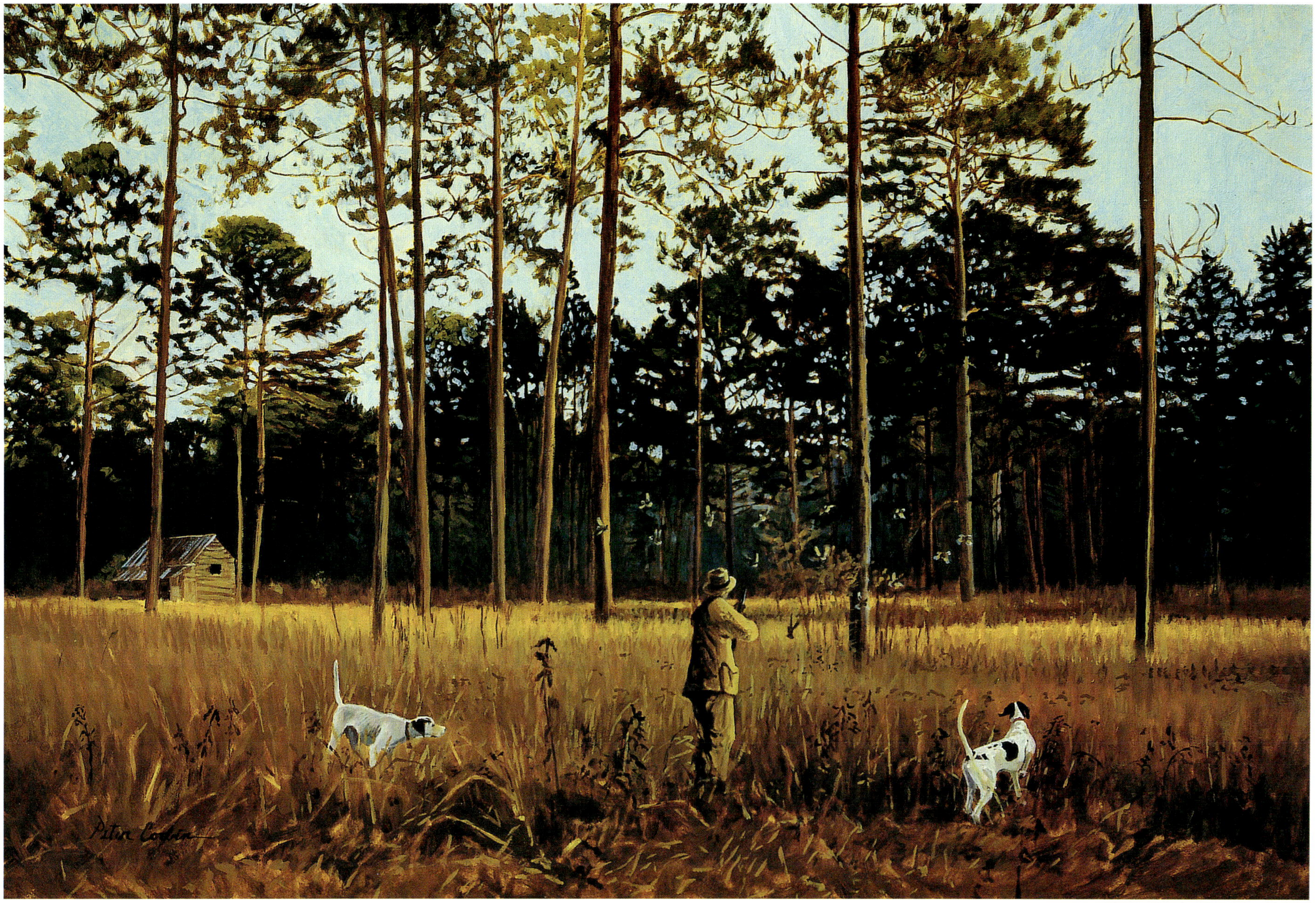

Old Cabin Covey, 2000
oil on canvas
20 × 30 inches
signed lower left

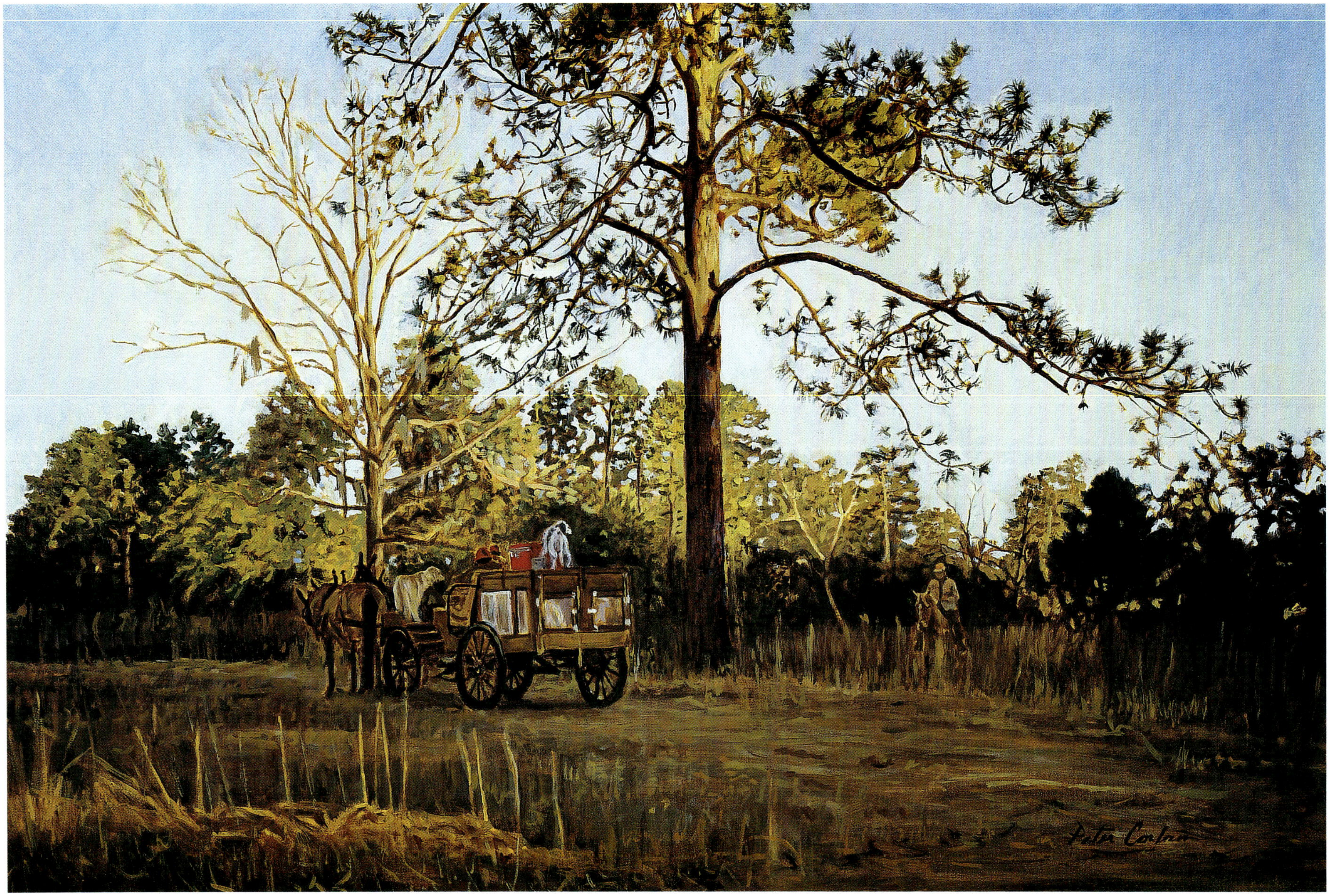

End of the Day—Quail Hunting, 2001
oil on canvas
20 × 30 inches
signed lower right

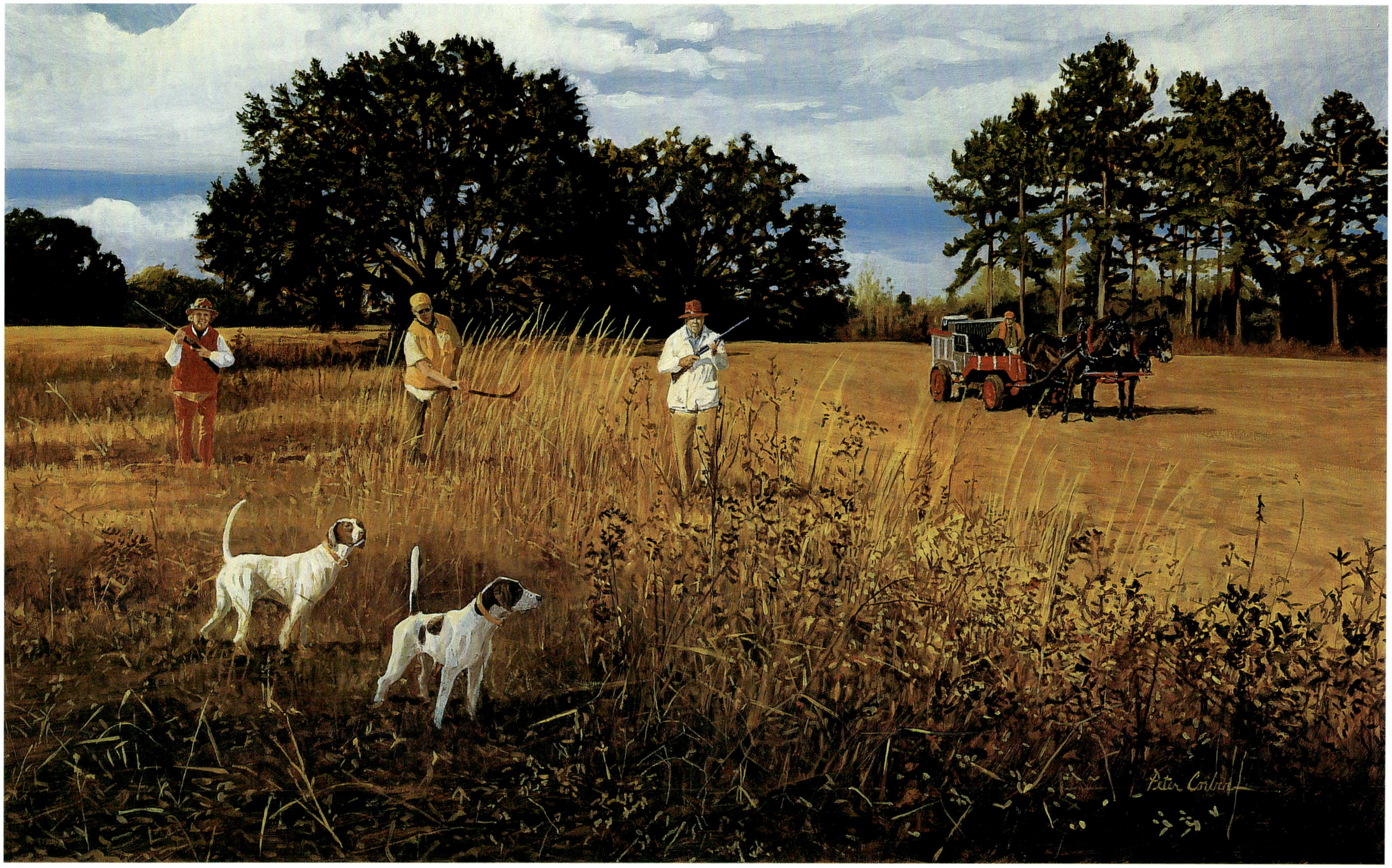

Loveridge Plantation, 2001
oil on canvas
24 × 40 inches
signed lower right

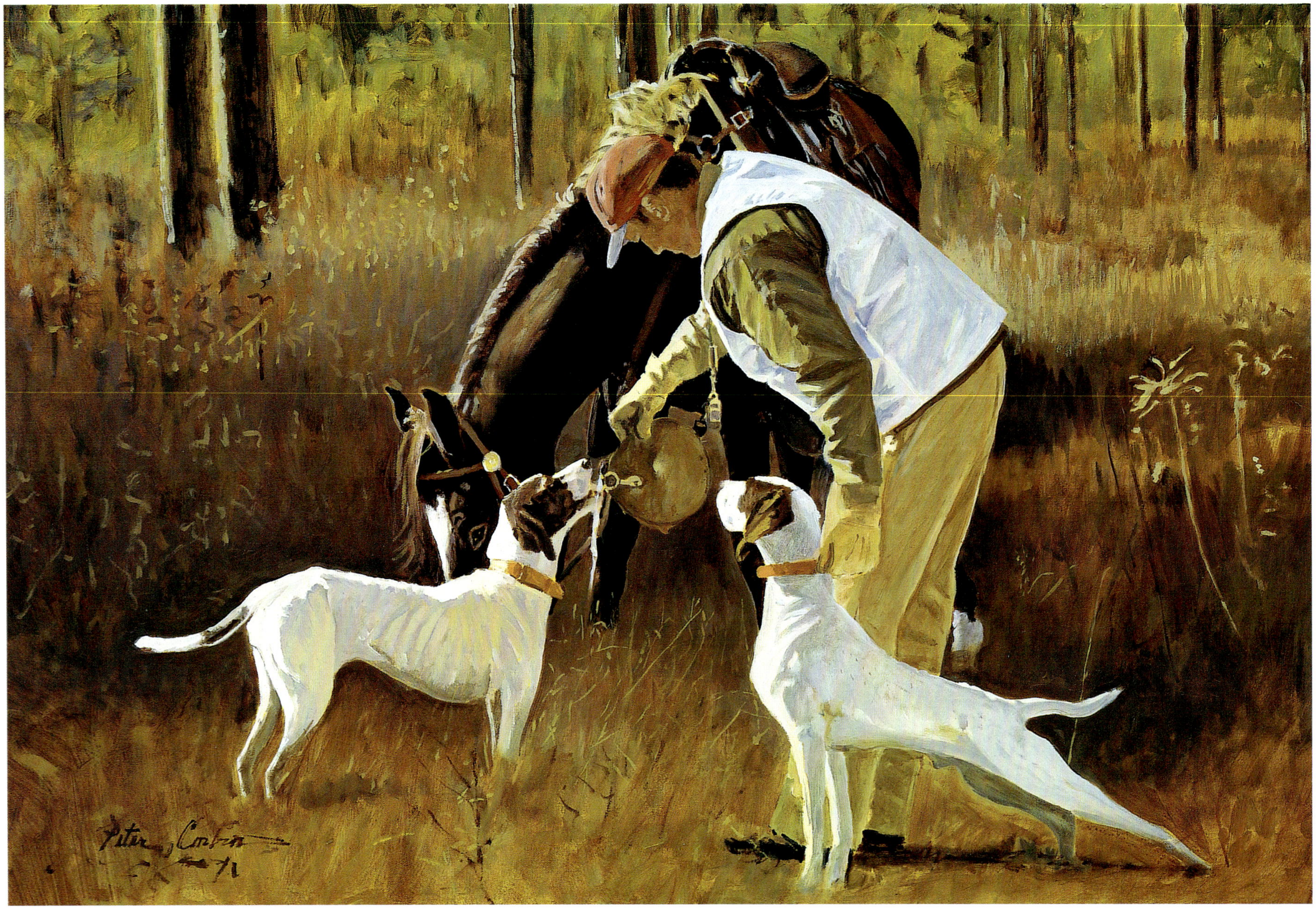

The Water Break, 2001
oil on canvas
20 × 30 inches
signed lower left

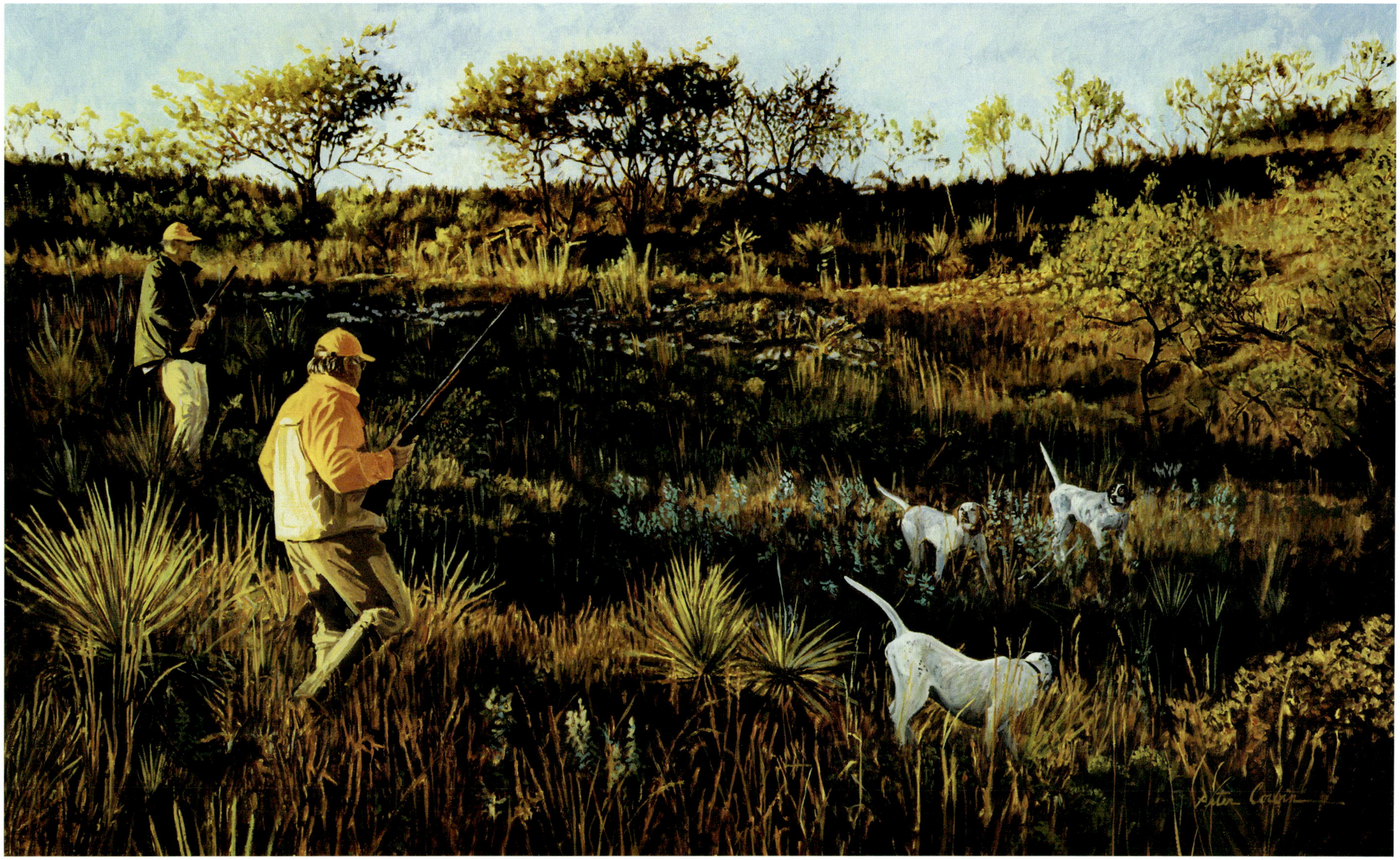

The Orange Coat, 2003
oil on canvas
24 × 40 inches
signed lower right

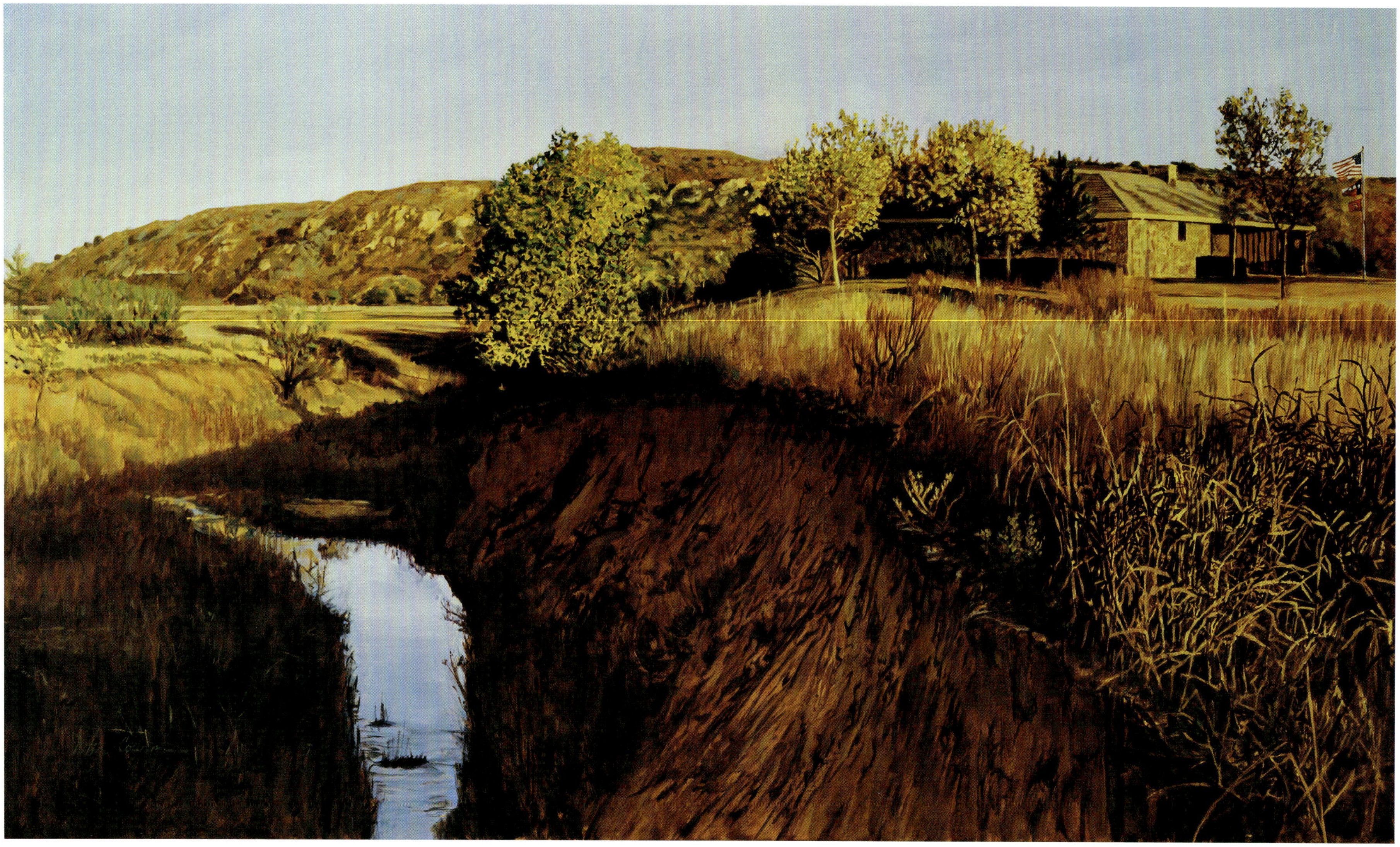

Elm Creek, 2003
oil on canvas
30 × 52 inches
signed lower left

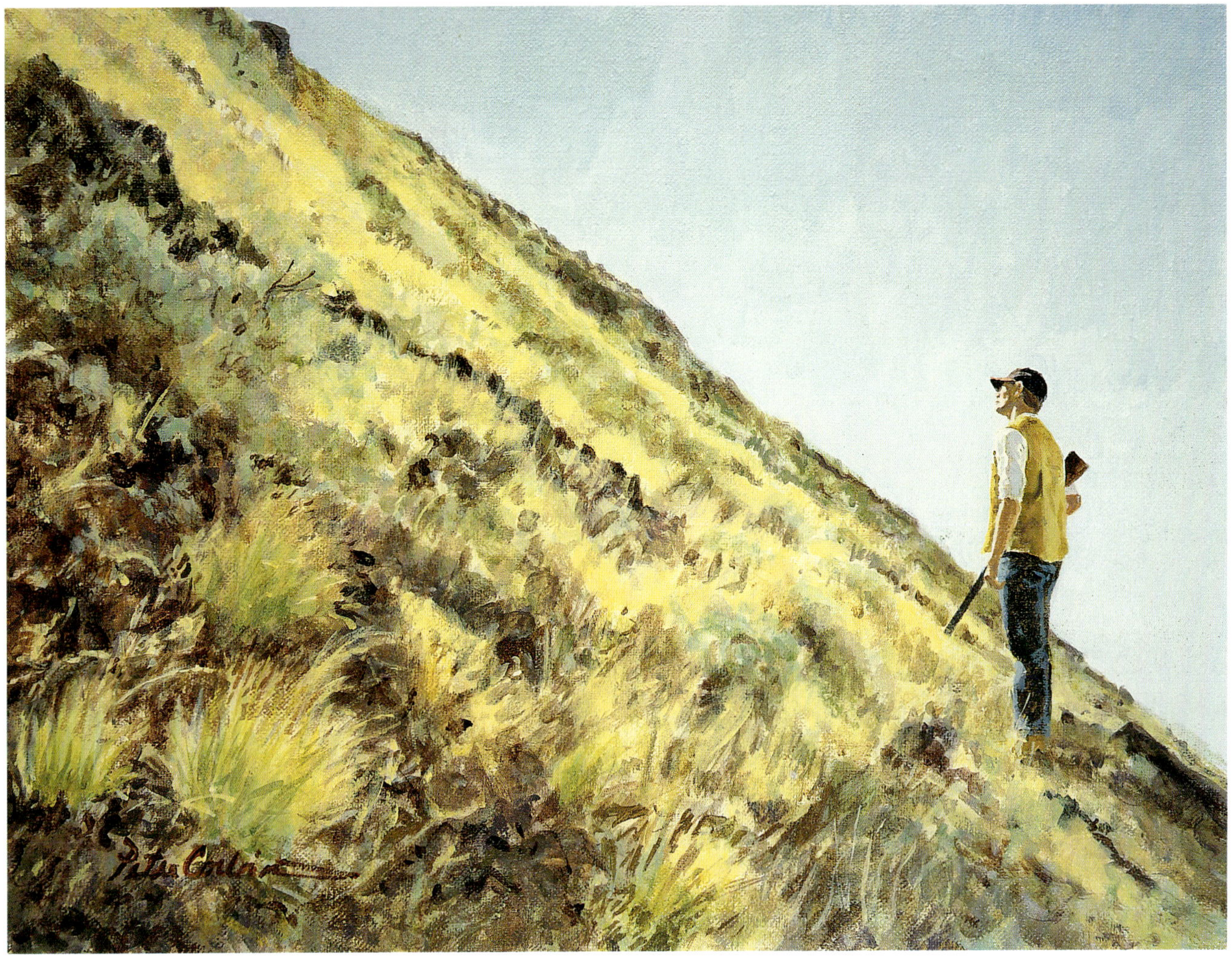

Chukar Hunter, 1992
acrylic on canvas
9 × 12 inches
signed lower left

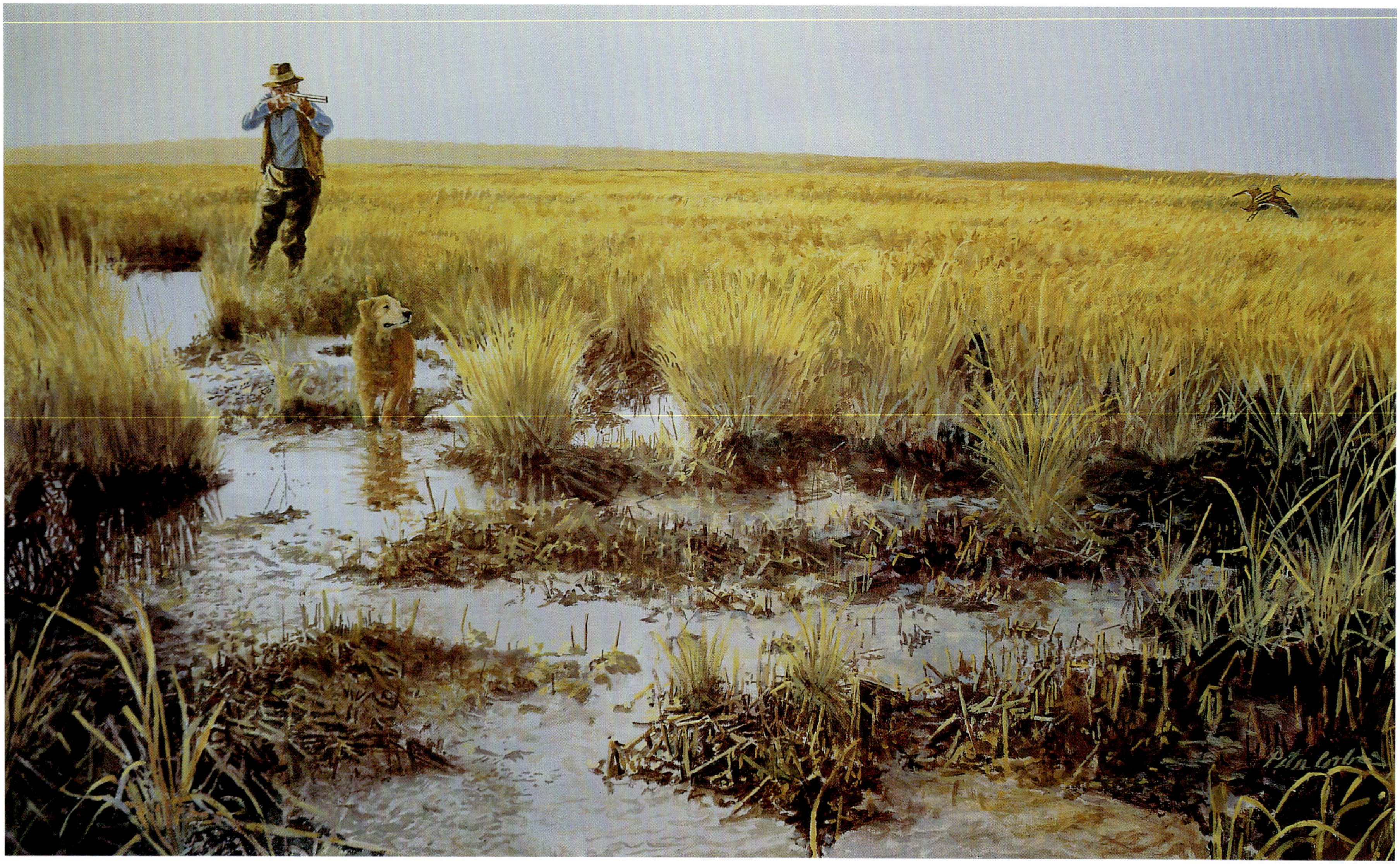

The Snipe Hunter, 1991
acrylic on canvas
20 × 36 inches
signed and dated lower right

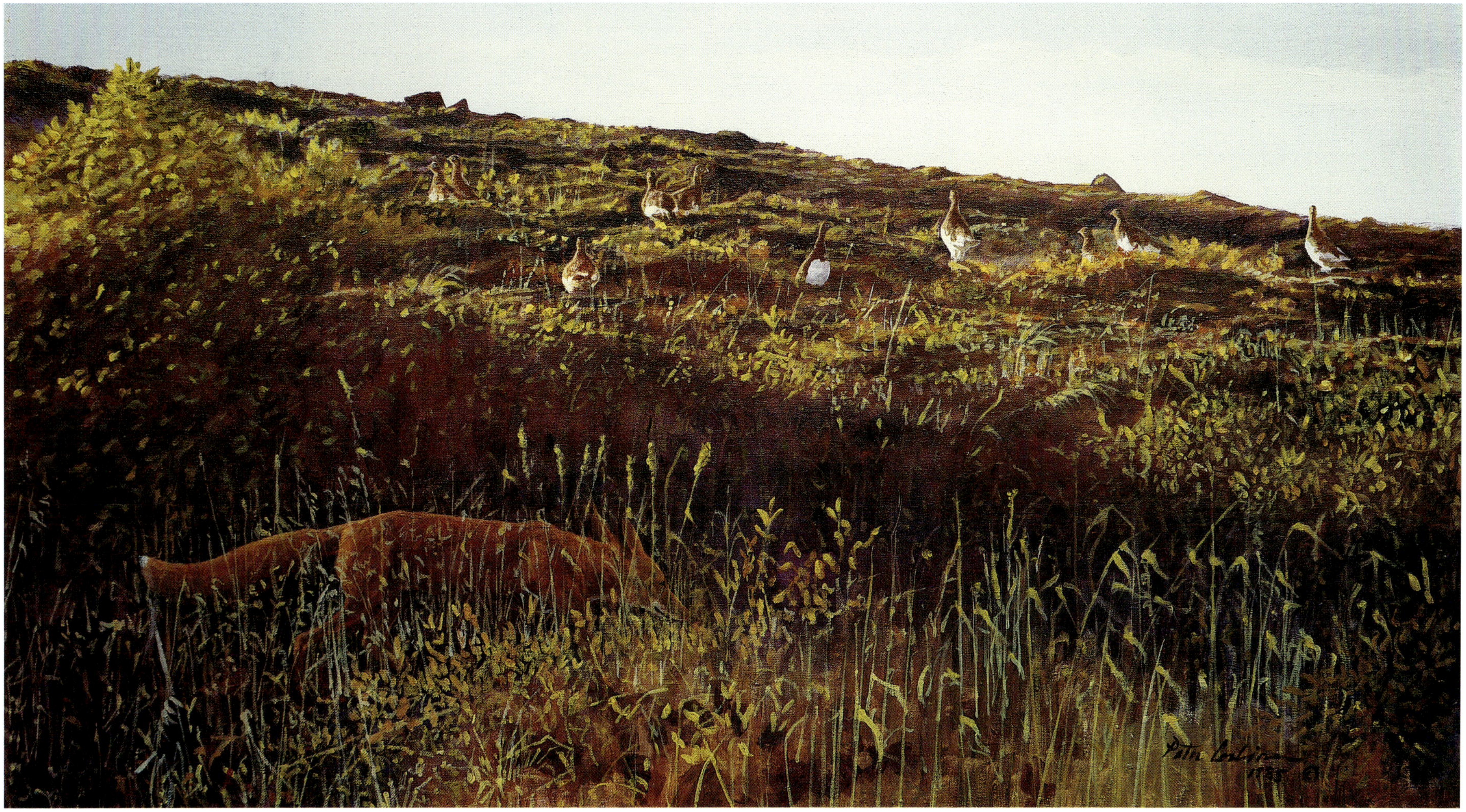

The Bird Hunter, 1985
acrylic on canvas
20 × 36 inches
signed and dated lower right

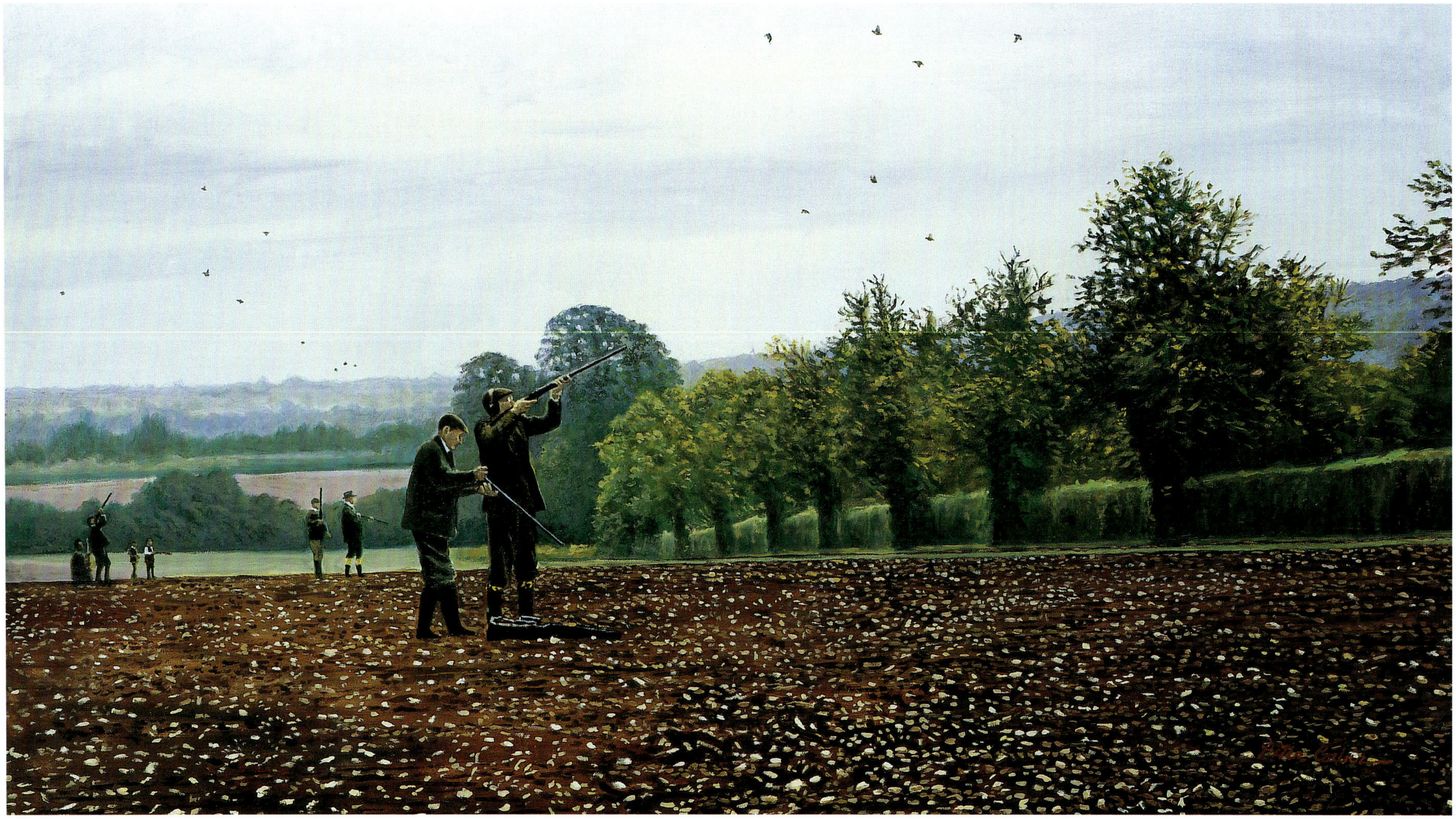

The Flint Field, 1998
oil on canvas
20 × 36 inches
signed and dated lower right

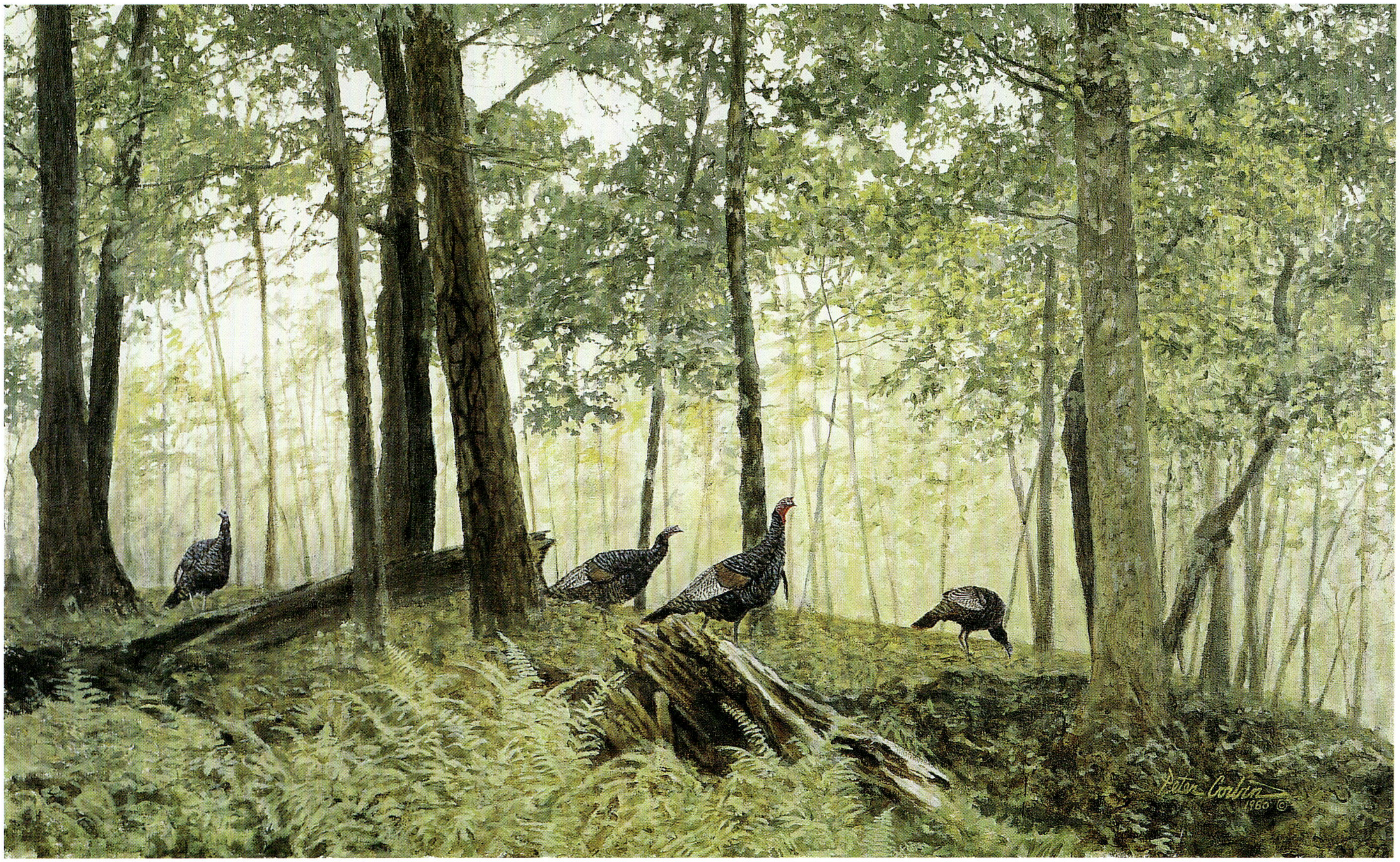

Morning Light, 1980
acrylic on canvas
24 × 40 inches
signed and dated lower right

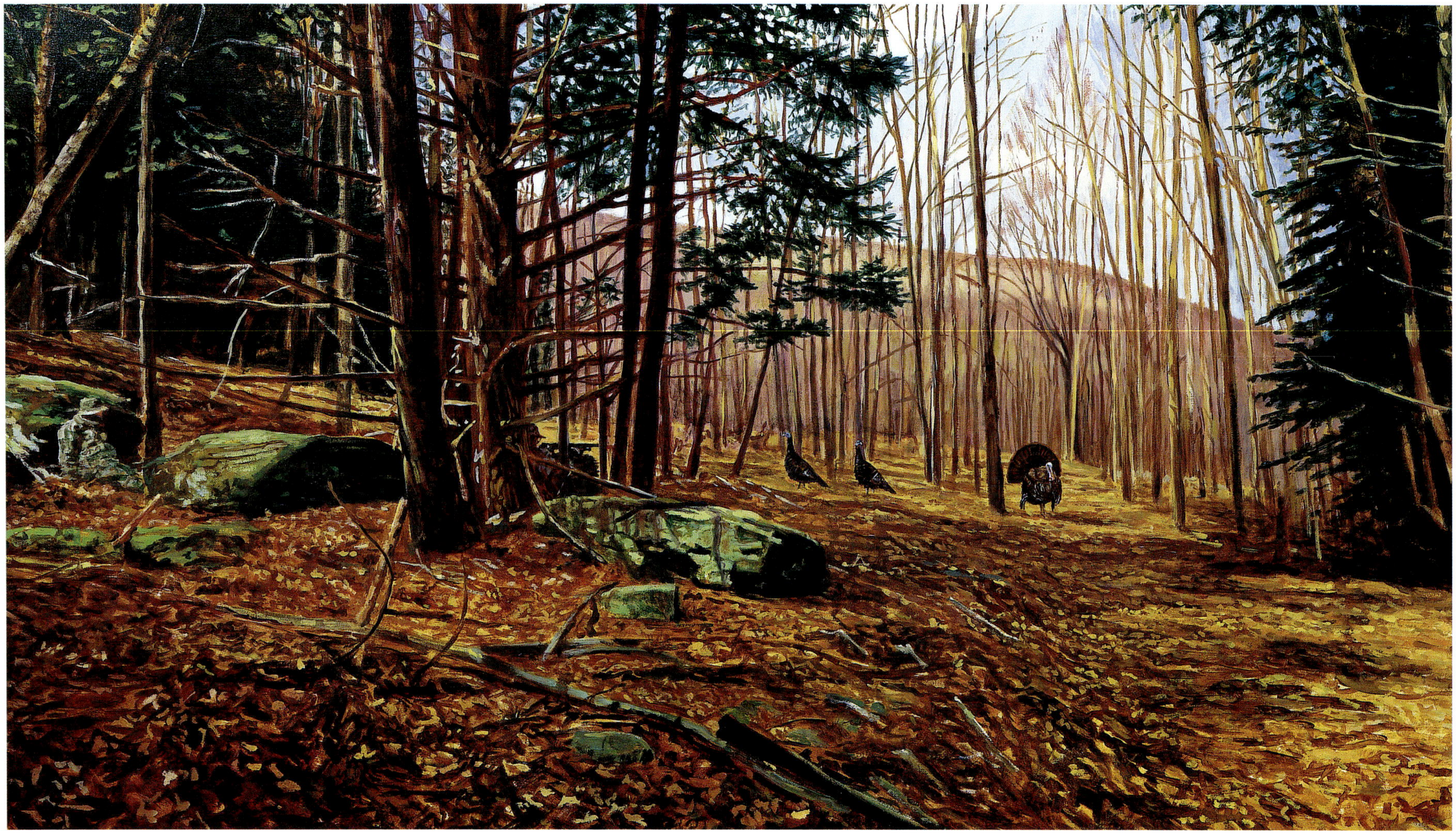

Best Bird, 1998
oil on canvas
20 × 36 inches
signed and dated lower left

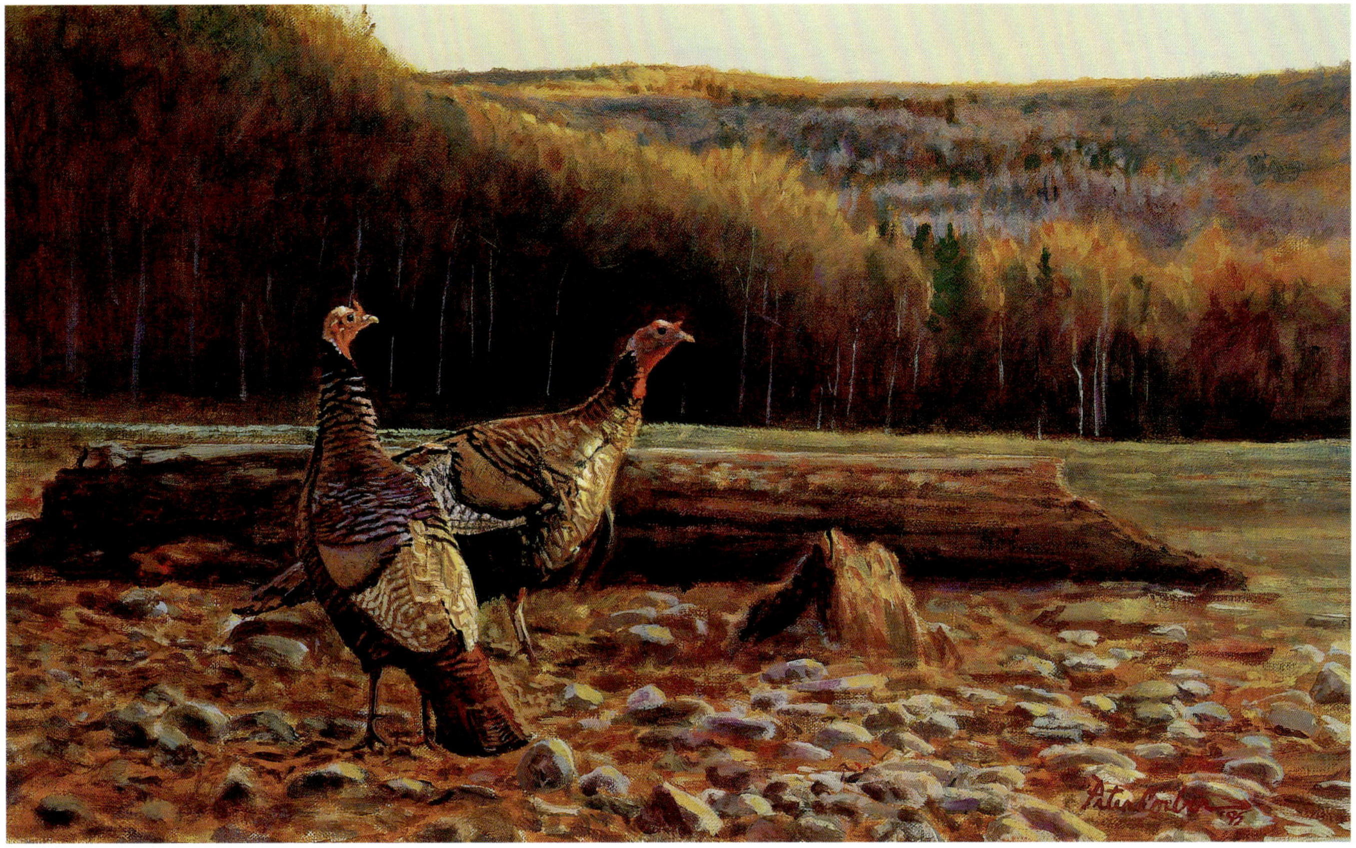

First Light—Turkeys, 1995
acrylic on canvas
12 × 20 inches
signed and dated lower right

Waterfowl

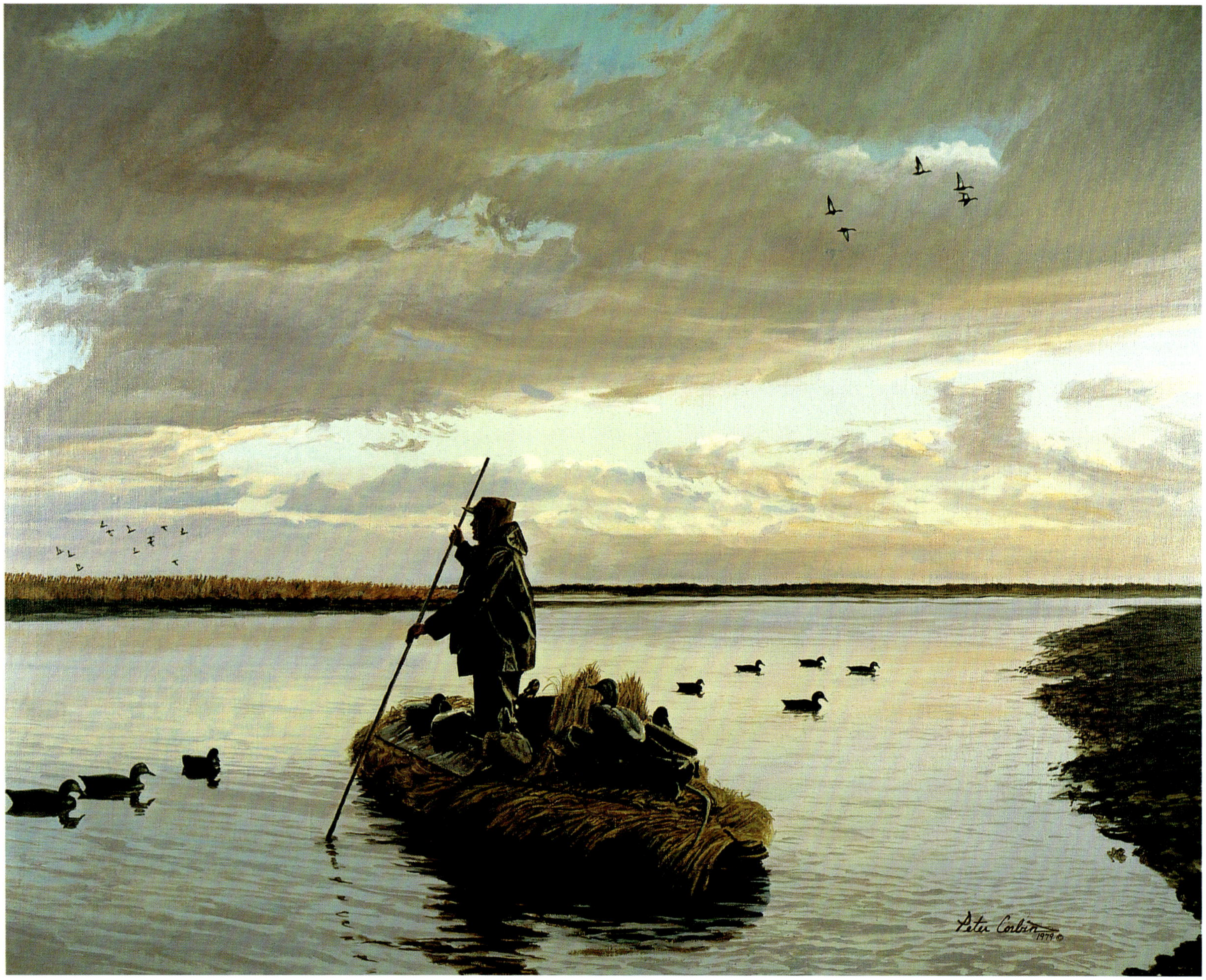

The Black Duck Gunner, 1979
acrylic on canvas
22 × 30 inches
signed and dated lower right

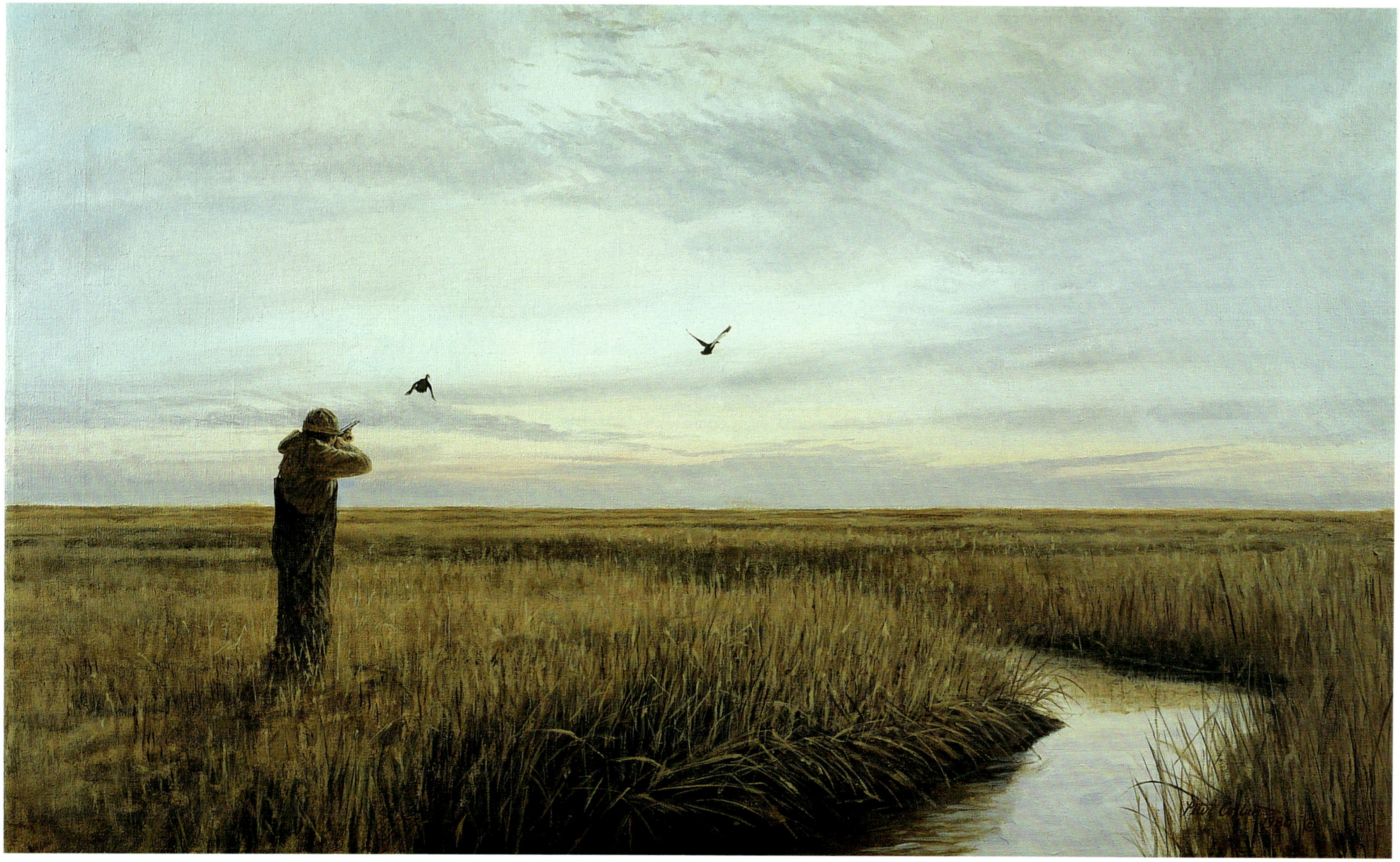

Jump Shooting, 1980
acrylic on canvas
24 × 40 inches
signed and dated lower right

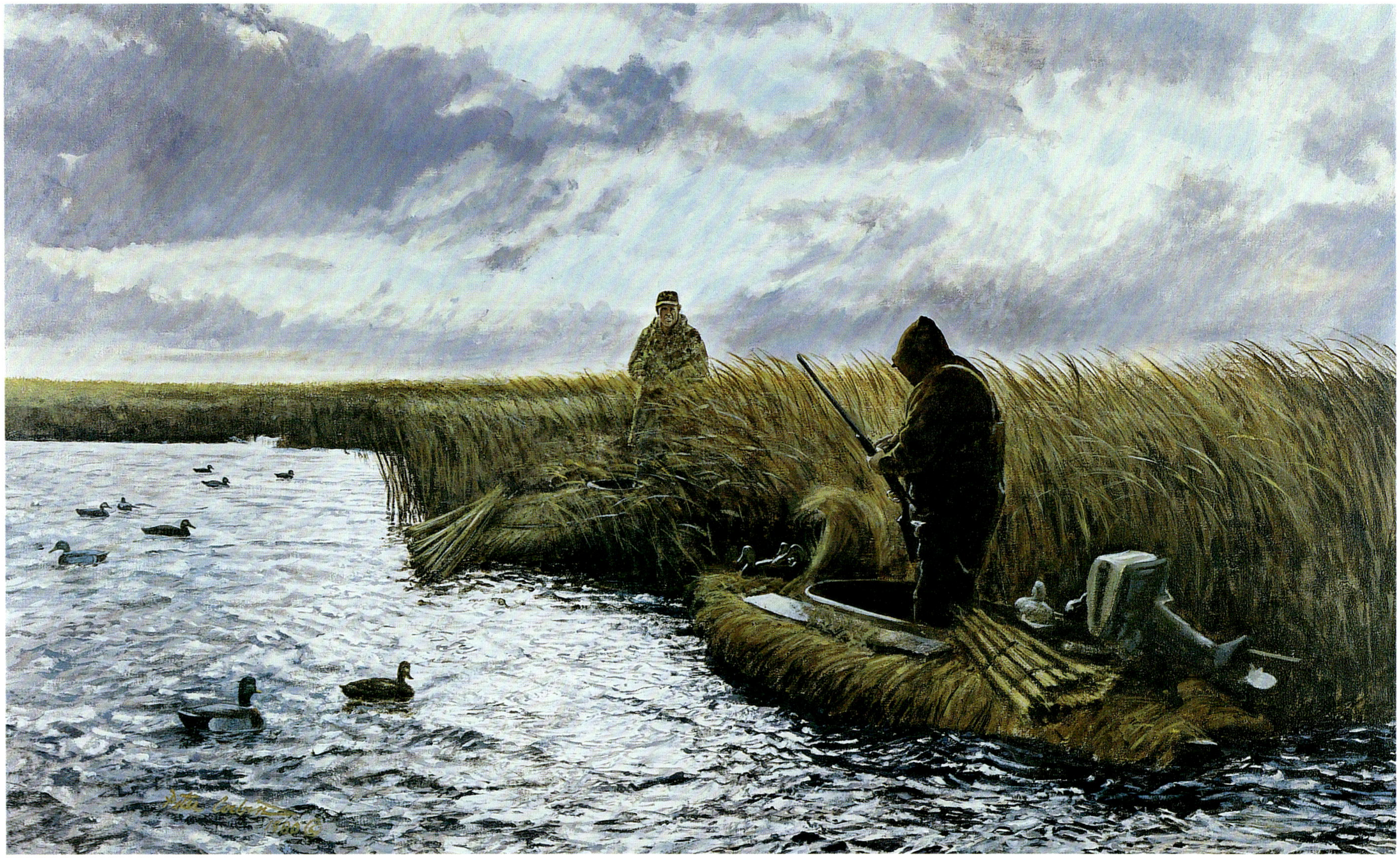

Gunning Partners, 1980
acrylic on canvas
24 × 40 inches
signed and dated lower left

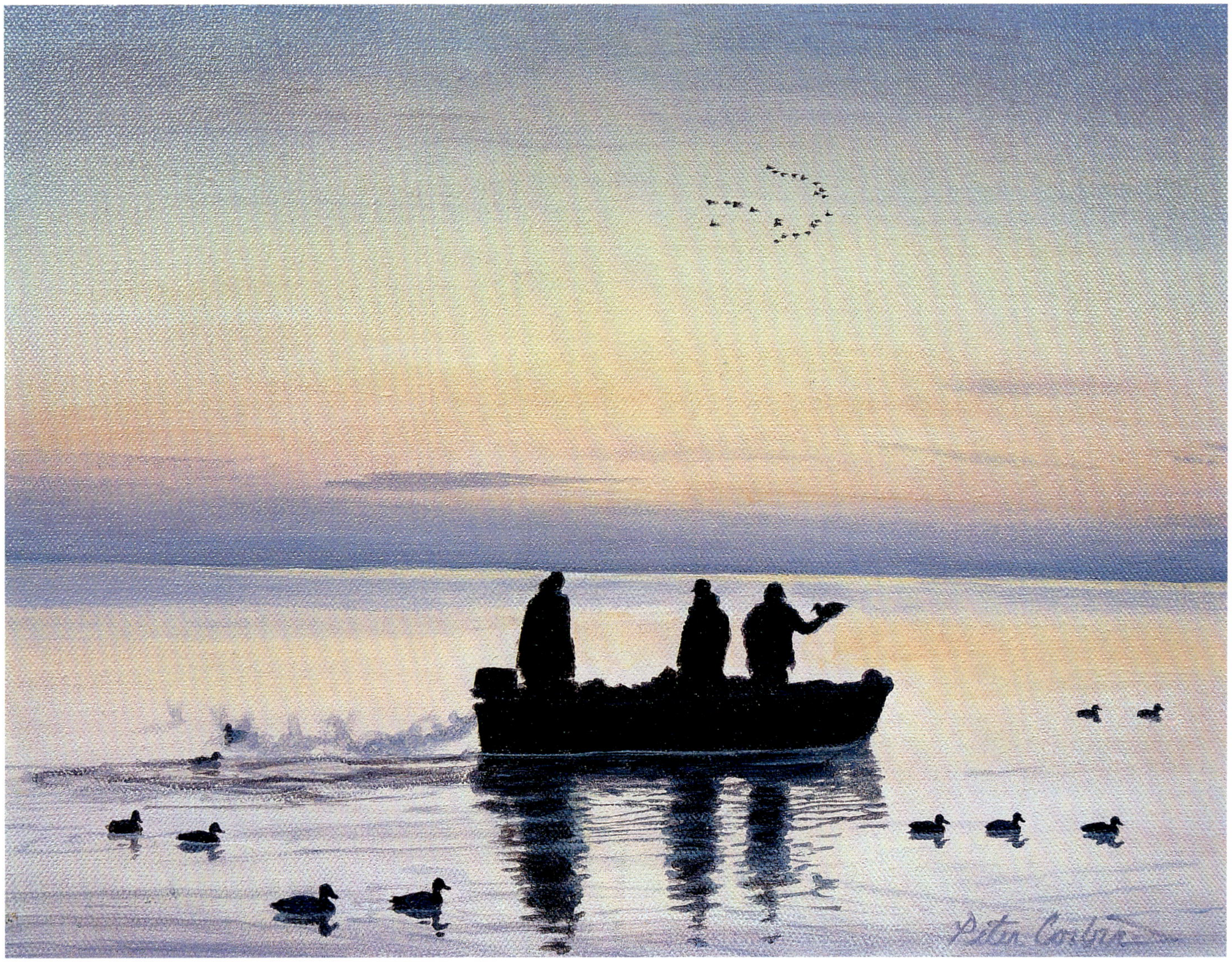

Setting the Rig, 1984
acrylic on canvas
9 × 12 inches
signed lower right

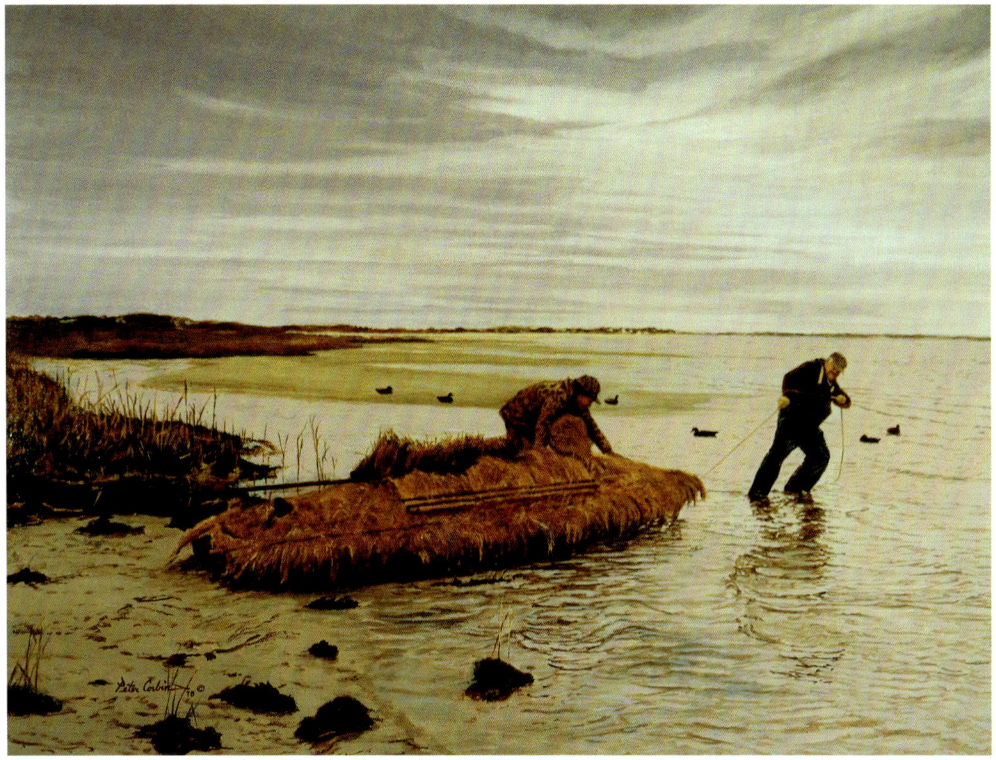

Tides Out, 1978
acrylic on canvas
22 × 30 inches
signed and dated lower left

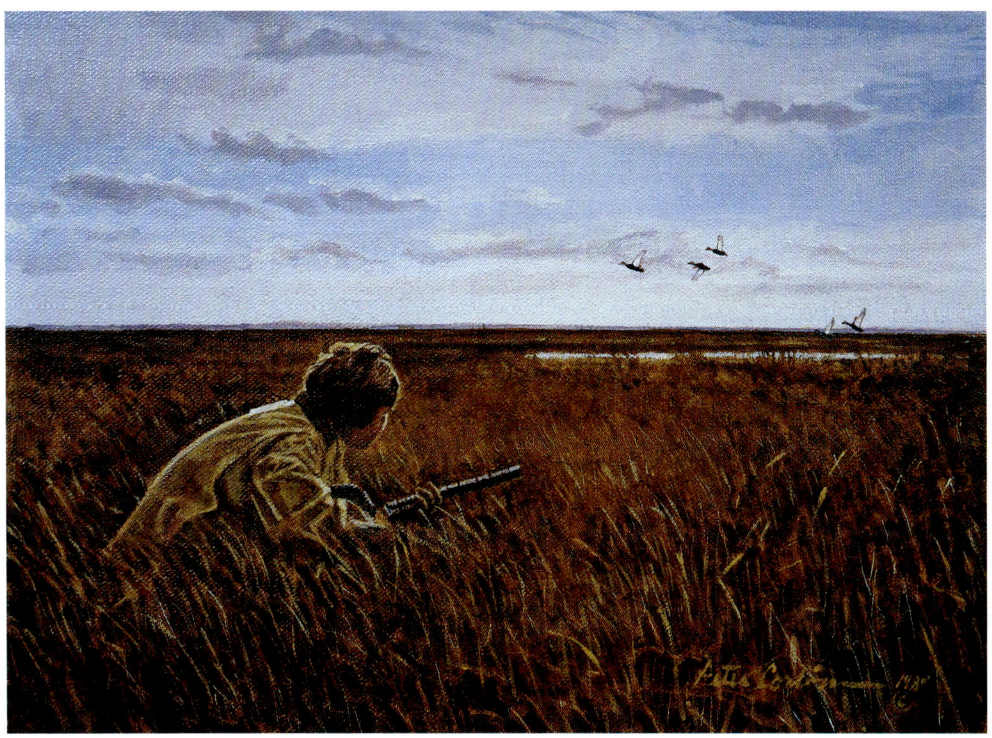

Hope Springs Eternal, 1984
acrylic on canvas
9 × 12 inches
signed and dated lower right

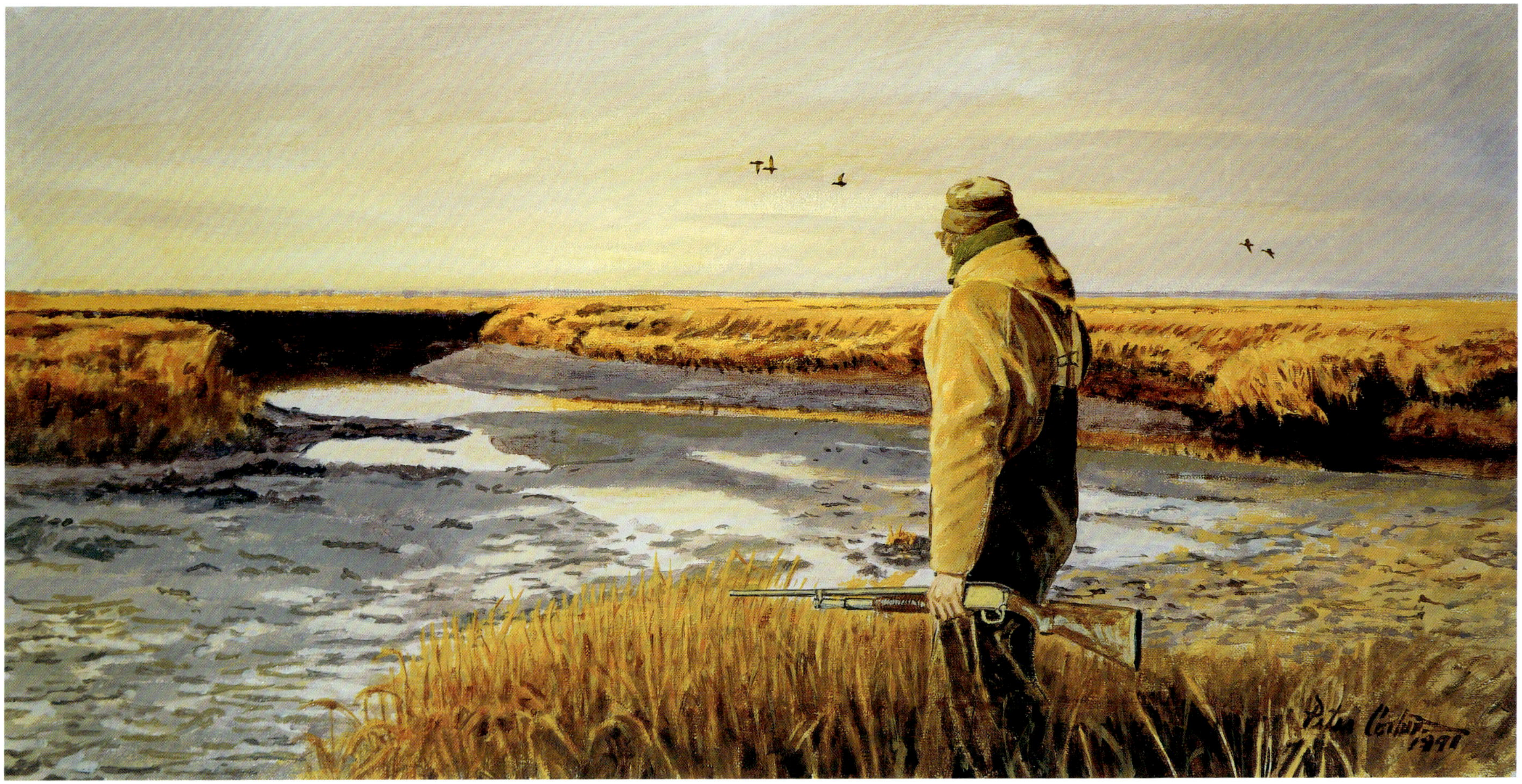

Salt Marsh Afternoon, 1991
acrylic on canvas
12 × 24 inches
signed and dated lower right

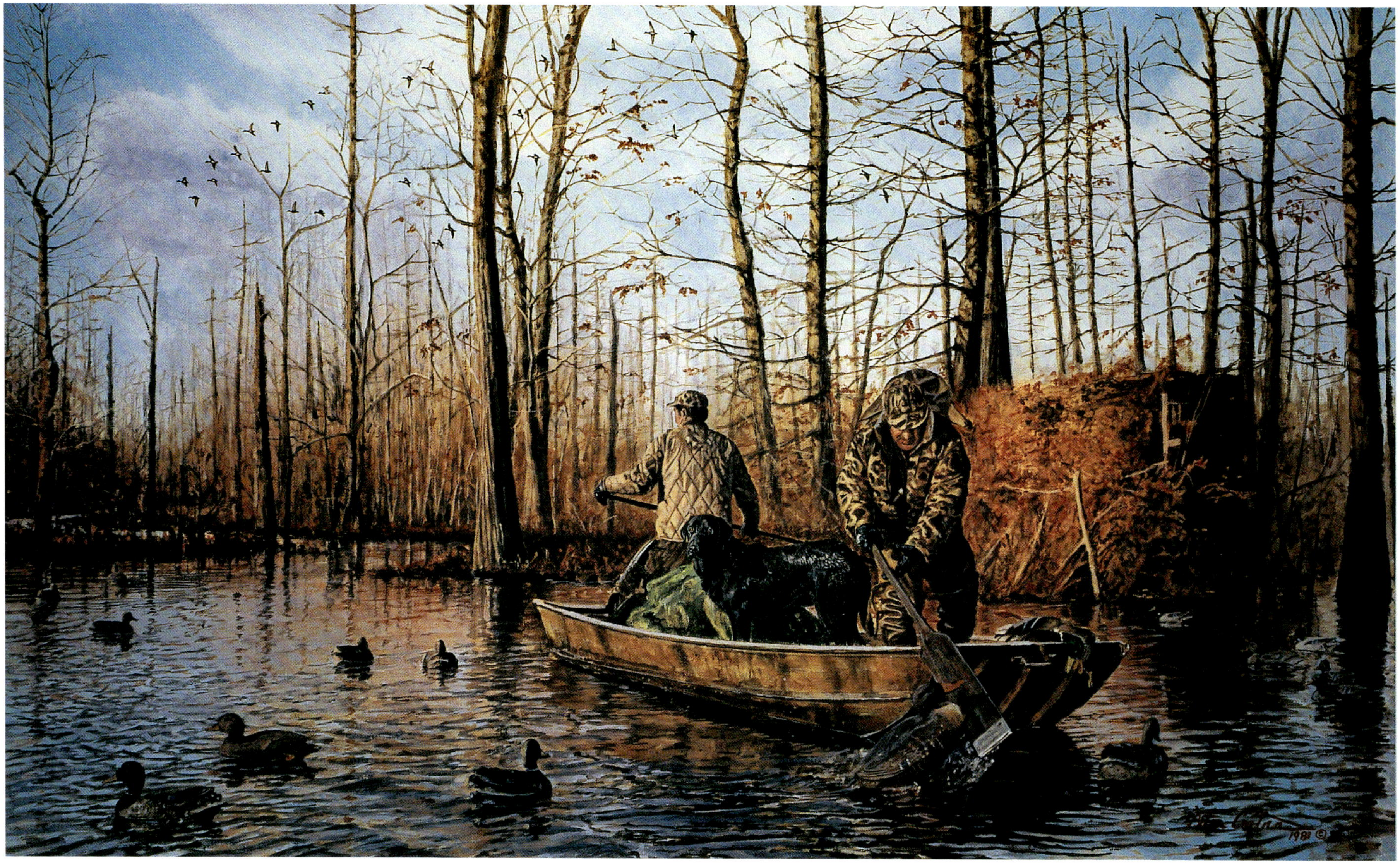

The Mallard Hunters, 1981
acrylic on canvas
24 × 40 inches
signed and dated lower right

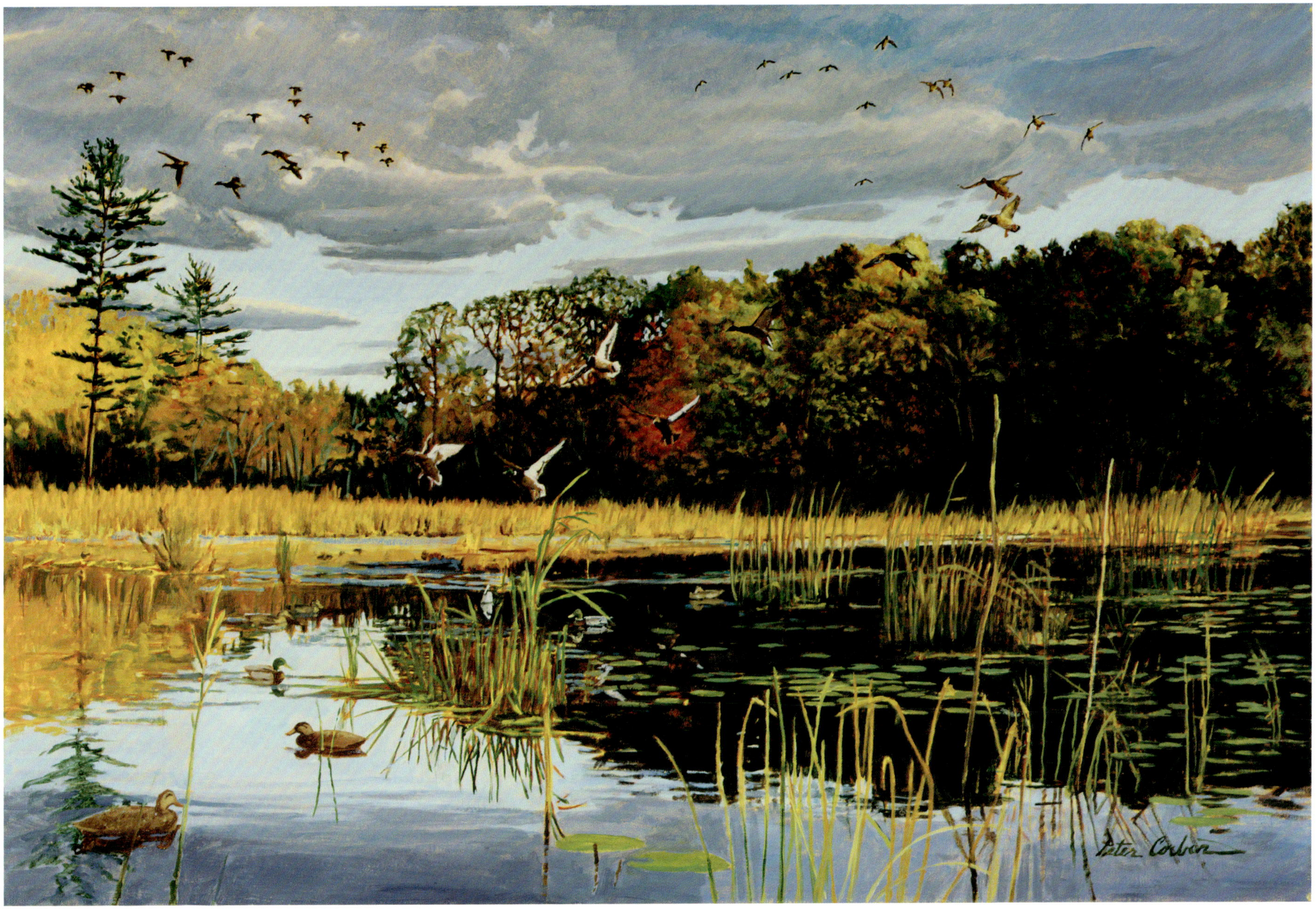

Flight Birds, 2003
oil on canvas
20 × 30 inches
signed lower right

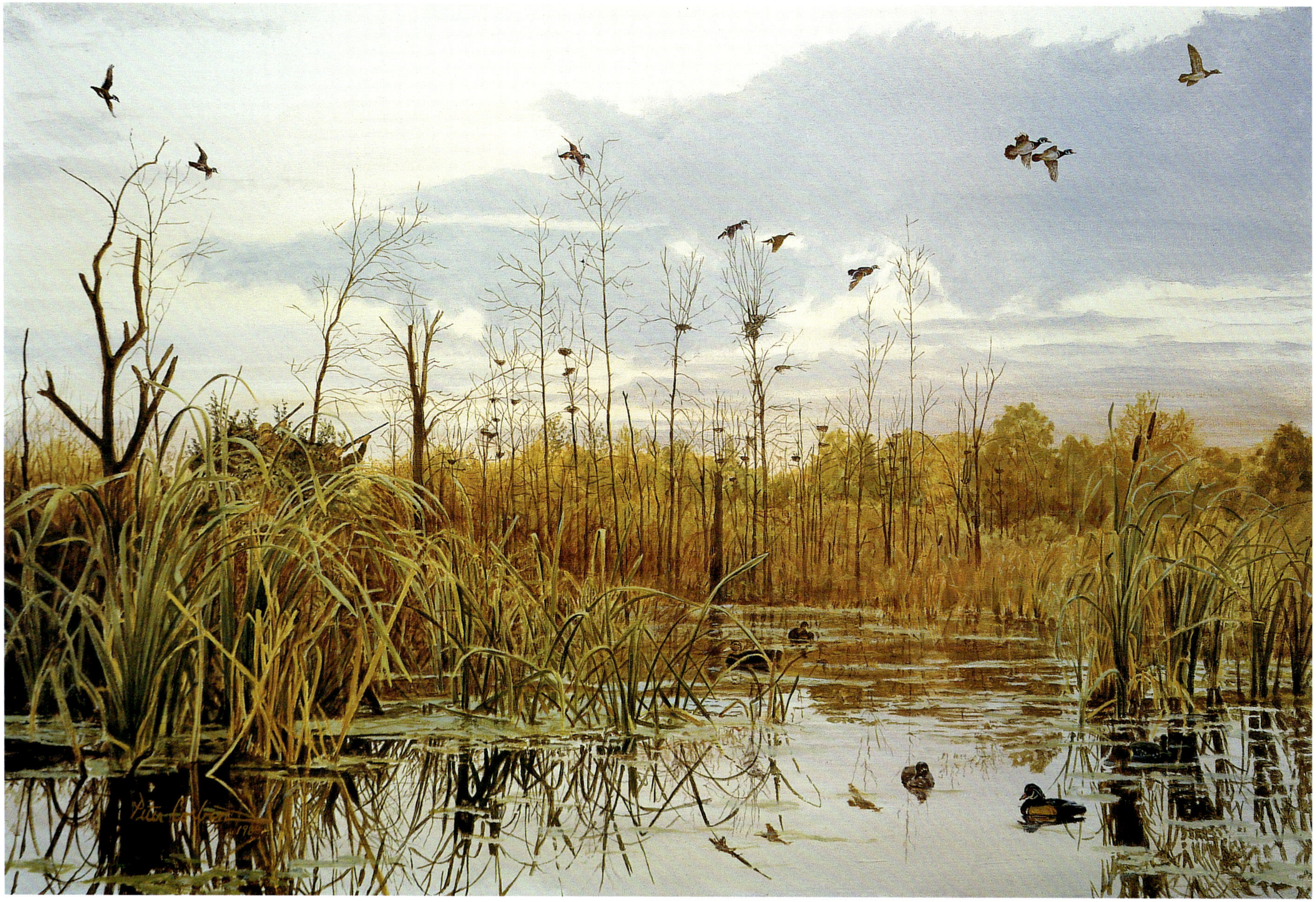

The Pothole—Wood Ducks, 1988
acrylic on canvas
24 × 36 inches
signed and dated lower left

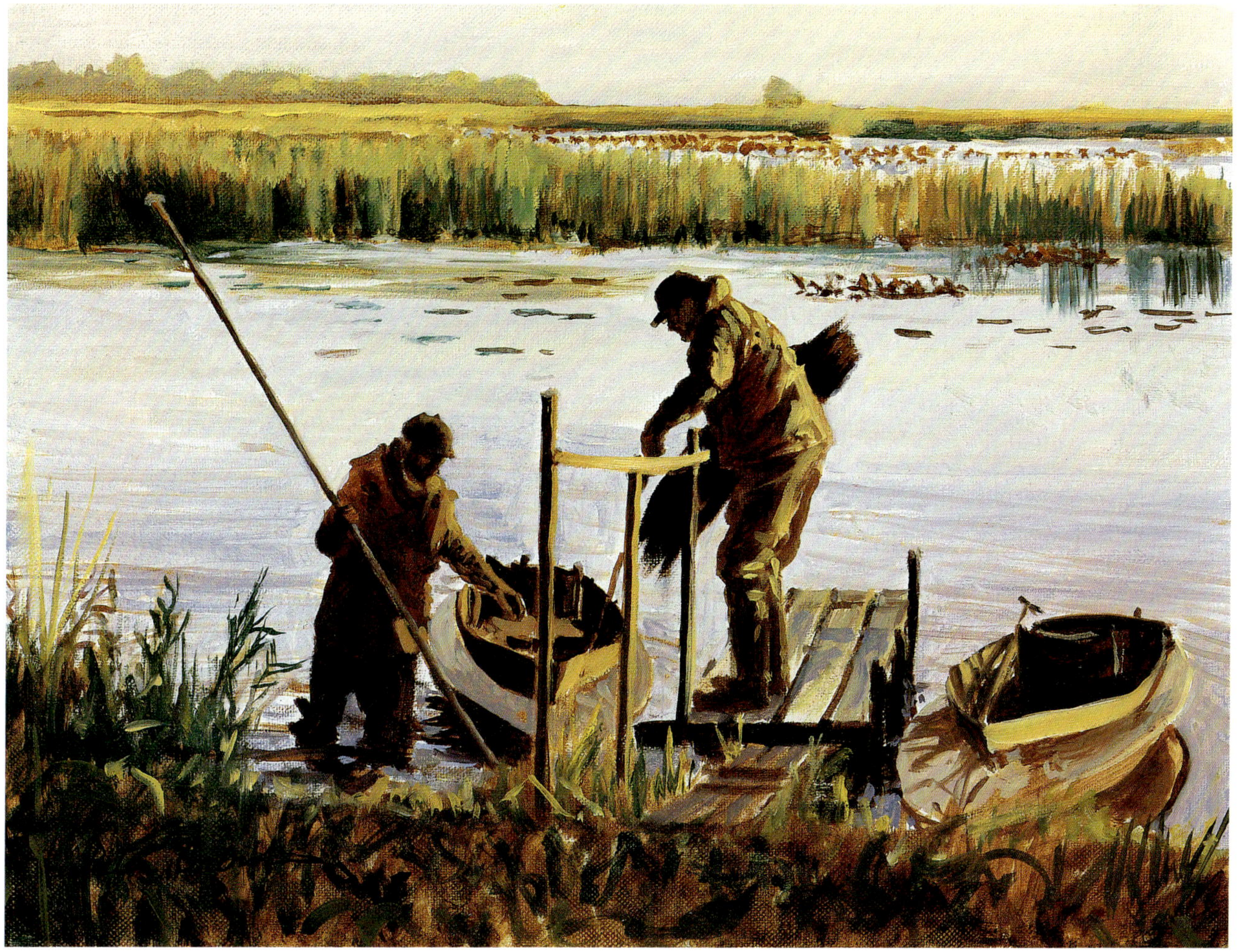

The Old Club Way, 1998
oil on canvas
9 × 12 inches
signed lower left

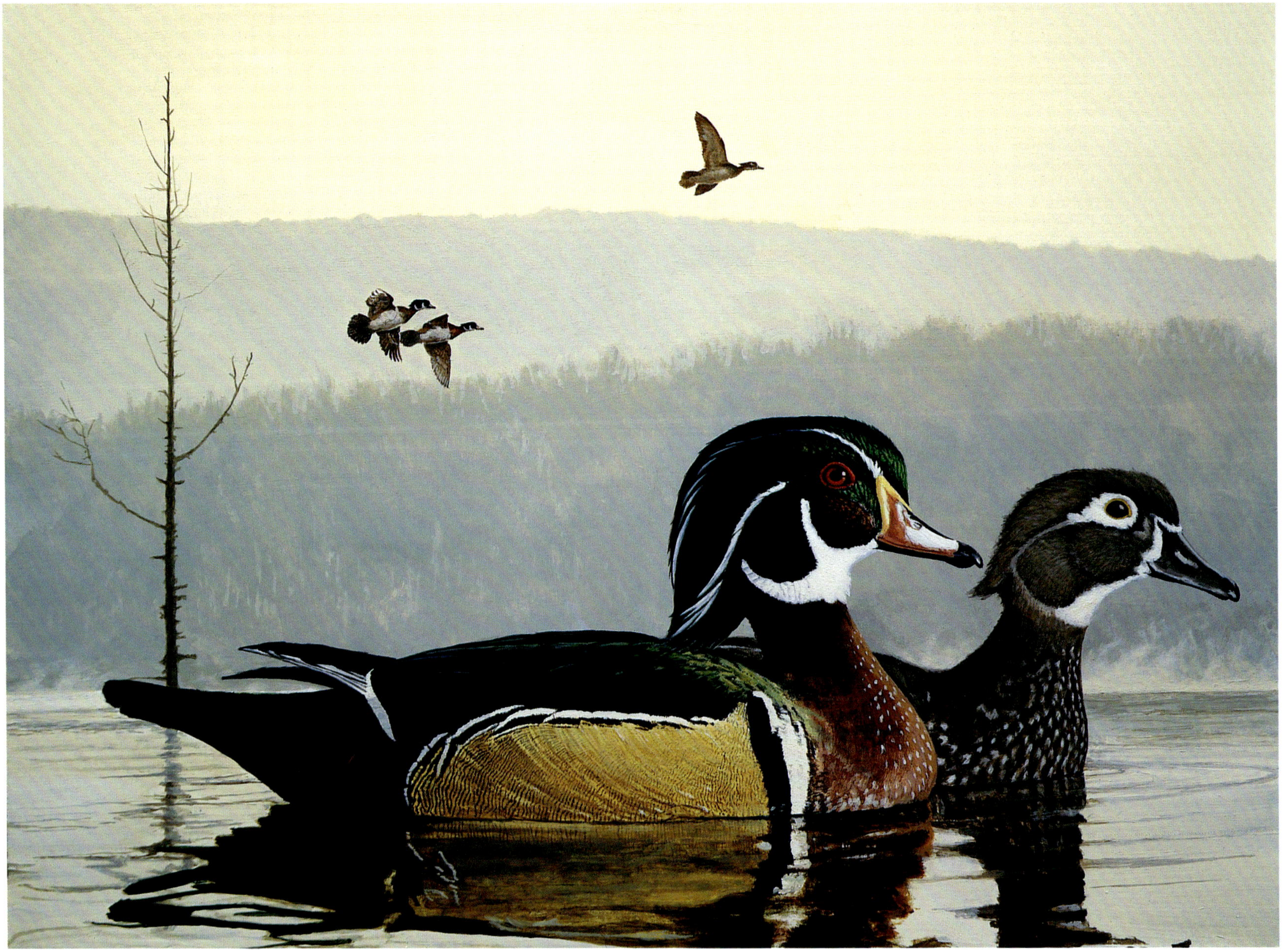

Wood Ducks, 1986
acrylic on masonite
13 × 18 inches
signed on back, duck stamp entry

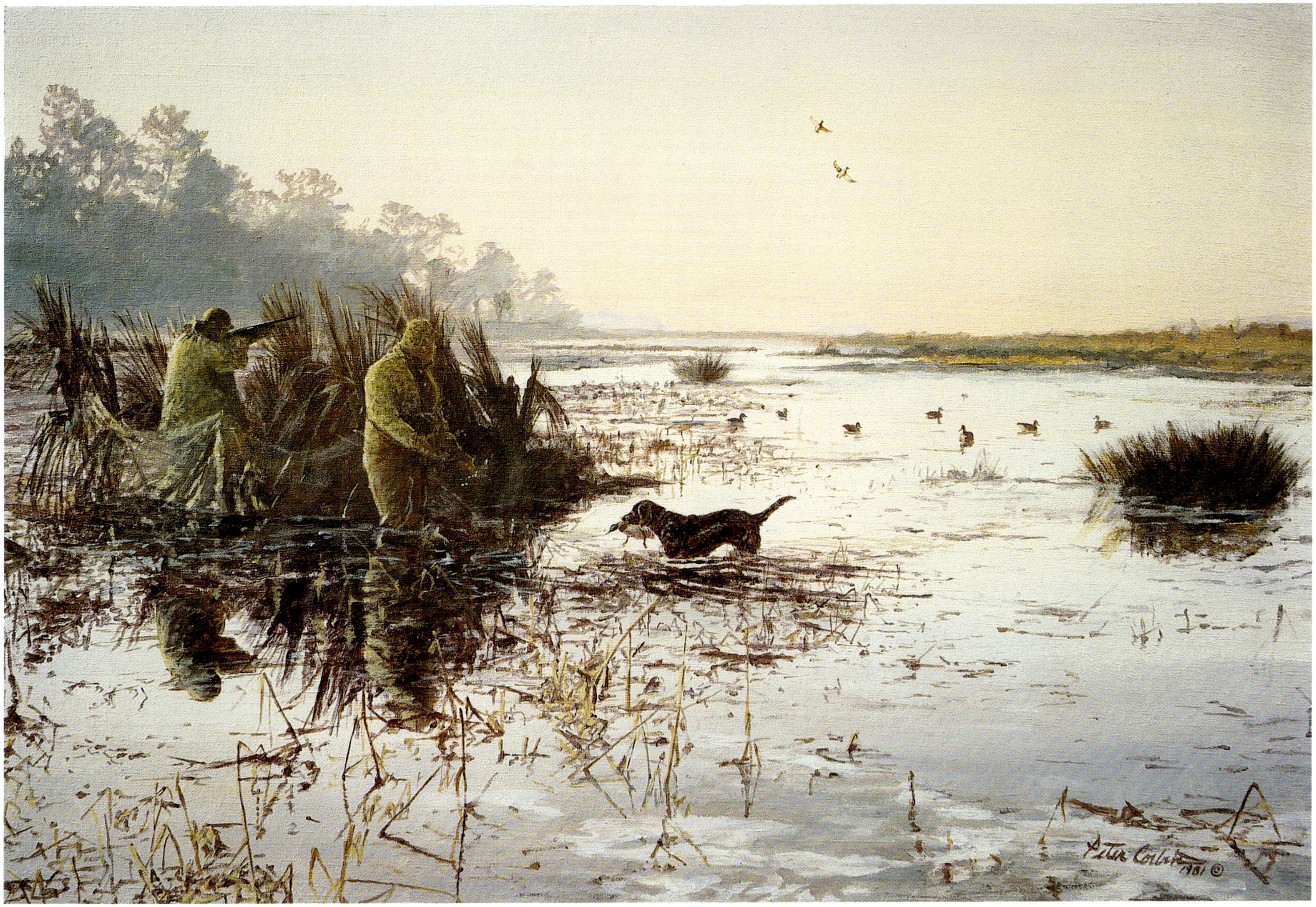

The Palmetto Blind, 1981
acrylic on canvas
20 × 30 inches
signed and dated lower right

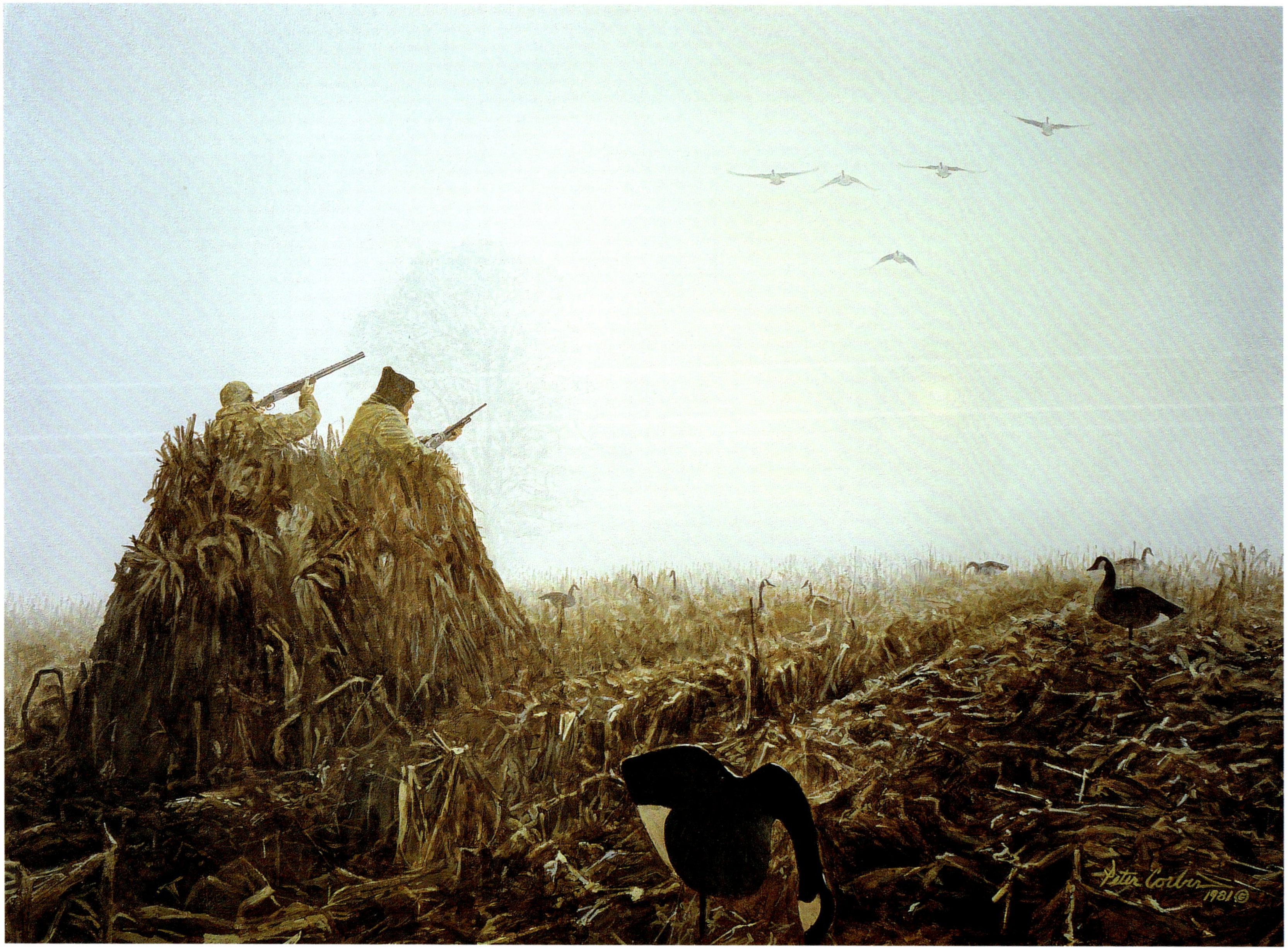

Out of Morning Mist, 1981
acrylic on canvas
30 × 48 inches
signed and dated lower right

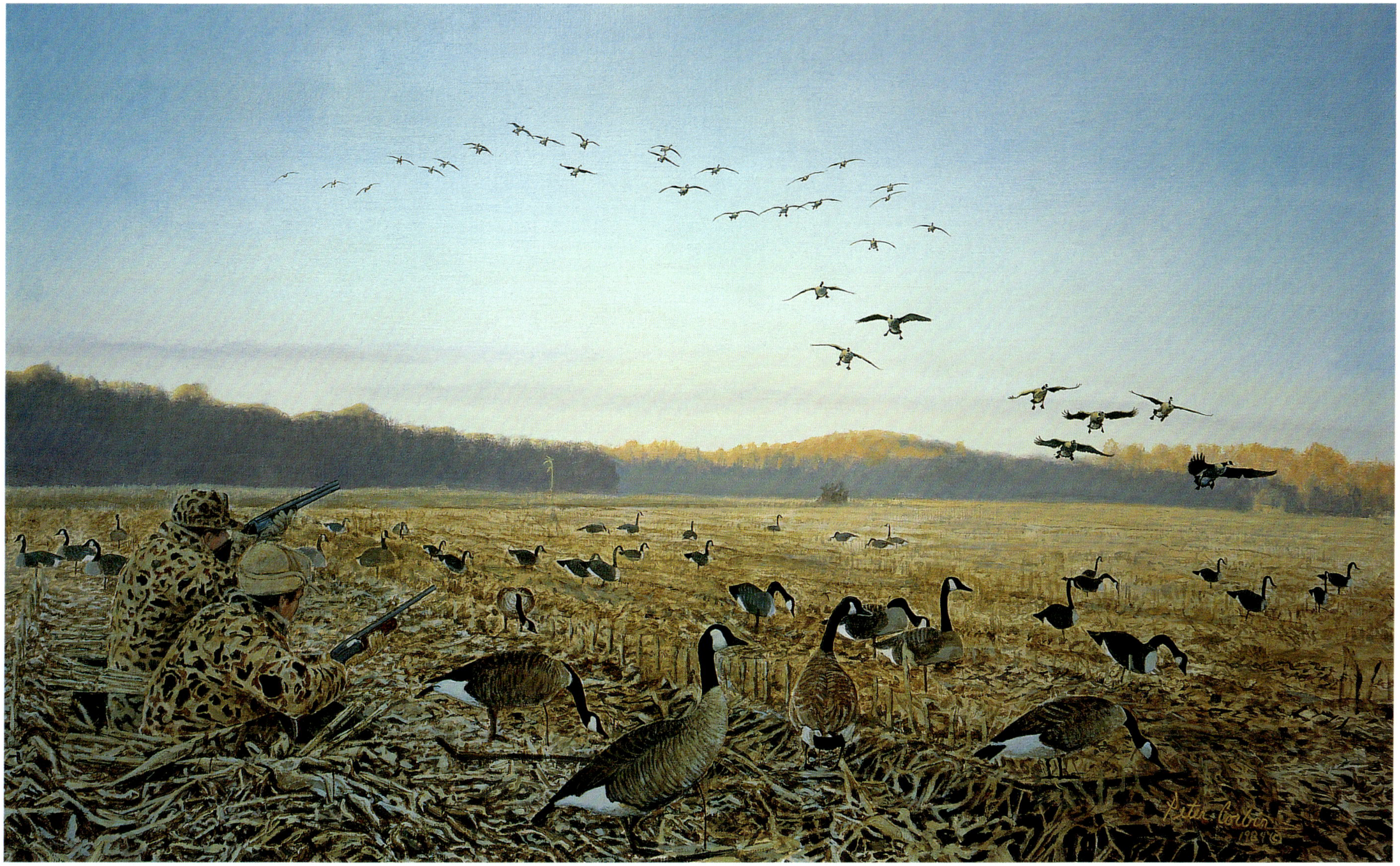

The Field Hunters, 1984
acrylic on canvas
24 × 40 inches
signed and dated lower right

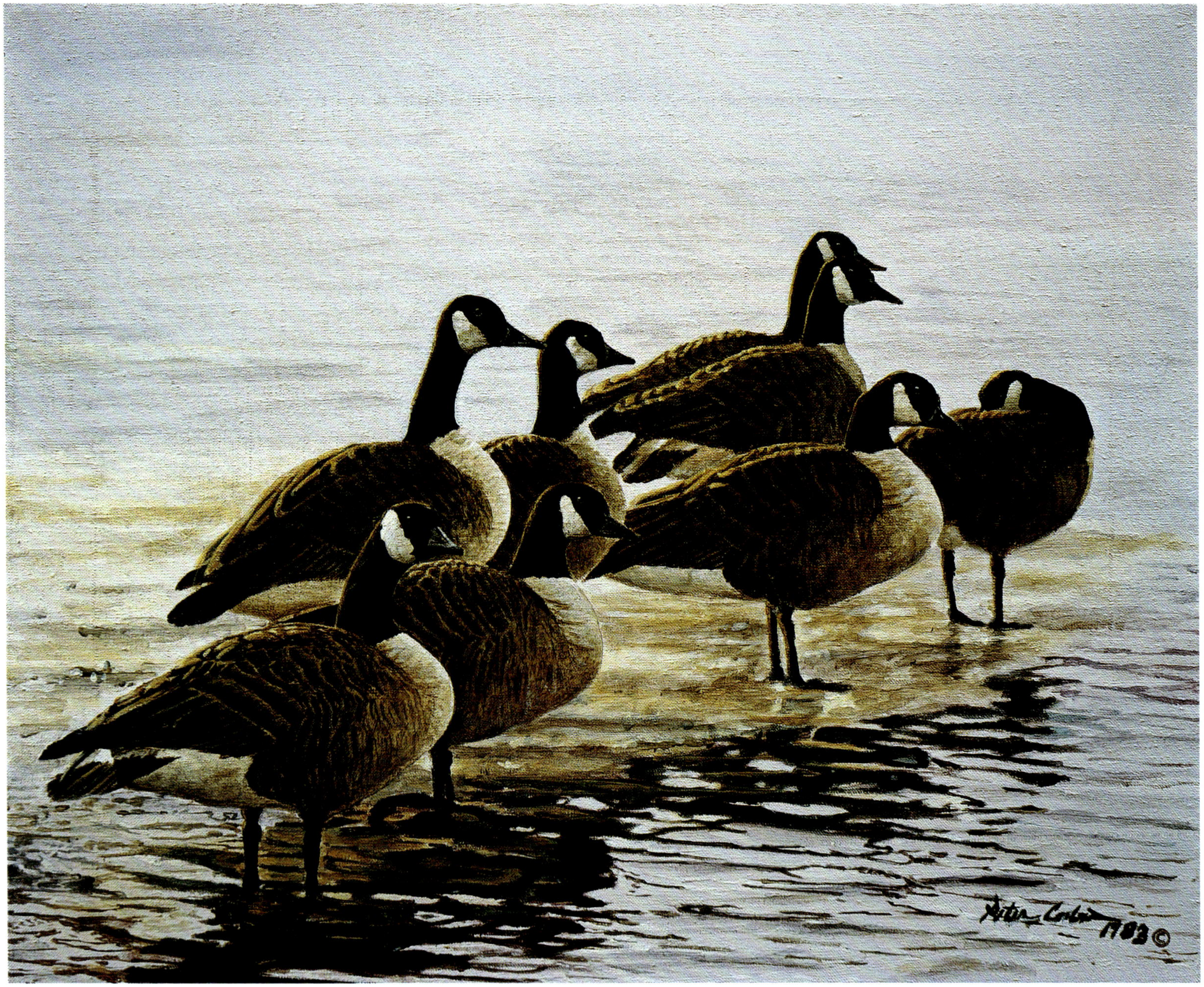

Edge of the Iceflow, 1983
acrylic on canvas
16 × 22 inches
signed and dated lower right

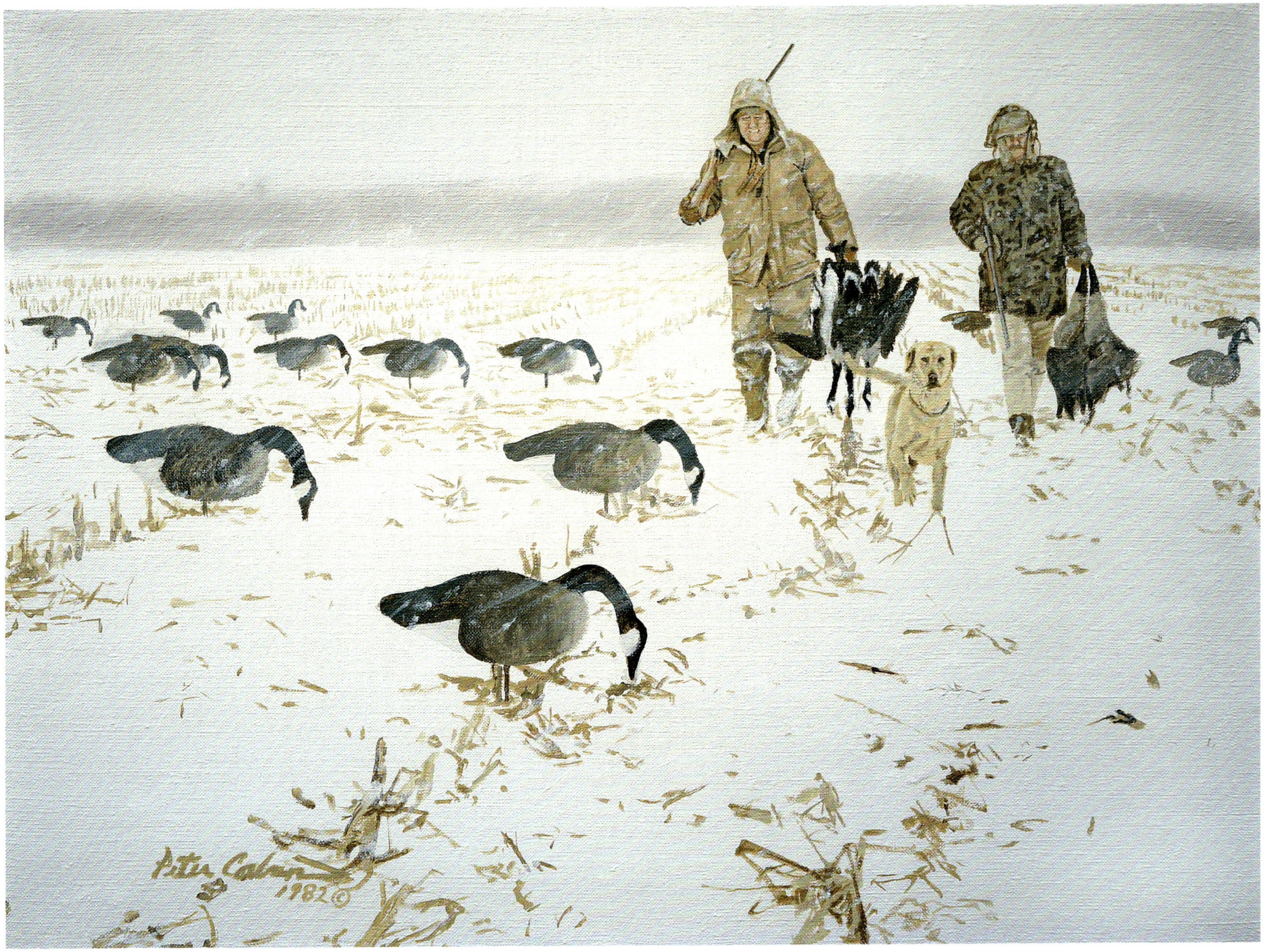

Bad Weather, Good Luck, 1982
acrylic on canvas
16 x 22 inches
signed and dated lower left

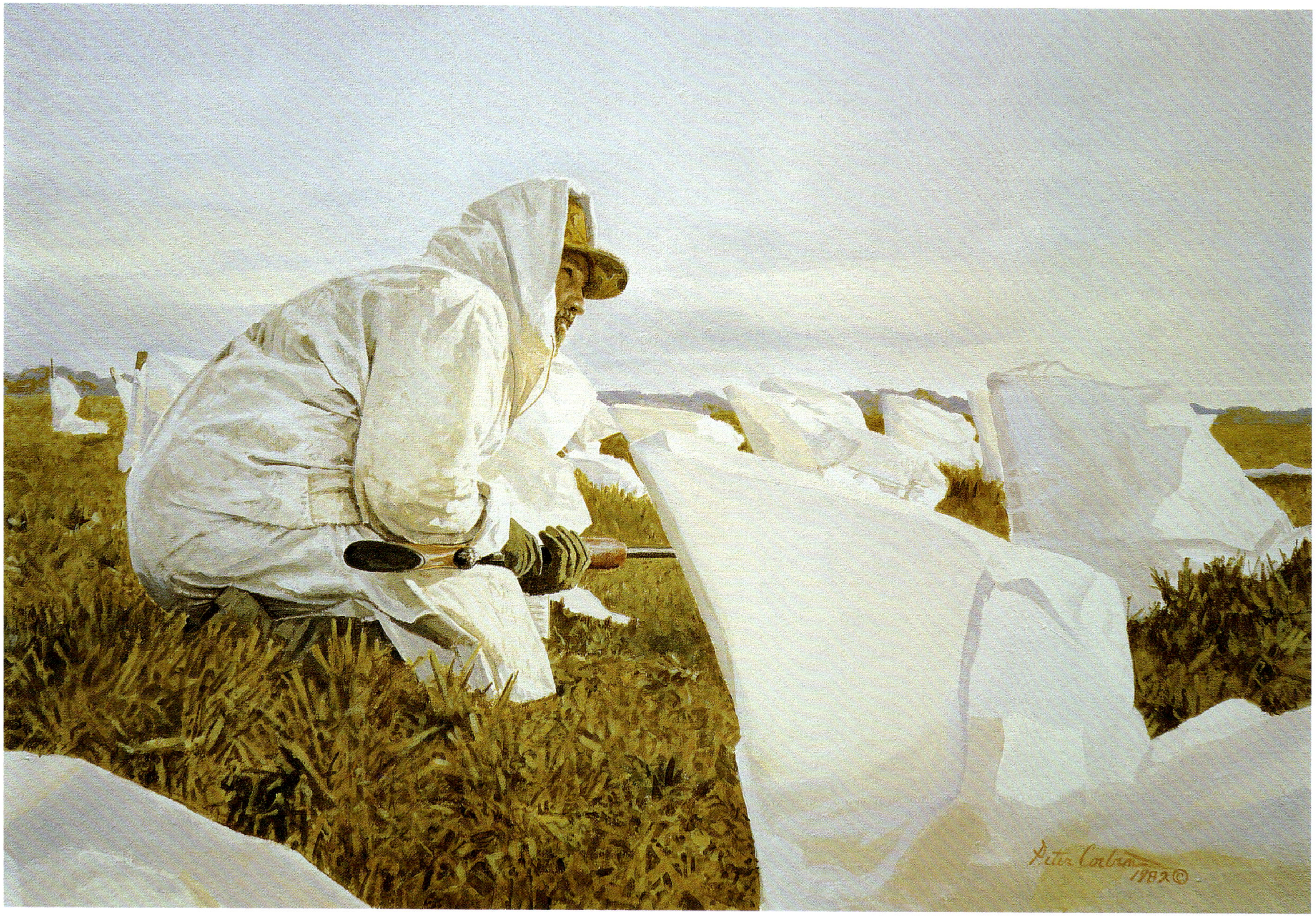

Study in White, 1982
acrylic on canvas
20 × 30 inches
signed and dated lower right

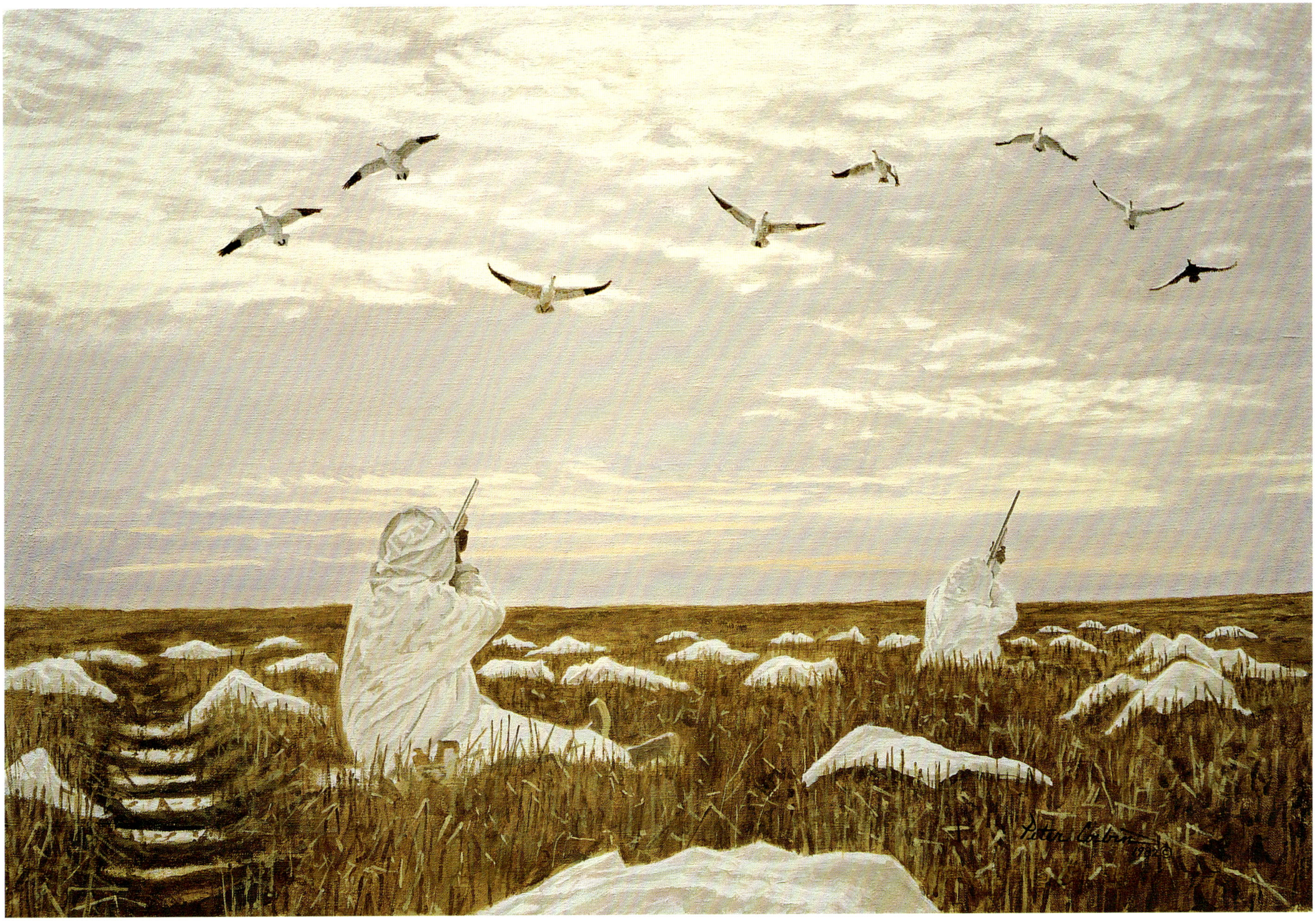

Just Right, 1982
acrylic on canvas
20 × 30 inches
signed and dated lower right

Equine & Portraits

When asked if I painted portraits, I often replied, "Yes, but mostly from the back or side. I don't like looking down a twelve-gauge."

Over the years I have painted a number of portraits of both field scenes and more formal intimate scenes. What I like to do most is record my subject's love of the place they have created or the sport they have chosen. The blessing of my work is that I have been allowed to visit many wonderful places; it is a great privilege to see these salmon rivers, plantations, and camps. I have met an array of amazing individuals of great achievement in environments where they are usually at their relaxed best as they show me what they treasure most about their lives. It is my job to capture that passion.

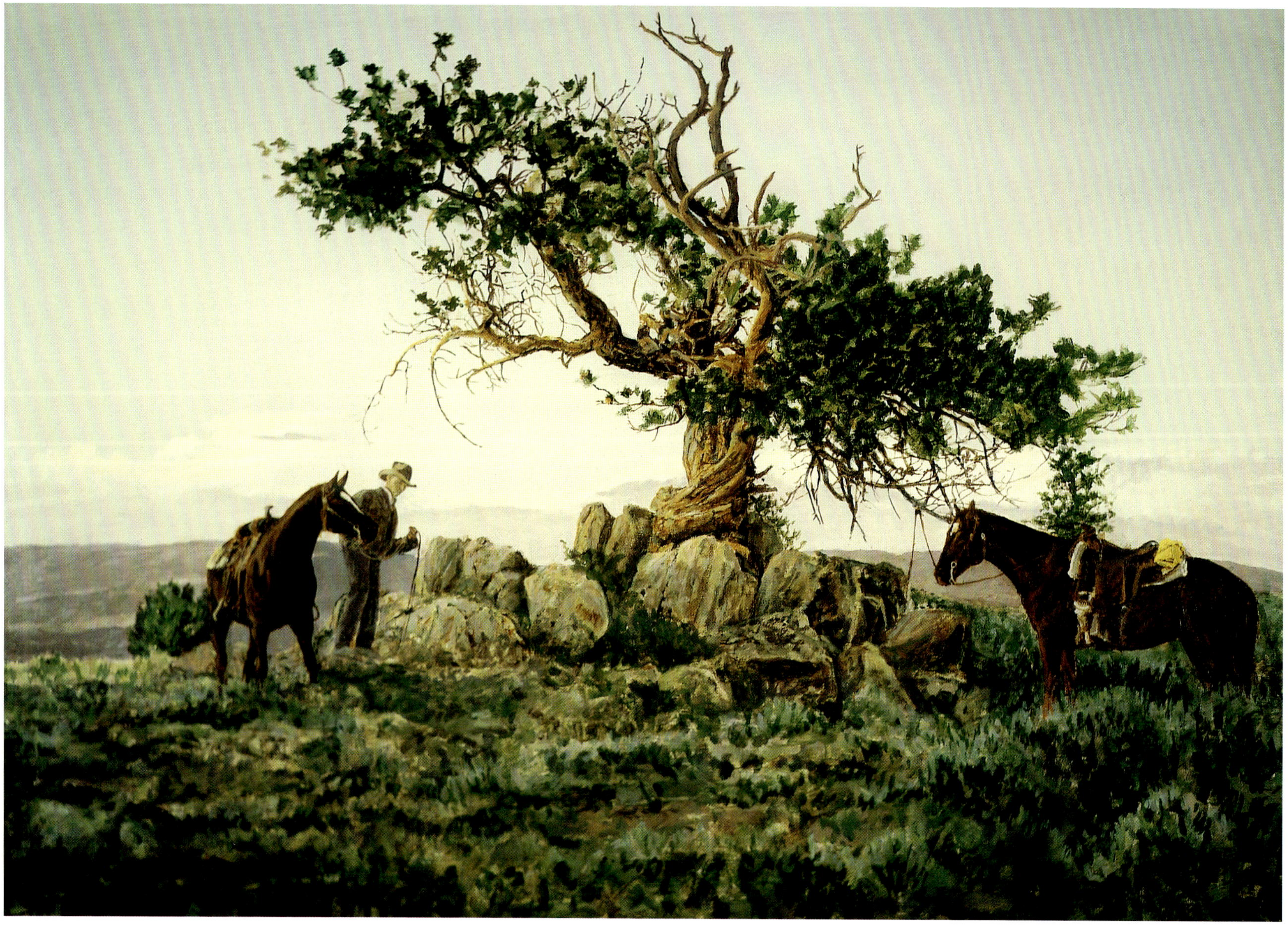

The Hitching Tree, 1977
acrylic on canvas
20 × 30 inches
signed and dated lower left

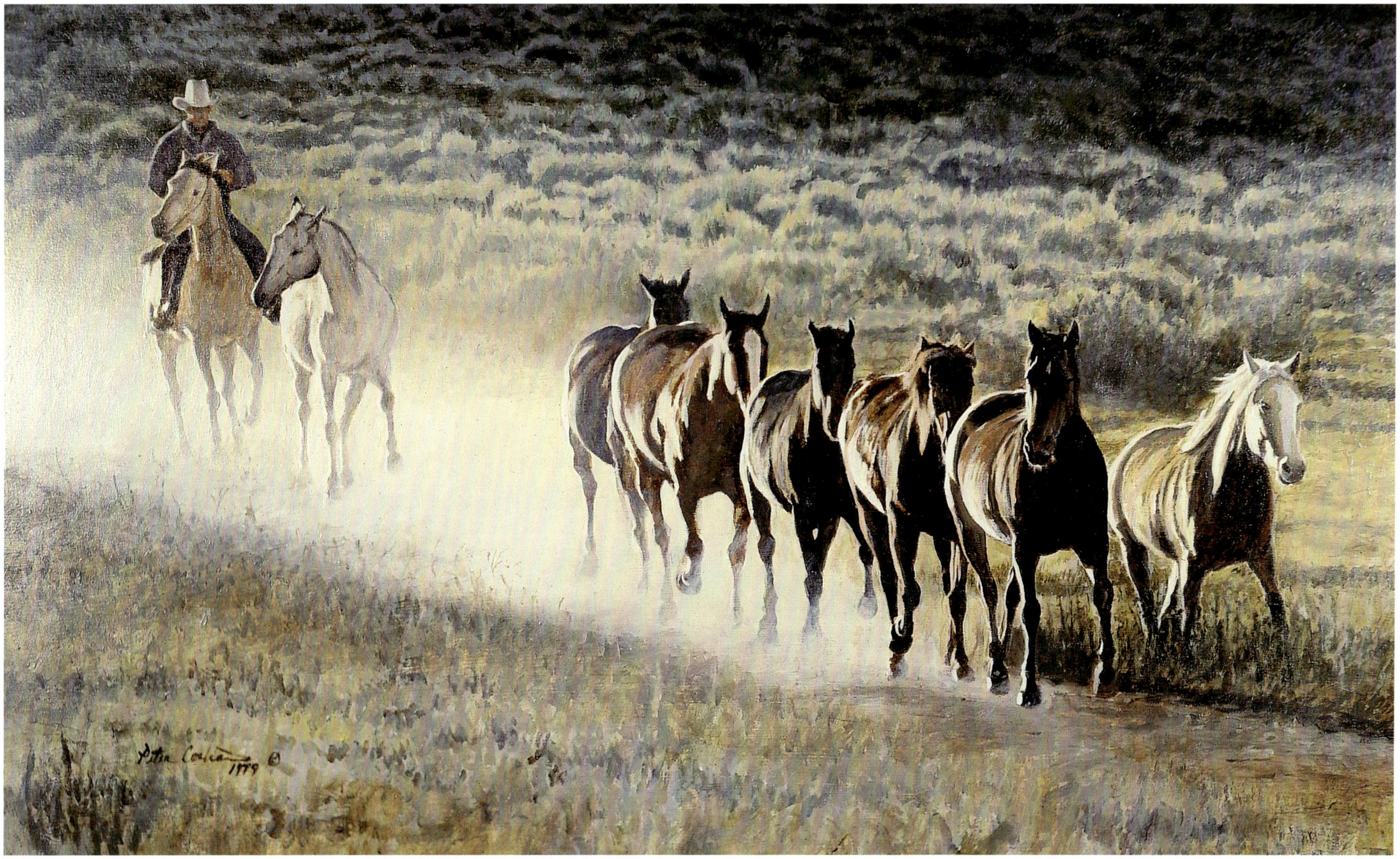

Running Them In, 1979
acrylic on canvas
24 × 40 inches
signed and dated lower left

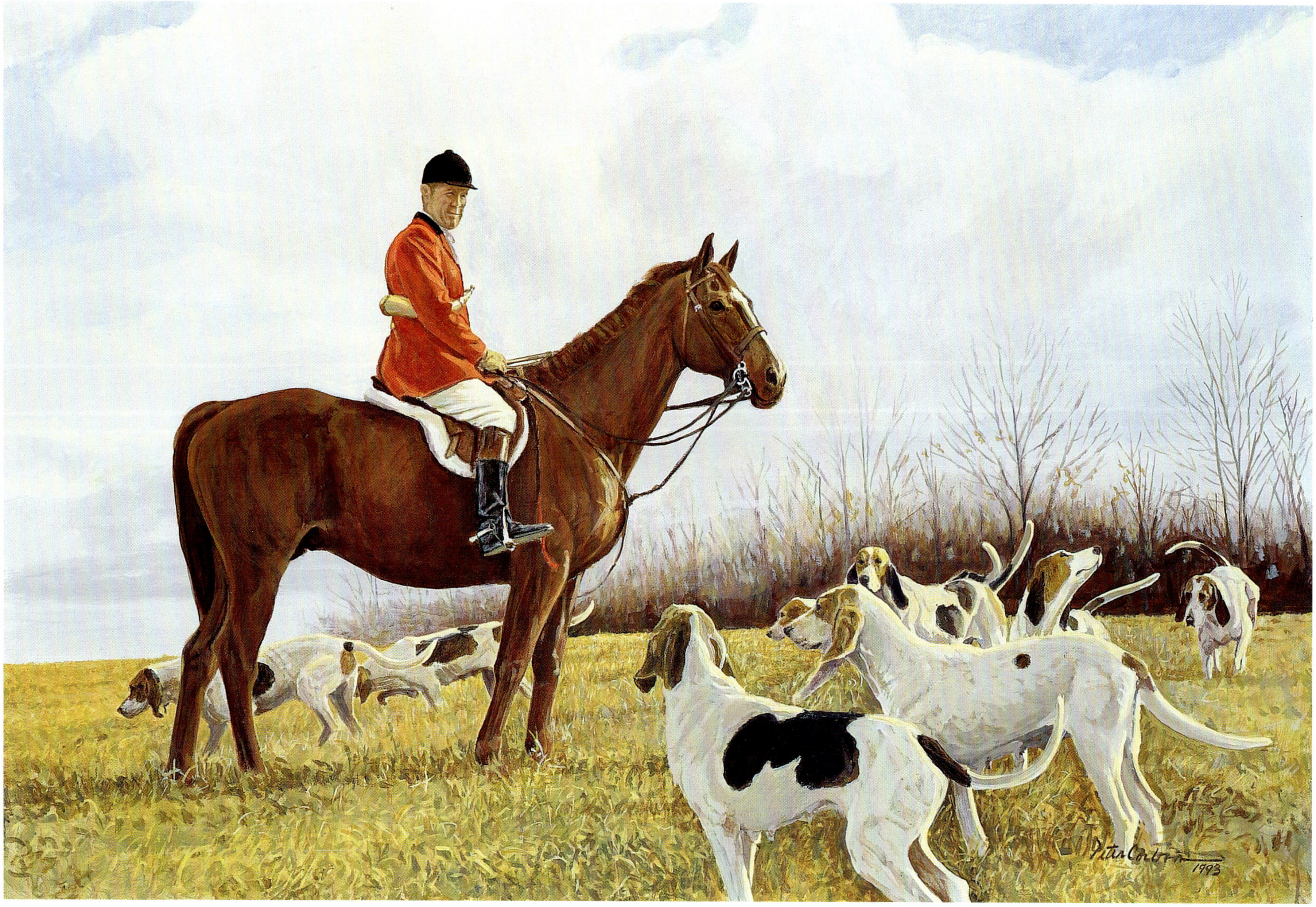

Before the Meet, 1993
acrylic on canvas
20 × 30 inches
signed and dated lower right

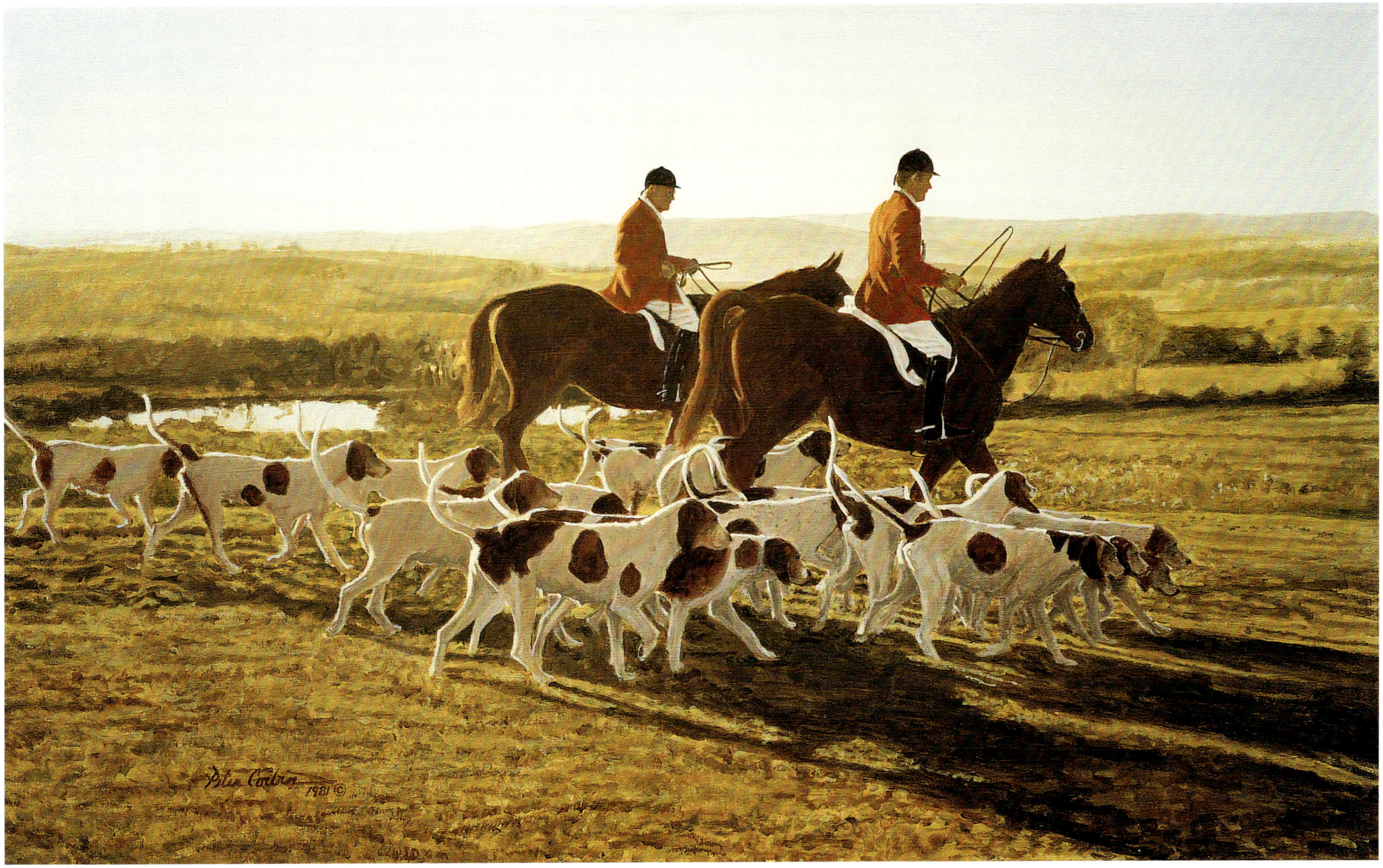

A Morning at Wethersfield, 1981
acrylic on canvas
24 × 40 inches
signed and dated lower left

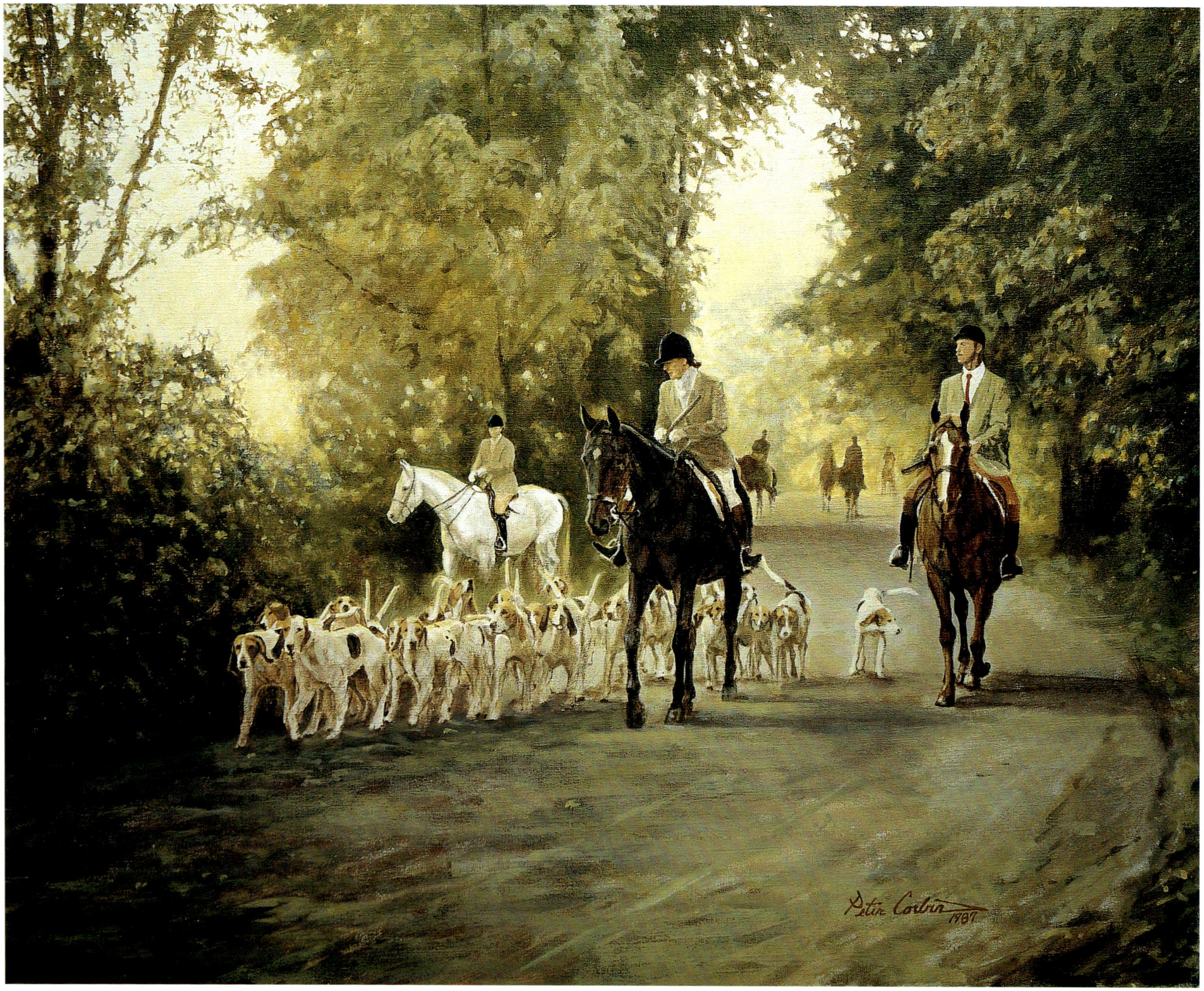

Cubbing, 1987
acrylic on canvas
24 × 30 inches
signed and dated lower right

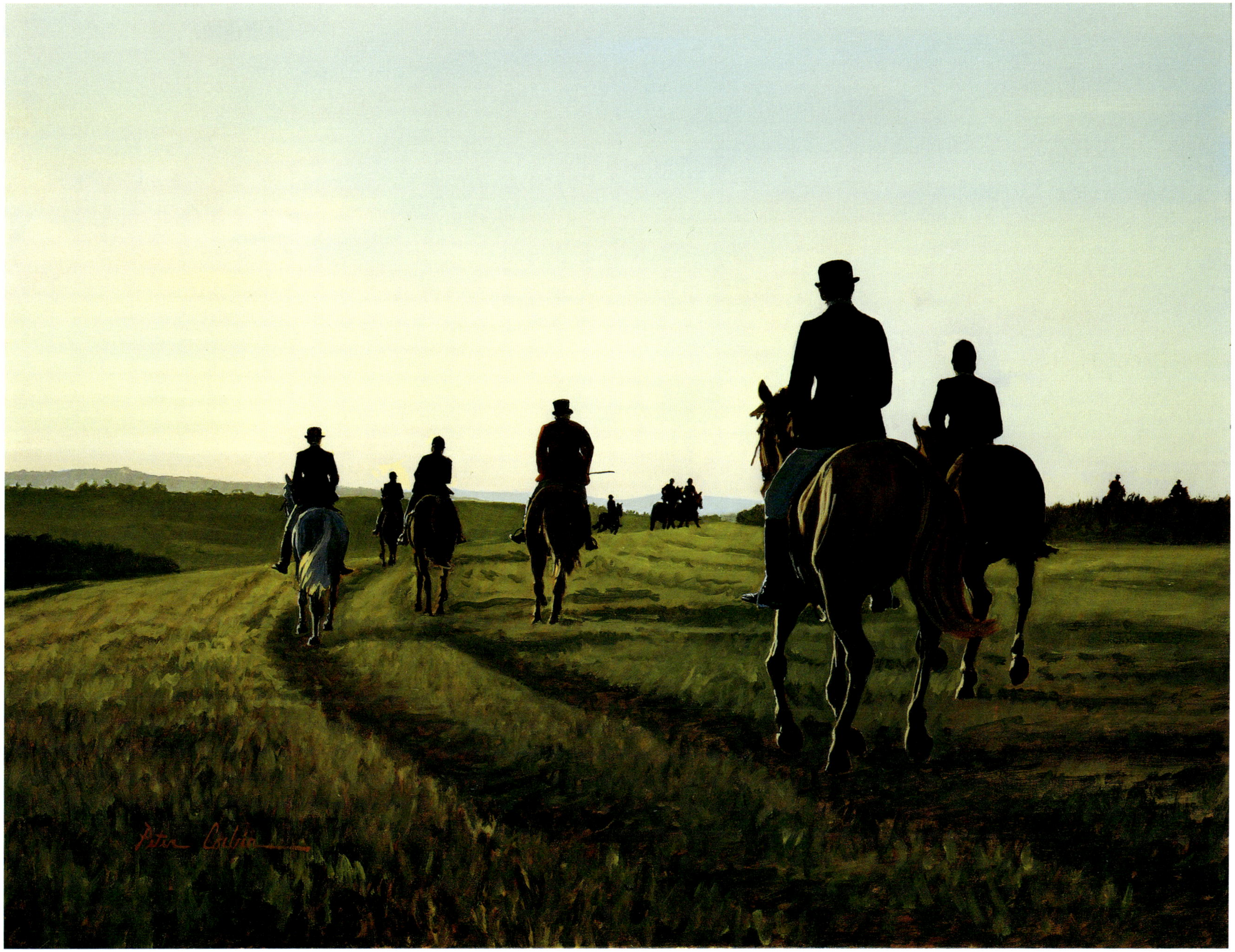

A Morning Run, 2004
oil on canvas
30 × 40 inches
signed lower left

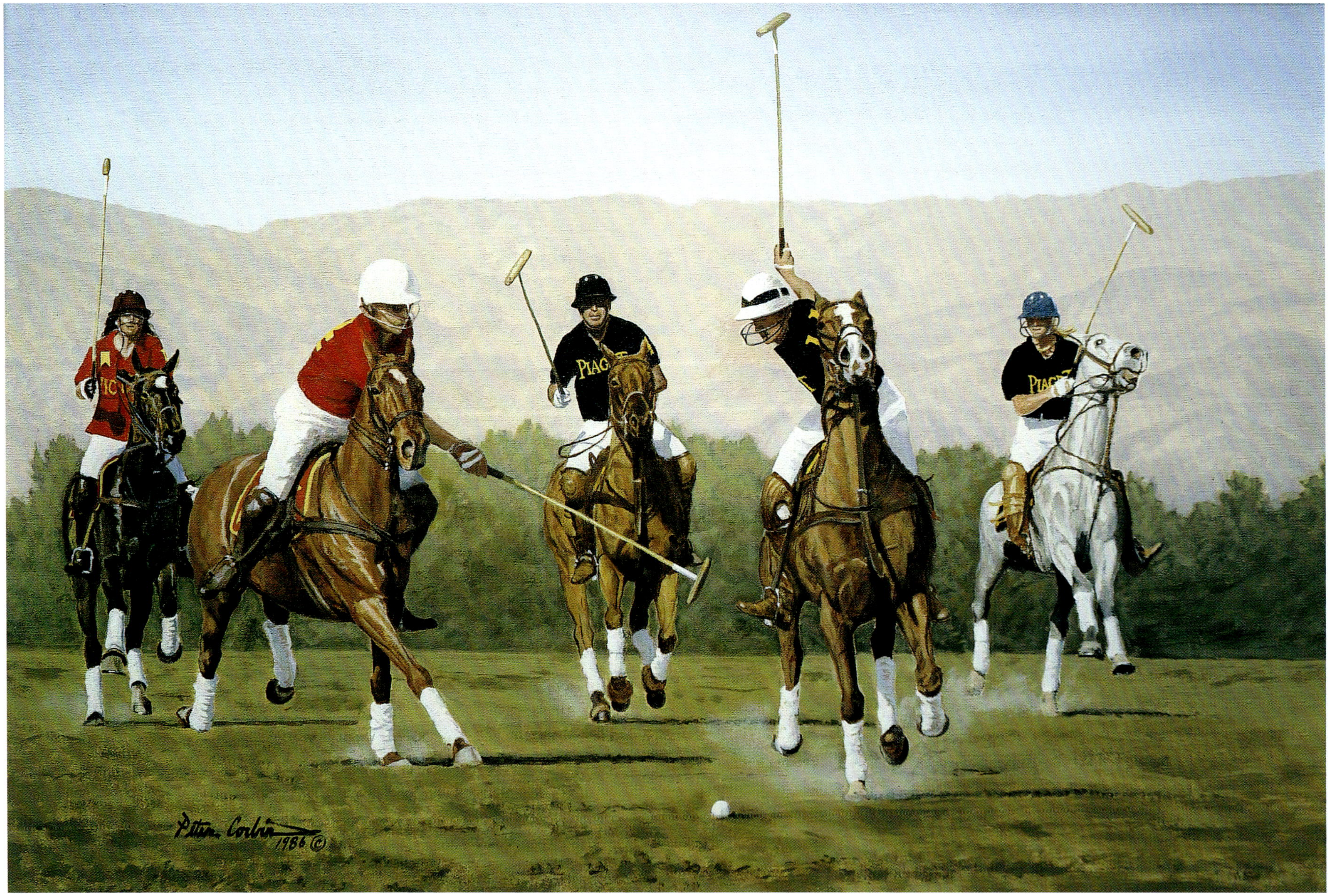

Chukkers for Charity, 1986
acrylic on canvas
24 × 36 inches
signed and dated lower left

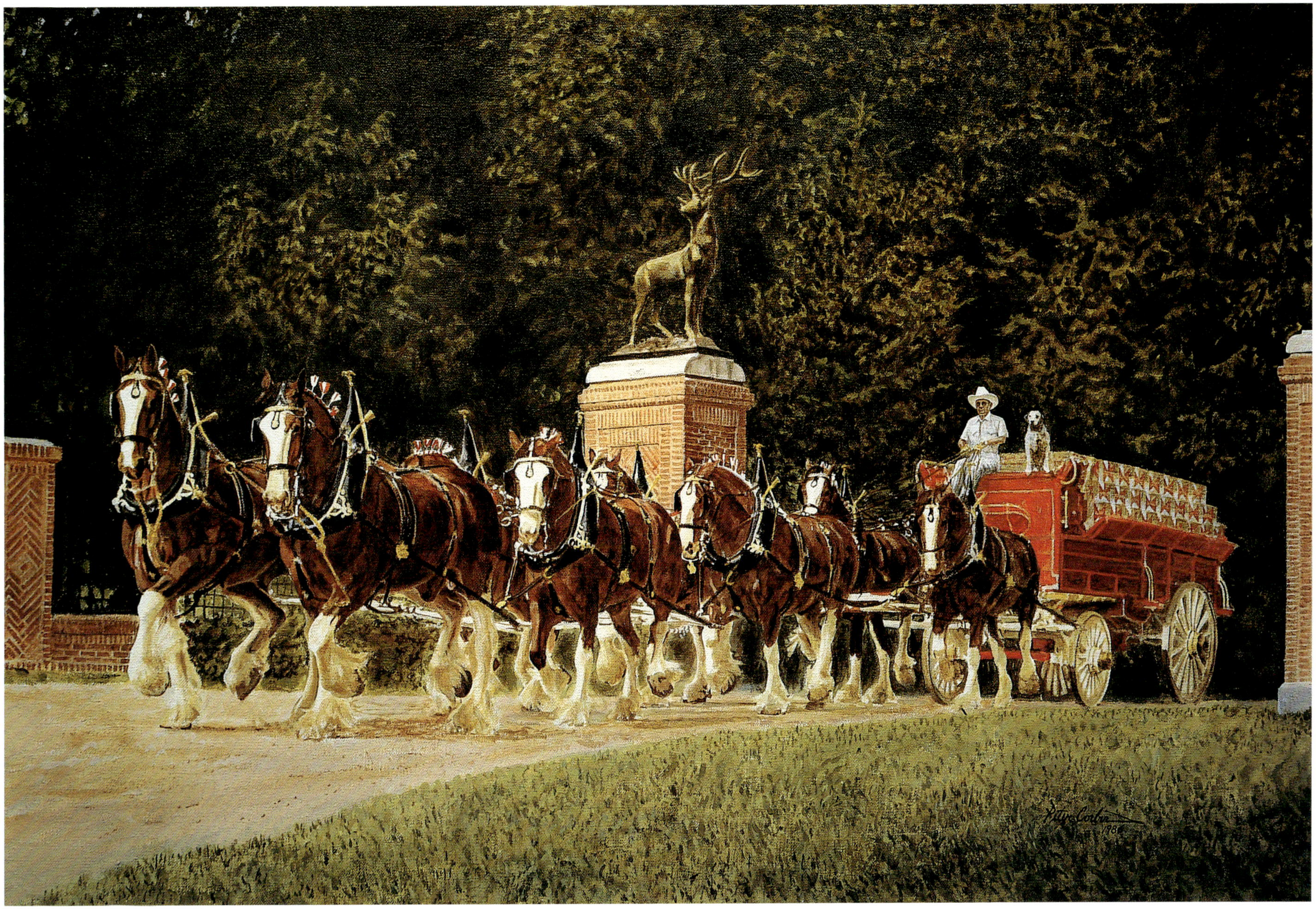

The Budweiser Clydesdales, 1986
acrylic on canvas
24 × 36 inches
signed and dated lower right

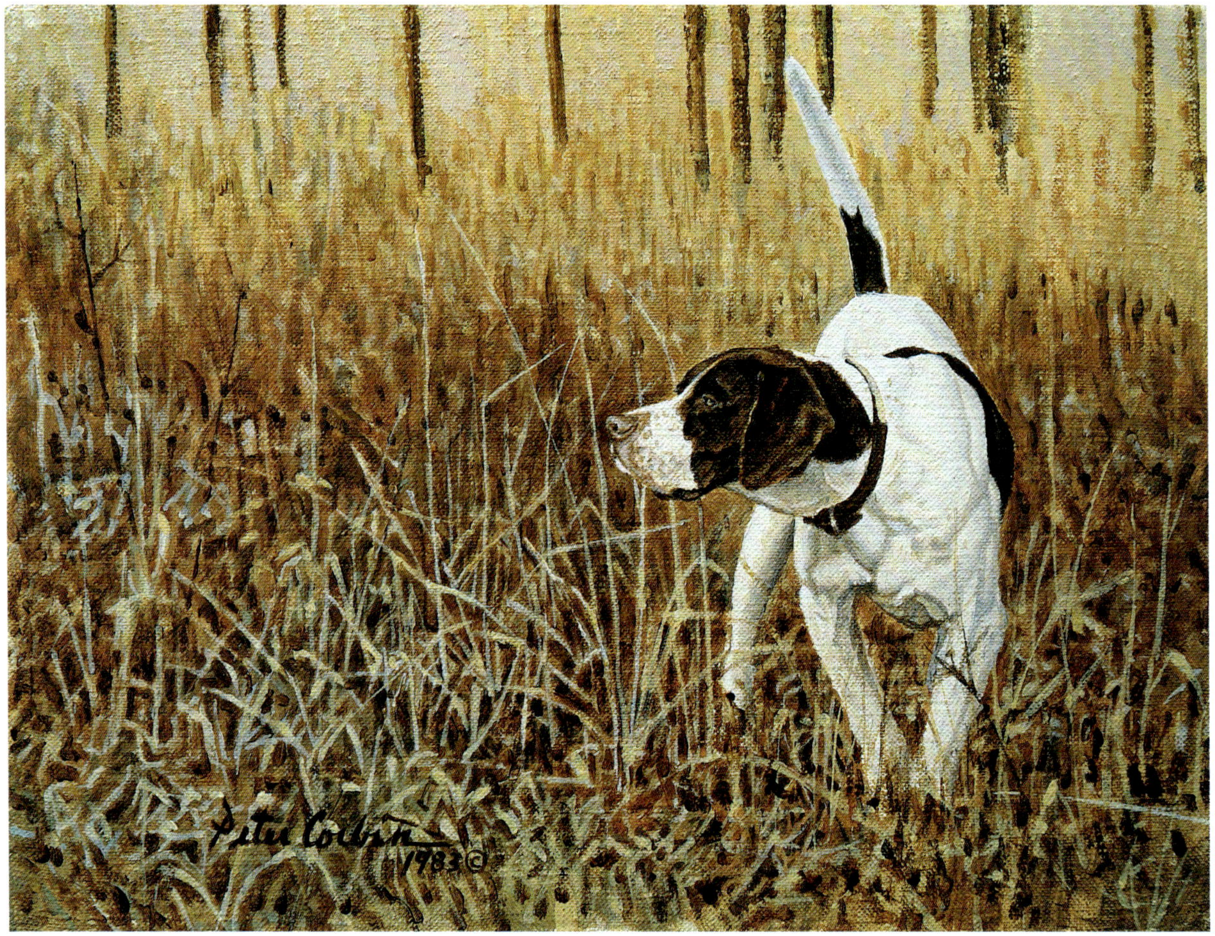

In His Prime—Staunch, 1983
acrylic on canvas
9 × 12 inches
signed and dated lower left

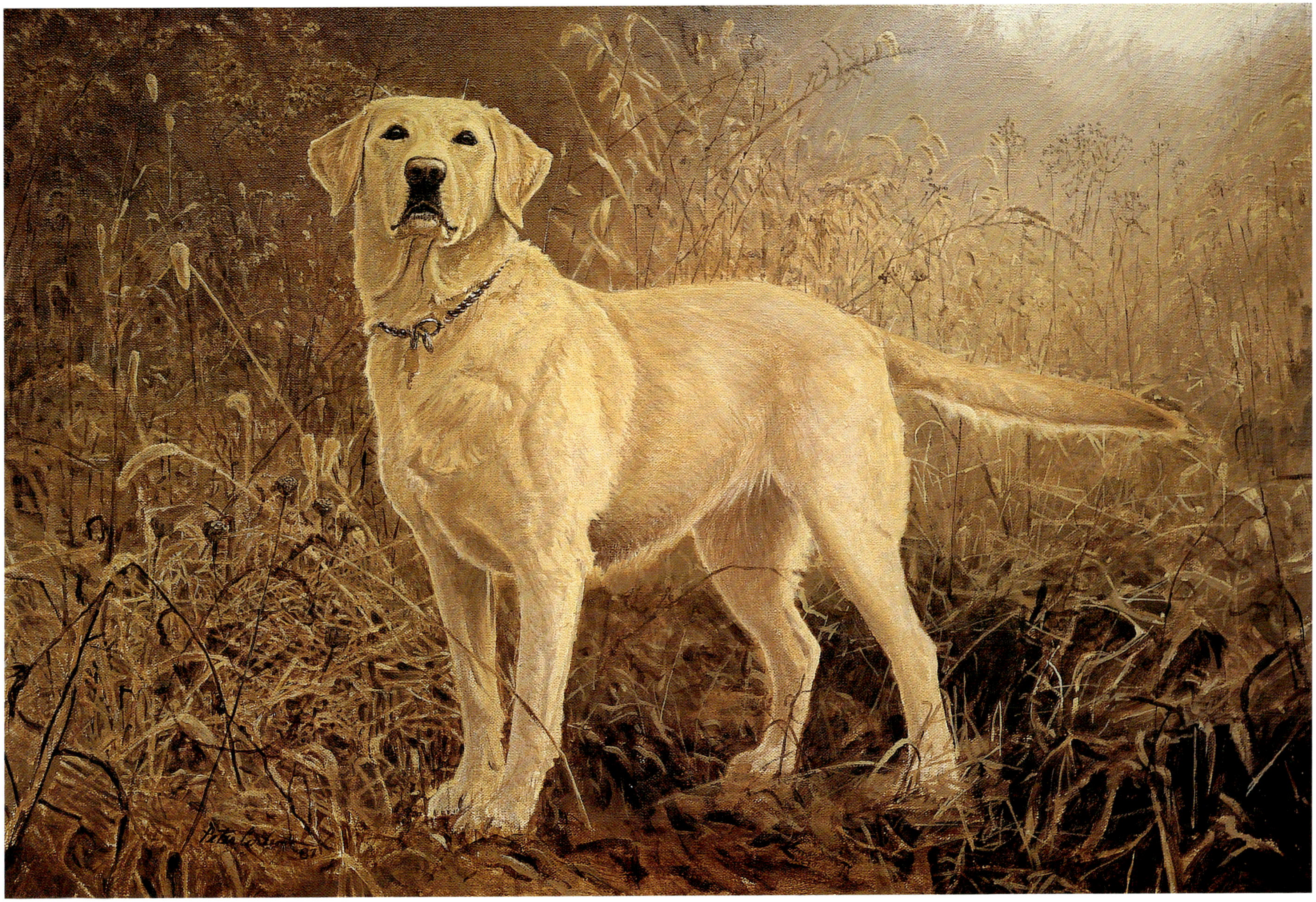

Anticipation, 1987
acrylic on canvas
20 × 30 inches
signed and dated lower left

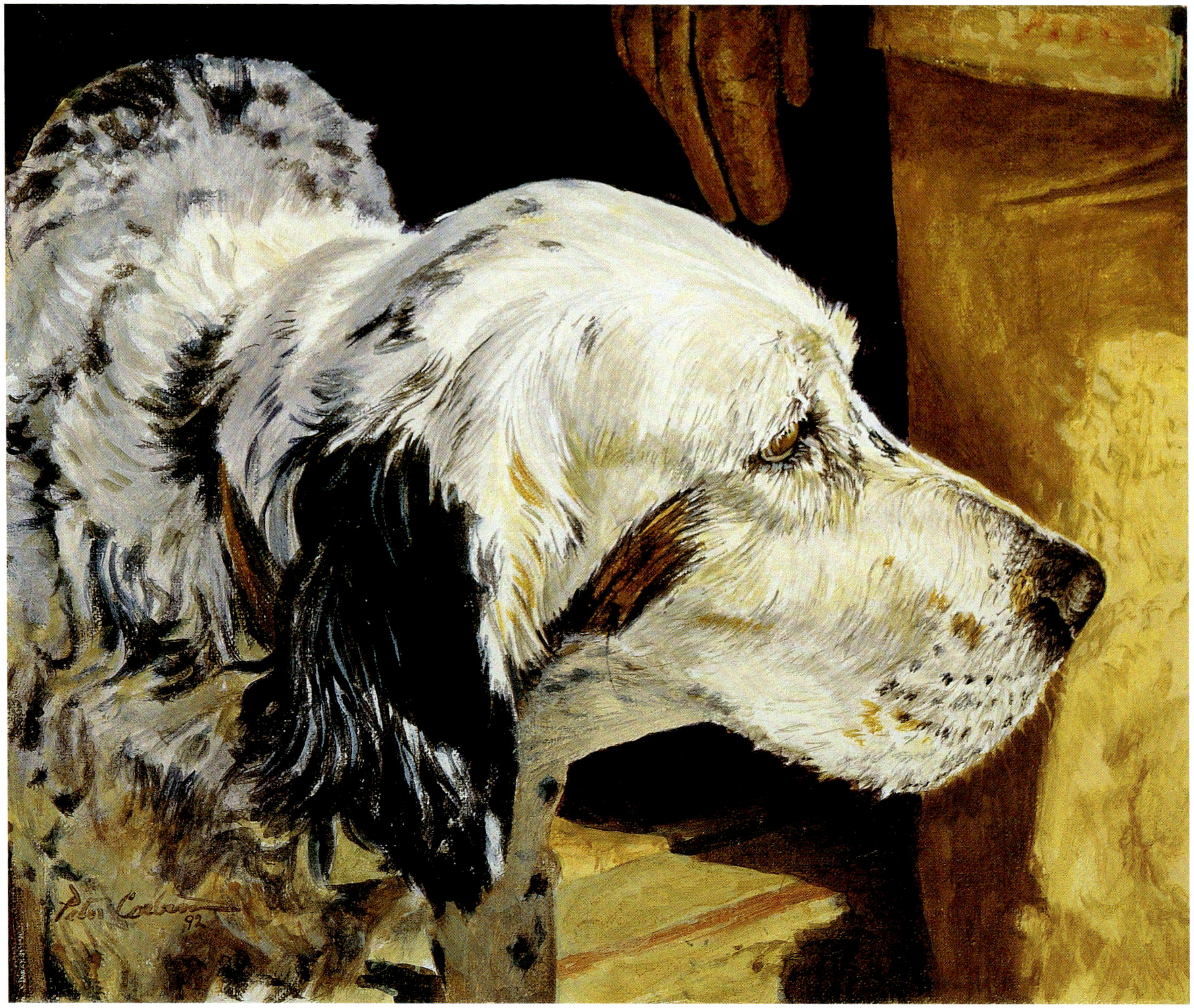

Sugar Maple, 1992
acrylic on canvas
9 × 11 inches
signed and dated lower left

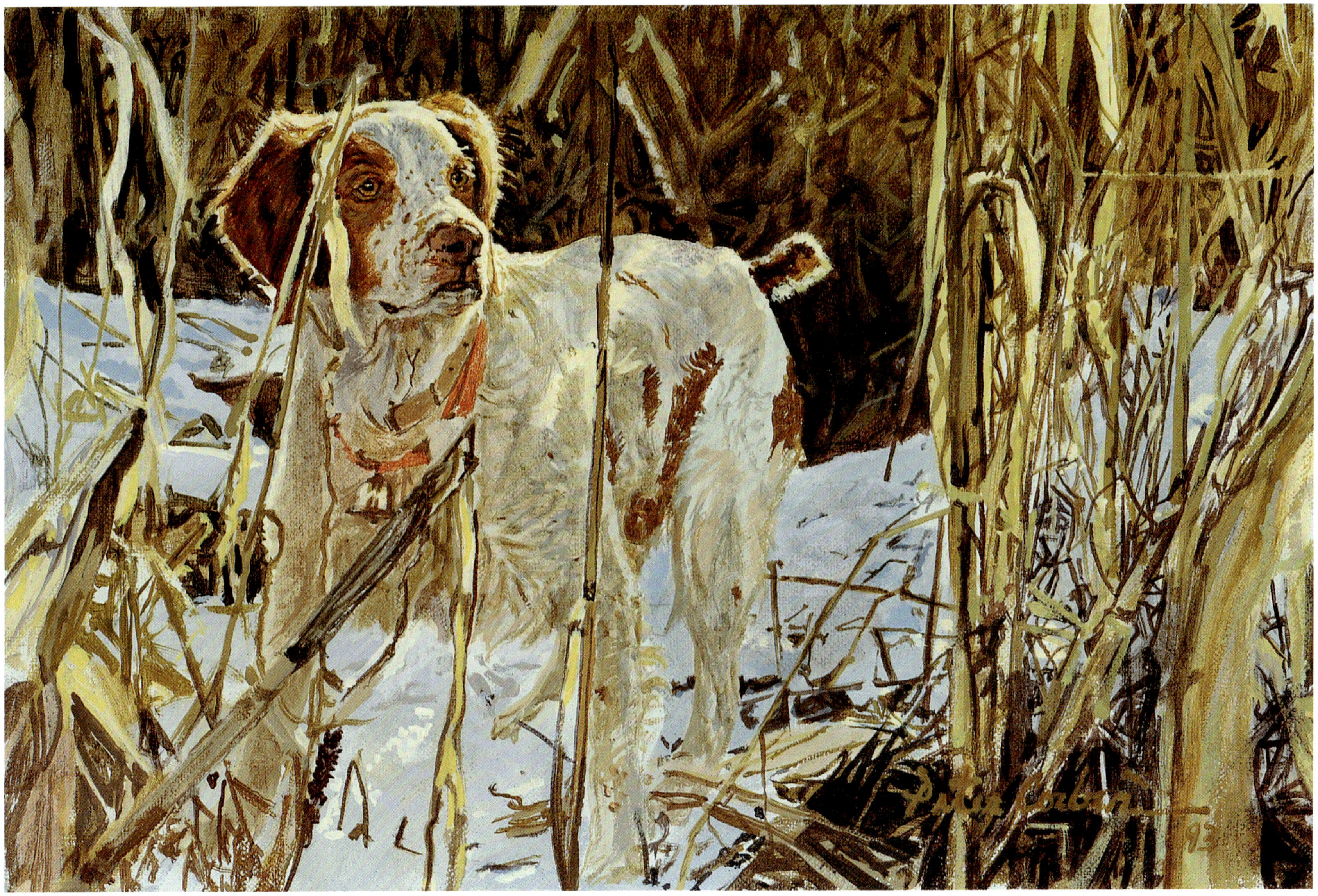

Russ, 1993
acrylic on canvas
8 × 12 inches
signed and dated lower right

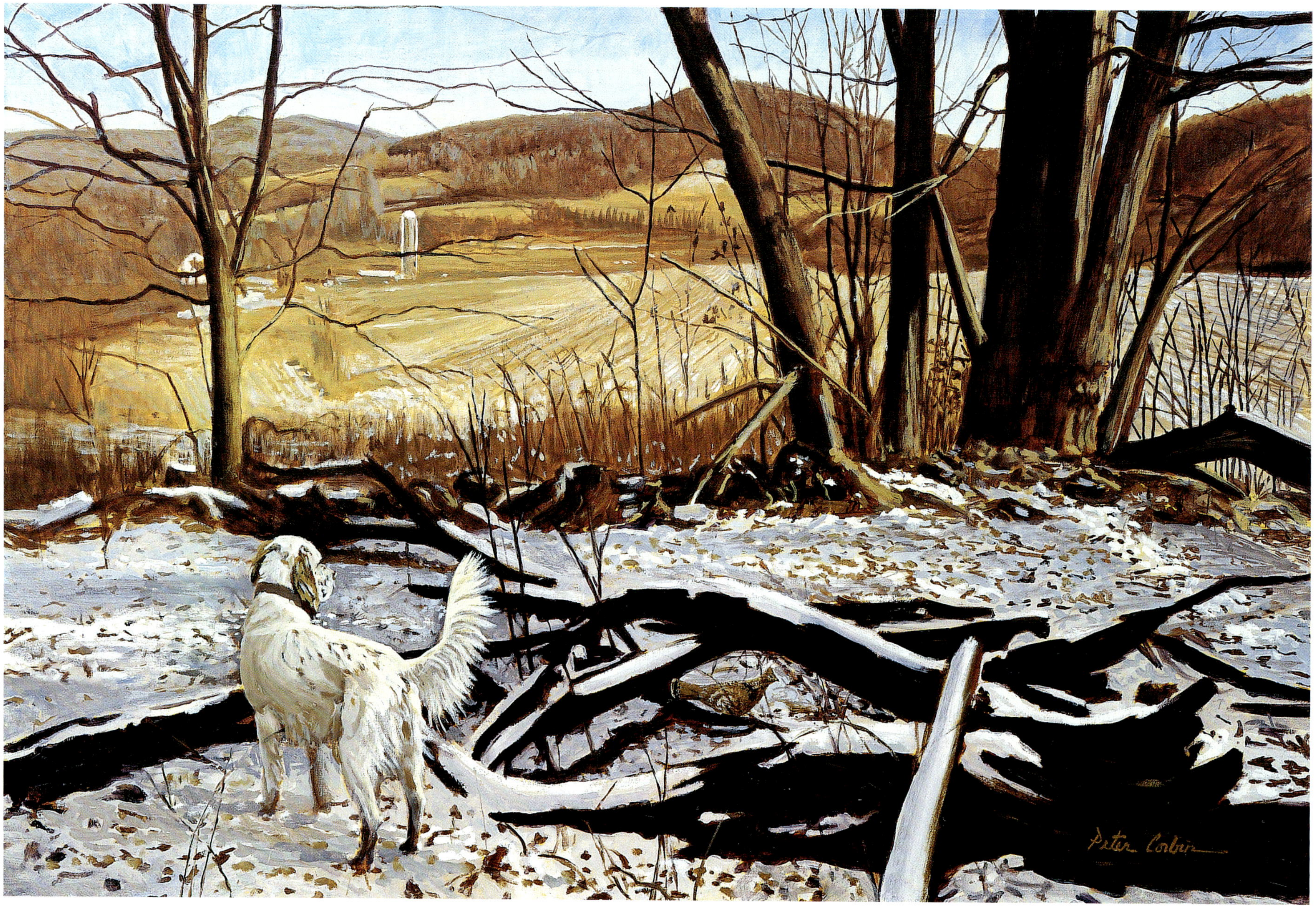

Rigby, 2001
oil on canvas
20 × 30 inches
signed lower right

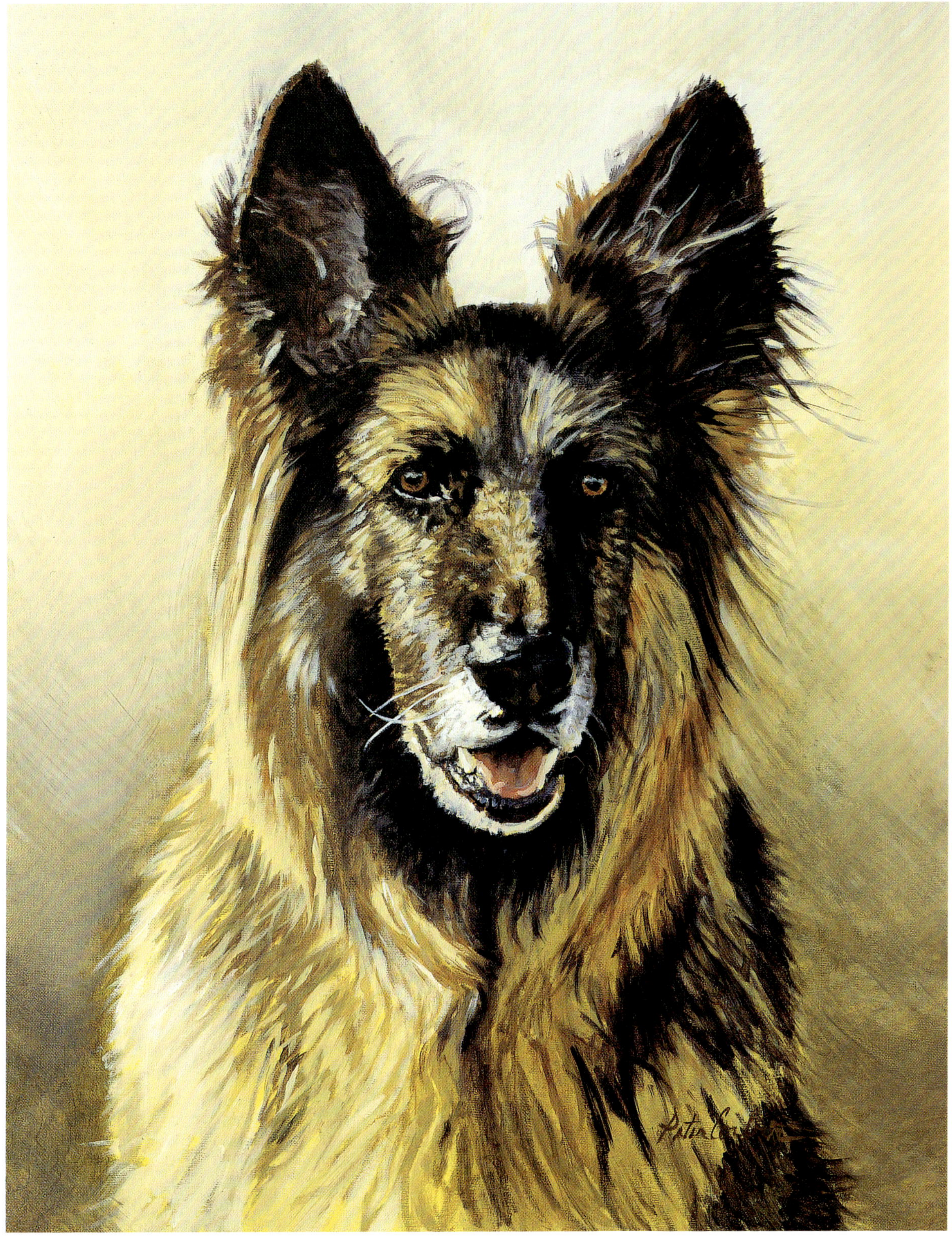

Buzz, 1998
oil on canvas
20 × 16 inches
signed lower right

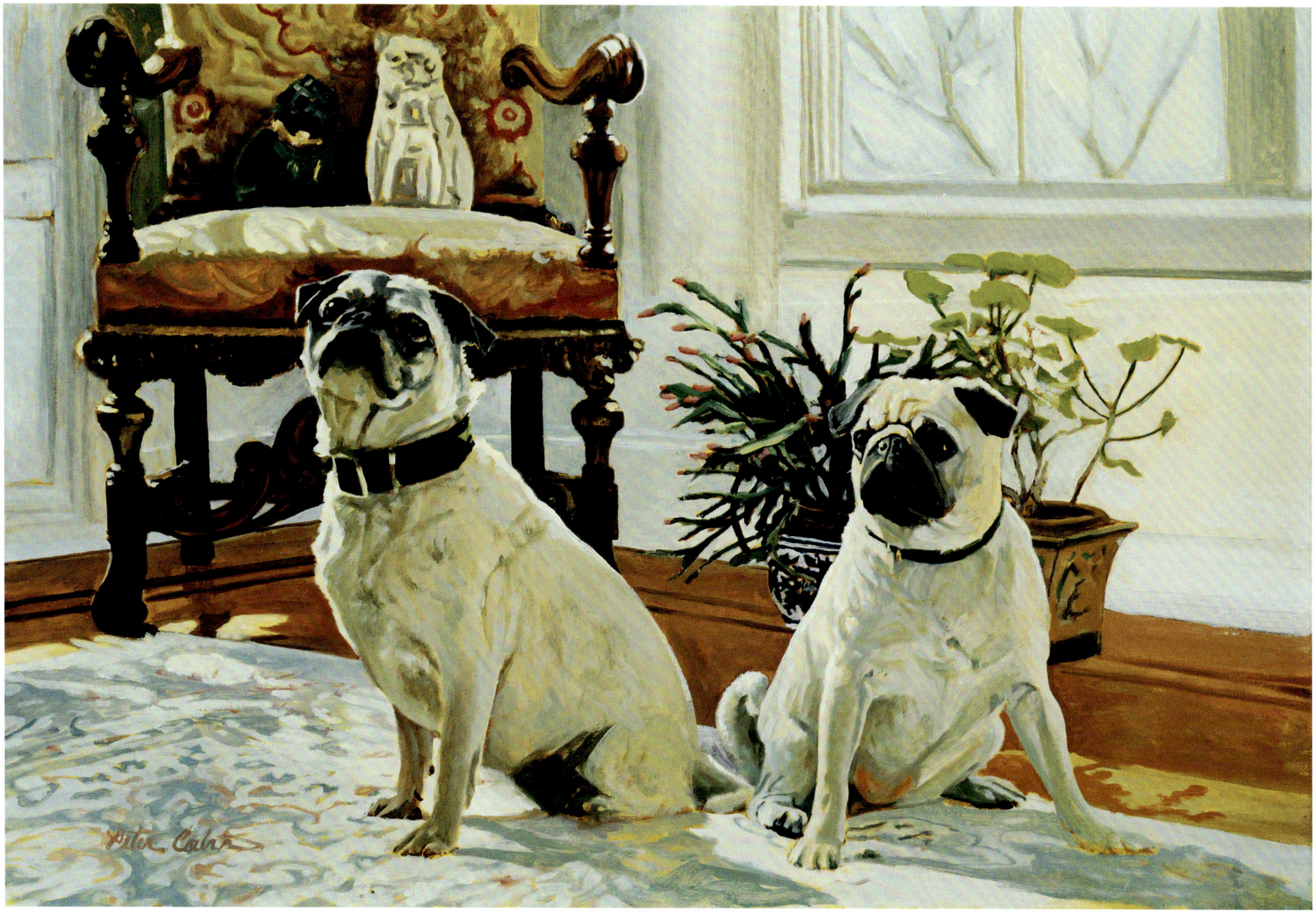

Ginger and Coco, 2003
oil on canvas
20 × 30 inches
signed lower left

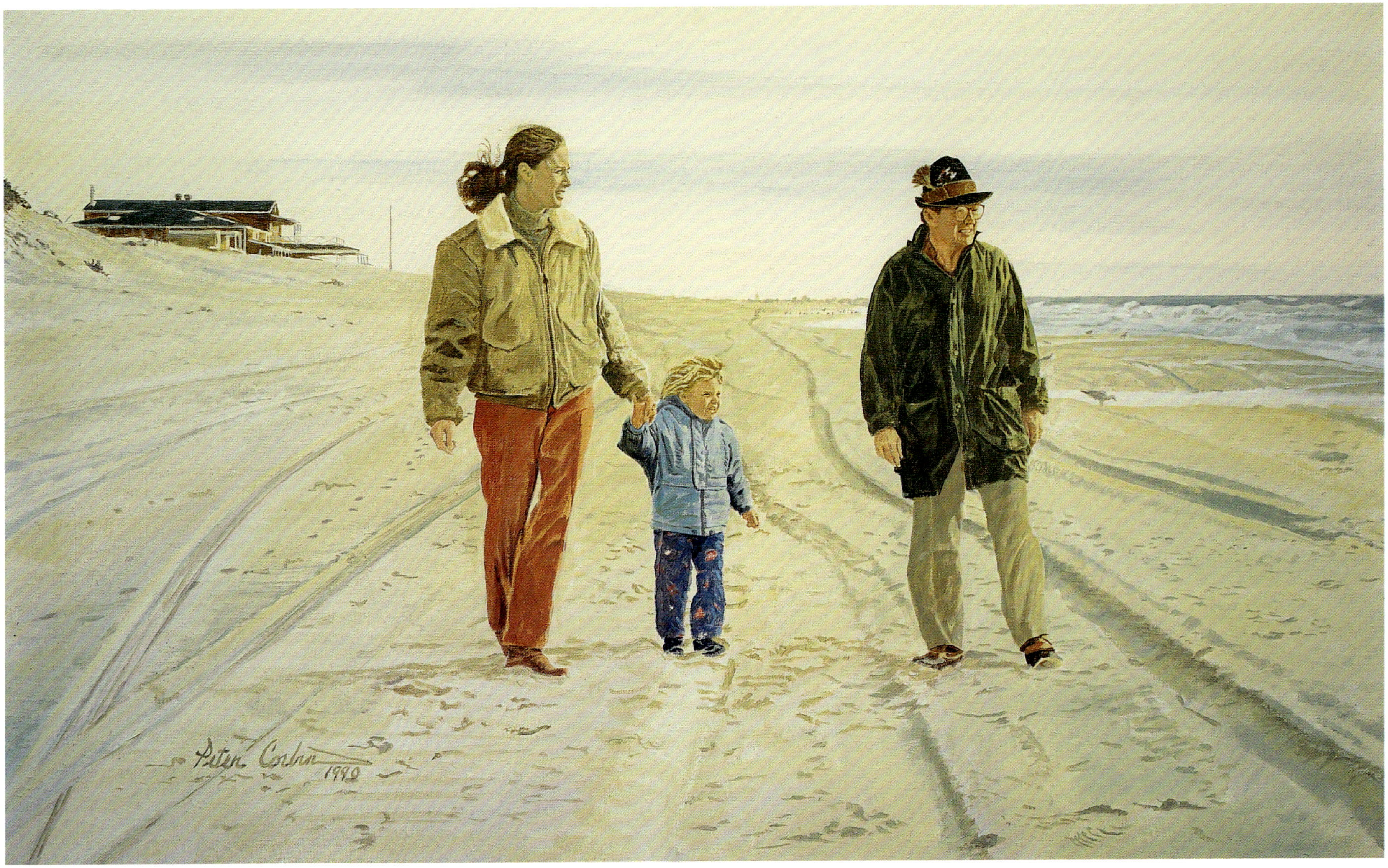

Winter Walk, 1990
acrylic on canvas
24 × 36 inches
signed and dated lower left

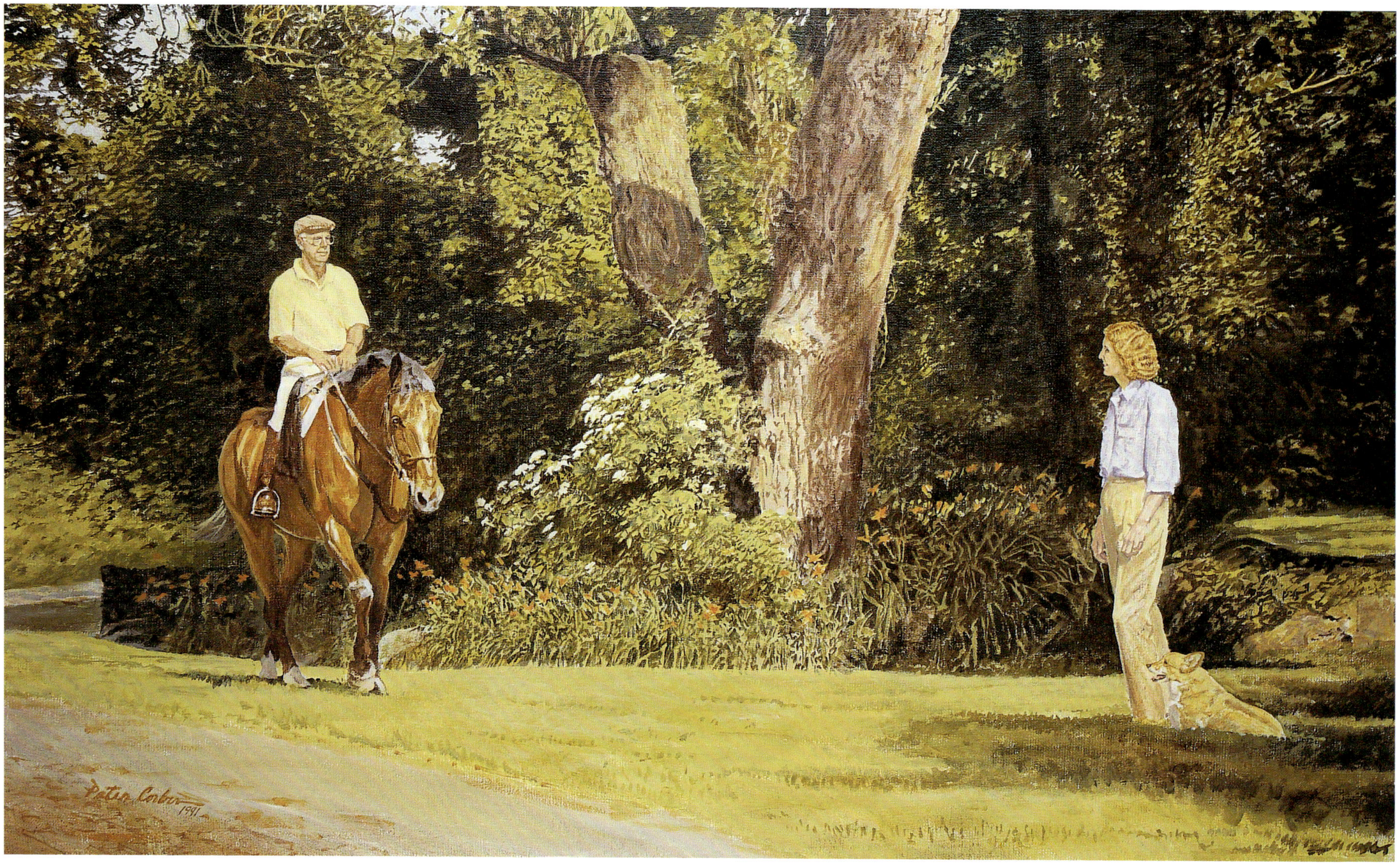

Portrait of Mr. and Mrs. Farnham Collins, 1991
acrylic on canvas
24 × 40 inches
signed and dated lower left

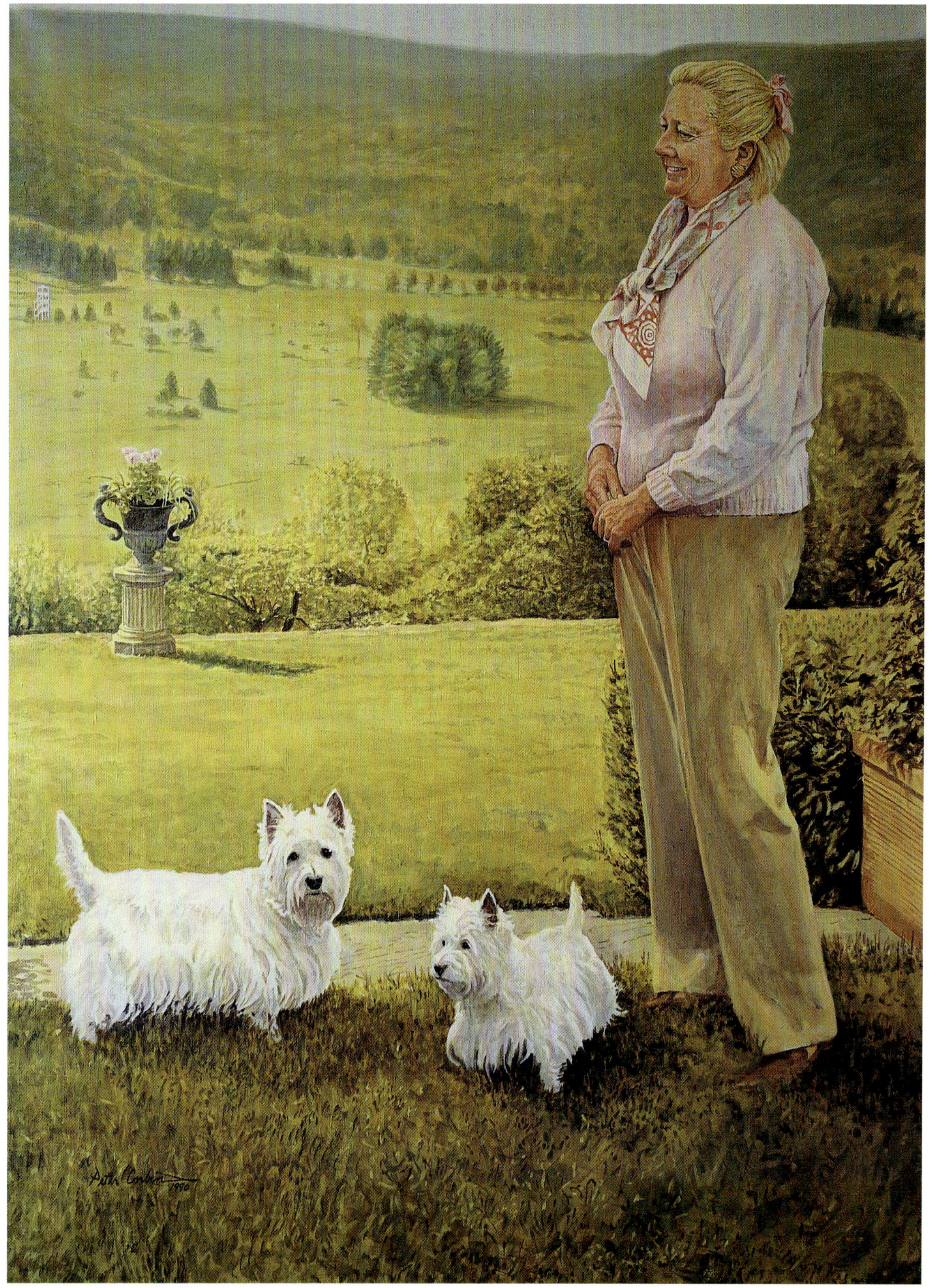

Portrait of Mrs. Cassandra M. Milbury, 1990
acrylic on canvas
48 × 36 inches
signed and dated lower left

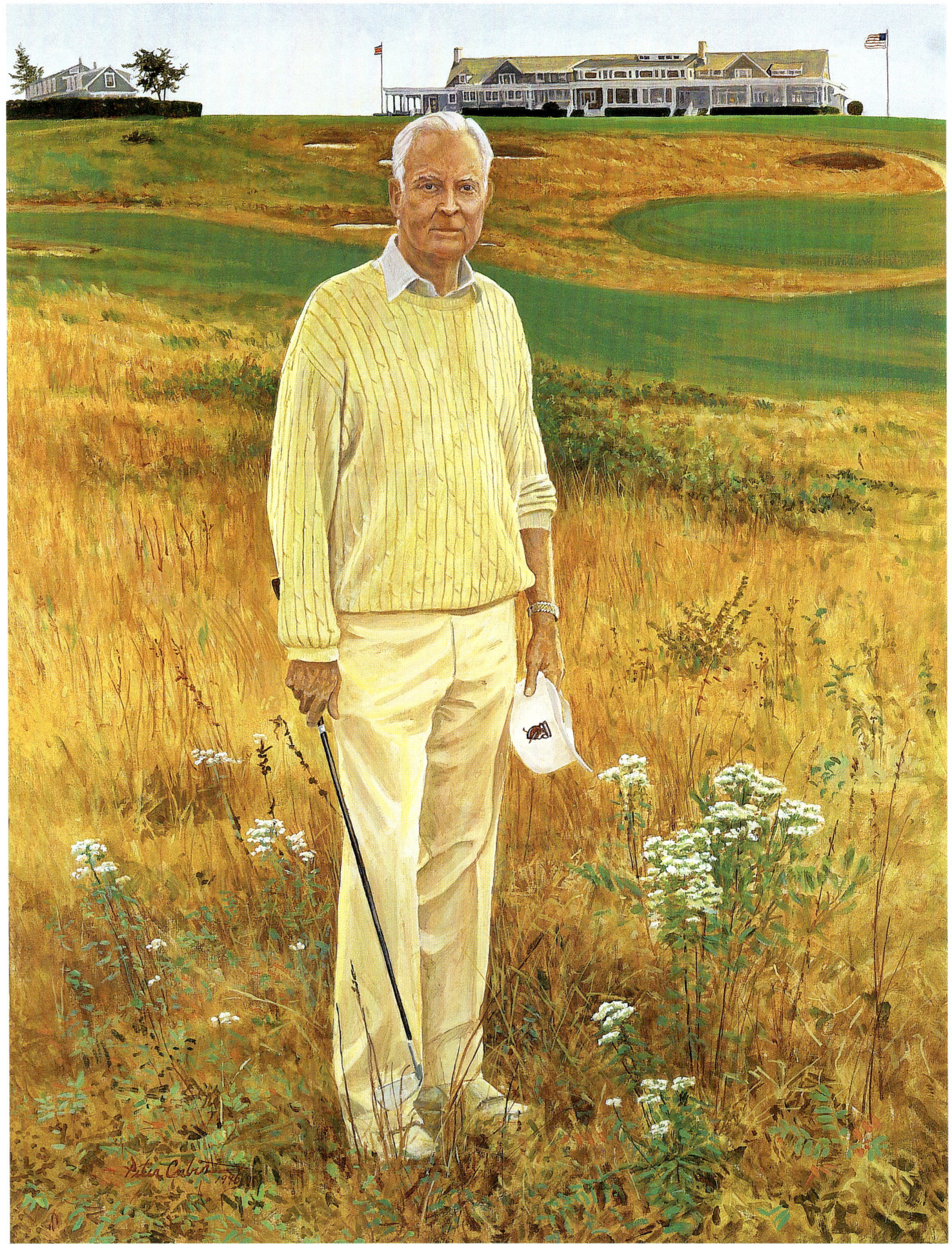

Mr. H. Virgil Sherrill at Shinnecock Hills, 1996
acrylic on canvas
36 × 28 inches
signed and dated lower left

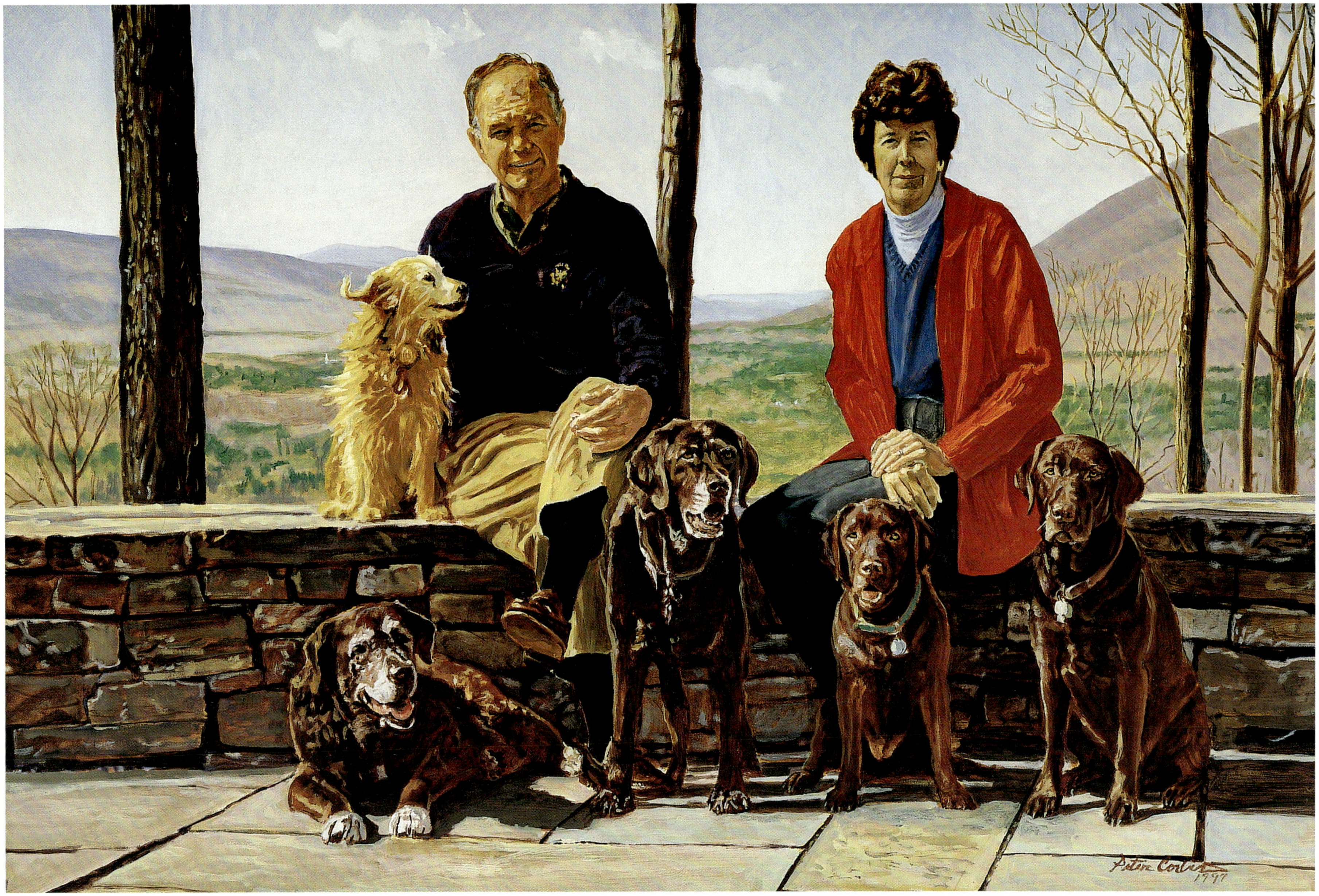

Portrait of Mr. and Mrs. John Runnette, 1997
oil on canvas
24 × 36 inches
signed and dated lower right

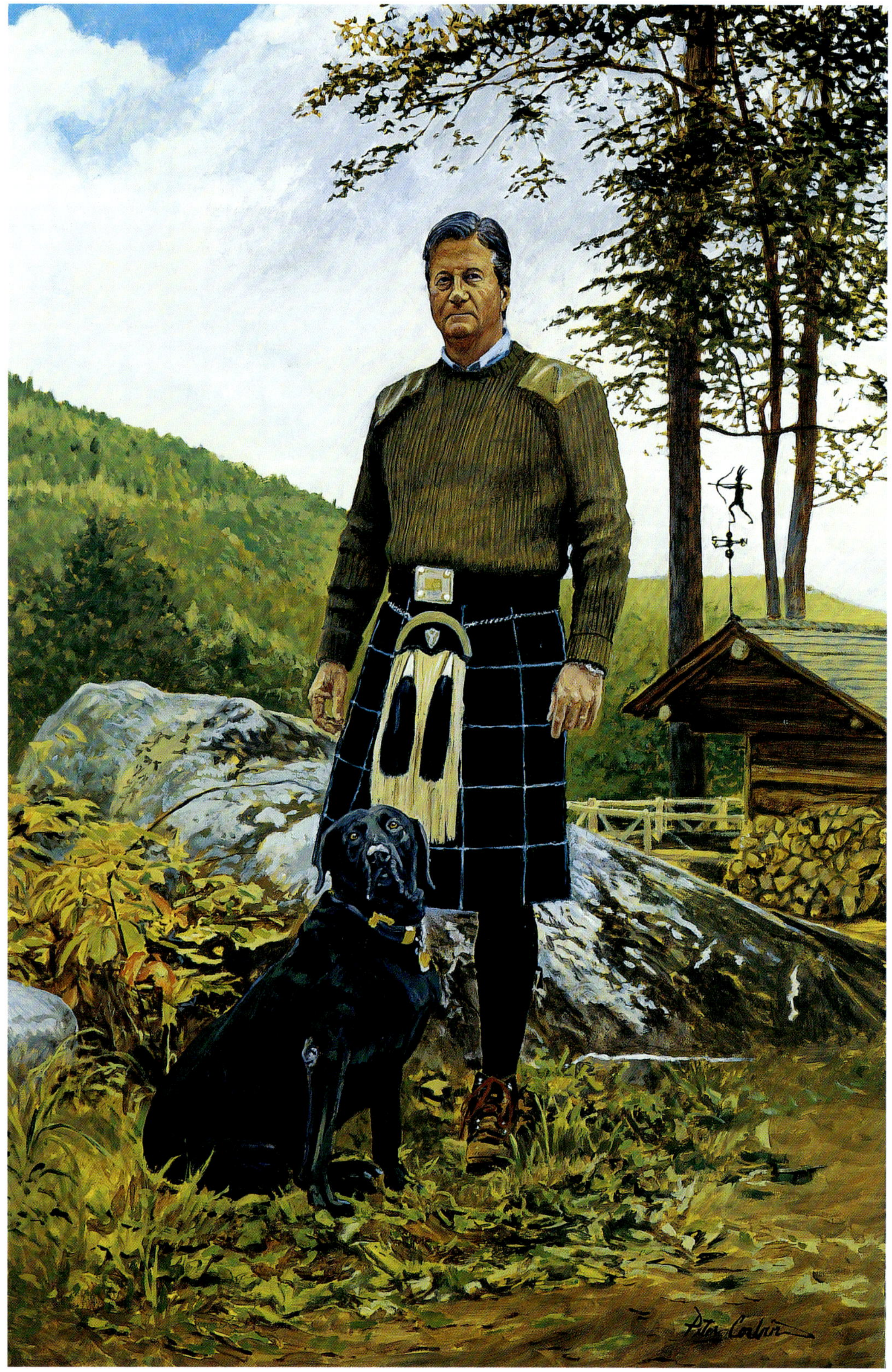

Portrait of Mr. Douglas Luke, 1999
oil on canvas
36 × 24 inches
signed lower right

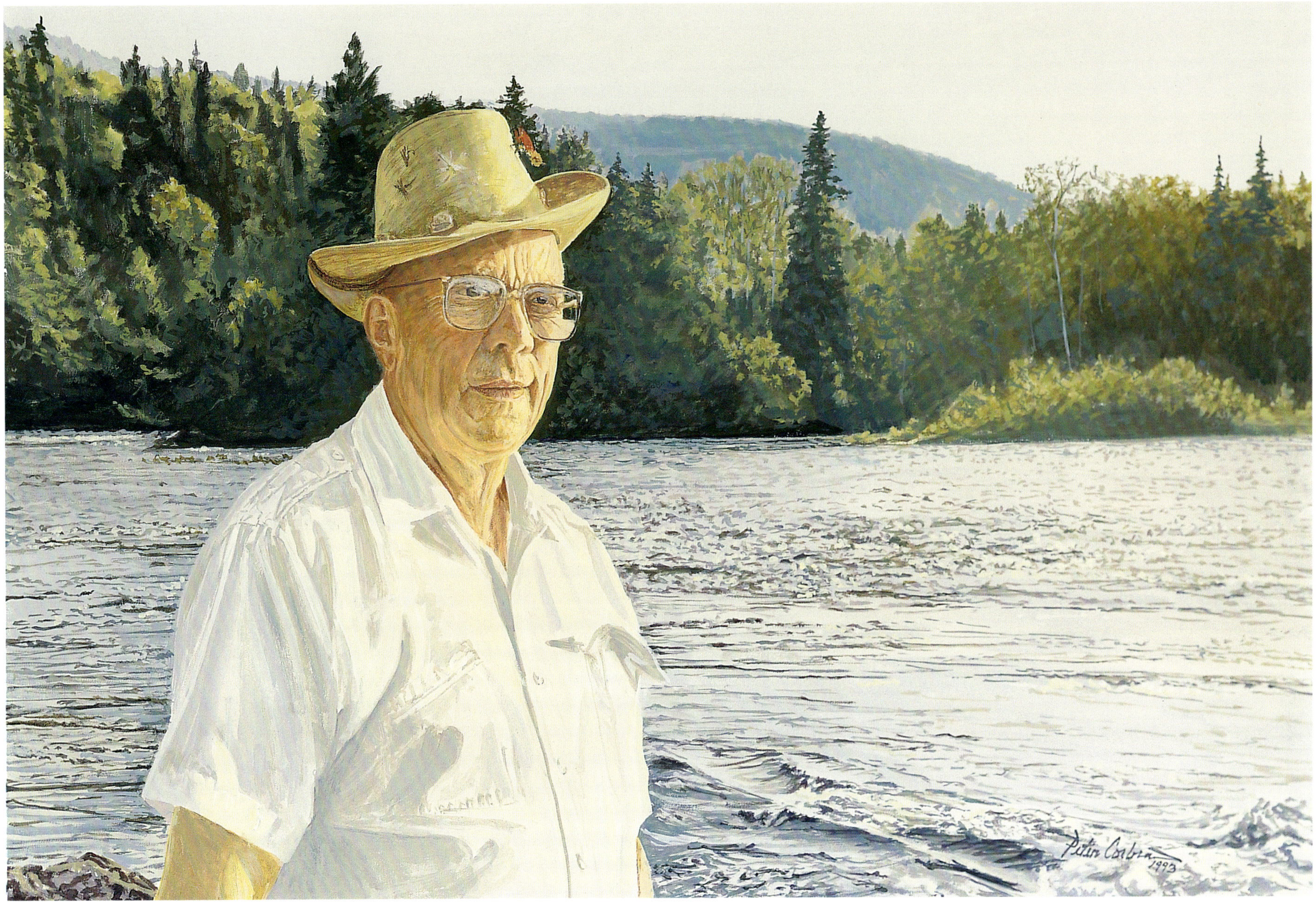

Keeper of the River, 1993
acrylic on canvas
20 × 30 inches
signed and dated lower right

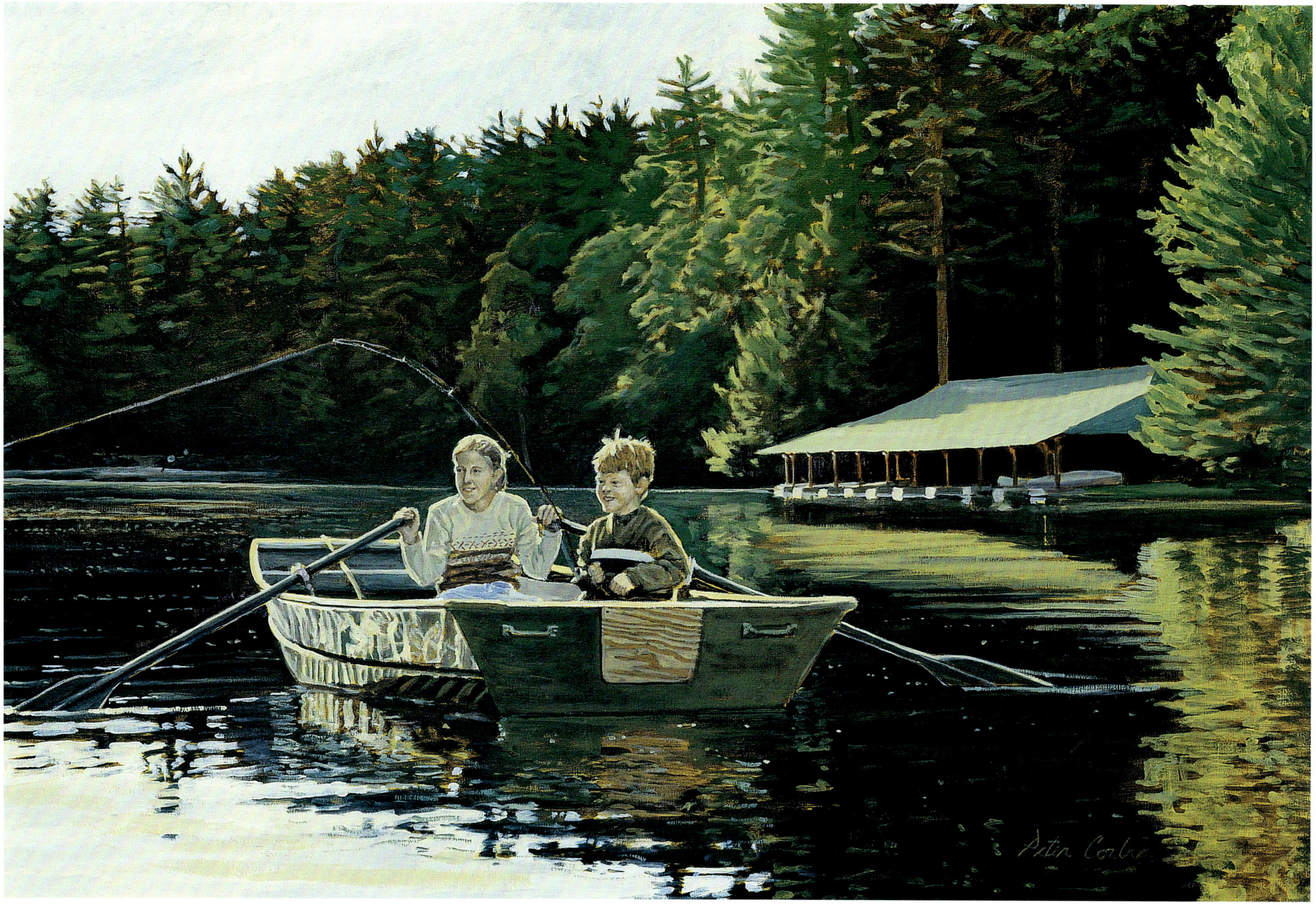

Hemlock Evening, 2002
oil on canvas
20 × 30 inches
signed lower right

Sculpture

My steel-and-fiberglass sculptures were simple forms taken to an extreme scale to show the drama of transmitted light. The early pieces had the heroic proportions of a young man's shouting. As the curvilinear pieces progressed in form to show transitions and linear tension, the polished surfaces provided the reflected light. My last sculptural pieces were jewelry made of precious material with a more complex design; only the butterfly pieces had the elements of realism to transcend the abstract form. My later paintings may seem less complex than my sculpture, but in reality the same abstract concepts have to work as well as does the illusion of narrative realism.

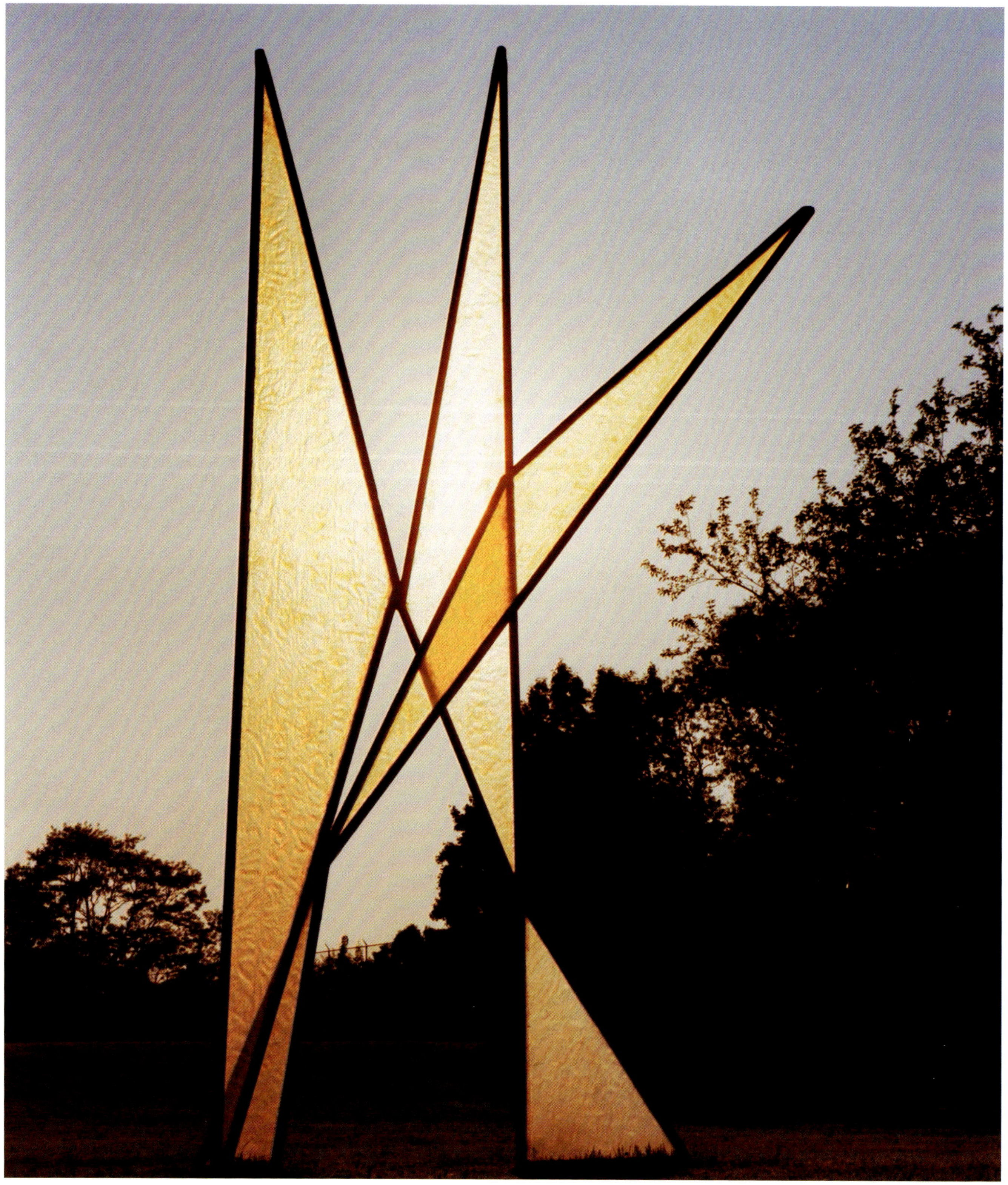

Transmitted Light Sculpture #1, 1968
steel and fiberglass

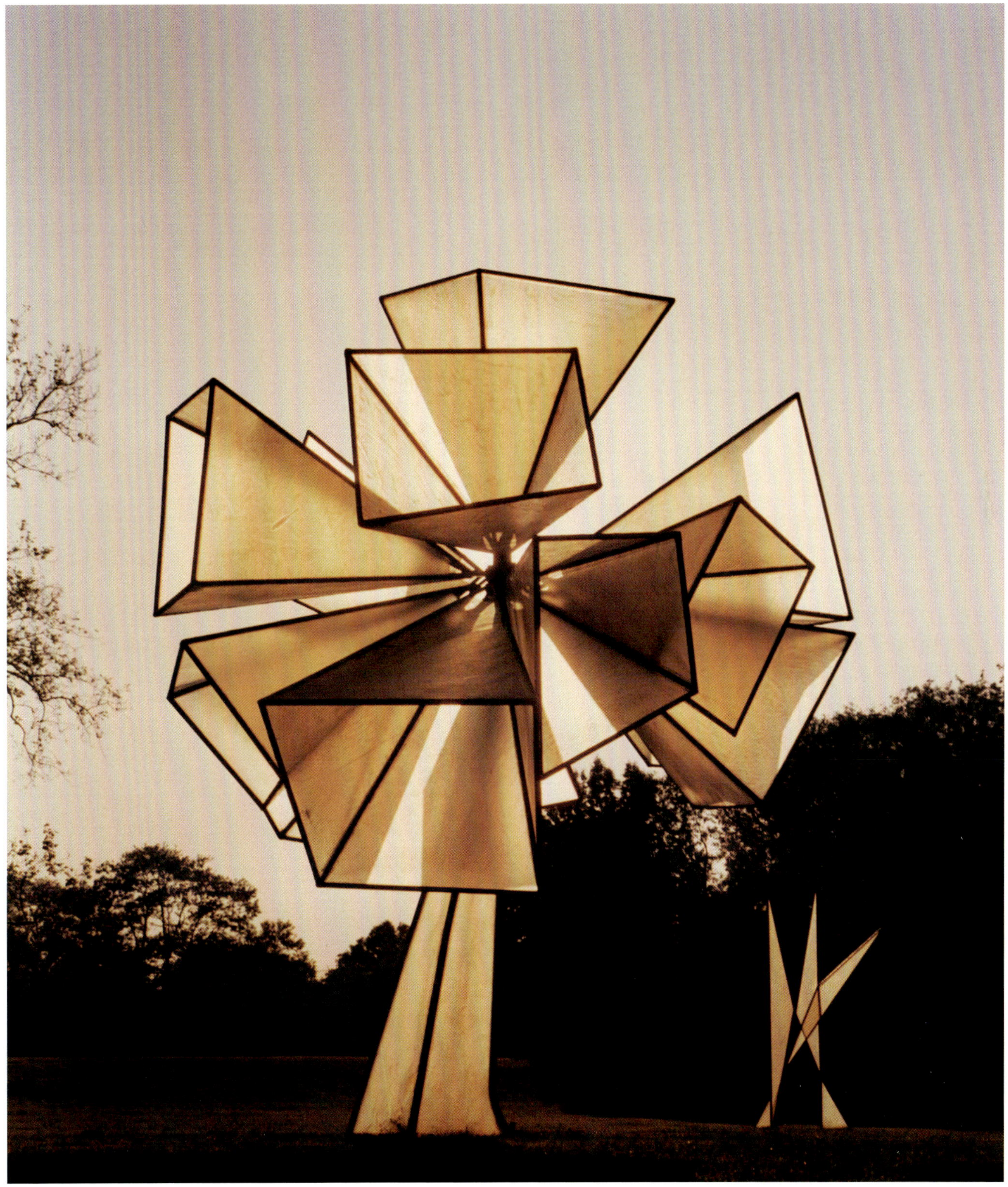

Transmitted Light Sculpture #3, 1968
steel and fiberglass

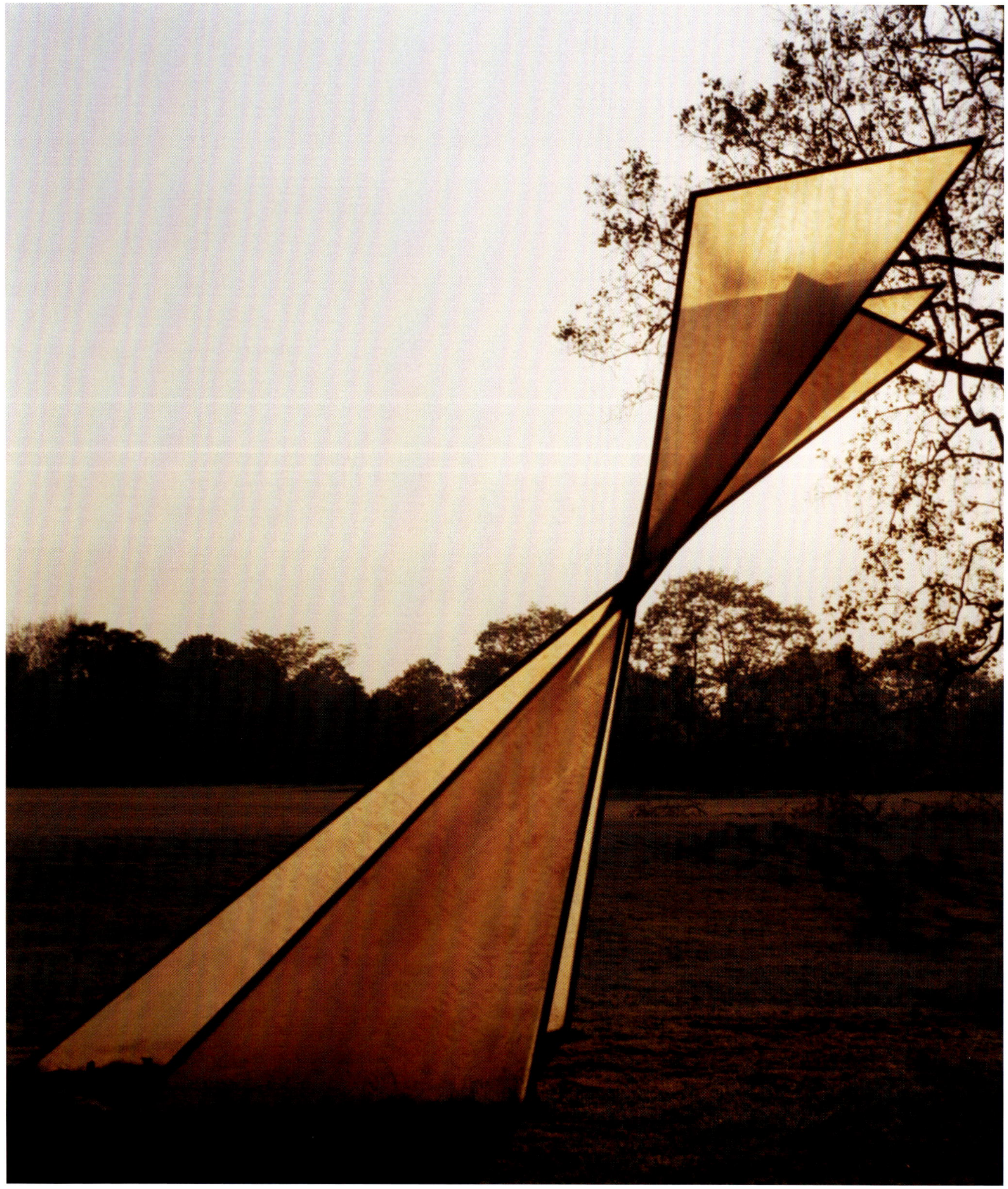

Transmitted Light Sculpture #2, 1968
steel and fiberglass

Reflected Light Sculpture #2, 1969
stainless steel

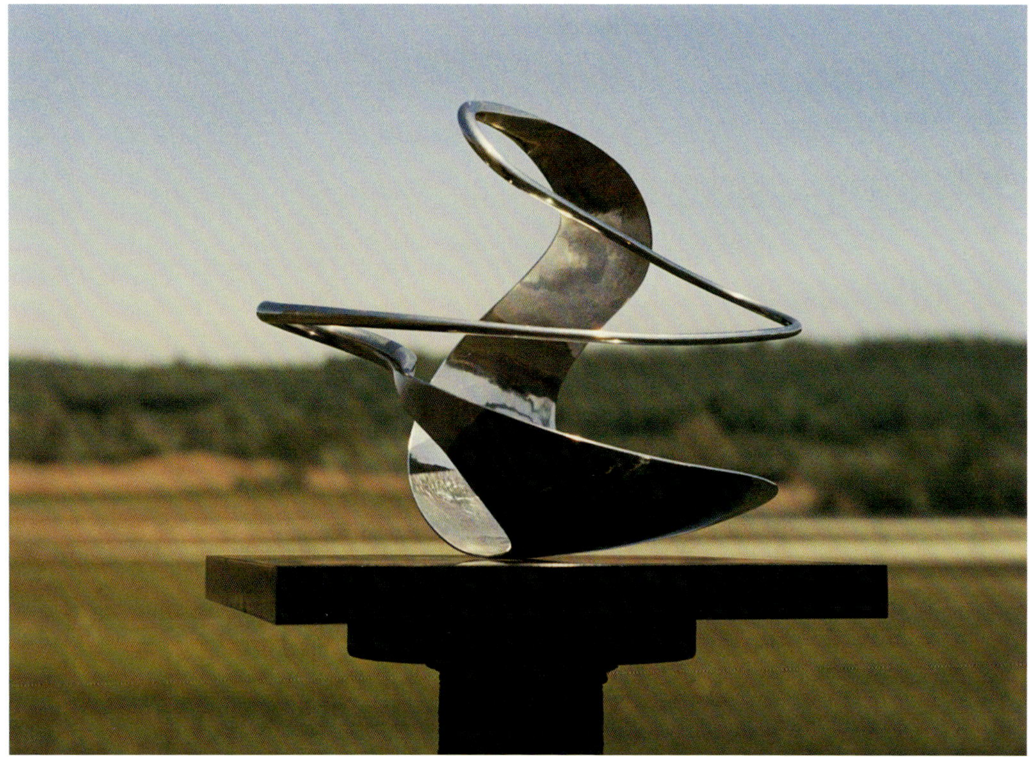

Reflected Light Sculpture #4, 1969
nickel silver and mild steel

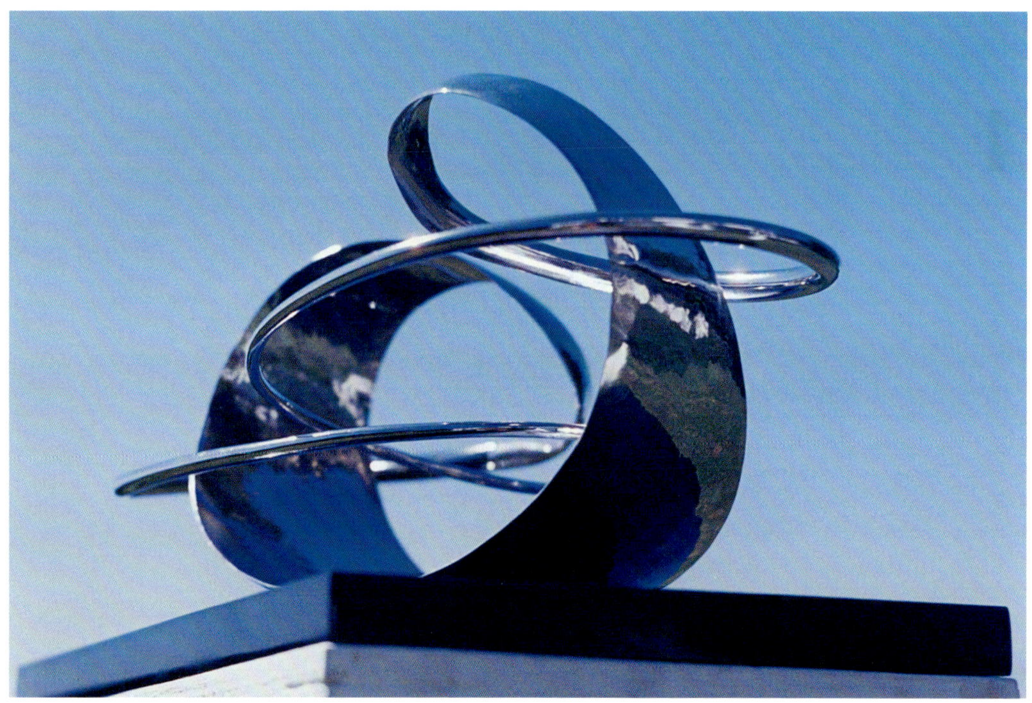

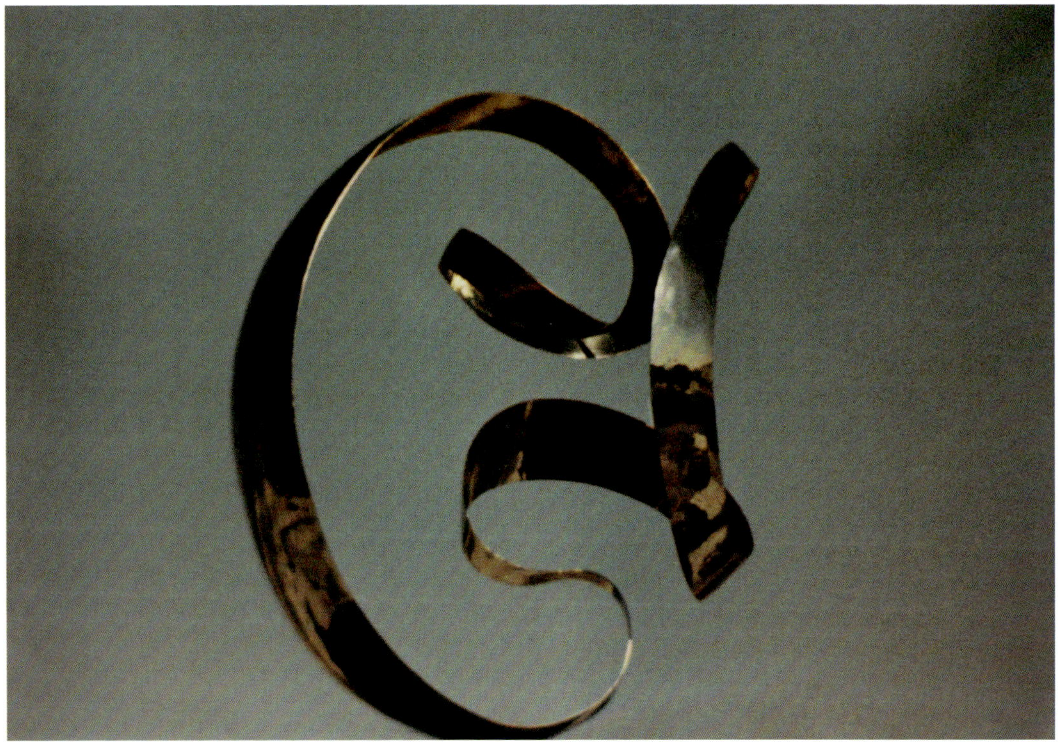

Reflected Light Sculpture #5, 1969
stainless steel

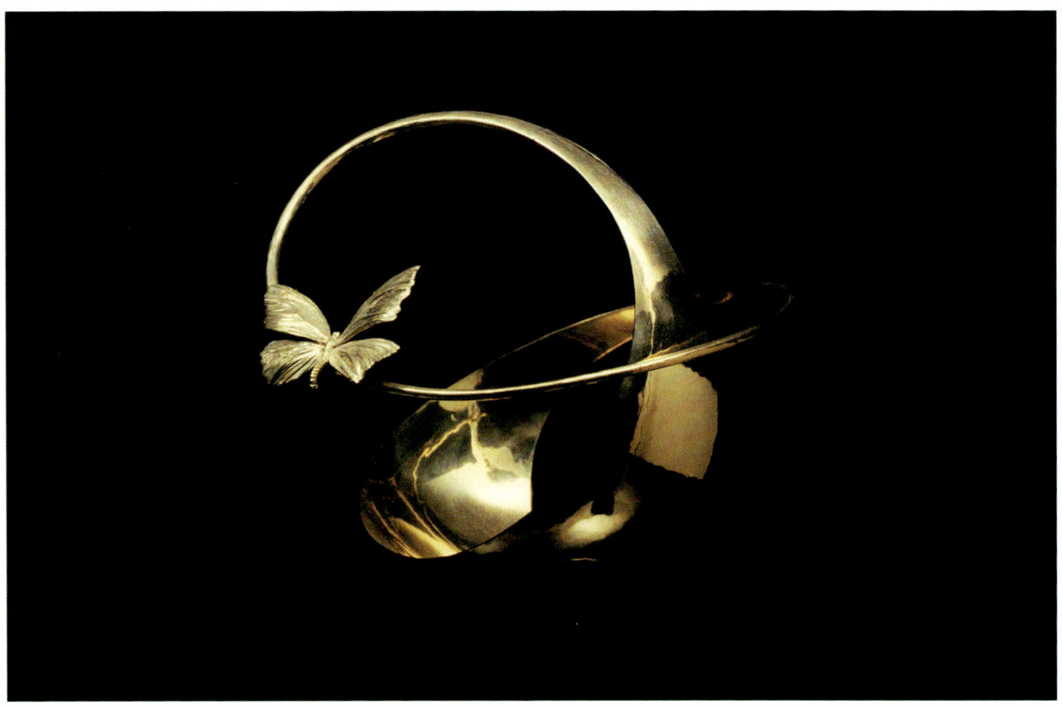

A Moments Rest, 1982
gold

Limited-Edition Prints

Atlantic Salmon

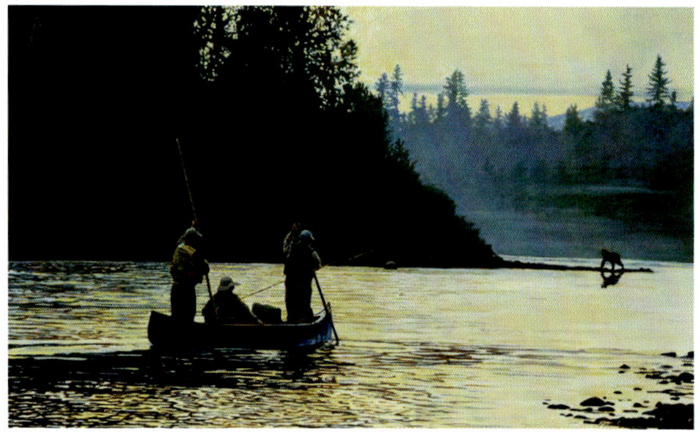

4

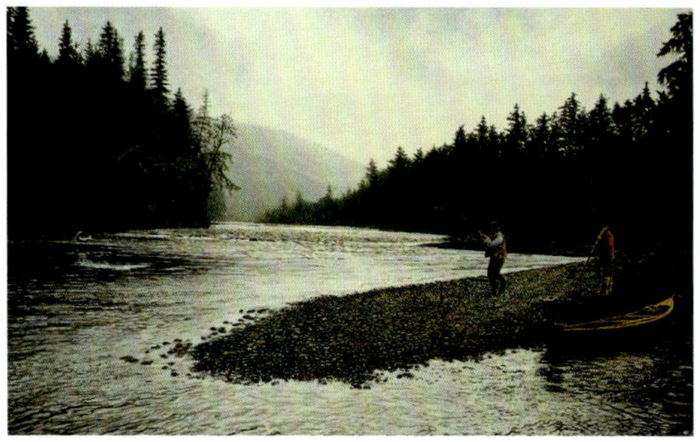

1

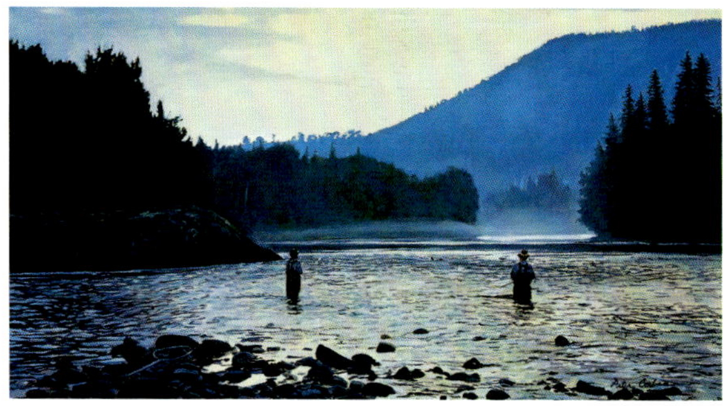

5

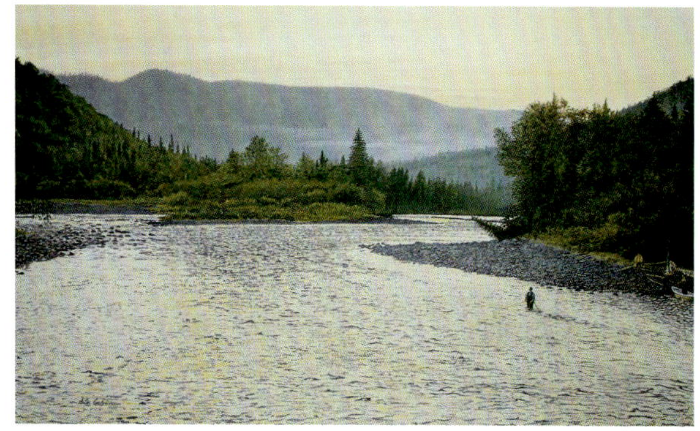

8

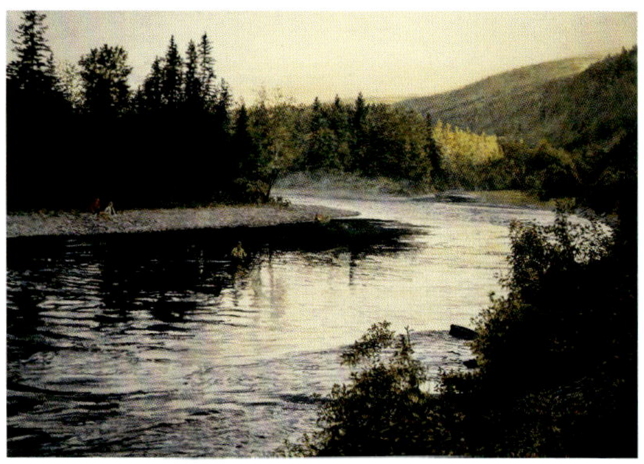

2

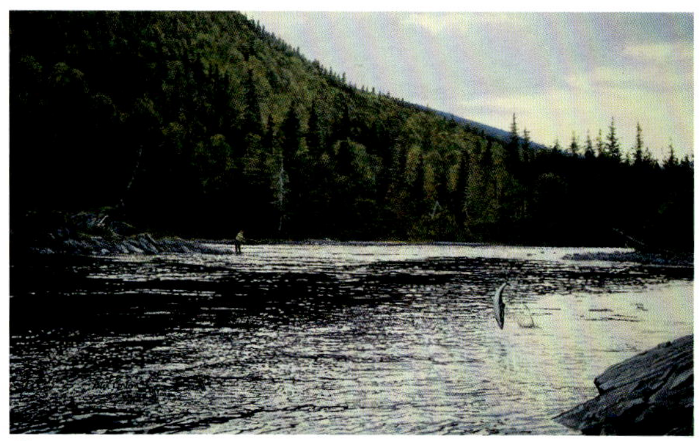

6

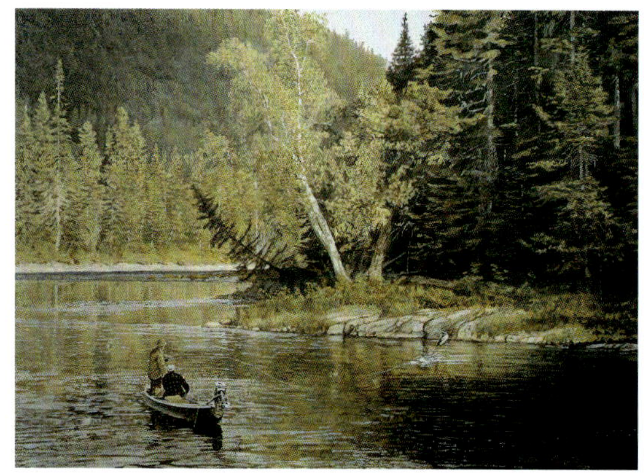

9

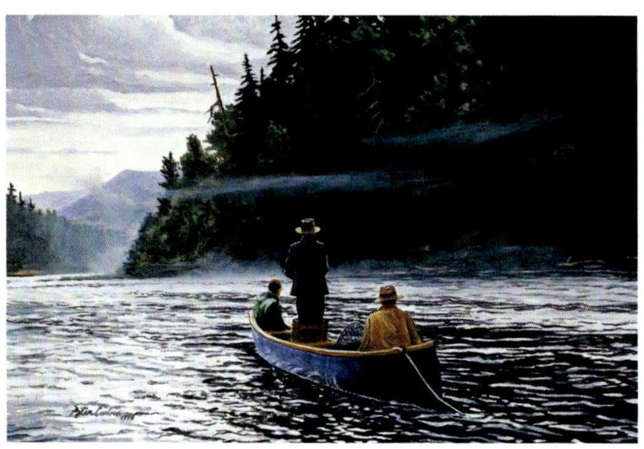

3

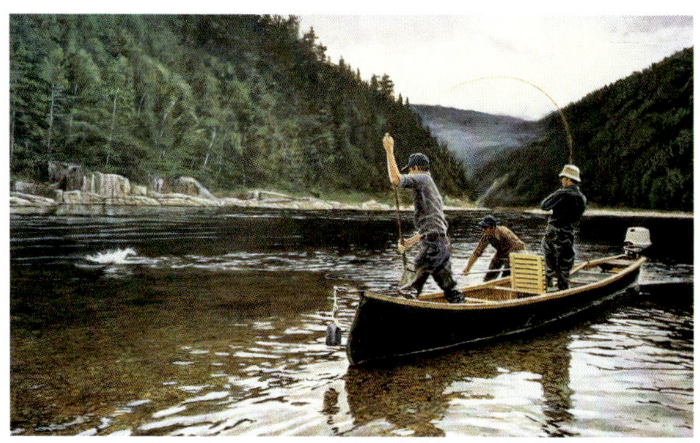

7

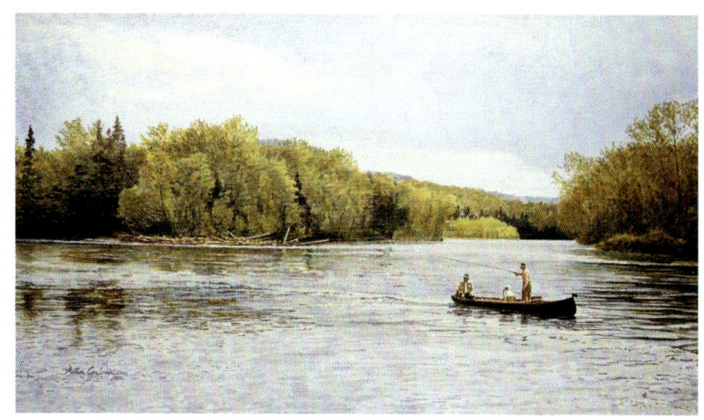

10

1. *A Cascapédia Morning*
   (Atlantic Salmon Federation 1989 Print of the Year)
   Published by Mill Pond Press
   Issue Date: 1988
   Edition Size: 950, 25 Artist's Proofs Remarqued
   Image Size: 17⅞ × 30 inches

2. *Shadow Water*
   Published by Shooter's Hill Press
   Issue Date: 1995
   Edition Size: 300
   Image Size: 16⅝ × 24⅞ inches

3. *The Blue Canoe*
   (Atlantic Salmon Federation 1999 Print of the Year)
   Published by Shooter's Hill Press
   Issue Date: 1998
   Edition Size: 300
   Image Size: 16⅝ × 25 inches

4. *Evening Encounter*
   Published by Shooter's Hill Press
   Issue Date: 2004
   Edition Size: 150
   Image Size: 15 × 25 inches

5. *Charlie Valley Rock*
   Published by Shooter's Hill Press exclusively for the Anglers Club of New York
   Issue Date: 2001
   Edition Size: 150
   Image Size: 13 × 25 inches

6. *One-on-One*
   Published by Shooter's Hill Press for the Catskill Fly Fishing Center
   Issue Date: 1990
   Edition Size: 250
   Image Size: 14⅞ × 24¾ inches

7. *Near the Net*
   (Atlantic Salmon Federation 1982 Print of the Year)
   Published by Atlantic Salmon Association
   Issue Date: 1981
   Edition Size: 200, 25 Artist's Proofs Remarqued
   Image Size: 14⅜ × 24 inches

8. *A Cascapédia Evening*
   Published by Shooter's Hill Press
   Issue Date: 1992
   Edition Size: 300
   Image Size: 17⅞ × 30¼ inches

9. *Wyers Pool*
   Published by Petersen Prints
   Issue Date: 1983
   Edition Size: 400
   Image Size: 14 × 19 inches

10. *Above the Fork*
    Presentation Series Print
    Published by Shooter's Hill Press
    Issue Date: 1993
    Edition Size: 950
    Image Size: 6½ × 9½ inches

Trout

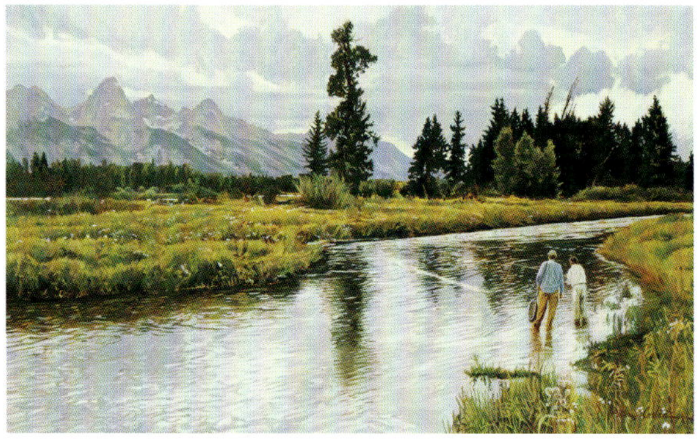

11

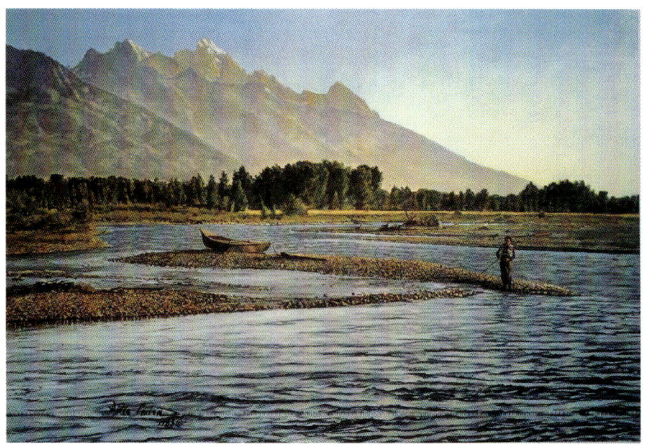

12

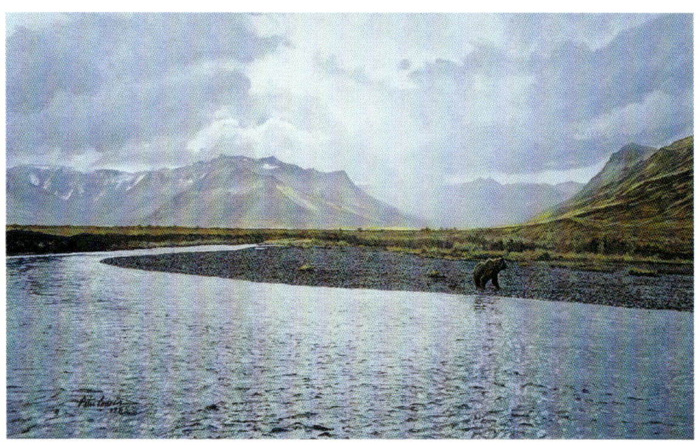

13

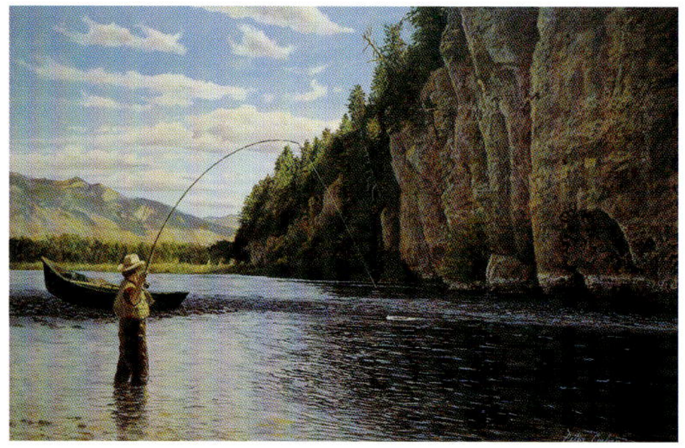

14

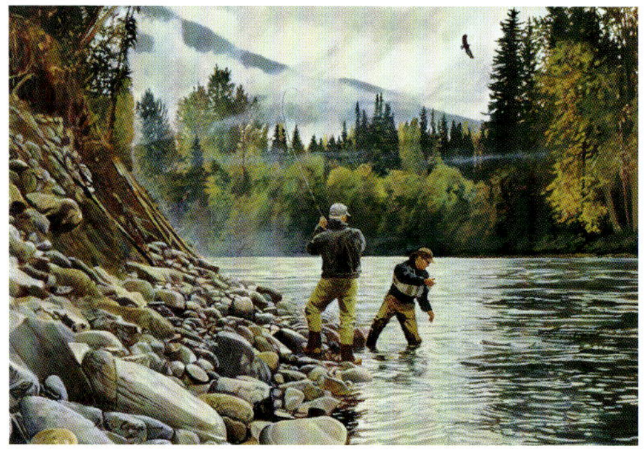

15

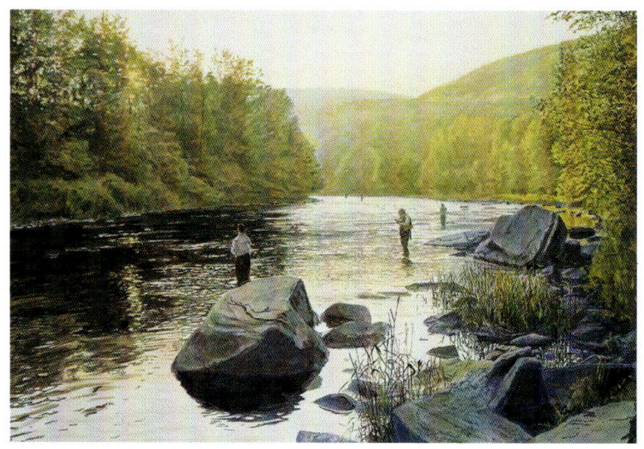

16

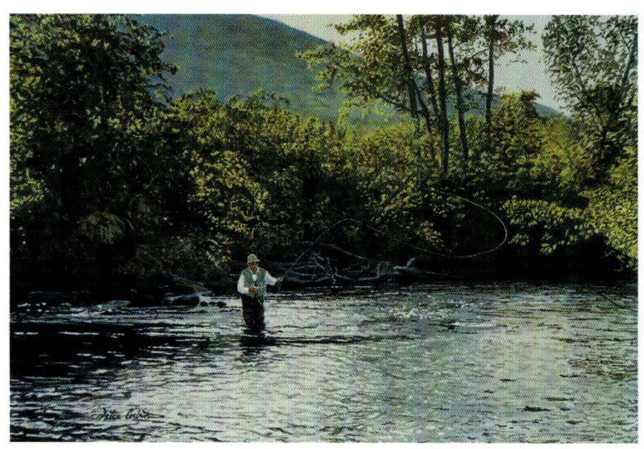

17

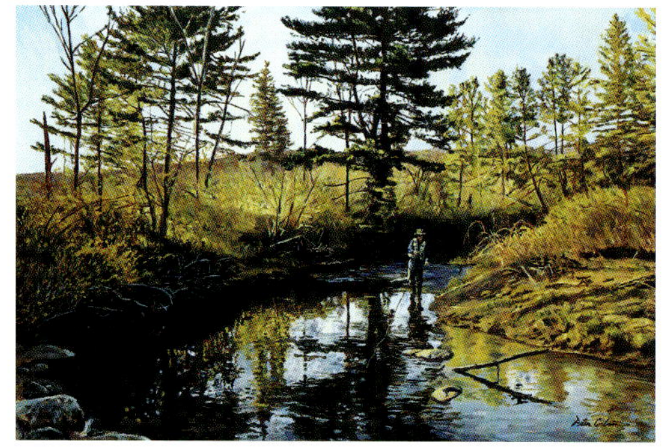

18

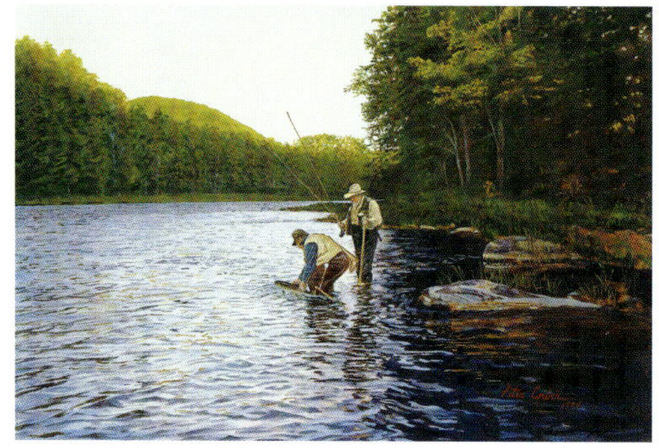

19

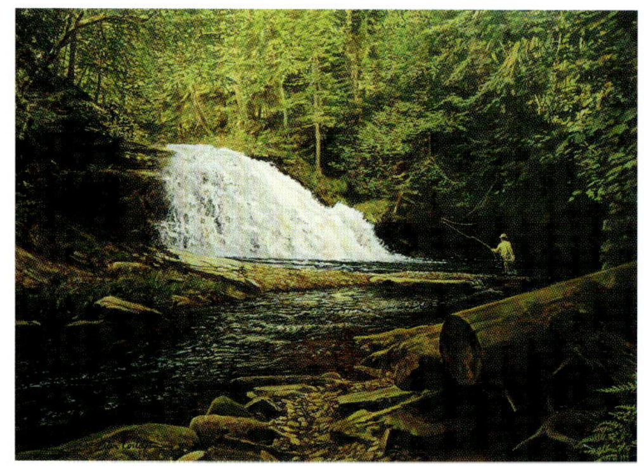

20

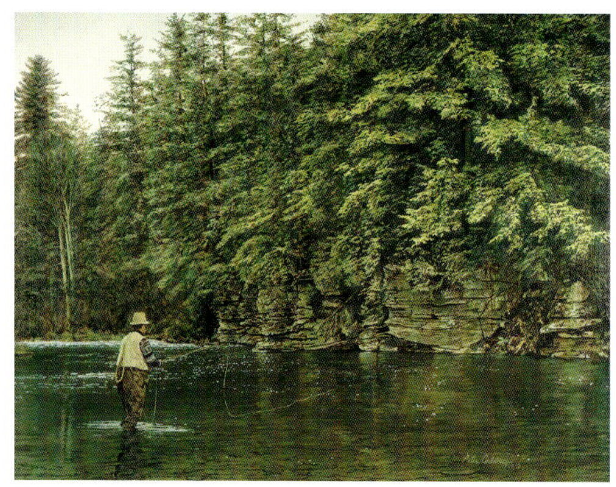

21

11. *Partners*
Published by Shooter's Hill Press
and matching numbered books of
PETER CORBIN: An Artist's Creel
Hudson Hills Press
Issue Date: 2005
Deluxe Edition Size: 150
Image Size: 15 × 25 inches

12. *The Gravel Bar*
Published by Petersen Prints
Issue Date: 1983
Edition Size: 400
Image Size: 14 × 21⅛ inches

13. *Alaskan Solitude*
Published by Shooter's Hill Press
Issue Date: 1995
Edition Size: 300
Image Size: 16⅝ × 24⅞ inches

14. *Head of the Canyon*
Published by Shooter's Hill Press
Issue Date: 1993
Edition Size: 300
Image Size: 16⅝ × 24⅞ inches

15. *Close at Hand*
Published by Shooter's Hill Press for
the Silver Hilton Steelhead Lodge
Issue Date: 2002
Edition Size: 200
Image size: 16 × 24 inches

16. *Beaverkill Afternoon*
Presentation Series Print
Published by Shooter's Hill Press
Issue Date: 1993
Edition Size: 950
Image Size: 6½ × 9½ inches

17. *Battenkill Afternoon*
Published exclusively for The American
Museum of Fly Fishing
Issue Date: 1993
Edition Size: 200
Image Size: 16⅝ × 24⅞ inches

18. *The Hollenbeck Club*
Published by Shooter's Hill Press exclusively
for The Hollenbeck Club
Issue Date: 2000
Edition Size: 50
Image Size: 16⅞ × 25 inches

19. *Releasing a Trophy*
Published by Shooter's Hill Press exclusively
for Theodore Gordon Fly Fishers
Issue Date: 1995
Edition Size: 250
Image Size: 14 × 21 inches

20. *The Falls*
Published by Shooter's Hill Press
Issue Date: 1989
Edition Size: 250
Image Size: 18 × 24⅞ inches

21. *The Ledge Pool*
Published by Petersen Prints
Issue Date: 1983
Edition Size: 400
Image Size: 12½ × 18 inches

Salt Water

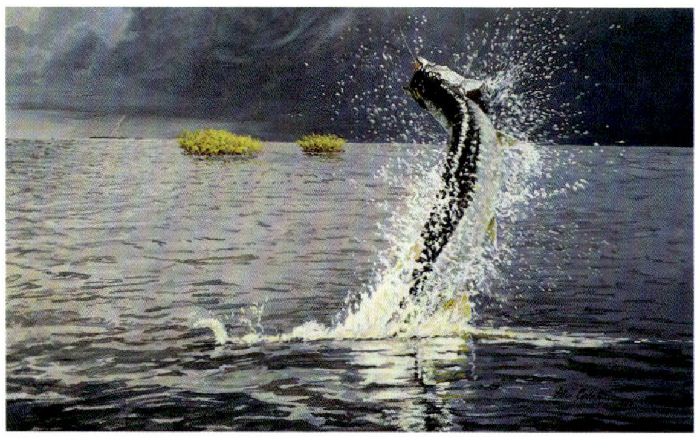
22

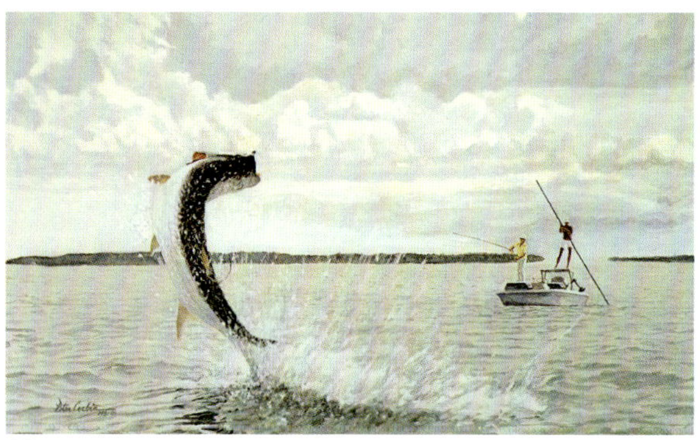
23

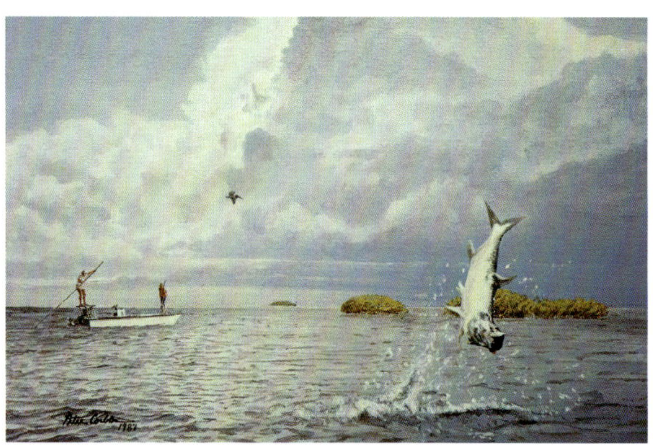
24

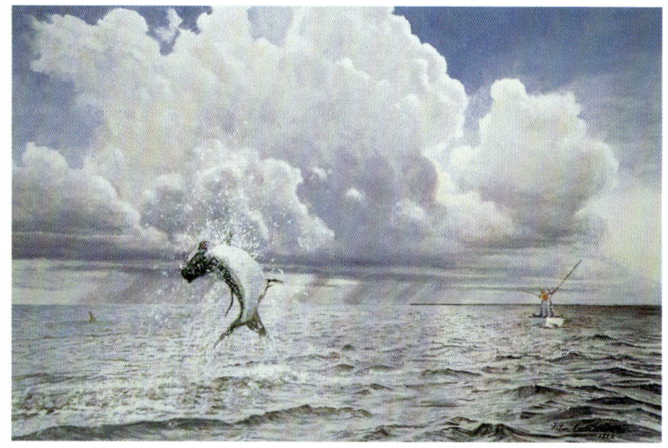
25

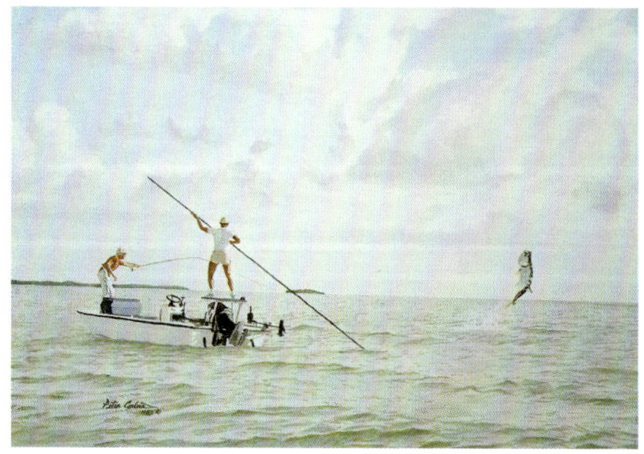
26

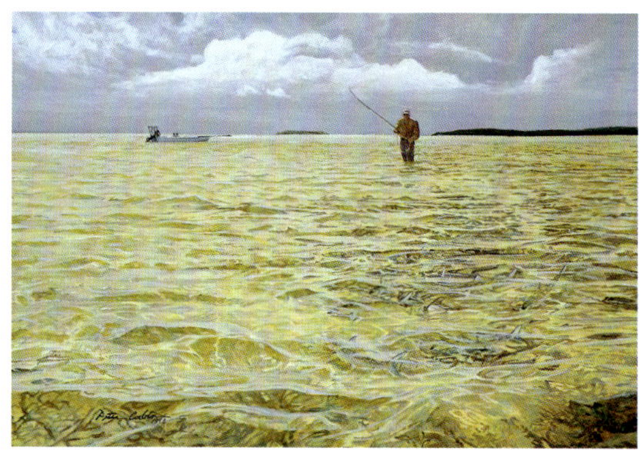
27

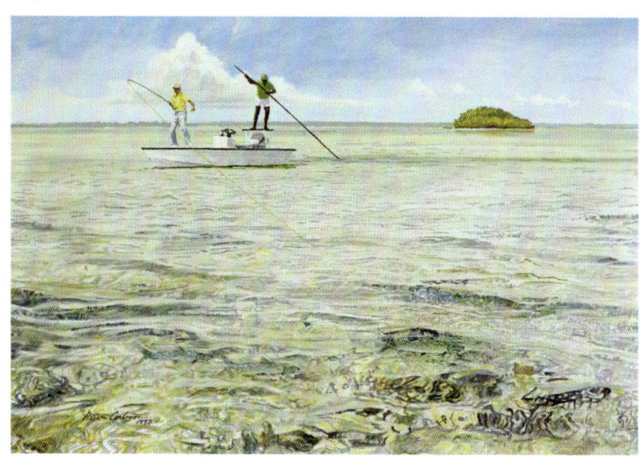
28

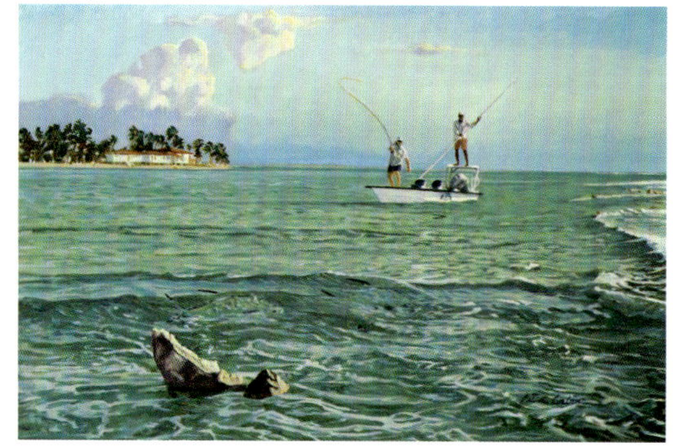
29

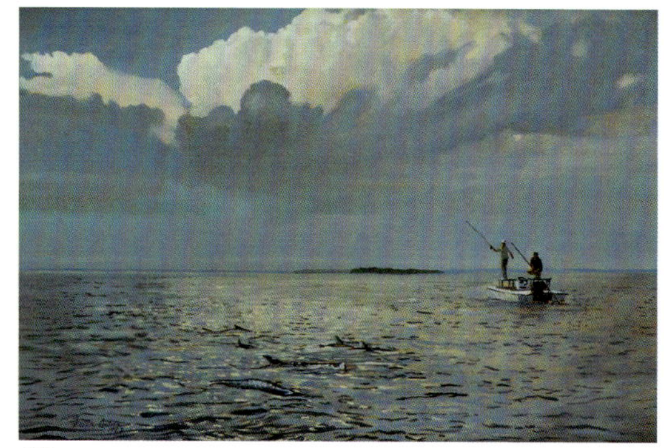
30

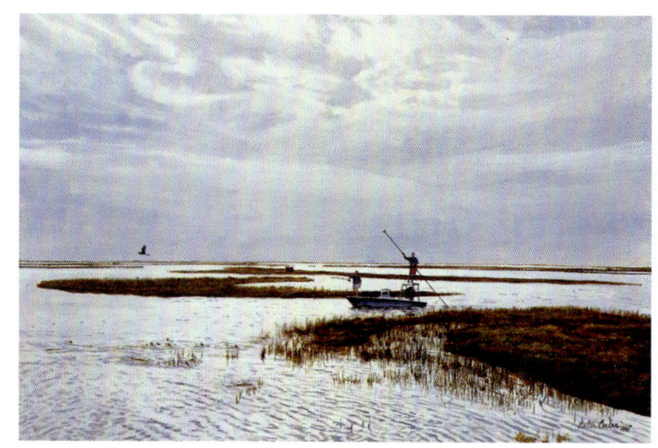
31

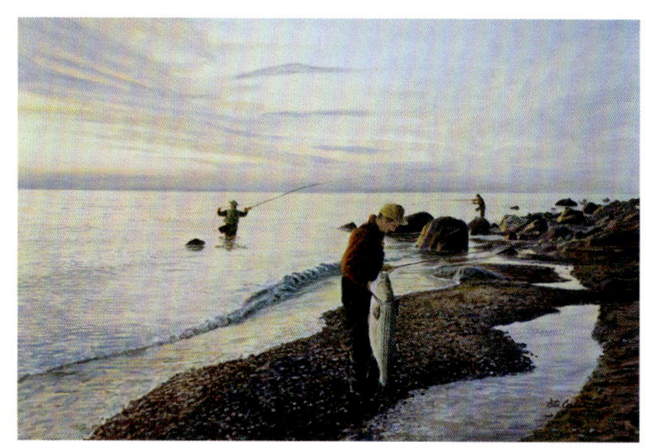
32

22. *Thunder & Lightning*
Published by Shooter's Hill Press
Issue Date: 1995
Edition Size: 300
Image Size: 16⅝ × 24⅞ inches

23. *First Run*
Published by Petersen Prints
Issue Date: 1983
Edition Size: 400
Image Size: 12½ × 20¼ inches

24. *Tarpon's Tempest*
Published by Shooter's Hill Press
Issue Date: 1990
Edition Size: 250
Image Size: 16¼ × 24⅜ inches

25. *Trouble Brewing*
Published by Shooter's Hill Press and Meadow Run Press, matching numbered books of *The Silver King*
Issue Date: 1993
Edition Size: 100
Image Size: 16⅝ × 24⅞ inches

26. *Straight Up*
Presentation Series Print
Published by Shooter's Hill Press
Issue Date: 1993
Edition Size: 950
Image Size: 6½ × 9½ inches

27. *Hard Light–Bonefish*
Published by Shooter's Hill Press
Issue Date: 1996
Edition Size: 300
Image Size: 16⅝ × 25 inches

28. *The Starting Gate*
Published by Shooter's Hill Press and Meadow Run Press, matching numbered books of *The Bonefish*
Issue Date: 1993
Edition Size: 100
Image Size: 16⅝ × 24⅞ inches

29. *Turneffe Permit*
Published by Shooter's Hill Press exclusively for Turneffe Flats Lodge
Issue Date: 2002
Edition Size: 150
Image Size: 16 × 24 inches

30. *Rolling Tarpon*
Published by Shooter's Hill Press
Issue Date: 2000
Edition Size: 250
Image Size: 13⅜ × 20 inches

31. *Edge of the Marsh–Redfish*
Published by the Coastal Conservation Association
Issue Date: 1997
Edition Size: 100, 25 Artist's Proofs
Image Size: 15 × 22 inches

32. *Trophy Fish*
Published by Shooter's Hill Press
Issue Date: 1996
Edition Size: 300
Image Size: 16⅝ × 25 inches

Upland

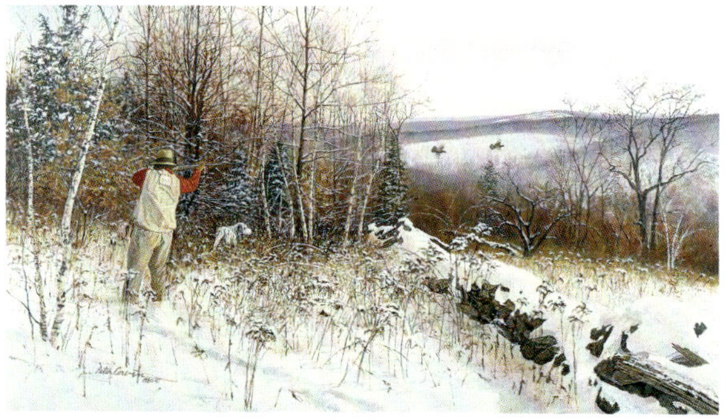

33

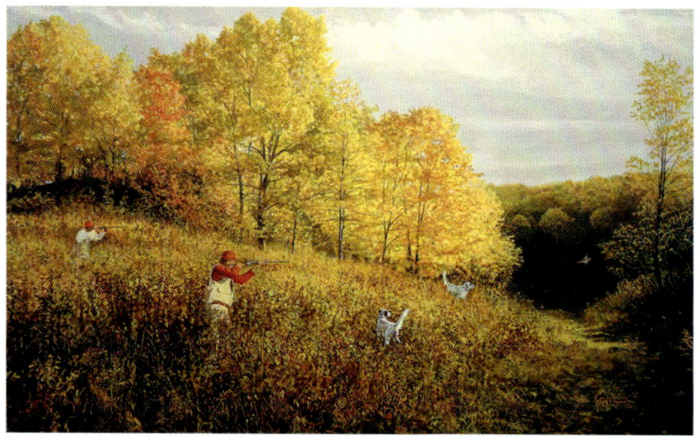

34

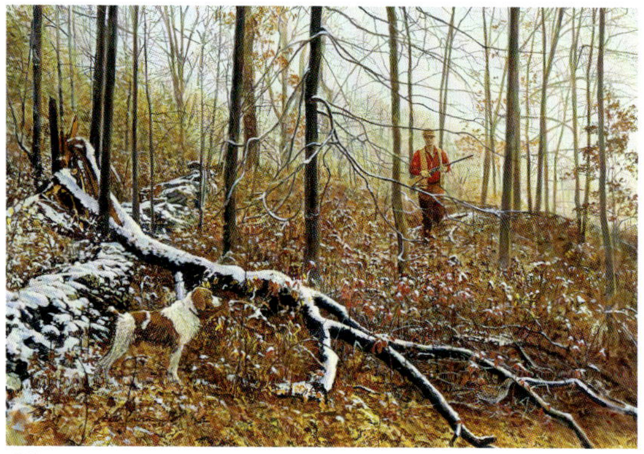

35

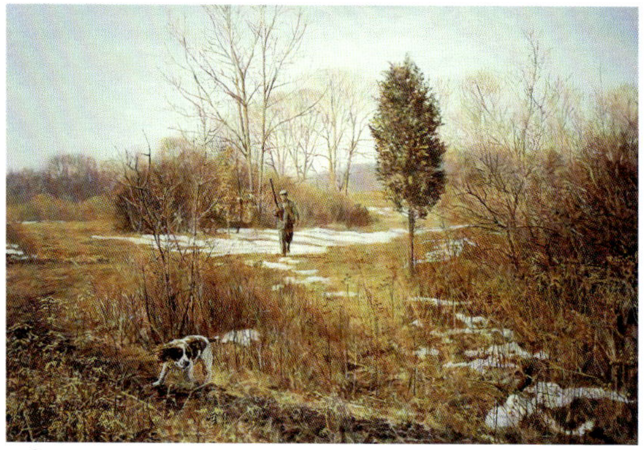

36

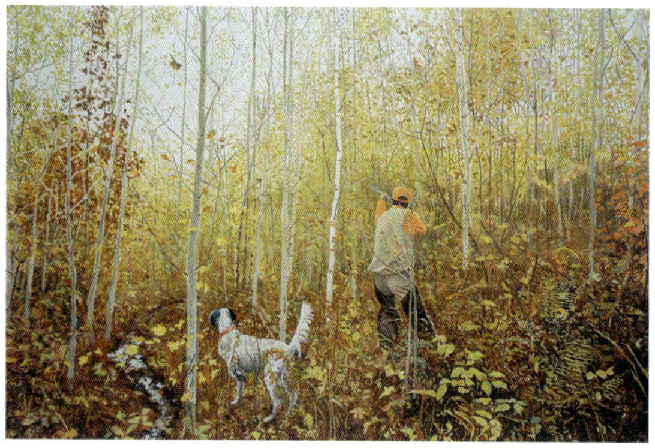

37

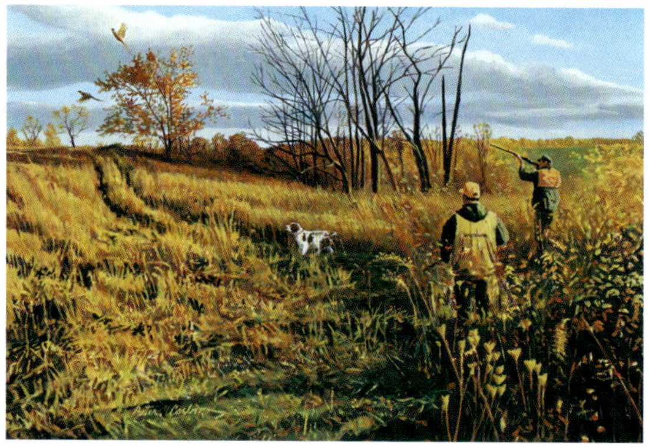

38

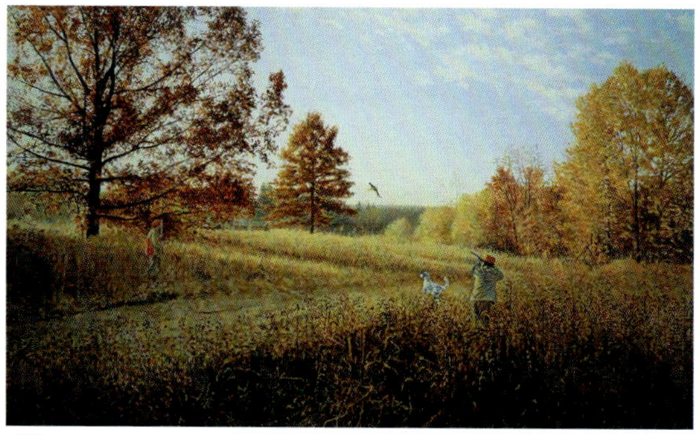

39

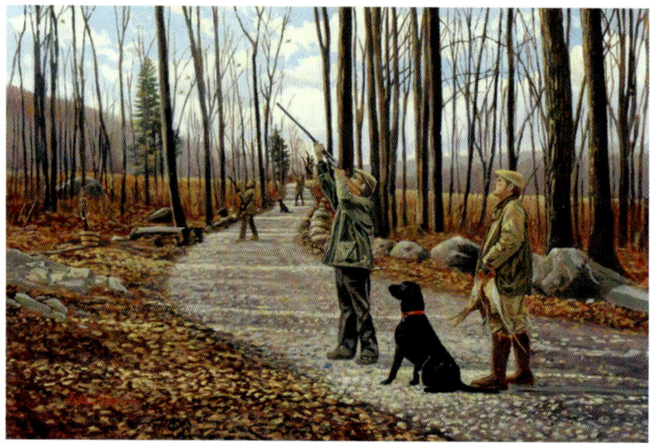

40

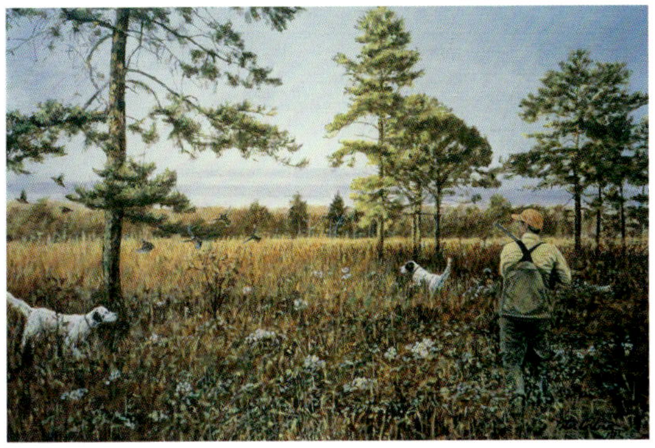
41

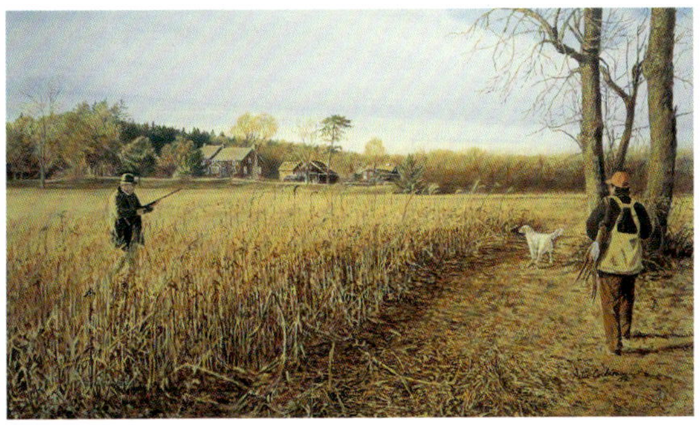
42

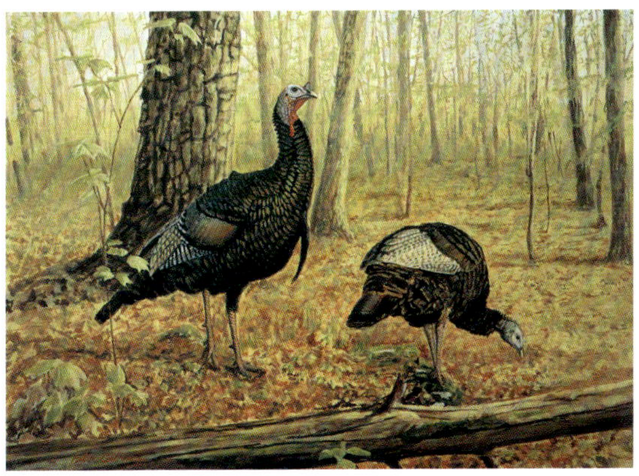
43

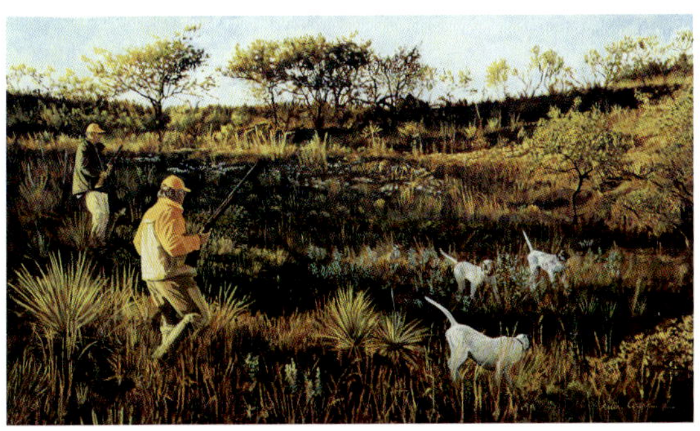
44

33. *A Chance to Double*
Published by The Orvis Company
Issue Date: 1980
Edition Size: 250, 50 deluxe
Image Size: 14¾ × 24¾ inches

34. *First of the Season*
Published by Shooter's Hill Press
Issue Date: 2000
Edition Size: 250
Image Size: 15 × 25 inches

35. *Stonewall Brittany*
Published by Shooter's Hill Press
Issue Date: 1993
Edition Size: 300
Image Size: 16⅝ × 24⅞ inches

36. *Three Seconds to Lift Off*
Presentation Series Print
Published by Shooter's Hill Press
Issue Date: 1993
Edition Size: 950
Image Size: 6½ × 9½ inches

37. *October Afternoon*
Published by Shooter's Hill Press
Issue Date: 1992
Edition Size: 300
Image Size: 16⅝ × 24⅞ inches

38. *Tamarack Double*
Published by Shooter's Hill Press
for "Friends of Corbin Shoot"
Issue Date: 2002
Edition Size: 25
Image Size: 16 × 24 inches

39. *Amwell Autumn*
Published by Shooter's Hill Press
Issue Date: 1989
Edition Size: 250
Image Size: 14¾ × 24¾ inches

40. *The Line*
Published by Shooter's Hill Press
for "Friends of Corbin Shoot"
Issue Date: 2004
Edition Size: 25
Image Size: 16⅝ × 25 inches

41. *Opening Day Bobwhites*
Published by Petersen Prints
Issue Date: 1985
Edition Size: 950, 25 Artist's Proofs
Remarqued
Image Size: 16⅝ × 25 inches

42. *Sandanona Sporting Club*
Published by Shooter's Hill Press exclusively
for Sandanona Sporting Club
Issue Date: 1990
Edition Size: 150
Image Size: 15 × 25 inches

43. *Spring Fever*
(First New York State Turkey Stamp Print)
Published by Sportsman's Specialty Company
Issue Date: 1982
Edition Size: 1,500
Image Size: 6½ × 9 inches

44. *The Orange Coat*
Published by Shooter's Hill Press
Issue Date: 2005
Edition Size: 150
Image Size: 15 × 25 inches

Water Fowl

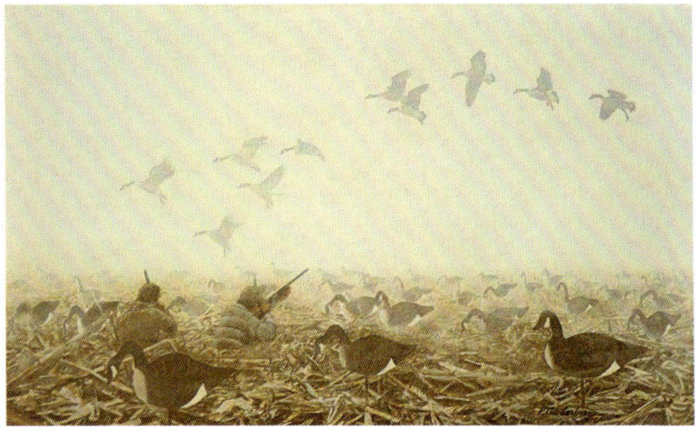

45

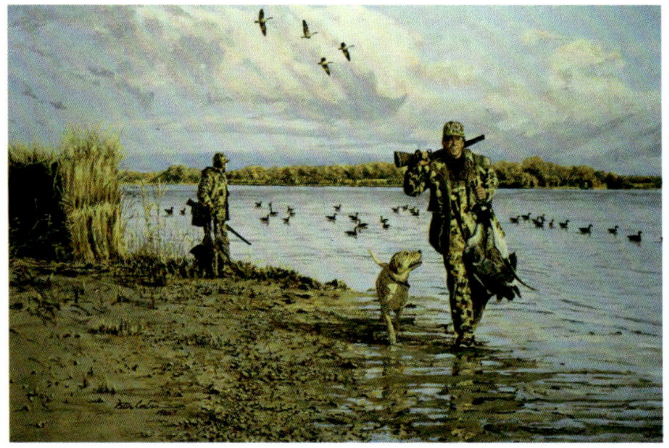

48

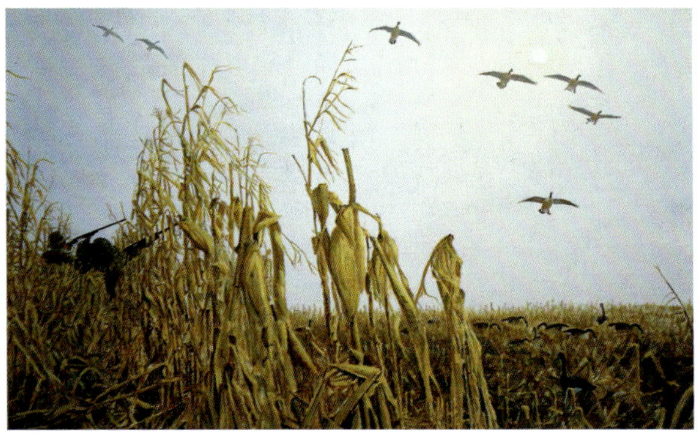

46

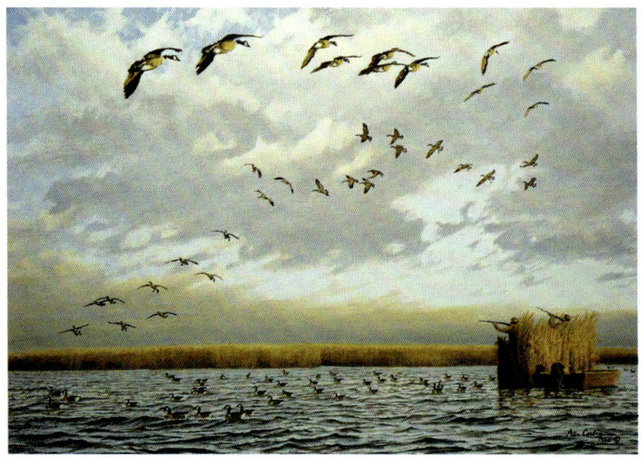

49

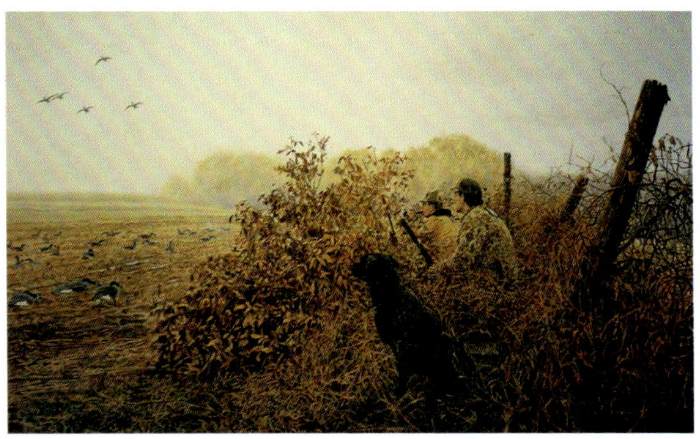

47

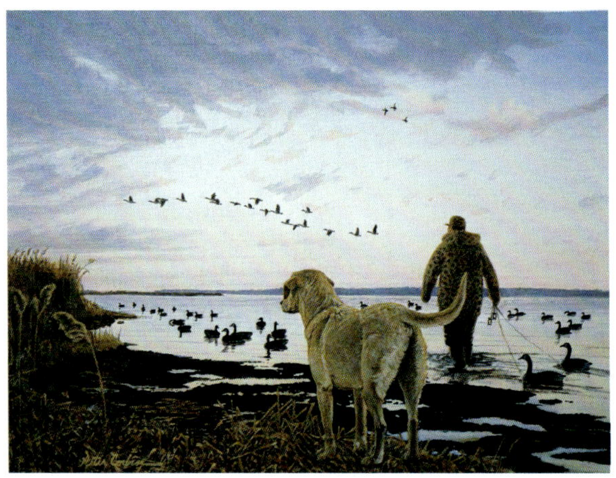

50

45. *Fogbound*
    Published by Petersen Prints
    Issue Date: 1982
    Edition Size: 800
    Image Size: 15 × 24¾ inches

46. *The Cornrow Blind*
    Published by Shooter's Hill Press
    Issue Date: 1990
    Edition Size: 250
    Image Size: 14¾ × 25 inches

47. *The Hedgerow Blind*
    Published by Mill Pond Press
    Issue Date: 1988
    Edition Size: 950, 25 Artist's Proofs
    Remarqued
    Image Size: 16 × 26¾ inches

48. *A Day to Remember*
    (National Ducks Unlimited Companion Piece)
    Published by National Ducks Unlimited
    Issue Date: 1987
    Edition Size: 4,500, 150 Artist's Proofs,
    25 Artist's Proofs Remarqued
    Image Size: 16 × 24 inches

49. *Flight Pattern*
    (First New York State Ducks Unlimited
    Sponsor Print)
    Published by New York State Ducks
    Unlimited / John Treiber Insurance Co.
    Issue Date: 1987
    Edition Size: 1,000, 50 Artist's Proofs
    Remarqued
    Image Size: 16⅜ × 24⅞ inches

50. *A Promising Day*
    Published by the Waterfowl Festival & Peter
    S. Corbin Inc.
    Issue Date: 1984
    Edition Size: 300
    Image Size: 12¾ × 17 inches

51. *Black Ducks–The Old Way*
(Second New York State Ducks Unlimited Sponsor Print)
Published by New York State Ducks Unlimited / John Treiber Insurance Co.
Issue Date: 1988
Edition Size: 1,250, 50 Artist's Proofs Remarqued
Image Size: 16⅜ × 24¾ inches

52. *Edge of the Bay*
Published by Mill Pond Press
Issue Date: 1988
Edition Size: 950, 25 Artist's Proofs Remarqued
Image Size: 14¼ × 19⅜ inches

53. *Broadbill Shooting on Barnegat Bay*
Published by Southern Ocean County Ducks Unlimited
Issue Date: 1978
Edition Size: 264, 35 deluxe
Image Size: 18⅜ × 27⅞ inches

54. *Opening Day Mallards*
Published by Petersen Prints
Issue Date: 1985
Edition Size: 950, 25 Artist's Proofs Remarqued
Image Size: 16½ × 25 inches

55. *The Mallard Hunters*
Published by Petersen Prints
Issue Date: 1981
Edition Size: 800, 25 Artist's Proofs Remarqued
Image Size: 15 × 25 inches

56. *The Pothole–Wood Ducks*
(Third New York State Ducks Unlimited Sponsor Print)
Published by New York State Ducks Unlimited / John Treiber Insurance Co.
Issue Date: 1990
Edition Size: 1,300, 100 Executive Edition, 50 Artist's Proofs Remarqued
Image Size: 16⅝ × 25 inches

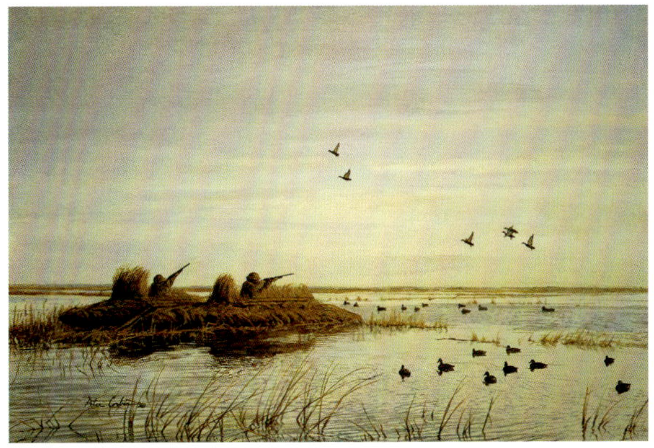
51

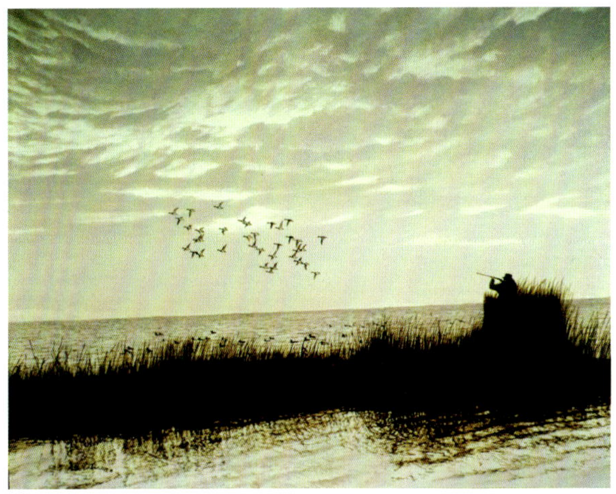
52

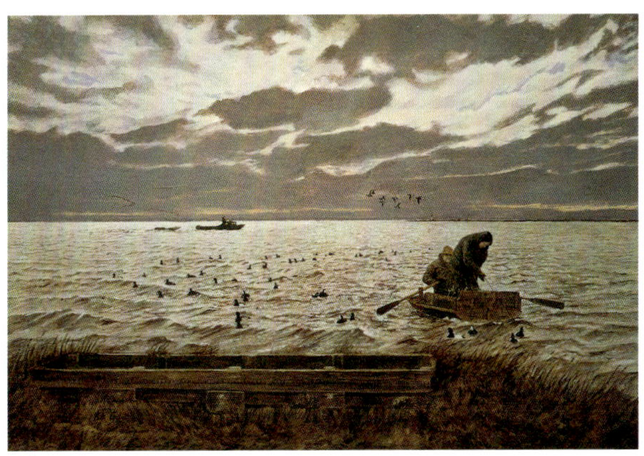
53

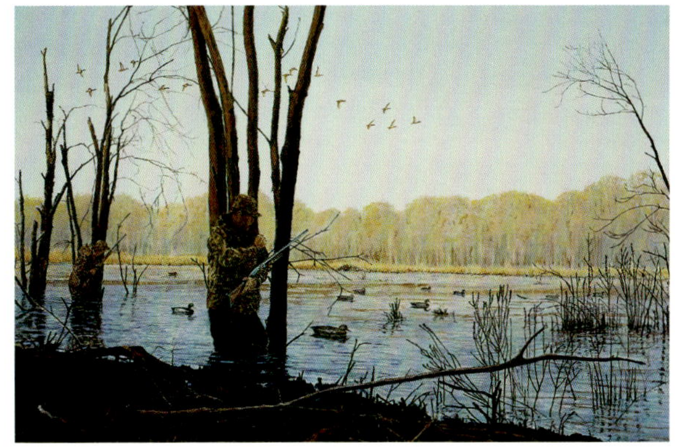
54

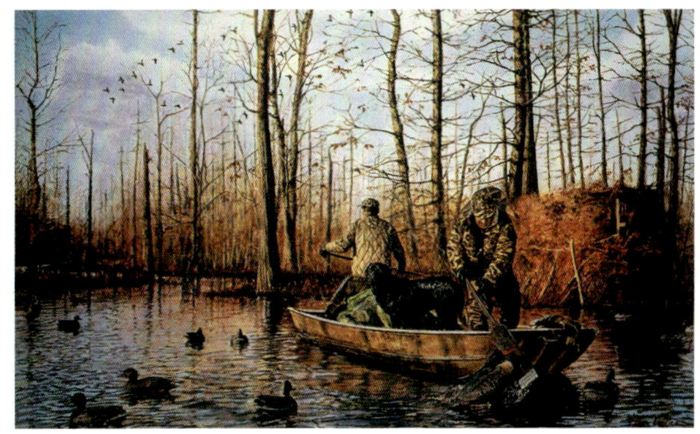
55

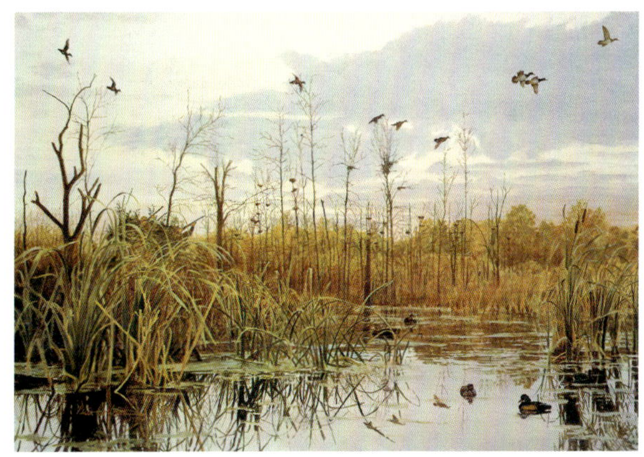
56

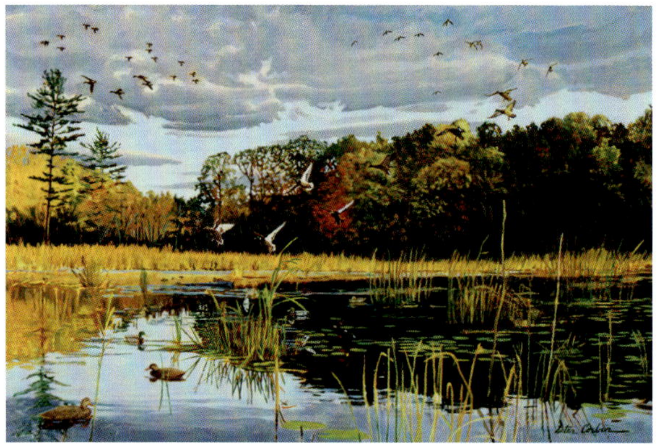

57

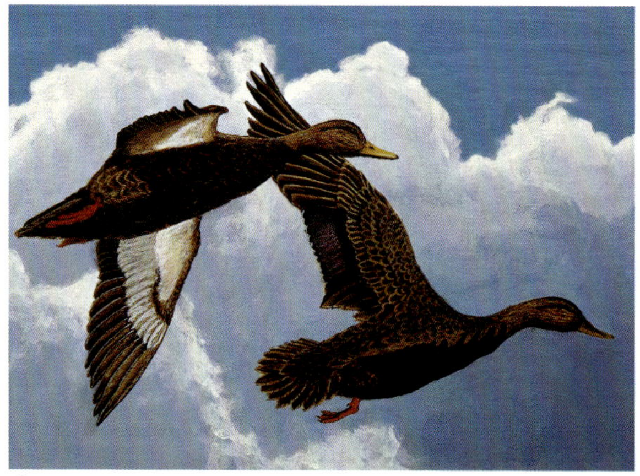

60

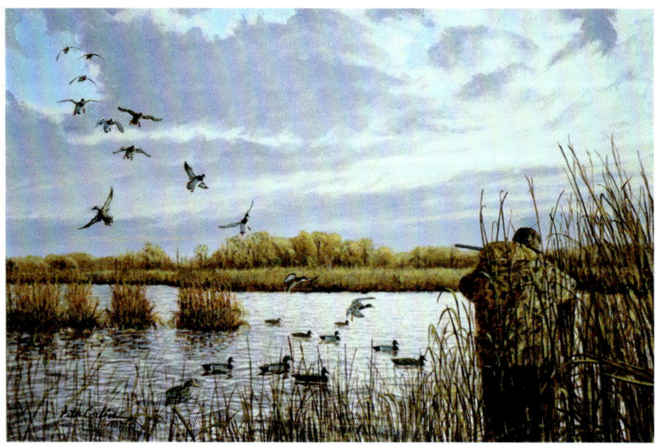

58

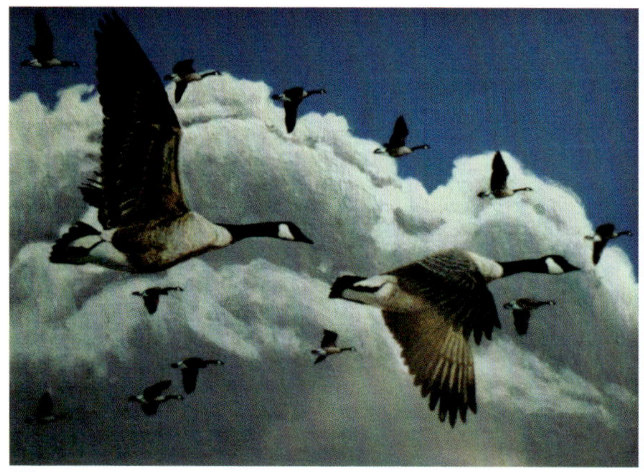

61

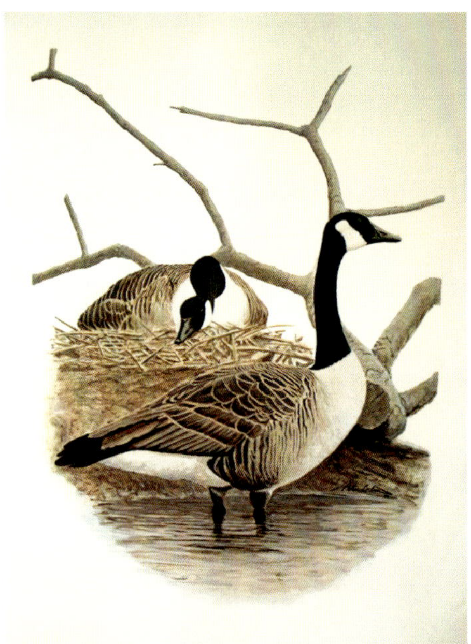

59

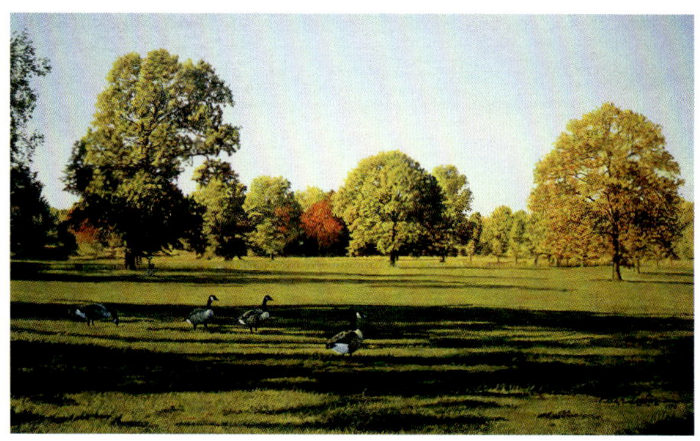

62

57. *Flight Birds*
    Published by Shooter's Hill Press for "Friends of Corbin Shoot"
    Issue Date: 2003
    Edition Size: 25
    Image Size: 16 × 24 inches

58. *Totally Committed*
    Published by Petersen Prints
    Issue Date: 1982
    Edition Size: 800
    Image Size: 16 × 24 inches

59. *The Stick Nest*
    Published by Phillip Morris Company
    Issue Date: 1976
    Edition Size: Unknown
    Image Size: 20 × 15½ inches

60. *Black Ducks*
    (First Long Island Wetlands and Waterfowl League Stamp)
    Published by A. J. Liu American Sporting Collector
    Issue Date: 1977
    Edition Size: 600, 50 deluxe
    Image Size: 6½ × 9 inches

61. *Canada Geese*
    (First New York State Ducks Unlimited Print of the Year)
    Published by New York State Ducks Unlimited / Genesee Brewing Company
    Issue Date: 1983
    Edition Size: 750
    Image Size: 7¼ × 10 inches

62. *Giralda Farms*
    Published by Shooter's Hill Press exclusively for The Prudential
    Issue Date: 1990
    Edition Size: 150
    Image Size: 15 × 25 inches

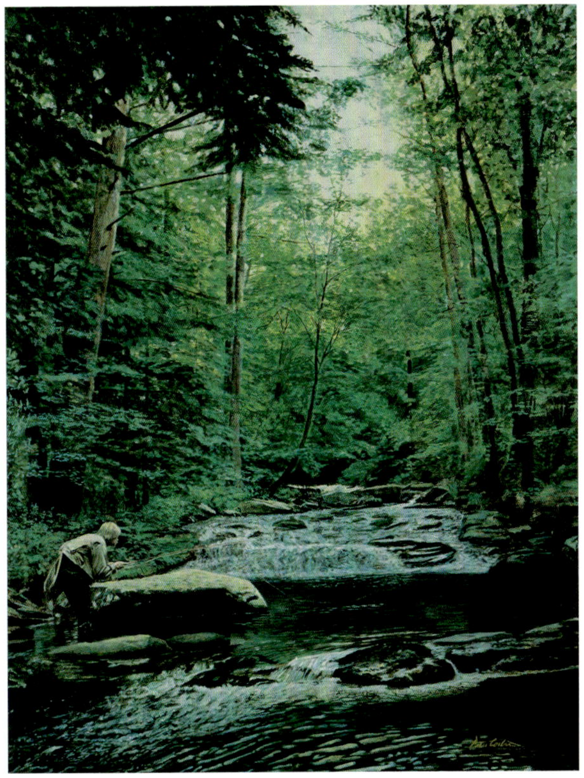
63

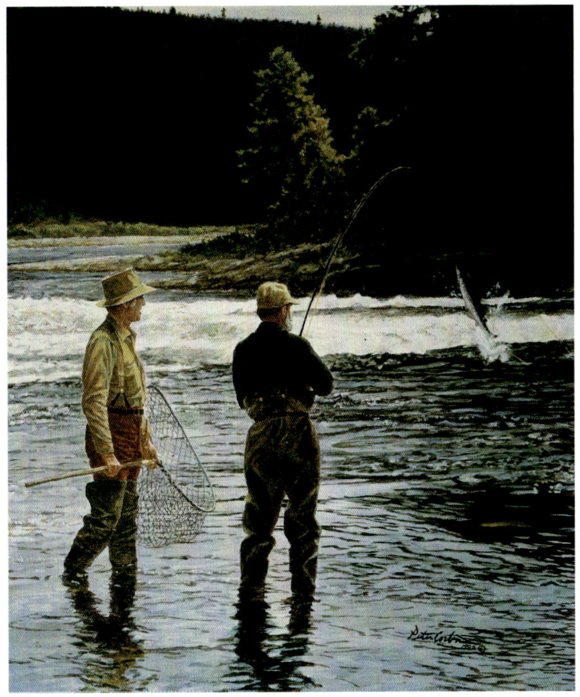
65

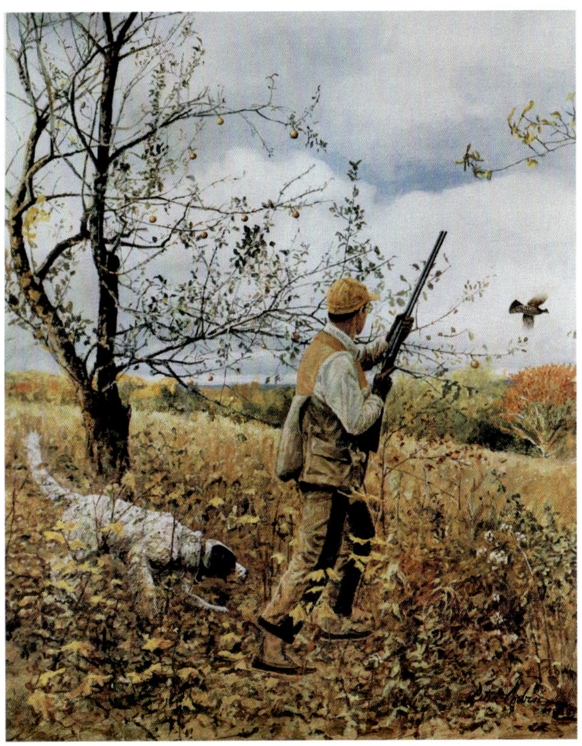
64

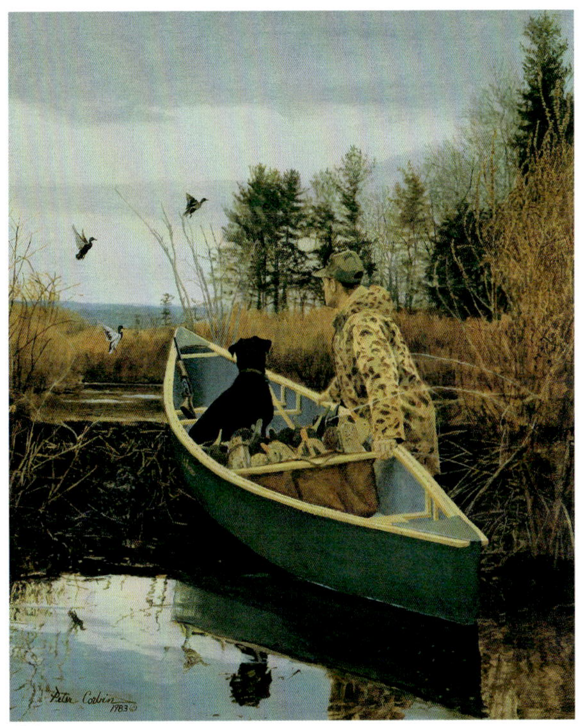
66

63. *Stalking*
    Published by Raventree Publications
        for L. L. Bean
    Issue Date: 1982
    Edition Size: 800
    Image Size: 23 × 18½ inches

64. *Edge of the Orchard*
    Published by Raventree Publications
        for L. L. Bean
    Issue Date: 1982
    Edition Size: 800
    Image Size: 21 × 18 inches

65. *Above the Rapids*
    Published by Raventree Publications
        for L. L. Bean
    Issue Date: 1983
    Edition Size: 375
    Image Size: 21⅛ × 18¼ inches

66. *Easing Them Out*
    Published by Raventree Publications
        for L. L. Bean
    Issue Date: 1983
    Edition Size: 375
    Image Size: 20⅞ × 18 inches

Chronology

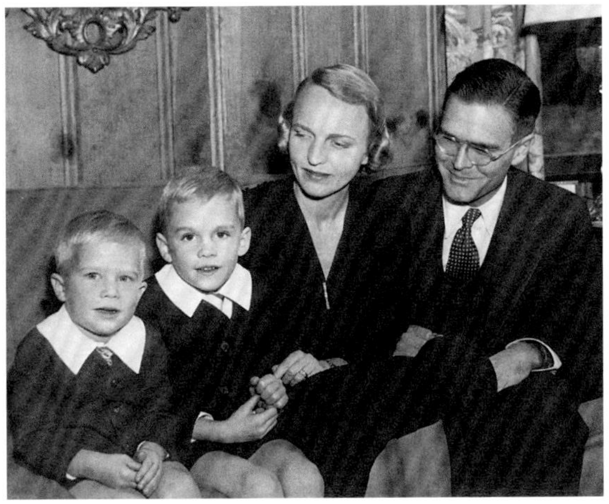

Peter (age two), Hunter, Elizabeth & Robert Corbin, 1947.

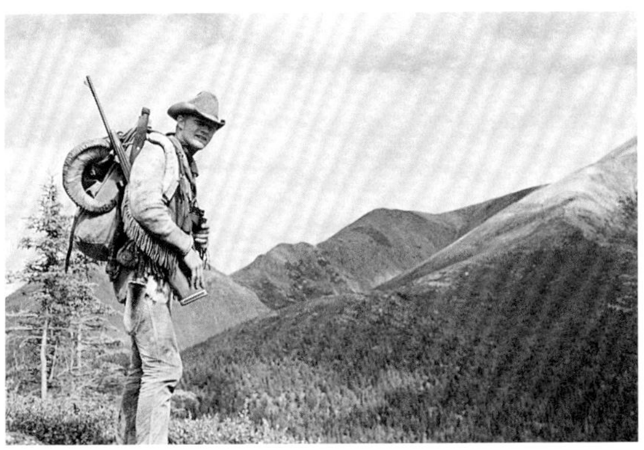

Cassiar Range, British Columbia, 1964.
Photo by George Galpin.

1945 Peter is born in West Orange, New Jersey, to Robert and Elizabeth Corbin of Llewellyn Park, West Orange, New Jersey. Peter has an older brother, Hunter.

Located approximately fifteen miles from New York City, Llewellyn Park, built in the 1870s, is one of the first planned communities in the country with miles of roads and large open, wild spaces.

Peter's father, a banker by trade, makes his own fly rods and collects A. B. Frost prints and books on Carl Rungius, Lynn Bogue Hunt, and Francis Lee Jaques. He paints and carves decoys.

1950 Peter is taken to the Hartwood Club in the Catskills, founded by Peter's great grandfather William O. Corbin, among others, in the late 1800s. This is Peter's first exposure to fishing, to deer, grouse, snakes, and to the deep woods of old pine trees.

1951 Father presents Peter with first shotgun. Peter learns to carry it properly in field for three years before he is allowed to have shells.

1955 Family travels to Miramichi River, New Brunswick. Peter lands first grilse and sees print by Ogden Pleissner.

1959 After attending day schools, Peter leaves home for Pomfret School in northeastern Connecticut, where a sculpture teacher, Alice Dunbar, and a painting teacher, Charles Cole, encourage his artistic exploration. Peter excels more on the athletic field than in the classroom.

1963 Peter goes to British Columbia with Gus Blagden, where they hunt Stone sheep and Rocky Mountain goat. He returns to the Cassiar Range the following summer.

1964 Enters Wesleyan University and plays football, hockey, track, and lacrosse. Peter fails freshman calculus and is allowed to enter art program early, where he studies under John Risley and Harry Nadler. He becomes interested in the study of light.

1966 The Corbin family takes air safari trip to game parks of Kenya and through Tanganyika. Peter deep-sea fishes in the Indian Ocean and then for Nile Perch in Lake Rudolph where he lands a giant Nile Perch, about eighty pounds. This trip begins a lifetime pattern of world travel and appreciation of the natural world.

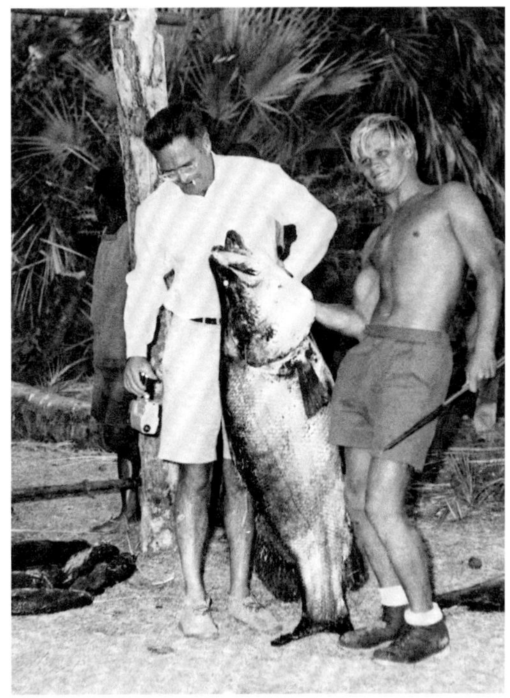

Peter with giant Nile Perch taken on family safari trip to Lake Rudolph, East Africa, 1966. Photo by Hunter Corbin.

1968 Peter has one-man show at Wesleyan University of his large outdoor abstract sculpture featuring transmitted light. He graduates with high honors in art.

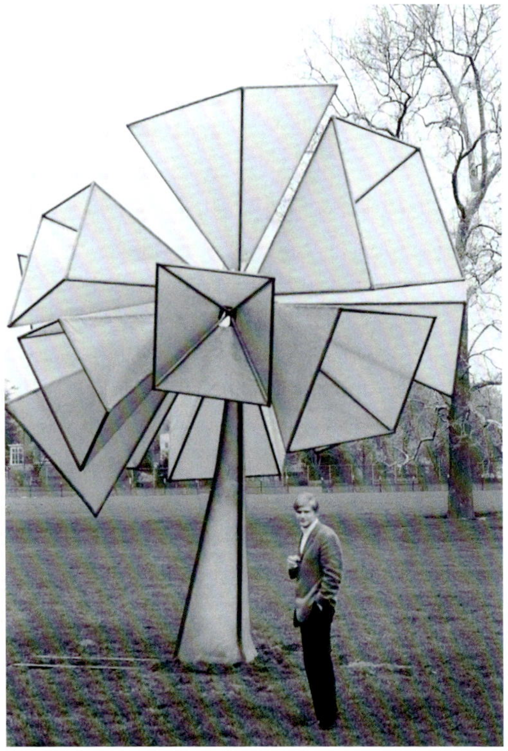

Show opening at Wesleyan University, May 1968

Parents divorce. Peter travels to Spain and Italy with mother, spending many long hours in El Prado and sketching in Florence. He finds motion study to start new series of sculpture from street sketch sheets. Returns to rented house in Connecticut and begins six-piece series of abstract sculptures dealing with reflected light and linear motion. This series of work lasts for two years.

1969 Peter moves to California and studies at California College of Arts and Crafts.

1970 Somewhat disillusioned with art scene in Bay area, Peter returns east and begins working for Robert S. Fisher & Co., a jewelry manufacturer in Newark, New Jersey. Although primarily involved with management, he designs a few jewelry pieces.

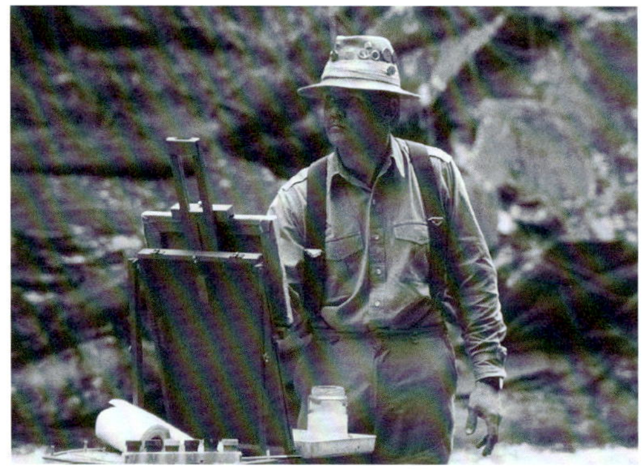

Peter Corbin in an early publicity photo. Photo by Gordon Allen

1973 Marries Lillian Stokes Pyne, October 6, a date chosen to give the newlyweds time to settle in together before the heart of the duck-hunting season arrives.

They spend their honeymoon on the Grande Cascapédia, where Lillian outfishes him. Upon their return, they move to New York City, where Lillian works at a New York bank. Peter reverses the commute to Newark.

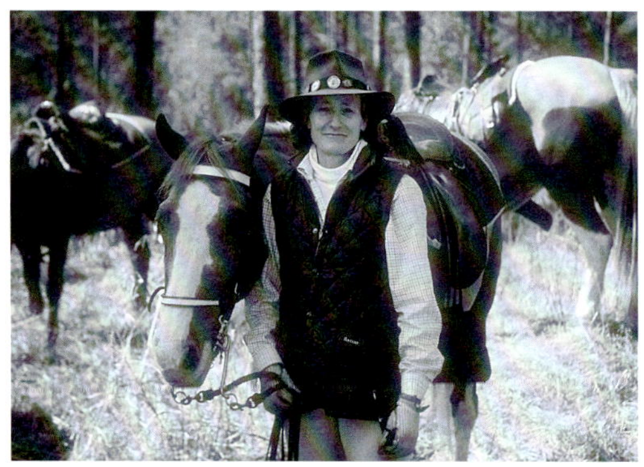

Lillian, an accomplished equestrian, on quail hunt, 2003. Photo by Peter Corbin.

1974 With Lillian's encouragement, both Peter and Lillian resign from their employers to live in weekend house at Hartwood Club in Catskills so Peter can paint full-time. He sells his first work at The Crossroads of Sport gallery in New York City.

1975 Peter and Lillian move to Rhinebeck, New York. Peter shows paintings at the Waterfowl Festival in eastern Maryland and the Game Conservation in San Antonio, Texas. Begins to receive commissions with reputation for sporting paintings of sky and water.

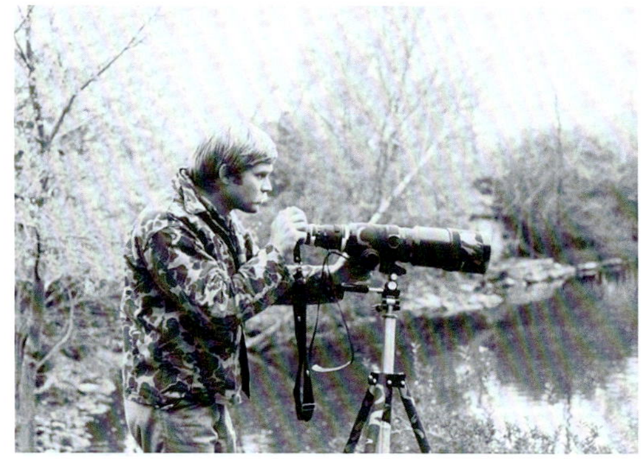

Peter Corbin, 1977

1979 L. L. Bean commissions Peter for first of four covers for its catalog.

Son, Parker Stockton Corbin, is born September 29.

1982 Daughter, Lindsey Pyne Corbin, is born May 29.

The family moves to Millbrook, New York, and names their new home "Shooter's Hill." Its one hundred acres is a haven for mallards, wood ducks, Canada geese, and green-winged teal.

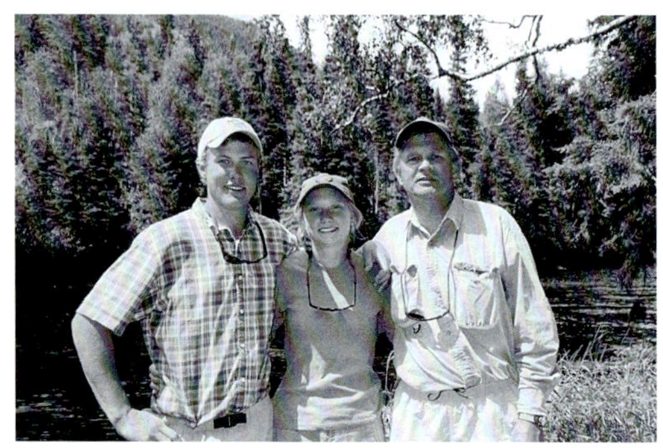

Peter, Parker, and Lindsey on the Grand Cascapédia, 2001. Photo by Donald Christ.

1985 Peter takes several trips to Alaska with old friend (and Parker's godfather) Lee Mortimer, inspiring several large paintings, the largest of which, *Crossing the Estuary*, is accepted to the *Birds in Art* exhibition of the Leigh Yawkey Woodson Museum and purchased for its permanent collection.

1987–1988 Peter takes two artist-in-residence trips to Jackson Hole, Wyoming, and studies horse anatomy there with Jon Zahourek. He paints several scenes of the Snake River and the Tetons.

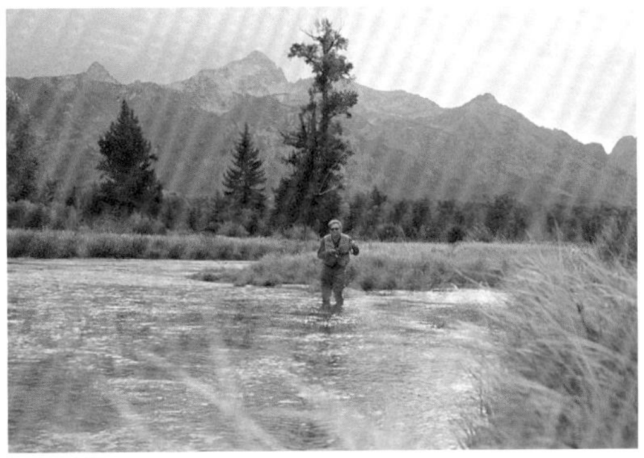

Jackson Hole, September 2003. Photo by Bill Egan.

1989 After having his paintings published by Petersen Prints and later by Mill Pond Press, Peter founds Shooter's Hill Press to gain control of his limited-edition prints to offer smaller editions for his collectors and private publishing for corporations, lodge owners, and clubs. There are essentially three components of Corbin's business: privately commissioned works, original paintings and drawings done "on spec," and limited-edition prints published under his own Shooter's Hill Press imprint.

1991–1995 Peter takes a number of trips to the Florida Keys and competes in several tarpon tournaments. He wins the Islamorada Irregulars Invitational, where he meets a number of future clients. The simplicity of the flats environment, with only sun, horizon, and water, becomes one of Peter's central landscape themes.

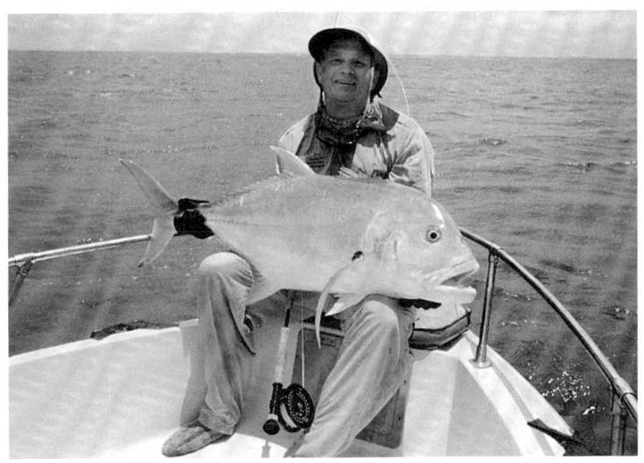

Giant Trevally, Christmas Island, 2001.
Photo by Joe Griffin.

1997 After working in acrylic paint for twenty-five years, Peter decides to go back to using oil paint with which he became familiar in college. His work develops softer edges and less detail, but more vibrancy and depth of color.

2000 Holds show at Deerfield Academy, Deerfield, Massachusetts.

2002–2004 Peter is invited to conduct a painting auction at Coeur d'Alene Art Auction in Reno, Nevada, now an annual event. Corbin's 2003 Coeur d'Alene entry, another salmon-fishing scene entitled *Evening Encounter* (for the bear that the guides and angler surprise), fetched the highest price a Corbin painting has ever commanded and more than double the pre-auction estimate.

Exhibitions

ONE-MAN EXHIBITIONS

1993 The Culinary Institute of America, Hyde Park, New York

1989 *An Artist's Creel*, The American Museum of Fly Fishing, Manchester, Vermont

1977 The Suffolk Marine Museum, Islip, New York

GROUP EXHIBITIONS

2001–2004 The Coeur d'Alene Art Auction, Reno, Nevada

2000 Deerfield Academy, Deerfield, Massachusetts

1996 *The Art of Fly Fishing—A Visual History*, Academy of the Arts, Easton, Maryland

1994 *Animals in Art*, Brookfield Zoo, Chicago Zoological Society, Brookfield, Illinois

1994 *The Sporting Life*, The Nabisco Gallery, Hanover, New Jersey

1994 *Prospectus 1994*, American Academy of Equine Art, International Museum of the Horse, The Kentucky Horse Park, Lexington, Kentucky

1993 *Pleissner Show*, The National Art Museum of Sport, Indianapolis, Indiana

1992 *Art and the Animal*, The Society of Animal Artists, 1992–1993 National Tour: Roger Tory Petersen Institute of Natural History, Jamestown, New York; The R. W. Norton Art Gallery, Shreveport, Louisana; Oklahoma Museum of Natural History, Norman, Oklahoma; Oshkosh Public Museum, Oshkosh, Wisconsin; Houston Museum of Natural Sciences, Houston, Texas

1992 *Naturally Drawn*, The Leigh Yawkey Woodson Art Museum, Wausau, Wisconsin

1991 *Art and the Animal*, The Society of Animal Artists, 1991–1992 National Tour: The Cleveland Museum of Natural History, Cleveland, Ohio; Virginia Museum of Natural History, Martinsville, Virginia; The Witte Museum, San Antonio, Texas; San Bernadino County Museums, Redlands, California; Anniston Museum of Natural History, Anniston, Alabama

1991 *Invited Artists Exhibition on Foxhunting Subjects*, American Academy of Equine Art at the Museum of Hounds and Hunting, Morven Park, Leesburg, Virginia

1991 *The World of Salmon*, The American Museum of Fly Fishing, Manchester, Vermont

1988 *The Art of Sport: Selections from the National Art Museum of Sport*, Colorado Springs Fine Art Center, Colorado Springs, Colorado

1987 *Birds in Art*, Leigh Yawkey Woodson Art Museum, Wausau, Wisconsin; Rochester Museum and Science Center, Rochester, New York; Natural History Museum of Los Angeles, Los Angeles, California; Chicago's Field Museum of Natural History, Chicago, Illinois

1986 *Birds in Art*, Leigh Yawkey Woodson Art Museum, Wausau, Wisconsin; Frye Art Museum, Seattle, Washington; The Santa Barbara Museum of Natural History, Santa Barbara, California; Bernice Pauahi Bishop Museum, Honolulu, Hawaii; The Beijing Natural History Museum, Beijing, China

1985 *Angler's All: Man and His Environment Through 500 Years of Fly Fishing*, The California Academy of Sciences, San Francisco, California

1984 *Selections from the National Art Museum of Sport in Celebration of the Olympic Year*, Fairfield University, Fairfield, Connecticut

1983 *Wildlife in Art*, National Wildlife Federation, Vienna, Virginia

1983 *The Artist's Eye on Sports*, City University of New York, New York

1980 *The Philadelphia Wildfowl Exposition*, The Academy of Natural Sciences of Philadelphia, Philadelphia, Pennsylvania

PUBLIC COLLECTIONS

Cascade Mountain Winery and Restaurant, Amenia, New York

Dana Corporation, St. Paul, Minnesota

Frazer Paper Company, Bridgeport, Connecticut

John Treiber Agency, Inc., Mineola, New York

L. L. Bean Inc., Freeport, Maine

Leigh Yawkey Woodson Art Museum, Wausau, Wisconsin

The National Art Museum of Sport, Indianapolis, Indiana

The Prudential, Giralda Farms, Madison, New Jersey

HONORS

1999 Atlantic Salmon Federation Print of the Year

1995 Atlantic Salmon Federation Artist of the Year

1995 Theodore Gordon Flyfishers' Print Artist

1993 The American Museum of Fly Fishing 25th Anniversary Print

1990 The Catskill Fly Fishing Center and Museum Print honoring Lee Wulff

1989 New York State Ducks Unlimited Sponsor Artist of the Year

1988 National Ducks Unlimited Companion Artist

1988 Atlantic Salmon Federation Artist of the Year

1988 New York State Ducks Unlimited Sponsor Artist of the Year

1987 New York State Ducks Unlimited Sponsor Artist of the Year

1984 Waterfowl Festival Cover Artist, Easton, Maryland

1983 First New York State Ducks Unlimited Print of the Year

1982 New York State Wild Turkey Stamp

1981 Atlantic Salmon Federation Artist of the Year

1977 Long Island Wetlands and Waterfowl League Stamp

1977 Drawings for the White House under President Carter

Bibliography

BOOKS

1998 *A Company of Anglers*, edited by Austin McK. Francis, privately published for The Anglers Club of New York

1996 *West of Key West*, edited by John Cole and Hawk Pollard, Stackpole Books, Mechanicsville, Pennsylvania

1994 *The Bonefish*, edited by George Reiger, Meadow Run Press, Stone Harbor, New Jersey

1993 *The Silver King*, edited by George Reiger, Meadow Run Press, Stone Harbor, New Jersey

1992 *The Starlight Creek Angling Society*, Harry Middleton, Meadow Run Press, Stone Harbor, New Jersey

1990 *The Compleat Schwiebert: A Treasury of Trout Fishing from Around the World*, by Ernest Schwiebert, Truman Talley Books/Dutton, New York

1983 *Who's Who in Waterfowl Art*, J. Ray Chapman, Ambassador Graphics and Wildlife, Summerville, South Carolina

1983 *The Georgia-Florida Field Trial Club 1967–1983*, edited by Charles M. Chapin III, Princeton University Press, Princeton, New Jersey

1976 *Trout Fishing*, Charles Waterman, Simon and Schuster, New York

1973 *An American Crusade for Wildlife*, James B. Trefethen, Winchester Press and the Boone and Crockett Club, New York

PERIODICALS

1996 September/October, *Wildlife Art News*, "The More Things Change: The New Art of Peter Corbin," by Michael McIntosh

1996 May/June, *Sporting Classics*, "Grand Slam on the Flats," story and art by Peter Corbin

1995 Summer, *Atlantic Salmon Journal*, "Peter Corbin," by Harry Bruce

1991 September/October, *Sporting Classics*, "Peter Corbin's Dirty Work," by Tom Davis

1986 September/October, *Wildlife Art News*, "The Sportsman's Legacy of Peter Corbin: A Whisper of Light," by Tom Davis

1985 August, *Sports Afield*, "The Paintings of Peter Corbin," by Lionel Atwill

1981 February, *Atlantic Salmon Journal*, "A Fascination of Light," by John Merwin

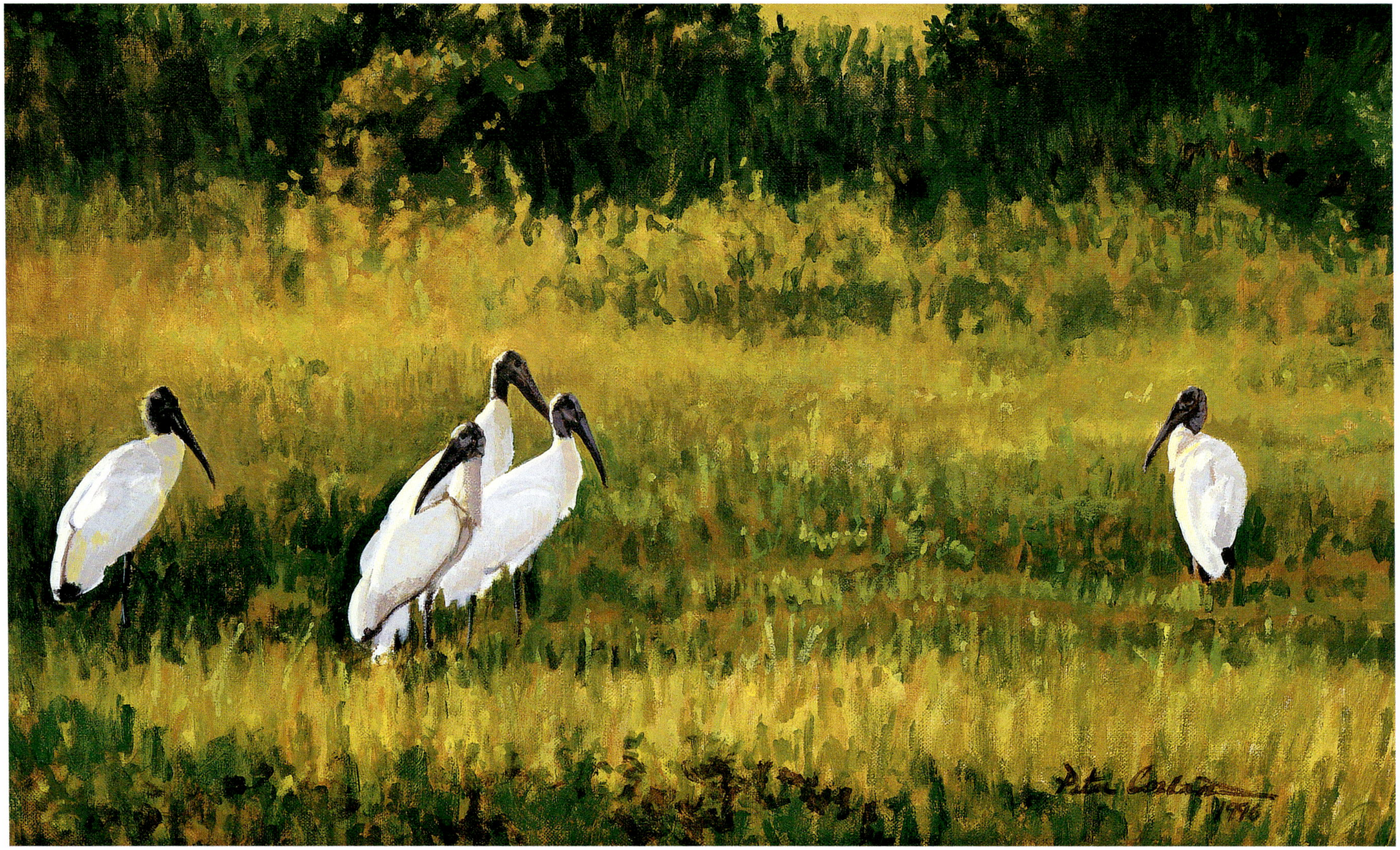

Wood Storks, 1996
acrylic on canvas
12 × 20 inches
signed and dated lower right

Index

PAGE NUMBERS IN *italics* REFER TO ILLUSTRATIONS.

A

Abbett, Bob, 30
Above the Fork, 172, 173
Above the Rapids, 183
abstract expressionism, 28, 33
abstraction, 22, 27, 28, 33, 34, 40, 163
acrylic painting, 16, 187
Adirondack Guide, 53
Adirondack Reflection, 45
Alaskan Solitude (painting), *10,* 13
Alaskan Solitude (print), *174,* 175
Albers, Josef, 36
American Museum of Fly Fishing, 30
Amwell Autumn (painting), *102*
Amwell Autumn (print), *178,* 179
angling, *see* fishing
Anticipation, 147
anticipation, scenes of, 19
Arrowhead Weed, 48
Atlantic salmon, *55–65, 172–73*
Atlantic Salmon Federation, 30
Atlantic Salmon Journal, 12
At the National, 37

B

Bad Weather, Good Luck, 133
Battenkill, 50
Battenkill Afternoon, 174, 175
Bean, L. L., 19, 30, 186
Beaverkill Afternoon (painting), *44*
Beaverkill Afternoon (print), *174,* 175
Before the Meet, 140
Best Bird, 116
Bird Hunter, The, 113
birds, *see* hunting
Black Duck Gunner, The, 118
Black Ducks, 182
Black Ducks—The Old Way, 181
Blagden, Gus, 27, 185
Blue Boats, 46
Blue Canoe, The (painting), *24*
Blue Canoe, The (print), *172,* 173
Bonefish Flats, 83
Broadbill Shooting on Barnegat, 181
Broken Sky/Broken Water, 81
Budweiser Clydesdales, The, 145
Buzz, 151

C

Calder, Alexander, 34
California College of Arts and Crafts, Oakland, 28, 186
Canada Geese, 182
Cascapédia Evening, A (painting), *58*
Cascapédia Evening, A (print), *172,* 173
Cascapédia Morning, A (painting), *25*
Cascapédia Morning, A (print), *172,* 173
Catskills, 29, 185, 186
Catskill Valley, A, 99
Chance to Double, A (painting), *18*
Chance to Double, A (print), *178,* 179
Changing the Fly, 33
Charlie Valley Rock (painting), *62*
Charlie Valley Rock (print), *172,* 173
Christ, Donald, 186
chronology, 185–87
Chukar Hunter, 111
Chukkers for Charity, 144
Close at Hand (painting), *74*
Close at Hand (print), *174,* 175
Coastal Conservation Association, 29
Coeur d'Alene Art Auction, Reno, Nevada, 22, 187
Cole, Charles, "Chick," 27, 185
color, 36, 187
Corbin, Elizabeth, 27, 185
Corbin, Hunter, 185, *186*
Corbin, Lillian, 29, 186
Corbin, Lindsey, 186, *186*
Corbin, Parker, 27, 36, 186, *186*
Corbin, Peter:
  chronology, 185-87
  exhibitions, collections, and honors, 189-90
  photographs of, *40, 185, 186, 187*
Corbin, Robert, 27, 185
Corbin, William O., 185
Cornrow Blind, The, 180
Crossing the Estuary, 26, 30, 187
Cubbing, 142

D

Daisy Chain, The, 86
Day to Remember, A, 180
Deadfall Flush, 95
Degas, Edgar, 36
dogs, paintings of, *32, 146–52*
Down River, 31
drawing, 32
Ducks Unlimited, 29
Dunbar, Alice, 27, 185

E

Eakins, Thomas, 11, 12, 34
Easing Them Out, 183
eastern trout, *42–54*
Edge of the Bay, 181
Edge of the Iceflow, 132
Edge of the Marsh, 176, 177
Edge of the Orchard (painting), *23*
Edge of the Orchard (print), *183*
Elm Creek, 110
End of the Day—Quail Hunting, 106
equine paintings, 12, 32, 36, *37,* 137, *138–45*
Evening at the Forks, 63
Evening Encounter (painting), *8,* 187
Evening Encounter (print), *172,* 173

Evening on Ladies Pool, 65
Evening on the River, 70
Evening Stripers, 20
Evening Tide, 91
exhibitions, 189–90

F
Falls, The, 174, 175
Field Hunters, The, 131
Firehole Evening, 69
First Light—Turkeys, 117
First of the Season, 178, 179
First Retrieve, 32
First Run, 176, 177
Fishcreek Evening, A, 67
Fisher (Robert S.) & Co., Newark, New Jersey, 28, 186
fishing, *frontispiece, 8,* 12, *13,* 15, *17,* 18, 19, *19, 20, 21,* 22, *22,* 24, *24, 25,* 27, 29, *31,* 33, *33,* 34, *35,* 36, 40, 41, *42–91,* 185, *185*
  Atlantic salmon, 55–65, *172–73*
  eastern trout, *42–54*
  salt water, *76–91, 176–77*
  trout, *174–75*
  western trout, *66–75*
Fishing the Edges, 72
Flats Fisherman, The, 79
Flight Birds (painting), *125*
Flight Birds (print), *182*
Flight Pattern, 180
Flint Field, The, 114
Florence (Italy), 28, 186
Fly Fisherman magazine, 11
fly fishing, *see* fishing
Fogbound, 180
Frost, A. B., 11, 18, 28, 30, 34, 185
  Duck Shooting from a Blind, 27
  Shooting Pictures, 18

G
Game-Coin, *29–30*
Georgia-Florida Field Trials, The, 29
Ginger and Coco, 152
Giralda Farms, 182
Grande Cascapédia River, 22, 24, 25, 29, 186, *186*
Gravel Bar, The (painting), *66*
Gravel Bar, The (print), *174,* 175
Great Expectations, 57
Gunning Partners, 120

H
Hard Day's Work, A, 94
Hard Light Bonefish, 176, 177
Harper's Weekly, 11
Harriman's Ranch, 12, *13*
Headed for Quiet Water (painting), 22, *22*
Headed for Quiet Water (print), *172,* 173
Head of the Canyon (painting), *71*
Head of the Canyon (print), *174,* 175
Hedgerow Blind, The, 180
Hemlock Evening, 160
Hill, Gene, 29
Hitching Tree, The, 138
Hollenbeck Club, The, 174, 175
Homer, Winslow, 11, 18
Hope Springs Eternal, 122
horses, *see* equine paintings
Hunt, Lynn Bogue, 18
hunting, 12, *14,* 15, *16,* 18, *18,* 19, *23,* 27, *27, 29, 32,* 33, 34, 36, 93, *94–135*
  upland, *94–117, 178–79*
  waterfowl, *118–35, 180–83*

I
illustration, 11, 12, 29
In His Prime—Staunch, 146

J
Jaques, Francis Lee, 18–19, 185
jewelry, 28, *28,* 163, 186
John's Rock, 73
Jump Shooting, 119
Just Right, 135

K
Keeper of the River, 159
Key West Sponger, 88
Kuhn, Bob, 15, 35

L
Landing, The, 60
Ledge Pool, The, 174, 175
Leigh Yawkey Woodson Art Museum, Wausau, Wisconsin, *Birds in Art* exhibition, 30, 187
light, 12, 15, 22, 27, 28, 33, 34, 40, 41, 163, 185, 186
limited-edition prints, 30, *171–83,* 187
Line, The, 178, 179
Long Cast, The, 64
Loveridge Plantation, 107
Lower Beat, 61
Low Water at the Point, 59

M
Madrid (Spain), 28, 186
Mallard Hunters, The (painting), *124*
Mallard Hunters, The (print), *181*
Michigan Morning, 98
Mill Pond Press, 30, 187
Miramichi Morning, 61
Mr. Sherrill at Shinnecock Hills, 156
moment, scenes of the, 19
Moments Rest, A, 168
Morning at Wethersfield, A, 141
Morning Coffee, 52
Morning Light, 115
Morning on the Grand, 59
Morning Run, A, 143
Mortimer, Lee, 187
motion, 28, 33, 41, 186
Mountain Pool, 51

N
Nadler, Harry, 36, 185
Near the Net (painting), *55*
Near the Net (print), *172,* 173

O
October Afternoon (painting), *96*
October Afternoon (print), *178,* 179
oil painting, 16, 187
Old Cabin Covey, 105
Old Club Way, The, 127
One Chance, 77
One-on-One, 172, 173
On the Edge—Bonefish, 82
Opening Day Bobwhites, 178, 179
Opening Day Mallards, 181
Orange Coat, The, 109
Orvis, 30
Out of Morning Mist, 130

P
Palmetto Blind, 129
Partners (painting), *75*
Partners (print), *174,* 175
Permit Fisherman, The, 20
Permit Flats, 78
Petersen Prints, 30, 187
Picasso, Pablo, 33
Pin, 28
plein air painting, 32
Pleissner, Ogden, 11, 17–18, 25, 28, 30, 34, 185
  Blue Boat on the Saint Anne, 17–18, *19*
Poling the Permit Flats, 84
Pomfret School, 27, 185
Portrait of Douglas Lukei, 158
Portrait of John Hettinger, 80
Portrait of Mr. and Mrs. Farnham Collins, 154
Portrait of Mr. and Mrs. John Runnette, 157
Portrait of Mrs. Cassandra M. Milbury, 155
portraits, 30, 32, 137, *153–60*
Pothole—Wood Ducks, The (painting), *126*
Pothole—Wood Ducks, The (print), *181*
Power and Grace, 21
prints, limited-edition, 30, *171–83,* 187
Promising Day, A, 180
Putting Down a New Pair, 104

R
Raphael, 28
realism, 12, 18, 33, 40, 163
Reflected Light Sculpture #1, 28
Reflected Light Sculpture #2, 167
Reflected Light Sculpture #3, 34
Reflected Light Sculpture #4, 167
Reflected Light Sculpture #5, 168
reflection, scenes of, 19
Releasing a Trophy, 174, 175
Rigby, 150
Risley, John, 27, 185
Rivera, José de, 34
Rolling Tarpon (painting), *87*
Rolling Tarpon (print), *176,* 177
Ruffed Grouse, 32
Ruffed Grouse Society, 29
Rungius, Carl, 19, 185
Running Them In, 139
Run on the Bank, The, 35
Russ, 149

S
salmon, Atlantic, *55–65, 172–73*
Salt Marsh Afternoon, 123
salt water, *76–91, 176–77*
Sandanona Sporting Club, 178, 179
sculpture, 27, 28, *28,* 30, 33, 34, *34,* 163, *164–68,* 185, 186, *186*
September's Song, 68
September Thunder, 97
Setting the Rig, 121
Shade Tree—Fall, 100
Shadow Water (painting), *17*
Shadow Water (print), *172,* 173
Sharp Tail Country, 16
Shooter's Hill Press, 12, 187
shotgunning, *see* hunting
Sleeping Indian—Rising Trout, 69
Smith, Steve, 34
Snipe Hunter, The, 112
Sound of the Falls, The, 54
South Bite—Andros, 85
Sporting Classics, 30
Sports Afield, 30
Spring Fever, 178, 179
Stalking (painting), *42*
Stalking (print), *183*
Standing Corn, 14
Starting Gate, The, 176, 177
Stick Nest, The, 182
Stonewall Brittany, 178, 179
Straight Up, 176, 177
Study in White, 134
Sugar Maple, 148
Summer Evening, 49
Summer Hatch, 49

T
Tamarack Double (painting), *103*
Tamarack Double (print), *178,* 179
Tarpon's Tempest, 176, 177
Three Seconds to Lift Off, 178, 179
Thunder & Lightning (painting), *76*
Thunder & Lightning (print), *176,* 177
Tides Out, 122
Titian, 28
Totally Committed, 182
Transmitted Light Sculpture #1, 164
Transmitted Light Sculpture #2, 166
Transmitted Light Sculpture #3, 165
Trophy Fish (painting), *90*
Trophy Fish (print), *176,* 177
Trouble Brewing, 176, 177
trout, *174–75*
  eastern, *42–4*
  western, *66–75*
Turneffe Permit, 176, 177
Two Loons, 48

U
upland, *94–117, 178–79*
Upper Falls, 43
Upper Lake, 52

V
Valley, The, 101
Velázquez, Diego, 28
Vermeer, Jan, 30

W
Wading for Bones, 89
Wading for Salmon—Iceland, 56
Water Break, The, 108
waterfowl, *118–35, 180–83*
Wesleyan University, 27, 33, 36, 185
  1968 Corbin exhibition, 185, *186*
western trout, *66–75*
White Skow, The, 47
Wildlife Art, 30
Winter Walk, 153
Wood Ducks, 128
Wood Storks, 192
Working for a Living, 91
Wyers Pool, 172, 173

Z
Zahourek, Jon, 36, 187